THE FRENCH LAUNDRY, PER SE

MDR Reservations

per se

Date
Monday, September 30th, Dinner

93

✱✱✱

2

2

2

2

3

2

Artis & Igor

Expeditor
Anna

Kitchen Servers
Zackery
Brandon
Joowon
Rashi
Mary

Indra & Israel

2

1

2

2

2

4

3

2

Training

3

2

Coffee Servers
Shakil - Coffee
Alberto - Buff

Alex G & Chan

Alex P & Andreas

2

2

Menu
Elaine

2

2

2

Talent Sets The Floor, Character Sets The Ceiling

A NOTE FROM THOMAS KELLER

TWO YEARS AGO, in what now seems like another lifetime, I began working on this book. My intent at the time was to celebrate two restaurants—The French Laundry and per se—by telling their stories within the broader context of the evolution of fine dining. Though I knew there would be wrinkles in the narrative (there always are), I could never have imagined how dramatically its arc was destined to change.

As I write today, the world is in the midst of a pandemic that has taken the lives of hundreds of thousands, sickened millions, and brought the global economy to its knees. While few sectors have been spared the devastation, fewer still have been hit harder than the profession I know best. The COVID-19 crisis has shuttered restaurants and their suppliers around the globe (many of them permanently) while upending countless lives and livelihoods. The depth of the damage is difficult to quantify yet impossible to ignore. One of the many truths the current crisis has revealed is the value of restaurants as a social force. Every single one—from sandwich shops to pizza parlors to chains that employ millions of people to the hundreds of thousands of independent restaurants—is more important than any of us realized. At some level, many of us recognized this all along, but we see it now more clearly than ever before.

Since July 1994, when we opened The French Laundry, I've spent the majority of my time there. Often, I've asked our guests, "What brings you here? Are you celebrating anything?" A common reply I hear is: "We're just celebrating being together." To me this is the most gratifying answer of all. It underscores what these places are all about: making memories.

That starts, of course, with friends and family gathered at a table for a meal. But it is more than that. It extends outward in a web of community and connectivity. Just as we feed our guests, they, in turn, feed us. We are joined in a symbiotic relationship that also helps sustain the farmers who grow our food, the fishermen who catch our lobsters and harvest our oysters, the foragers who gather wild mushrooms and mulberries, the wineries who supply our cellars. And

on and on. Those who choose to have a meal at our restaurants support the cleaners who wash our linens and the artisans who make our porcelain, the florists who fill our rooms with beauty, the truckers who deliver our food, the manufacturers of our culinary tools, the companies that recycle our boxes and cans. The nourishment provided by a meal does not begin or end with the food served on a plate.

We are all in this together. That we hear this phrase so frequently does not make it any less true. Never has it resonated with me more profoundly. In the midst of this pandemic, our team would like to recognize the heroic work of healthcare professionals and first responders who put their lives on the line to tend to others. We'd also like to express our gratitude to essential employees everywhere—from the grocery store clerk and postal carrier to the pharmacist and delivery driver to the barista who makes your morning coffee—who ensure that we receive our daily necessities and sometimes small comforts.

In every disaster and national emergency, the restaurant community has stepped up. After 9/11, after Hurricanes Sandy and Maria, after wildfires and floods—we were there. We continue to do our part today, even as our own lives and businesses have been so critically affected. Now it is time for everyone who cherishes their time in a restaurant, whether at a French Laundry or that local pizzeria or taqueria or family-owned diner, to join us in supporting this community and do what they can to make sure that its workers stay safe, its businesses stay healthy, and its intricate network of farmers, artisans, suppliers, and more remains intact. When this pandemic recedes, we want to be ready to open the doors and say, "Welcome."

Much has changed in the world over the past two years. What remains unaltered is our shared humanity, our need for community, and our capacity for generosity. This book, like the two restaurants at its center, is meant as a tribute to these traits.

April 2020

Also by Thomas Keller

Bouchon Bakery
with Sebastien Rouxel, along with Susie Heller,
Matthew McDonald, Michael Ruhlman, and Amy Vogler

Ad Hoc at Home
with Dave Cruz, along with Susie Heller,
Michael Ruhlman, and Amy Vogler

Under Pressure
with Jonathan Benno, Corey Lee, and Sebastien Rouxel,
along with Susie Heller, Michael Ruhlman, and Amy Vogler

Bouchon
with Jeffrey Cerciello, along
with Susie Heller and Michael Ruhlman

The French Laundry Cookbook
with Susie Heller and Michael Ruhlman

THE FRENCH LAUNDRY, PER SE

THOMAS KELLER

David Breeden, Corey Chow,
and Elwyn Boyles

with Susie Heller *and* Michael Ruhlman
Photography by Deborah Jones

Artisan Books · New York

Library of Congress Cataloging-in-Publication Data.
Names: Keller, Thomas, 1955- author.
Title: The French laundry, Per Se / Thomas Keller.
Description: New York : Artisan, a division of Workman Publishing Co.,
   Inc., 2020. | Includes index.
Identifiers: LCCN 2020019707 | ISBN 9781579658496 (hardcover)
Subjects: LCSH: Cooking, French. | French Laundry (Restaurant) | LCGFT:
   Cookbooks.
Classification: LCC TX719 .K35 2020 | DDC 641.5944—dc23
LC record available at https://lccn.loc.gov/2020019707

Design by Volume Inc.

Artisan books are available at special discounts when purchased in bulk for premiums and sales
promotions as well as for fund-raising or educational use. Special editions or book excerpts also
can be created to specification. For details, contact the Special Sales Director at the address
below, or send an e-mail to specialmarkets@workman.com.

For speaking engagements, contact speakersbureau@workman.com.

Published by Artisan
A division of Workman Publishing Co., Inc.
225 Varick Street
New York, NY 10014-4381
artisanbooks.com

Artisan is a registered trademark of Workman Publishing Co., Inc.

Published simultaneously in Canada by Thomas Allen & Son, Limited

Printed in China

First printing, October 2020

10 9 8 7 6 5 4 3 2 1

This book is dedicated to all our teams, past and present, for the contributions they have made to the lives of so many; to our partners, farmers, fishermen, foragers, and gardeners; and finally to our guests, who have supported us throughout the years. I am grateful to call you my friends and colleagues.

—Thomas Keller

To my dudes. E, M, and Q. Love you.

—David Breeden

To my wife, Kaeleigh, and my son, Caelan. Without your support, I wouldn't be able to do what I love to do.

—Corey Chow

I would like to dedicate this book to my aunt Camilla Broadbent, whose help and support during my apprenticeship in London allowed me to step into the world of pastry and never look back.

—Elwyn Boyles

CONTENTS

PREFACE

WHEN WE BEGAN BUILDING a new restaurant in the Time Warner Center in New York in the early 2000s, people invariably asked me, "Is it going to be The French Laundry?" And my response was always, "Well, not The French Laundry, per se."

Because it wasn't. But it wasn't *not* going to be The French Laundry, either, because the restaurant I envisioned had a similar cuisine and style and refinement. The two restaurants, and the teams that ran them, would be joined by a set of standards, a philosophy, and a culture. I wanted the two restaurants to be connected but to have their own personalities. The restaurants' current chefs, David Breeden in California and Corey Chow in New York, are very different people who bring different styles of cooking to their dining rooms, but their interpretations of the food fall within the framework of The French Laundry, which I opened in 1994. Which is why I could only answer that frequent question as I did. Here, then, is an attempt to capture both of them in one book, as well as an opportunity to reflect on the evolution of The French Laundry and on fine dining generally over the past twenty-six years.

Thomas Keller

THE CORNET

YOU COULD SAY A TUILE RECIPE from *Gourmet* magazine in the late 1980s launched The French Laundry. And that the very same tuile recipe remains a philosophical touchstone.

I'd loved serving rabbit ever since my days at La Rive, a tiny family-run restaurant in the Hudson Valley where I cooked on my own and taught myself how to dress rabbits, which in turn taught me about using the entire animal. By the time I was chef of Rakel, at Clarkson and Varick Streets in New York City, I was serving rabbit loin perfumed with rosemary. But I wanted to put all of the rabbit on the plate, so I made a *salpicón* of its liver and kidney and onion to go with it. All of this was soft food—I needed some crunch. I remembered reading a tuile recipe in *Gourmet*, so I found it and turned it into a savory tuile. It was so delicate and crisp, perfect for the *salpicón*.

It was also pliable when it came out of the oven, an idea that stayed with me.

Rakel couldn't survive the recession at the beginning of the 1990s, and my partner, Serge Raoul, wanted to turn it into a more casual restaurant, as many restaurants of the time were doing. I love casual dining, but that's not the style of food I wanted to cook.

Just five years earlier, I'd been in one of the most dynamic kitchens in New York, the Polo Lounge at Westbury Hotel, run by chef de cuisine Patrice Boely. Nouvelle cuisine was new and exciting; I couldn't go backward. I told Serge no—going casual wouldn't feel true to my ambition. (Little did I know that Serge would return to my life and become instrumental in my being able to open The French Laundry—he was not only a mentor and friend but a great supporter of what I hoped to achieve.)

So there I was in 1990. I'd basically failed at the two restaurants I'd run. I was unemployed and alone in New York. I was thirty-five, and going nowhere.

I landed a job at Checkers, a small hotel in Los Angeles run by Bill Wilkinson, who invented what we now call the boutique hotel when he opened Campton Place in San Francisco. He was the first to put a dynamic American chef—Bradley Ogden—in a hotel, and it was at Campton Place that Ogden made his name. Checkers was Wilkinson's second hotel. He had high expectations for me.

The hotel was hosting a huge event the week I was to arrive, and Bill had asked me to develop a canapé that would wow Los Angeles and announce my arrival. So on top of all my anxiety and fear about uprooting and starting anew, leaving my friends and a city I loved, I needed a showstopper.

I didn't have one.

Just before I left New York, some friends took me to lunch at Phoenix Garden in Chinatown, where we'd eaten once a month. As was our custom, we went across the street for ice cream afterward.

You have to understand where my head was at this moment. I was leaving New York for a new city and new employer. I was sad to be leaving my close friends, sad to be leaving this amazing city. I was frightened. I was challenged. I felt enormous anxiety over the responsibility I was about to take on.

So when my friends and I went to the Baskin-Robbins across from Phoenix Garden, and the person behind the counter handed me my cone in its little plastic holder, I smiled—*There's my canapé! I'll make my tuile into a cone—a cornet.* I smiled, and I was happy. I'd been so depressed and unhappy for so long, I almost didn't recognize the feeling.

I decided to fill the cornet with tuna tartare (it was the nineties), wasabi cream, and chive oil, and it was the hit Bill had wanted.

The tuiles were a little too fragile, but the pastry chef at Checkers and I worked together to refine the batter so that they were durable enough to hold a heavy protein, but were still delicate, and could be made in large numbers. I asked the engineers at the hotel to cut me two triangles of Plexiglas with half-inch-wide holes to hold the cones, and used those to serve them. The tuna tartare cone became such a hit, I served it to VIPs at Checkers—until management cut me loose for insubordination. I was different then. I was a little less mature, a little more short-tempered. I had ambition, but had yet to learn how to *manage* that ambition (for more on that, see page 152).

Two years later, in 1992, I was trying to impress potential partners who could help me buy The French Laundry, and the cornet was the first thing I served them. I couldn't afford tuna for the tartare, so I went with salmon, which was less expensive. I had no money. I had no job. All I had was an idea. And the cornet that always made them smile.

I'VE TOLD this story before, but I tell it again because like everything, this cornet has evolved, just as my profession, the world of fine dining, has evolved. And yet, after twenty-six years, the cornet still makes *me* smile. Everyone who dines at The French Laundry in Yountville, California, and at per se in Manhattan is offered this bite first precisely *because* it's meant to make them smile. The cornet not only reflects this joyful connection to food, but also symbolizes what this book is about: awareness, inspiration, interpretation, and evolution—namely, the evolution of fine dining. And the more people you work with, the more likely you are to experience evolution and improvement.

I call these improvements "green tape moments," because they're not only about the food. We had always used painter's tape—first blue, then green (less expensive!)—to mark deli containers and hold menus down at the pass, simply tearing the tape and leaving the jagged edges. After ten years of this, the expediter from The French Laundry, Zion Curiel, was setting up the pass at per se for its very first service, taping the night's menus to the white linen. He decided to cut the tape so that we had clean right angles everywhere. It was a small change, but for me, it was like the shot heard round the world: those right angles and clean lines impact the way you *think* at the pass. I'd charged the French Laundry staff who had come to help open per se to push themselves to find new ways to improve. This was Zion's contribution. Everyone felt it, and the revelation extended to all reaches of our team. I'd been tearing tape for twenty years, and this had never occurred to me. Eric, Jonathan, Grant, Mark, Shuna—how many chefs had never thought to do this? This simple act said to everyone, *If something as small as taking a pair of scissors to tape could have such a huge impact, what more could we do?*

In the same way, we continued to improve the cornet in response to our drive for efficiency and more refined service, and even to Americans' changing diets. Initially, one of the chefs would spend a half hour or more chopping salmon by hand, then had to spend more time picking out the many white sinews that separate the layers of flesh. Today, we grind the salmon through a super-chilled grinder, then pass it through a tamis, a drum sieve, which catches all those sinews, a process that results in an extraordinarily delicate texture and reduces the time it takes to prepare the salmon. Our method evolved.

We used to make stencils for the cornet tuile using Kendall Farm crème fraîche lids, which were just the right size, but that meant the chef making the tuiles each day would need to spread the batter one circle at a time. Now we've engineered sheet-pan-size silicone stencils so the chef can make dozens at a time.

We're also now able to preserve the cooked cornet with our chamber vacuum sealer, one of the great technologies to enter the professional kitchen. If we're doing a party, we can make a thousand cornets over the course of a week and put them in a container, gas flush them, and seal them, and they'll stay fresh.

We used to serve the cornet from a little Plexiglas tray—that was all we could afford. We then designed a silver service piece with Christofle called "The Cadillac" to serve multiple guests. We also designed a piece called "The Bouchon" (French for "cork"), which holds the individual cornet set down before each diner.

As the American diet has evolved, more people have stopped eating gluten. This forced us to develop a gluten-free tuile. Our R&D team combined a mixture of nongluten grains that would work just like flour in the tuile batter, giving birth to our product called Cup4Cup, which at the time was the first completely gluten-free flour that could be used cup for cup as you would use wheat flour. The diner spurred the cornet's evolution.

And while the concept of the cornet remains the same—crispy cracker, creamy texture, savory salmon, and a tuile batter unchanged for twenty-six years—the ingredients change, as a way to express each of our chefs' personal visions. If salmon is on the menu in another form, we may serve a fluke tartare. We make a vegetarian cornet. The version photographed here is David Breeden's cornet at The French Laundry, the Everything Bagel Cornet—which takes the dish into the realm of the bagel with lox and cream cheese.

Culturally it's a dish associated with New York City, home of per se, not Northern California. But it creates a connection between the two restaurants that is really important to me and to our team. Corey Chow, chef de cuisine at per se, solidifies that connection by doing his own Everything Bagel as a caviar course, making the two restaurants work, in a way, as fraternal twins.

All this evolution, embodied in a single dish that came out of a very sad time in my life three decades ago.

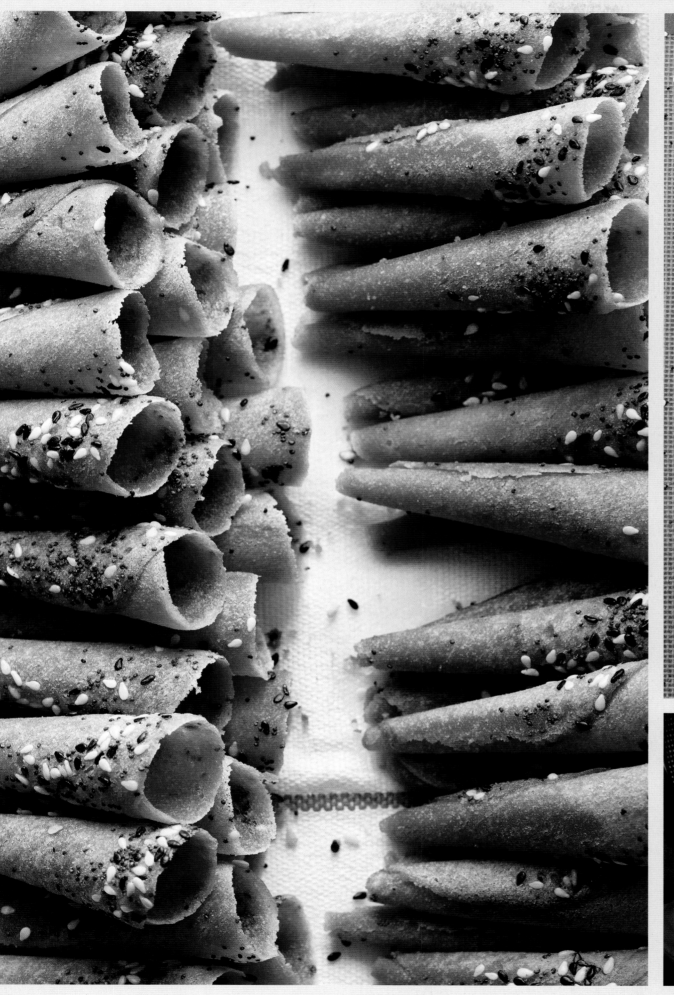

THE CHEFS

TWENTY-SIX YEARS AGO it dawned on me that the business I run is like a sports franchise. We hire chefs, servers, and managers—our athletes—and need to do so with a philosophy of not only winning in the present but building for success in the future: succession planning.

Everyone who works here enters with different life experiences and different skills that they apply to a range of tasks. We hire them, we train them, we mentor them, whether they are young chefs at Bouchon or Ad Hoc or more mature chefs arriving at per se or The French Laundry. Some are akin to AAA ballplayers, working their way up from the minors; others have already played in the majors. Our job is to reinforce their strengths and help them overcome their weaknesses. All of them are part of a team, whether they're in AAA or in the top echelon. Even Stephen Strasburg, the MVP of the Washington Nationals, said after winning the 2019 World Series, "I'm just here to be part of the team."

I think about the kids in the major leagues. Imagine staring down a 95-mile-per-hour fastball with fifty thousand people screaming around you. That's composure. I feel the same for my chefs—every member of the team is under pressure to perform at a very high level. When they land in positions of responsibility at our restaurants, they show the same amazing composure, discipline, and skill as an elite athlete. They all understand the importance of being part of a team, and I'm so proud of them for it.

And it's not only about the performance of the chefs, but about the coaches and managers as well. When I or one of my senior staff hires someone, we expect that new hire to surpass what we can do. It's the only way to keep improving. If that person you've hired, trained,

and mentored does not, over time, become better than you, then *you* haven't done your job.

I LEARNED THIS LESSON through a painful experience. We opened the restaurant per se overlooking Manhattan's Columbus Circle in February 2004. One week later, a fire devastated the restaurant, and it almost devastated me. But as chefs, we come together in times of crisis.

Eric Ziebold had been my longtime chef de cuisine at The French Laundry and helped me open per se. Though he had plans to move on to open his own restaurant after the launch of per se, he offered to return to The French Laundry while I stayed in New York to work on rebuilding per se and manage the situation. We reopened, happily, and when per se was running smoothly, I returned to Yountville, to The French Laundry, expecting to take the pass for that night's service, which I'd been doing for ten years.

But I saw Eric standing there. *He* had the pass. He'd been at the pass all the time I was reopening per se. In that moment, I realized I didn't have a job anymore, at least not the same job that I'd held for so long. I'd moved from player to coach. And not simply because I'd had to let someone else play in a crisis, but because there were younger chefs who could do what I used to do better than I could do it now.

At the time, we were all just reacting to an urgent situation, but once I was able to reflect, I saw the bigger picture, the greater need for succession planning, long-term team building . . . the same thing a successful sports franchise does. More than just determine who will be the next chef to fill a role, we need to determine how to help the new players build on and surpass their predecessors. How can Timothy Hollingsworth surpass Corey Lee at The French Laundry? How can Eli Kaimeh move beyond Jonathan Benno, and then Corey Chow beyond Eli?

The new chefs aren't by nature so superior to the former ones, but the tools and equipment improve, the ingredients grow increasingly fine, and—most important—the training and mentorship we practice allow them to advance. This is how you build excellence in a team, excellence that endures and is sustainable, even if one key player—like me standing at the pass in the kitchen of The French Laundry—moves on.

IN THE FALL OF 1999, I was on the book tour for *The French Laundry Cookbook*. One of the stops was the Williams Sonoma in Pasadena. In line with his mom, waiting to get a book signed, was twenty-year-old Corey Chow, a psychology major at Cal Poly Tech in Pomona, California. He didn't know he wanted to be a chef yet—his mom just knew he loved food.

Eight years later, during family meal at per se, I got my plate and took it to the kitchen to eat. It was Chinese food—beef and broccoli, fried rice, fish with scallions, steamed and finished by flash frying. I asked Jonathan Benno, chef de cuisine, "Who made family meal?" and he pointed to a commis, the lowest rung of the brigade. It was Corey Chow, who now had my attention.

Corey had graduated from Poly Tech, then gone to Le Cordon Bleu in Pasadena. He externed at Alan Wong's Honolulu and loved it so much he stayed for six years. During that time, Wong closed the restaurant for two days so that Jonathan and per se pastry chef Sebastien Rouxel could put on a special dinner there. Corey had never seen such perfect culinary execution. He was astonished, and so he set his sights on per se.

He staged at per se, and Benno gave him a job. He moved quickly up to sous chef, but, not seeing a path for more advancement, he left to work with Rich Torrisi and became a chef de cuisine for the Michelin-starred restaurant Torrisi Italian Specialties. I ate there and had the same experience I'd had when Corey made family meal. *This guy can cook*, I thought, *and he's also running a kitchen.*

When Corey asked to return to per se, as executive sous chef under Eli Kaimeh, I said, "You can cook, but can you lead a team?" He said, "Yes, Chef." And when Eli left, Corey advanced to become chef de cuisine, a place he never dreamed he'd be when he was in line waiting with his mom for his book to be signed eighteen years earlier.

Around the time Corey came to work as a commis, David Breeden was already a chef de partie on his way to becoming sous chef and, ultimately, executive sous chef at per se. David had had a rough upbringing in the hills of eastern Tennessee—so rough, in fact, that he left home at age fourteen with $21 in his pocket. Somehow, he made his way, living on his own, often working at restaurants. He applied to the best restaurant in his area, Club LeConte, run by a chef named Seth Simmerman, but never heard back, so he decided to join the United States Navy. He didn't know that his application to the chef had been shunted to the manager of the dining room rather than the chef. On the very day David, newly eighteen, was set to enlist in the navy, Chef Simmerman called to

offer him a job. David said, "I can't, I'm joining the navy today." Chef Simmerman said, "I was in the navy, I cooked on submarines, and believe me, you don't want to do that. Get your ass in here."

The year was 1998, and Chef Simmerman became David's mentor. Because David didn't have a car and it took so long for him to get to the restaurant using public transportation, he asked the chef if he could catch a ride to the restaurant. The chef said, "I leave at eight a.m.—your shift doesn't start till three." David said, "If you drive me to the restaurant, I'll work for free until three." And that's how David learned to cook—working for free from nine to three, then minimum wage from three to eleven.

David set his sights on a job at The French Laundry after reading an article about me in *Gourmet*, in which I talked about the importance of killing rabbits. He managed to talk his way in via Devin Knell, one of our longtime chefs, a great technician, who was looking for a butcher. "I can butcher," David fudged. ("I could *maybe* French a rack of lamb," he says now, "but really, I didn't even know how to cut a chicken efficiently and well.")

(opposite) David Breeden
(above) Elwyn Boyles
(above right) Corey Chow

I remember walking into the old screened-in porch and seeing him butchering every day, but I thought he was a culinary student on an externship. He was good, so I asked him when he was going back to school.

He said, "I'm not in school."

I said, "Where do you work?"

He said, "I'm hoping to work here."

I asked if he was considering moving out here. He said, "I already did. My girlfriend arrives with all my stuff tomorrow."

Like I said, people catch your attention. I began to watch him, saw the way he took ownership of every task, mastered it, did it better than anyone. He eventually became a chef de partie, moved all the way up to saucier, before the stresses of cooking at this level took their toll. He took six weeks away from the restaurant to decompress and visit family.

He wanted to move to New York, and so, with my blessing, he went to see Jonathan Benno, and Chef Benno hired him. David knows both kitchens really well now.

Corey and David are two very different chefs, but they work well within the framework of the restaurants—David ingeniously figuring out how to serve the food of his rural background (pole beans, pork shank) in a Michelin three-star restaurant, Corey likewise maintaining a connection to his Chinese American heritage.

I'VE ALWAYS BEEN GOOD at surrounding myself with people who are smarter than me, and Elwyn Boyles is one of those people. In 2008, I'd been advertising in trade magazines for a pastry chef, and I got a call from Tom Aikens, in London, who had been the youngest chef to earn two Michelin stars. He told me of a very talented pastry chef named Elwyn Boyles who had worked for him and who was ready for a change and wanted to spend time in the United States.

Elwyn was raised first on a farm in Wales, then in the little village of Horseheath, England, a half hour south of Cambridge. He began washing dishes at the local country inn, the Red Lion, during high school. By the time he was finishing high school and taking his A Levels, he was the chef, cooking simple pub food six nights a week—prawn cocktail, mushroom stroganoff, steak and kidney pie, apple crumble.

After graduating, he spent nearly four months in Australia, and on his return he had decided university was not for him. He wanted to cook. Through a government apprenticeship program, he was placed at the Café Royale, a posh hotel right off Piccadilly Circus, and started, as many apprentices do, in pastry. But just four months in, Elwyn said, "Hey, I really like it here. And I'm good at it." So he stayed in the pastry arts during the three-year apprenticeship.

He then worked in upscale hotels in London—The Four Seasons and The Connaught—then at smaller Michelin-starred restaurants, Midsummer House, led by Daniel Clifford, and Tom Aiken's eponymous restaurant in Chelsea.

He arrived at per se in New York in 2008 and persevered as he adjusted to a new country, a new restaurant group, and a new management style. After about a year, he came into his own.

I knew by then that if I wanted to keep Elwyn on my team, I'd have to keep him interested, keep giving him new projects to work on, so I charged him with unifying the dessert programs of The French Laundry and per se. It's important to me to keep my kitchens connected, that they feed one another. This is why we have live screens of each kitchen, so one can see what the other is doing at any time. Elwyn achieved that unity with our desserts and has become, in my mind, a pastry chef second to none.

These three chefs lead the French Laundry–per se team and, along with me, are the voice of this book. But three people don't make two Michelin three-star restaurants. Everyone who works at the restaurants helps to shape those restaurants. Every single person. From the dishwasher to the chef to the woman in Petaluma who makes the cheese and the man who created an oyster farm in Duxbury, Massachusetts, where never an oyster had grown before he grew one, to the accountants and the service staff to the whole team in the garden to the GM at our new Mexican restaurant and the bartender and chefs *there*. Please understand how important it is for me to express this. Everyone who works at these restaurants *shapes* these restaurants. A little better each day, that's the goal—a little better this morning than yesterday.

Special mention must also be made of two chefs who worked behind the scenes to develop the recipe portions for this book—Elaine Smyth and Alison Beazley (left), who did all their work for the book while maintaining their daily duties at per se and The French Laundry.

I thank them all.

DAVID BREEDEN

MY JOURNEY TO THE FRENCH LAUNDRY

MY FIRST MEMORY of The French Laundry was as a guest on August 6, 2004. I had started in kitchens as a dishwasher in my mid-teens, and now had gotten a stage at The French Laundry, to begin the following January. I was in San Francisco with my girlfriend exploring the culinary scene, and we got a last-minute reservation due to a cancellation and drove up for lunch. Kevin Macway, a longtime French Laundry associate, was our captain. We had, of course, an amazing meal (my first "Peas and Carrots," originated by then poissonier Jonathan Benno). But that was not the highlight. At the end of the meal, Kevin, who knew I'd be staging there, asked if I'd like to meet Chef.

I was so nervous. What if my granddad's suit makes me look unprofessional? What if he grills me on the classical repertoire? What if I've had too much wine?

Suddenly I beheld the most beautiful kitchen I had ever seen. Chef was on the pass cutting romano beans. He looked at me, smiled, and said, "Chef! How was your meal?" Then he said, "I look forward to your joining the team." I don't remember much else—I was so nervous. It was like meeting Michael Jordan.

SIX MONTHS LATER, January 25, 2005, I arrived at 5:00 a.m. for my 5:30 start, having scoured again my copy of *The French Laundry Cookbook*.

I entered the copper door to the kitchen, and even now I distinctly remember the smell—not like a kitchen but rather like someone's home. There were two enormous 100-liter pots of veal stock simmering away, and the beautiful smells of the mirepoix and aromatics were wafting through the air. A butcher with a huge kit of rabbits cut each into precise pieces. A commis cut the brunoise for the chefs de partie on a mandoline.

My first-ever task was to prepare the pommes Maxim for the famous Beets and Leeks lobster dish. I also had to juice beets and chiffonade leeks. I was terrified. Walter Abrams, the poissonier, a buff Colombian dude from South Florida, arrived and looked at the pommes Maxim, evaluating the texture and seasoning. "Not bad, rookie," he said.

It was an amazing kitchen. Every service was dynamic. The food was . . . perfect. And in a way I'd never seen before, everything we did in the French Laundry kitchen was about the guests.

AFTER TWO YEARS, the intensity of the work and serious family issues led me to take a break, regroup in my mind, be with family and my beloved East Tennessee hills.

But I'm a cook and quickly grew restless. I had to keep moving. I took a break from Tennessee to stage in New York (Daniel, Jean-Georges) but didn't feel comfortable in those kitchens. Against my instinct, because The French Laundry had been so hard, I went to see the per se kitchen and introduce myself to its chef de cuisine, Jonathan Benno.

He was at the sous chef's desk, next to the pass, on the phone. I waited. When he hung up, I introduced myself. He gave me the same smile Thomas Keller had given me, shook my hand in the same way. I gave him my resume. This was where I wanted to be. And a few weeks later, Chef Benno called and asked when could I be in New York.

Some kitchens you just fit into. And Jonathan became a mentor, even a father figure, to me. And by chance, he, I, and our late dear colleague Chris L'Hommedieu were the only people working at per se who had also worked at The French Laundry.

When Thomas was at per se, we had a special relationship because of this. I spoke the French Laundry language, and Thomas strove to keep the two restaurants spiritually joined. This sounds trite but it's a fact: Thomas taught me more than anyone in my life about how to become a leader, a compassionate human, and a mentor to my own team.

In November 2012, Thomas called me into the office of the general manager at per se, where we could speak alone. I'd been at per se four years and had risen to executive sous chef under Eli Kaimeh. Thomas did this a lot, with all of us, making sure we were good, asking about our goals, our challenges.

But this time he had a funny smile. He said, "Chef, are you ready to come home?"

I said, "Absolutely," not quite understanding.

Timothy Hollingsworth, the hugely respected chef de cuisine of The French Laundry, was leaving, Thomas explained, and then asked, "Would you consider returning to The French Laundry as chef de cuisine?"

I almost swallowed my tongue.

THE FRENCH LAUNDRY KITCHEN I returned to lead was not what I'd left five years earlier. It no longer had the walk-in, since replaced by six Traulsen reach-ins designed by Chef, which were far more efficient. The porch had been enclosed to create a space for the commis to prep, and the chefs de partie could do their mise en place at their stations. It had a Rational combi oven and a blast chiller, essential

tools for precise cooking. Those stockpots, though, were still there simmering away. That familiar aroma was still in the air and that beautiful breeze was still blowing through the open windows to the courtyard.

And I was chef de cuisine. Rather than the pressure cooker I remembered as a young commis, the kitchen was an intensely professional environment. Chef had set everything up for everyone to succeed. All I had to do was support my team and let them flourish.

In late 2014, Chef and I had dinner at Bouchon, as we often did. But this time he had something important to ask me. "How would you like a new kitchen, Chef?"

I said, "What do you mean? We do need a new stove."

He said, "No, think of the Louvre. And I. M. Pei's pyramid."

In February 2017, after two years of difficult work in a temporary kitchen and the supporting buildings, we moved into the new kitchen. It was like walking into a palace. We had all the tools that we had ever wished for. We had a Rational on the line for the fish station, a rotisserie, and a wood-burning hearth. The commis and pastry kitchens had many improvements as well, such as a large twelve-burner stove, full-size blast chiller, chocolate shop, meat maturation cooler for dry-aging meats, and temperature-controlled butchery. We also expanded our wine cellar to accommodate up to 20,000 bottles.

But most of all, we had space. The space allowed us to hire more chefs, which gave us fewer working hours but more time to prep, more room in which to work, more time to take care, more time to think of and better serve the guest.

For Chef, and therefore me, it was, is, and always will be about the guest.

COREY CHOW

MY JOURNEY TO PER SE

FOR CULINARY SCHOOL, I did my externship at Alan Wong's in Honolulu and I loved it so much, I stayed for six years. But things changed for me when three chefs from per se—Chung Chow, pastry chef Sebastien Rouxel, and chef de cuisine Jonathan Benno—came to do a special dinner. There was something about the way they worked, their precision and professionalism, that told me I had to make it out to per se. And because I'd assisted Chung and Jonathan, I had an in, and I earned a stage, which led to a job offer as a commis, the entry-level position.

I was scared. The kitchen was so intimidating. I'd never been in an environment like this. Three Michelin stars. Thomas Keller. Jonathan Benno. New York City. Everyone was better than me. At twenty-eight, I was the oldest commis, but the least experienced with fine dining at this level. The culture, the terminologies, the sense of urgency. It was all a weird dream.

I kept my head down and worked. You do one thing right and then another, and you begin to build a little confidence. You also develop trust among your peers. What I was unprepared for was the generosity of the mentoring I received. David Breeden was a chef de partie when I arrived. Chung Chow. Matt Orlando. Eli Kaimeh. These guys were the badasses. They were, and I mean this as a term of high respect, animals. They studied technique relentlessly and were constantly learning from and teaching one another.

David taught me classical technique and the cuisine of the South. Chung, he just knew everything—everything about the food, his technique was flawless, and he even knew maintenance for all the equipment. If you had a question about anything, you went to Chung. Matt had worked at Noma and The Fat Duck, and so he brought a

new way of thinking to our ever-evolving food. And Eli had a kind of confidence in his cuisine that mixed Jonathan's Italian with the melting-pot food of his native New York City and Syrian heritage. What a mix.

It was all about the team. Chefs from all over the world filled the per se kitchen, from all walks of life, passionate about food, sharing ideas and experiences. We began to seriously embrace the important tools of modernist cuisine, the ingredients that allowed us to further control texture and the tools like the Rational combi oven, which allowed for more precise cooking than sous vide. Everyone wanted to outdo each other. We were all super-competitive. And because of this, the kitchen was stimulating and exciting. I wanted to be in this so badly.

In 2009, Jonathan Benno left and Eli took over as chef de cuisine. He had his own plating style and flavor combinations and a fascination with the new techniques. He wasn't better than Jonathan, just different. The chefs were always like that. Jonathan had his Italian and French influences and a devotion to the classics. Eli was an evolved version of Jonathan. Eli was already the voice of that kitchen and when he took over, it was a surprise to no one.

His presence was the same as Jonathan's and the restaurant didn't change—it evolved. He made it his own. That's what we learned from Thomas: "Treat it like it's yours, and one day it will be." That's how the restaurant evolves. And it starts with the chef and the brigade. We kept pushing and evolving. Getting better, just a little better each day.

I was the first chef Eli promoted to sous chef. It was such an honor, a dream to reach that achievement. Never would I have thought to make it that far. And I couldn't have done it without great support from the team.

David continued to mentor me, taught me about leadership and camaraderie. He created a relationship between us that has influenced my career to this day.

When David became executive sous chef at per se, you could tell he was ready to be a chef de cuisine. He just acted like one, the way he led and mentored, the way he himself continued to evolve. He was surprised when Thomas Keller tapped him to become chef de cuisine at The French Laundry, but I wasn't. What an achievement for him, to go back to where he came from and be the boss. I was sad to see my comrade and mentor go but I was stoked for him. It was his time to make something his own.

AFTER NEARLY SIX YEARS at per se, I decided to leave. There wasn't room to advance and I wanted a shot at running my own kitchen. I worked for a time at Nomad, and then became chef de cuisine at Torrisi Italian Specialties. It was a good opportunity and I continued to grow. But my wife, Kaeleigh, whom I'd met at per se and who still worked there, knew how much I'd loved per se and suggested I go back. I'd kept in touch with Eli and I knew that the executive sous, Matt Peters, was about to start training for the Bocuse d'Or competition, which would take him away from per se. And with everyone's blessing, I was back again. Not very many people get that chance and I had to grab it right away.

IN JANUARY 2016, three months after I'd returned as executive sous chef, the *New York Times* review came out, and it devastated us.

Everything changed. We would always maintain our three Michelin stars. But how do you keep yourself and your people motivated when we just got shat on by the *New York Times*? How do you bounce back?

We all looked to Chef and the amazing way he handled the situation. New York is tough; the restaurant business cutthroat. But Chef didn't start screaming or railing against the *Times*. He was so incredibly calm, it calmed all of us. He treated the reviewer as he would have any other guest. He wrote him a personal apology. And then he brought us all together and said we will get through this one guest at a time. We continue to up our game.

David flew back to work at per se for two weeks, to collaborate with the team as we evaluated and analyzed the food, and, most important, to come together in a unified way. The review had forced us to rethink our food, our leadership, our teamwork, and the guest experience. What did we need to do to get the guests back and show why we are who we are? We kept doing our job, striving to be a little better every day.

Within the year, though, Eli decided to step away. I was now chef de cuisine.

I was chef de cuisine and I was scared. I was now in charge of a Michelin three-star restaurant, and because of the lingering effects of the review, I was in the crosshairs. But I had incredible support from my family, my team, and Chef.

I was able to make it my own. Because in the end, it's not about the food—though of course the food is important. What it's really about is respect. If there's one thing I want to teach the next incoming commis, it's just that. Respect for ingredients. Respect for technique. Respect for your colleagues and the hard work that they do. Respect for the openness of ideas, respect for the importance of teamwork, respect for teaching and mentoring.

That is how we continue to evolve.

MY JOURNEY TO AMERICA

WHEN I WAS A YOUNG COOK in London, The French Laundry was not a real place for me; it was a mythical restaurant that I had read about and seen photos of, a place of bright sunshine in an idyllic village on the other side of the world. Something you hear stories about but know you will never see. Little did I realize that it would be a major part of my life for eleven years.

Like Thomas and David, my first experience of kitchens was washing dishes, when I was fifteen and still at school, and I have to say that I loved it. The concentration it took to work a busy evening service effectively—the satisfaction at the end of the night when you leave with stacks of bright white plates, piles of glistening cutlery and a workstation of shiny stainless steel—just made me happy and left me fulfilled. Eventually, John and Angela, the owners of the Red Lion restaurant just outside Cambridge, and the first of many amazing people to support me, taught me to help them in the kitchen with actual cooking—and that started me on an incredible journey.

This part-time job as a cook led me to decide that I wanted to make a career out of cooking. Resolute in my goal, I hopped on a train to London to live with my aunt Camilla and began my three-year apprenticeship at the Café Royal. During these informative London years, I was lucky enough to work for some amazing chefs: Herbert Berger at the Café Royal, Michel Bourdin at the Connaught, Daniel Clifford at Midsummer House, and Tom Aikens at his eponymous restaurant. Michel Bourdin once told me that it is better to work in a few great places for a long time than a great many places and gain lesser experience. I really took this to heart and worked hard to gain the most from each establishment.

There came a point in 2008, after I had been working in some of the best restaurants and hotels in England for thirteen years, where I did not see what was next on my path. I was a little lost and didn't know where to take my career next—all I knew was that I wanted to carry on learning and gaining new experiences, and had a desire to gain these outside England. My friend Natalie showed me an advertisement in a UK catering magazine for a head pastry chef at per se in New York. I dared to dream for a moment of a new adventure in a new country, and I applied! With a recommendation from Tom Aikens I got the position and moved across the pond to New York City.

April 2008: I still remember vividly walking into the kitchen at per se for the first time. The walls gleaming and sparkly clean under the bright lights, the space open but organized and the cooks busy and focused like a well-oiled machine. David was on the meat station, Corey on the fish station. They stood out instantly, and it has been an absolute pleasure to travel the road with both of them. Throughout our work together, they have inspired me so many times and I am always grateful for that.

I CERTAINLY WAS NOT PREPARED for the difference in culture that I would experience by moving to America. I had visited on holiday before, and we all watch American films and TV shows, so how different could it be? As I found out, the answer is very different. My first year was a huge learning curve, and I had to adapt quickly just to get my head above water. But I was not alone: the team at per se was amazing, and they all helped me through it. With a lot of advice, listening, learning, and inspiration from the people around me, such as Jonathan Benno and Eli Kaimeh, after a year I finally felt like I was swimming with the current.

The next ten years were a whirlwind of activity: expanding the per se pastry program, taking on the challenge of aligning the per se and French Laundry pastry teams, helping to open four new restaurants, and eventually moving to California to assist the French Laundry pastry team through the renovation and to land in one of the most beautiful kitchens I have ever seen. I really had made it to that faraway place that I first saw just a glimpse of in *The French Laundry Cookbook* twenty years ago.

IT IS THE PEOPLE who made my time at per se and The French Laundry so memorable. Working with so many talented cooks, leaders, and mentors has been a pleasure and an honor. When people are always looking to help one another, teach each other, and learn from each other, something as simple as a casual five-minute conversation with David or Corey about food can lead to a month's worth of new dishes, experimentation, and refinement.

Truly, though, it was the cooks of the pastry teams at per se and The French Laundry that led my journey through those two great kitchens. I learned from them every day. Some of them taught me to listen more, some to talk more. Some taught me what it truly means to be a leader, others taught me about trust. And I think every single one of them taught me something new about pastry that reminded me that I still have so much to learn.

ABOUT THE RECIPES

THIS BOOK CONTAINS RECIPES for more than seventy fairly elaborate dishes, which include equally elaborate components. One of the goals of this book is to provide a glimpse into our kitchens, a look at the actual ingredients, recipes, and processes we use. Therefore, we did not significantly alter the recipes so they'd be easier for home cooks.

Indeed, the dishes in this book are even more complex than in *The French Laundry Cookbook*, reflecting the evolution of fine dining. The recipes have more components, and the components themselves have become increasingly refined, because they can be, because the tools are better and our kitchens are more advanced. Most important, there are more ingredients to work with that are of a quality that would have astonished me twenty-six years ago. I'm astonished even today. This is not because of our chefs; it's because of the farmers, foragers, fishermen, and gardeners who raise and grow this food, and our meaningful partnerships with them. It's an extraordinary symbiosis.

That said, all the recipes in this book—and in all my books—have been tested by Susie Heller and her team. She wanted to make these recipes accessible to those who want to cook the dishes in full, or even just some of their fantastic components (there was a time when Susie wouldn't stop talking about the kale aïoli, for instance). Susie found alternatives to some of the more challenging professional equipment, for example the combi oven, with which we can precisely control temperature and humidity—a game changer for us. But most of what we cook in the combi oven can be cooked using an immersion circulator, a tool that is now widely available and affordable, and that's how the recipes for this book have been developed.

So for those chefs and ambitious and talented home cooks who want to know exactly how our dishes come together, these recipes are exact, and Susie has worked hard to make sure they work in these quantities. The following is advice from her on cooking from the recipes:

Read the recipes before you begin to cook to be certain that you have the necessary equipment, and refer to the timing of each component. In many cases, components can be made days ahead—some require advance preparation—and some freeze well for longer storage.

Yields. In most cases, the recipes serve six as part of a multicourse dinner. You can easily increase the serving size of proteins, if you wish. The component quantities within a recipe can vary, however. Some yield just the amount needed for the recipe; others make more, because you need to work with larger quantities in order to get the correct result. Whenever possible, we've given you storage information for extra product.

Oven temperatures. The oven temperatures given are for a convection oven with the fan running, unless otherwise stated in the recipe.

Cookware sizes. We usually provide the size of the pan used in the development of the recipe. It's not crucial that you have the size listed, but do take the size difference into consideration as you cook. For instance, if you use a pot smaller than what is called for, it may take longer to reduce a liquid; if you use a larger one, the quantity will reduce more quickly.

Measurements. In the kitchen, our chefs most often use metric measurements, and in this book, we do, too. Most cookware is listed in US measures, with the closest metric equivalent in parentheses.

For very small measurements such as 1, 2, and 3 millimeters, there is no direct US correlation, so we give those measurements in metric only. Also, when a piece of equipment, such as a confectionary ruler, is sold only in metric sizes, we have given only the metric measure.

Blending. We always use a Vitamix blender, which is considerably more powerful than most home blenders. Because quantities are often small, we suggest that you use the smaller blender container, if you have multiple sizes, to make it easier to remove the finished product from the container, and use the tamper that comes with the Vitamix to help blend small quantities.

Sous vide. Many of our recipes use the process of cooking food sous vide: vacuum sealed in a bag and cooked in a water bath using an immersion circulator that maintains a precise water temperature. We'll list immersion circulator, as well as chamber vacuum sealer or any other professional-grade equipment, under "Special Equipment" at the start of each recipe when necessary. If an alternative cooking method can be used, the recipe will explain that.

Sources. If a specific brand has a flavor profile that is necessary for the correct recipe result, it will be noted in the ingredient list. A general list of preferred equipment, tools, and ingredient brands can be found on page 367.

The rest of my notes are standard: all eggs are large, all butter is unsalted, all kosher salt is Diamond Crystal, all sugar is granulated—unless stated otherwise.

I urge you to try some of the recipe components even if you aren't preparing the entire dish.   —*Susie Heller*

CANAPÉS

CANAPÉS

*The Spirit of
Generosity and
Graciousness*

IN THE BEGINNING, it was the cornet, and that was it (see page xviii). But as with everything we do, we continued to push ourselves to do more, to be more generous. The amuse-bouche was customary at a lot of fine-dining places at the time. But we loved our canapés so much that sometimes we'd serve guests nine canapés before the menu began. Pickled oysters, *gougenettes*, shrimp with avocado salsa served on a fork. Canapés began as a way for us to use the excellent products we had discovered in new ways, and to introduce our guests to the philosophy of The French Laundry.

The canapé station remains the hardest station for a chef de partie to work. It's usually manned by the youngest and least experienced chef in the kitchen after the commis. It's rapid-fire: three, four, even five courses you're responsible for as soon as the guest is seated. If you're successful on canapé, you may be in charge of turning out as many as twelve. They have to be ready the moment the restaurant opens. The chef de partie's work will set the tone for the rest of a guest's meal. We put the young chefs on the canapé station because if they can be successful there, they can be successful at any station in the restaurant. And yes, they work right next to me or the chef de cuisine and so are scrutinized, but they also have our support—we can help them as they find their legs.

Today our canapés are much more refined. We don't do the crazy stuff we used to do, sending out four different soups to a party of four. But canapés still have that same spirit of spontaneity and dynamic technique. They've become more composed the way other dishes have.

We have a large array of canapés now, but a meal at The French Laundry or per se still always opens with a cornet, either the classic or a variation, such as the Everything Bagel Cornet (salmon and cream cheese, which led to Corey's Bagel and Cream Cheese course—one idea always leading to another). We used to serve a cheese-filled gougère, which goes so well with the champagne we like to serve to begin a meal. When we began serving a more elaborate gougère as the cheese course, we had a void in our canapé repertoire, which led to much experimentation. One evening, we had a guest in for dinner, a golfer just finishing the Masters Tournament in Georgia, so we made a fun Southern canapé of pimento cheese and crackers. The guests dining at a table beside his saw the presentation and asked if they could have one as well, and we were happy to oblige. And we knew the search for our new cheese canapé was over. We now serve a "Ritz cracker" canapé that's filled with a mousse made from grated cheddar, toasted dehydrated onions, mayonnaise, and crème fraîche in place of the pimento cheese filling. This, too, will continue to evolve.

What follows are several of our plated canapés—small, light courses that welcome you into the meal. Caviar courses are included in this category as well.

SMOKED STURGEON RILLETTES ON AN EVERYTHING BAGEL

Everything Bagel, Pickled Pearl Onions, and Regiis Ova Caviar

Makes 36 bagels

EVERYTHING BAGEL CRUMBLE

Canola oil, for deep-frying

15 grams peeled garlic cloves

25 grams peeled shallots

Wondra flour, for dredging

33 grams sunflower seeds, toasted and minced

33 grams poppy seeds, toasted

13 grams white sesame seeds, toasted and minced

1.5 grams caraway seeds, toasted

Kosher salt

BAGELS

Sponge

150 grams bread flour

150 grams tepid water (about 80°F/27°C)

0.55 grams SAF instant yeast

2 grams malt syrup

Dough

315 grams bread flour

125 grams tepid water (about 80°F/27°C)

4 grams malt syrup

10 grams sea salt

2 grams SAF instant yeast

SMOKED STURGEON RILLETTES

335 grams smoked sturgeon, homemade (see page 239) or store-bought

155 grams cream cheese, at room temperature

25 grams whole butter, at room temperature

3 grams minced shallot

9 grams Agrumato lemon oil

Kosher salt

TO COMPLETE

36 chives

Regiis Ova caviar, 10 to 12 grams per portion

15 red pearl onions, 10 cut into petals, 5 cut into rings, pickled (see page 184)

Onion blossoms, for garnish

SPECIAL EQUIPMENT

Japanese mandoline

Thirty-six ½- to ⅝-inch-wide (13- to 16-millimeter) food-safe copper cutters or couplings, about 1⅛ inches (3 centimeters) long

Two 5-millimeter-thick confectionary rulers

This is a classic New York City staple: smoked fish and cream cheese on a bagel. Here it's an everything bagel, with pickled pearl onions to add acidity. And of course, these very components go well with caviar, and it's a link to the Everything Bagel Cornet at The French Laundry.

Our "everything" mix combines chopped fried garlic and shallot and sunflower, poppy, sesame, and caraway seeds. We buy sturgeon whole, skin and bone them, then smoke them over applewood. After the fish has cooled, it's simply paddled with about a third as much softened cream cheese and some butter, and finished with minced shallot and Agrumato lemon oil. For a perfect presentation, we roll out the rillettes on parchment, freeze them, then use a ring cutter to make discs the exact size as the halved bagel.

To serve, we simply halve the bagel, top it with a disc of the rillettes, add a sprinkle of the "everything" crumble, top it with quenelle of Regiis Ova caviar, and garnish it with pickled onion and a split chive tip.

FOR THE EVERYTHING BAGEL CRUMBLE

Fill a small saucepot with 2 inches (5 centimeters) of canola oil. Heat the oil to 300°F (150°C). Thinly slice the garlic on a Japanese mandoline. Thinly slice the shallots and separate them into rings. Fry the garlic for about 1 minute, until golden brown, and drain on paper towels. Coat the shallots in Wondra flour, then fry for about 2 minutes, until golden brown. Remove from the oil, drain on paper towels, and let cool. Mince the garlic and shallots.

In a bowl, combine the minced shallots and garlic, the sunflower seeds, poppy seeds, sesame seeds, and caraway. Mix until evenly distributed. Season to taste with salt. Store in an airtight container at room temperature for up to 3 days.

FOR THE BAGELS

Make the sponge: In a bowl, stir together the flour, water, yeast, and malt syrup. Transfer the sponge to a covered container and proof in a warm spot for 2 to 3 hours, until it has doubled in size and has a delicate aerated structure with a lot of bubbles.

(continued)

Make the dough: Transfer the sponge to the bowl of a stand mixer fitted with the dough hook. Add the flour, water, malt syrup, sea salt, and yeast. Mix the dough on medium speed for about 2 minutes. Stop the machine and use the dough to press and pick up any stray pieces on the bottom of the bowl. Mix for 2 minutes more. The dough will pull away from the sides of the bowl and form a smooth ball.

Remove the dough from the mixer bowl, shape it into a ball, and transfer it to an oiled bowl. Cover with plastic wrap and proof in a warm spot for 1 to 2 hours, until doubled in size (the time can vary greatly depending on the temperature of the kitchen).

Turn the dough out onto a very lightly floured board and divide it into about thirty-six 20-gram pieces. Cup your fingers around a portion of the dough and, using the palm of your hand, roll the dough against the board to form a perfectly smooth ball. As they are shaped, arrange the balls of dough on a parchment-lined sheet pan and cover with a lightly dampened kitchen towel to prevent a skin from forming.

If you will be cooking the bagels within a few hours, cover the balls of dough with the lightly dampened towel and proof in a warm spot for about 15 minutes, then refrigerate for at least 1 hour and up to 4 hours before cooking. There will not be a dramatic change, but they should have a slight rise. The dough can also be shaped, covered with plastic wrap, and refrigerated directly (without proofing) for up to 1 day. With either method, the dough will be cooked directly from the refrigerator.

We bake the bagels in deck ovens, with the top deck at 470°F (243°C) and the bottom deck at 450°F (232°C). If you do not have deck ovens, preheat your oven to 475°F (246°C). Line two sheet pans with parchment paper. Spray the inside and outside of thirty-six ½- to ⅝-inch-wide (13- to 16-millimeter) food-safe copper cutters or couplings, about 1⅛ inches (3 centimeters) long, with nonstick spray.

Bring a large saucepot of water to a boil. Working in batches, add 6 bagels to the water and adjust the heat to maintain a rapid simmer. Cook for about 1 minute on each side. Transfer the bagels to the prepared sheet pans and use the cutters to punch through the centers of the bagels, leaving the cutters in place. Remove the dough from the center of each cutter.

Place the bagels in the oven. If using a deck oven, release a 6-second injection of steam into the oven and bake for 10 to 12 minutes, until the bagels are a light golden brown. If you don't have a deck oven, bake for 8 to 10 minutes, until golden brown. The bagels should have a classic chewy texture. Remove from the oven, remove the copper cutters, and let cool.

FOR THE SMOKED STURGEON RILLETTES

Remove any skin from the sturgeon and cut into 1-inch (2.5-centimeter) pieces. In the bowl of the stand mixer fitted with the paddle attachment, mix the sturgeon on low speed to break it up. Add the cream cheese and butter. Begin mixing on low speed, gradually increasing the speed to medium to aerate the rillette, and mix until smooth, about 4 minutes in total.

Scrape down the sides and bottom of the bowl. With the mixer running, add the shallot and stream in the lemon oil. Season to taste with salt.

Place a piece of parchment paper on the work surface. Transfer the rillettes to the parchment and position two 5-millimeter-thick confectionary rulers parallel to each other on either side of the rillettes. Top with a second piece of parchment. Lay a rolling pin over the rulers and roll the rillettes into an even layer. Remove the rulers, transfer the parchment with the rillettes to a sheet pan, and freeze until firm.

Remove the rillettes from the freezer, lift off the top piece of parchment, and use a plain round cutter the same size as the bagel to punch out discs of the rillettes. Use one of the copper cutters you used for baking the bagels to cut out the centers of the rillettes (the hole in the rillettes should match up with the hole in the bagel). Cover the rillettes with plastic wrap and freeze until completely frozen, about 2 hours or up to 1 week. The trimmings can be combined and rerolled to punch out more discs or served as a spread.

TO COMPLETE

Cut about ¾ inch (2 centimeters) from the top of each chive. Using a sharp tourné knife, slice each chive tip lengthwise, beginning ⅛ inch (3 millimeters) from the bottom and cutting upward, to create a V shape.

Cut the bagels in half crosswise. You will only use the bottom half; the tops can be reserved for another use. Top each bagel bottom with a ring of frozen rillettes and sprinkle some everything crumble over the rillettes. Top with a quenelle of caviar and garnish with the chive tips, pickled onions, and onion blossoms.

DÉGUSTATION OF ENGLISH PEAS

Charcoal-Grilled Petits Pois, Pea Shoots, and English Pea Granité

Makes 6 servings

ENGLISH PEA STOCK

225 grams English pea
shells (pods with the
peas removed)

315 grams water

ENGLISH PEA GRANITÉ

½ sheet silver leaf gelatin

20 grams sugar

5 grams kosher salt

2 grams Pre-Hy (page
109)

1 gram Agrumato
lemon oil

PEA PUREE

120 grams kosher salt,
plus more to taste

60 grams sugar

250 grams shelled
English peas

13 grams Agrumato
lemon oil

5 grams Pre-Hy (page
109)

PEA POWDER

120 grams kosher salt,
plus more to taste

60 grams sugar

250 grams shelled
English peas

**CHARCOAL-GRILLED
PETITS POIS**

Extra-virgin olive oil

Kosher salt

TO COMPLETE

18 pea shoots

Extra-virgin olive oil

Kosher salt

SPECIAL EQUIPMENT

Dehydrator

Mortar and pestle

This dish shows how Corey is able to utilize every single part of a vegetable, even the parts one would assume you couldn't extract flavor from. He uses the pods for stock. He makes a puree with the stock and peas. He makes a granité from the stock, and he lightly smokes and grills the peas. It is a zero-waste dish. Pea shoots and pea flowers, when in season, finish the dish, an all-encompassing display of the textures and flavors of fresh peas.

FOR THE ENGLISH PEA STOCK

Trim and discard the ends of the pea shells, removing any woody stems and dirt. Thoroughly wash the pea shells and drain in a colander. Coarsely chop the shells into ½-inch (1.25-centimeter) pieces. In a blender, blend the pea shells and water until the shells have broken down.

Line a fine-mesh strainer with a dampened tea towel and set it over a medium bowl. Pour the pea stock through the towel; discard the solids. Refrigerate the stock in an airtight container for up to 3 days or freeze for up to 3 months. The stock will separate as it sits, so whisk it well before using.

FOR THE ENGLISH PEA GRANITÉ

Submerge the gelatin in a bowl of ice water to bloom (soften) for about 5 minutes. Pour about 50 grams of the pea stock into a bowl and warm in the microwave for about 30 seconds. Remove the softened gelatin from the ice water and squeeze out the excess water. Stir the gelatin into the warm stock to dissolve.

In a blender, blend 150 grams of the pea stock, the warm stock-gelatin mixture, the sugar, salt, Pre-Hy, and lemon oil. Blend for about 30 seconds, until homogenous, then strain through a chinois into a small bowl. Nestle the bowl in an ice-water bath and chill for about 10 minutes, until it is very cold.

Wrap the bowl well with plastic wrap and freeze the granité until solid, about 3 hours. The granité may be kept frozen for up to 2 days before serving.

(continued)

FOR THE PEA PUREE

Bring 2 quarts (2 liters) water to a boil with the salt and sugar. Add the peas to the boiling water and cook until tender, about 5 minutes. Drain the peas and, while they are hot, place them in the blender with 38 grams of the pea stock, the lemon oil, and the Pre-Hy. Blend until smooth, using the tamper to keep the puree moving. Taste and season with salt. Immediately pour the puree into a bowl and nestle the bowl in an ice-water bath to preserve the color and chill the puree. Pass the chilled puree through a chinois and refrigerate in an airtight container for up to 3 days.

FOR THE PEA POWDER

Bring 2 quarts (2 liters) water to a boil with the salt and sugar. Add the peas to the boiling water and cook until tender, about 5 minutes. Drain the peas, transfer to a small bowl, and nestle the bowl in an ice-water bath until cool.

Set a colander over a bowl. Place a handful of the peas in the colander. Gently shake the colander and massage the peas until the smallest peas, the petits pois, fall through the holes of the colander into the bowl. Repeat with the remaining peas. Reserve 30 grams of the smallest peas for charcoal grilling.

Squeeze the remaining, larger peas to release the two halves of the pea from the skins; the pea halves will not be used for this recipe but can be reserved for another use. Place the pea skins on a sheet pan lined with a nonstick silicone baking mat and dry in a dehydrator at 140°F (60°C) for 24 hours. (If the pan doesn't fit in your dehydrator, line the dehydrator with parchment paper and spread the pea skins on the paper.)

Grind the dried pea skins to a fine powder using a mortar and pestle. Sift the pea powder and store it in an airtight container in a cool, dry place for up to 2 weeks.

FOR THE CHARCOAL-GRILLED PETITS POIS

Prepare a fire (see page 270).

Make an open foil pouch by pressing two layers of aluminum foil over a pint (500-milliliter) container or a small bowl. The pouch should be large enough to accommodate the peas in a single layer. Poke small holes in the foil using a cake tester or toothpick to allow the smoke to penetrate the foil. Flatten the bottom of the pouch so that the peas can cook evenly over the grill.

Put the reserved 30 grams blanched small peas in the pouch. Season with olive oil and salt and place over the fire. Grill, stirring the peas often, for about 5 minutes, until they take on a pleasant smoky flavor. Refrigerate until cold.

TO COMPLETE

Thirty minutes before serving, scrape the granité with a fork and return it to the freezer until serving. Put six serving bowls in the freezer to chill for about 20 minutes.

Spoon about 10 grams of the pea puree into each chilled bowl. Spoon the granité over the puree and sprinkle with the grilled peas. Dress the pea shoots lightly with olive oil and salt and scatter them over the dish. Using a small fine-mesh sieve, dust the surface with pea powder.

FIG LEAF GRANITÉ

Fig Puree and Candy-Striped Figs

Makes 6 servings

FIG LEAF GRANITÉ

200 grams coconut water

300 grams water

100 grams sugar

40 grams chiffonade of
    fresh fig leaves

50 grams lemon juice

6 grams fleur de sel, or to
    taste

FIG PUREE

400 grams diced overripe
    figs

200 grams beet juice

50 grams sugar, plus
    more to taste

1 gram ascorbic acid

6 grams agar-agar

Fleur de sel

Lemon juice

TO COMPLETE

3 candy-stripe figs, stems
    removed, chilled until
    ice cold

SPECIAL EQUIPMENT

Chamber vacuum sealer
    (optional)

Figs grow beautifully all over Northern California, so when they're in season, we use them a lot. We like to serve this dish at the end of the season when the sun starts to set earlier. This results in a slower growth of the fig, and they almost bake on the tree. There is also little precipitation in the valley at that time, so the figs' natural flavor becomes intensely concentrated. This is nature's version of Corey's dehydrated-rehydrated honeynut squash (see page 200).

The leaves of the tree also offer great flavor. When you tear a fig leaf, you'll smell a hint of coconut, which gave us the idea to use them to infuse coconut water. We bring the coconut water just to a simmer with salt, sugar, and lemon, then add the sliced leaves and steep for about 10 minutes. The infused coconut water is strained, frozen, and served as a granité with the "late harvest" figs, seasoned with a little sea salt, and a jammy fig puree, made with beet juice to give it an earthy flavor.

FOR THE FIG LEAF GRANITÉ

Put the coconut water, water, and sugar in a 2-quart (2-liter) saucepot and bring to a boil over medium heat. Add the fig leaves to the pot, remove from the heat, cover with a lid, and steep for 10 minutes. Season with the lemon juice and fleur de sel. Strain through a chinois into a small bowl and discard the fig leaves. Cover the bowl with plastic wrap and place in the freezer until frozen completely.

FOR THE FIG PUREE

Put the figs, beet juice, sugar, and ascorbic acid in a 2-quart (2-liter) saucepot and bring to a boil over medium heat. Whisk in the agar-agar and boil, whisking continuously to prevent scorching or boiling over, until the agar-agar is activated, 2 to 3 minutes. Transfer to a bowl and nestle the bowl in an ice-water bath. Chill, undisturbed, until the fig puree base is completely firm and set.

Coarsely chop the fig puree base and transfer it to the blender. Beginning on low speed and gradually increasing to high, blend the puree until it is completely smooth, using the tamper to keep the thick puree moving. Pass the puree through a chinois into a container. Taste and adjust the seasoning with sugar, fleur de sel, and lemon juice.

If you have a chamber vacuum sealer, place the container, uncovered, in the sealer chamber. Run a complete cycle on full pressure to remove any air bubbles incorporated during blending. This will give the puree clarity and shine.

The puree can be refrigerated in an airtight container for up to 3 days.

TO COMPLETE

When the granité has frozen completely, use a fork to quickly scrape along the surface, creating a slushy consistency; work quickly so the granité does not begin to melt. Return the granité to the freezer. At least 30 minutes before serving, put six serving bowls in the freezer.

Cut the candy-stripe figs into small, bite-size pieces that will fit in the bottom of the serving bowls. Spoon a 15-gram dollop of the fig puree into the bottom of each chilled serving bowl and arrange the fig pieces next to the puree. Finish with a large spoonful of the granité over the top.

TOMATO CONSOMMÉ

Vine Consommé with Early Girl Tomato Bavarois and Plump Tomato Seeds

A SIDE SPOON OF TOMATO BAVAROIS
Whipped cream infused with tomato essence, set with gelatin.

CONSOMMÉ BASE
Green (unripe) tomatoes and some of the vine are salted and pulsed in a food processor with onion, garlic, and fennel seeds to a salsa-like texture and allowed to macerate.

FINISHED CONSOMMÉ
The "salsa" is strained, the solids are cooked, and water is added. We combine the liquids and clarify them with egg whites. The green vines are then steeped in the consommé like tea. We serve the consommé simply, in a small bowl with basil seeds.

In very early summer when the tomato plants are growing, but long before the tomato harvest, those vines in the hot sun send off an intoxicating perfume, a promise of summer. David and Corey would watch the gardeners prune the young, tender vines to keep the tomato plants from becoming gangly. They loved the smell and, with their insistence on using everything the plant or animal has to offer, wanted to put them to use. The result is a small miracle from what once went to the compost.

FROST-KISSED GARDEN CAULIFLOWER

Tender Bavarois and Green Orange Gelée

Makes 6 servings

CRISPY CAULIFLOWER

100 grams cauliflower

300 grams prepared veg blanc (see page 185)

TINY CAULIFLOWER FLORETS

24 tiny cauliflower florets, about ⅜ inch (1 centimeter) in diameter

100 grams prepared veg blanc (see page 185)

CAULIFLOWER BAVAROIS

2 sheets silver leaf gelatin

250 grams cauliflower florets

300 grams heavy cream

70 grams water

50 grams whole butter

10 grams sugar

6 grams fleur de sel

10 grams lemon juice

GREEN ORANGE GELÉE

½ sheet silver leaf gelatin

2 large green (underripe) oranges, or ripe oranges if green are unavailable

5 grams yuzu juice

5 grams sugar

2 grams kosher salt

30 grams water

TO COMPLETE

Canola oil, for deep-frying

Kosher salt

Sorrel leaves and blossoms

SPECIAL EQUIPMENT

Japanese mandoline

Dehydrator

Chamber vacuum sealer (optional)

Six 65-gram glasses

One chilly winter morning, our gardener came into the kitchen, thinking his cauliflower had been destroyed by an unexpected frost. But when David tasted it, he found that it was almost sweet. He loved it. Our gardener later figured out that the sudden cold had sent a signal to the cauliflower that made its carbohydrates spike—thus the term "frost-kissed." That very day, it was served as a salad that included black truffle and hazelnuts to Michael Bauer, former restaurant critic for the *San Francisco Chronicle*. The cauliflower's natural sweetness worked beautifully. Today we serve it as a bavarois, or light mousse, for a canapé. We glaze it with a barely set gelée made from unripened green oranges picked from a tree in our neighborhood. The green orange has a pleasantly sour flavor that marries well with the garden sorrel and crispy puffed cauliflower. The bavarois is a lot like the cauliflower panna cotta I originally served as a companion to the Oysters and Pearls in the early days of The French Laundry.

FOR THE CRISPY CAULIFLOWER

Cut the cauliflower into large florets. Using a Japanese mandoline, thinly shave the florets to about 1 millimeter thick. The size does not need to remain uniform, but the thickness should be consistent.

Place the shaved cauliflower in a bowl large enough to hold the cauliflower and the veg blanc. In a saucepot, bring the veg blanc to a boil, then pour it over the cauliflower and stir two or three times. Steep for 2 minutes. Drain in a colander and lay the cauliflower on a clean kitchen towel to dry. Arrange the cauliflower in a dehydrator and dehydrate at 160°F (71°C) overnight. The cauliflower will become completely dry and crisp with a light golden brown color.

The crispy cauliflower can be stored in an airtight container at room temperature for up to 3 days.

FOR THE TINY CAULIFLOWER FLORETS

If you have a chamber vacuum sealer, place the florets and the veg blanc in a sous vide bag, place in the sealer chamber, and vacuum seal. If you don't have a chamber vacuum sealer, combine the cauliflower and the veg blanc in a container and cover.

Refrigerate for at least 6 hours or for up to 1 day.

(continued)

Submerge the gelatin in a bowl of ice water to bloom (soften) for about 5 minutes.

Combine the cauliflower, 200 grams of the cream, the water, butter, sugar, and fleur de sel in a 1-quart (1-liter) saucepot and bring to a boil over medium-low heat. Reduce the heat and simmer for 5 minutes, or until the cauliflower is just tender. You should have 400 grams.

Meanwhile, whip the remaining 100 grams cream to soft peaks.

Transfer the cauliflower-cream mixture to a blender and blend on medium speed until smooth. Remove the softened gelatin from the ice water and squeeze out any excess water. Add the gelatin and the lemon juice to the blender and blend for 1 minute to incorporate. Strain the cauliflower cream into a bowl and nestle the bowl in an ice-water bath. Gently stir with a silicone spatula for 1 to 2 minutes to cool to room temperature; the gelatin should not begin to set.

Remove the bowl from the ice-water bath and, using a whisk, fold in the whipped cream in two additions. Divide the bavarois among six 65-gram glasses and refrigerate until completely set.

FOR THE GREEN ORANGE GELÉE

While the bavarois sets, submerge the gelatin in a bowl of ice water to bloom (soften) for about 5 minutes.

Juice the green oranges and strain the juice through a chinois. Combine 60 grams of the orange juice, the yuzu juice, sugar, and salt in a 1-quart (1-liter) saucepot. Heat over low heat, stirring, just to dissolve the sugar and salt. Do not boil or reduce the liquid. Remove the softened gelatin from the ice water and squeeze out any excess water. Add the gelatin to the juice mixture and stir just until dissolved.

Stir in the water and pass the mixture through a chinois into a spouted measuring cup. Let cool to room temperature (if it is hotter than that, it could melt the bavarois). Pour the gelée down a side of each glass to spread evenly over the bavarois. Refrigerate until set, for at least 30 minutes or for up to 1 day.

TO COMPLETE

Fill a deep fryer with 2 to 3 inches (5 to 7.5 centimeters) of canola oil. Heat the oil to 375°F (190°C). Put the dehydrated cauliflower in a small strainer and lower it into the fryer. Fry until the cauliflower puffs and becomes golden brown and crispy, less than 30 seconds. Remove from the fryer, drain on paper towels, and lightly season with salt.

Remove the tiny cauliflower florets from the veg blanc and lay them on a clean kitchen towel to dry; discard the veg blanc.

Place 4 or 5 tiny florets and 3 or 4 pieces of crispy cauliflower on top of the gelée in each glass. Garnish with sorrel leaves and blossoms.

PURVEYORS
AS PARTNERS

IN 2017, we lost one of our dearest partners, Ingrid Bengis, whose fish set the standard for fine-dining quality in the early 1980s. She had to approve of the chef before she'd sell him or her such pristine products! Among the many products she delivered was amazingly sweet peekytoe crab, which is tricky because it's so hard getting all the shell fragments out of the meat. As a chef aspiring to four-star status, I couldn't risk a patron (or critic!) getting a piece of shell in his or her crab salad with cucumber jelly and frisée. There was one picker who was flawless, Tina Gray, and I made sure each pint of picked crabmeat that arrived at The French Laundry was personally signed by her.

When Tina, who didn't have health insurance, became ill, Ingrid called me asking for help with Tina's medical bills; we didn't think twice about helping. I couldn't do my job if Ingrid couldn't do hers, and Ingrid couldn't do her job if Tina couldn't do *hers*.

When I was opening per se, I spoke to our beloved butter maker, Diane St. Clair, and told her I'd be needing to double our butter order. She said, "I'm giving you all the butter I can make. I only have four cows!" I said, "You need to buy more cows!" And she did.

Both stories are a reminder to me about how it's all interconnected. And why I think of them as partners, not purveyors.

They, more than any of us, devote their lives to their work. Those people who work with living things must always be engaged, and not just during a forty-hour workweek. They are successful because of this devotion, and if they don't succeed and thrive in their work, we certainly can't.

So here, I believe, is the ultimate way to think of Ingrid, of Soyoung Scanlan, Skip Bennett, the Pryzants, and Brent Wolfe, who in this book represent the hundreds of farmers, fishermen, foragers, and gardeners upon whom we rely: they are the gatekeepers of our health, and we need to support them in every possible way.

SKIP
BENNETT

*Island Creek Oysters,
Duxbury, Massachusetts*

Skip Bennett was born in the Island Creek neighborhood of Duxbury, Massachusetts, in 1965. His dad was a lobsterman, and Skip virtually grew up on Cape Cod Bay. While studying finance at Merrimack College, north of Boston, he made money by doing what he'd *been* doing for fun since he was a boy: digging for clams and mussels on the beach. Only now, he sold them. "I made *good money*," he recalls, important for a man long intent on moving to New York City's Financial District.

When he graduated, though, he decided to take a year off before heading to Wall Street to begin his professional life. He moved back to Duxbury, wanting a little more time on his beloved bay. He heard about a man on Cape Cod, in Wellfleet, who sold clam seed. Skip thought he'd experiment with clam farming, rather than digging, during his year off.

He found he loved physical work and working outdoors. The clams flourished in his bay, and he knew he could sell them, just as he had in college. By 1993, he realized he grew enough clams to make a living from it. Forget Wall Street. He was going to be a clam farmer! And he was—for two years, until 1995, when a parasite wiped out all his clams.

Devastated, desperate, not knowing what to do but not wanting to restock his beds with vulnerable clams, he remembered hearing about a man in Maine, someone named Mook. So he did what you did back then—he dialed 4-1-1, the general information number, and asked the operator, "Mook? Somewhere in Maine?" Sure enough, he was told, that would be Bill Mook of Mook Sea Farm in Walpole, Maine. Skip bought his first oyster seed from Bill.

Would this even work? Oysters didn't grow wild in the bay. Oysters don't grow wild in Duxbury because the water never gets warm enough for them to spawn, and even if they were to spawn, it would be

too cold for the larvae to thrive. But as spring turns to summer, the winds change and the bay becomes colder—temperatures perfect for oysters.

The bay proved to be a nutritious environment for oysters that have already formed a shell. Skip could start the oysters in a controlled environment and seed the beds once they were ready, when the oysters were less vulnerable. Cape Cod Bay proved to be an ideal environment for *farming* oysters.

By 1996, Skip was able to begin selling oysters. Were they any good? He had no idea. He hadn't eaten more than a few in his life. But at the time, it almost didn't matter—wholesalers bought all the oysters and distributed them without much regard for quality or origin, which was why so few restaurants had oysters on their menus, Skip explained. Chefs could only buy from wholesalers because at the time there weren't any oyster farmers selling direct to restaurants.

In the fall of 2001, Skip had one of his strongest crops ever, but after 9/11, as he put it, "You couldn't sell anything to anyone. The world kind of stopped."

What to do with all his oysters? He had no idea. He wasn't a foodie. There was no farm-to-table ideology in the air. Maybe a restaurant in a big city would take them? A buddy of his who worked in tech in Boston told him about Chris Schlesinger's East Coast Grill and Raw Bar over the river in Cambridge. Schlesinger was one of the most popular and best-known chefs in Boston. Skip hadn't heard of him, but the man had a raw bar, so he must've been purchasing oysters from somebody.

Skip drove some of his Island Creek oysters up to Cambridge and found Schlesinger. Schlesinger opened a few, paused after eating the first oyster, then ate a second. "I'll take them all," he said instantly. A mystified Skip remembers, "Chris was blown away."

So now Skip knew he had good oysters—really good oysters. He found some names of well-known restaurants in the back of an oyster book and started calling them. Soon his oysters were in the best seafood restaurant in the country, the Michelin three-star Le Bernardin in New York City. Its chef, Eric Ripert, became an immediate customer. From there, Skip could go anywhere, from New York's Grand Central Oyster Bar to restaurants in Philadelphia, Washington, and, after figuring out how to air ship his oysters, Los Angeles.

By 2004, not only was Island Creek thriving, but its name was spreading.

In February 2002, one week after the opening of per se in New York City, a fire tore through the kitchen, forcing us to close the restaurant. We would remain closed for months during the repair and reconstruction.

What to do with all the servers and chefs—they needed to work but didn't want to leave the company, and I didn't want to lose them. One thing I did was line up jobs for them at other restaurants, but two sous chefs, Rory Herrmann and Chris L'Hommedieu, set out to explore the Eastern Seaboard, looking for new, unusual, or little-known purveyors. (Chris, beloved by us all, would die of cancer in 2014 at age forty-four.)

They had heard about Island Creek. They had a close look at the operation, tasted the oysters, saw Skip's stock and how much he produced.

When per se reopened, Island Creek oysters were on the menu. Chris and Rory knew exactly the size and shape they needed for one of our signature dishes, Oysters and Pearls, and when they saw how Skip harvested the oysters, they asked him for a specific size and shape. Pretty soon, Island Creek was shipping to both restaurants. The flavor is just so clean, a heady whiff of the sea, slightly briny, with just the right salinity for the savory tapioca sabayon in which they rest.

Skip is now back to selling about a hundred thousand oysters in a busy week. He serves eight hundred chefs around the country.

It makes my heart glad that Skip and other purveyors like him no longer have to travel to chefs. They need only do their work well, and we find them.

CHILLED BRENTWOOD CORN SOUP

Celery Branch Salad, Piedmont Hazelnuts, and Celtuce Oil

Makes 6 servings

CHILLED CORN SOUP

80 grams kosher salt, plus more to taste

2,000 grams corn kernels

Cornstarch, if needed

Corn essence (page 288), if needed

CELTUCE OIL

225 grams peeled celtuce

175 grams canola oil

10 grams kosher salt

CELERY BRANCH SALAD

3 celery stalks, with leaves

Kosher salt

1 piece celtuce

45 grams corn kernels

TOASTED PIEDMONT HAZELNUTS

200 grams blanched hazelnuts

Hazelnut oil

Kosher salt

SPECIAL EQUIPMENT

Masticating juicer

Immersion circulator

Chamber vacuum sealer

This canapé soup is thickened by the starches of the main ingredient as they heat. The composition mirrors the French Laundry Corn Parfait canapé with its use of celtuce, sometimes called stem lettuce. Corey also likes to dehydrate all the pulp from straining the pureed corn and turning it into a powder to add to polenta for the freshest-tasting "grits" possible, or making a corn waffle with the dehydrated pulp in place of some of the flour for the bread element in a cheese course. The corn itself is from the French Laundry side of the country, Brentwood, California, about an hour east of San Francisco, and is available early in the season, before most restaurants have fresh corn on their menu. It's some of the sweetest, most tender corn I've tasted.

FOR THE CHILLED CORN SOUP

Bring 8 quarts (8 liters) water to a boil in a large blanching pot. Add the salt and the corn kernels to the pot. Return the water to a rolling boil and cook until the kernels are tender, about 5 minutes. Drain the corn and immediately, while the corn is still hot, juice it with a masticating juicer into a saucepot. Heat the corn juice over low heat, whisking continuously and increasing the heat until it barely simmers and has thickened to the consistency of heavy cream. The natural starch in the corn will thicken the juice into a soup; the consistency could vary depending on the starchiness of the corn. If the soup needs further thickening, cornstarch mixed with a small amount of cold water can be stirred in; if the soup is too thick, it can be loosened by the addition of corn essence. Season with salt to taste. Transfer the soup to a container and nestle the container in an ice-water bath to chill. Cover and refrigerate for up to 3 days. The soup will be served cold.

FOR THE CELTUCE OIL

Set an immersion circulator in a water bath and heat the water to 80°C (176°F). Cut the celtuce into 2-inch (5-centimeter) pieces. Pulse in a food processor, scraping the sides as necessary, until finely minced. Place the celtuce, canola oil, and salt in a sous vide bag. Place in a chamber vacuum sealer and vacuum seal. Cook in the water bath for about 30 minutes, until tender. Pinch the celtuce through the bag to gauge the tenderness. Remove from the water bath and let cool in the bag to room temperature. Strain the celtuce oil through a chinois; discard the solids. Refrigerate the celtuce oil in an airtight container for up to 3 weeks or freeze for up to 3 months.

FOR THE CELERY BRANCH SALAD

Pick the yellow celery leaves from the stalks and submerge them in a bowl of ice water to crisp. The leaves can be refrigerated in the water for up to 1 day.

Up to 1 hour before serving, bring a pot of salted water to a boil. Peel the celery stalks, squaring off the rounded side of the stalks as you peel them. Cut the celery into cubes the size of corn kernels. Blanch the celery in the boiling water until tender. Remove the celery with a strainer and submerge the strainer in an ice-water bath to chill. When the celery is cold, dry it on paper towels and sprinkle with salt to taste.

Peel the celtuce and cut it into cubes the size of corn kernels. Blanch the celtuce as you did the celery and dry it on paper towels.

Blanch the corn as you did the celery and celtuce and dry it on paper towels.

FOR THE TOASTED PIEDMONT HAZELNUTS

Preheat the oven to 350°F (180°C).

At the top of the hazelnut there is a small line, which marks the spot where the two halves of the hazelnut come together. Using a paring knife, cut each hazelnut in half through the line.

Place the hazelnuts in a dry sauté pan and put the pan in the oven. Toast the hazelnuts, tossing every 5 minutes, for about 15 minutes, until golden brown. Season the hazelnuts with hazelnut oil and salt to taste.

TO COMPLETE

Arrange the celery, celtuce, hazelnuts, celery leaves, and corn kernels in the bottom of each serving bowl. Drizzle with the celtuce oil. Pour the corn soup over the vegetables and hazelnuts at the table.

REEBOKS IN THE KITCHEN

Jean-Louis Palladin and the
Evolution of Fine Dining

YOU CAN'T TALK ABOUT FINE DINING IN AMERICA without paying tribute to Jean-Louis Palladin. He was the game changer for my generation. A tall, skinny chef with wild hair and round glasses who wore Jordache jeans and Reeboks with his kitchen whites, he was an entirely different species from the tyrannical French chef of haute cuisine. He hailed from Gascony in southwestern France, the land of duck confit and Armagnac and the Three Musketeers, and had a swashbuckling personality to match. He was thirty-three years old in 1979 when he opened his restaurant, Jean-Louis, in the Watergate Hotel in Washington, DC. So many features of fine dining today owe their origins to Jean-Louis and that restaurant—the celebration of food, the quality of the ingredients, the relationships with farmers, fishermen, gardeners, and foragers—that I don't hesitate to call him the father of modern fine dining in America. What Alice Waters did for California cuisine, Jean-Louis did for fine dining as a leading figure in the farm-to-table movement. He made us all aware that we had to know our farmers; his work demanded that we cultivate a more intimate relationship with ingredients and, in turn, a closer connection to our food.

I must pause here to acknowledge the other huge influence on me and my generation of chefs, a book called *Great Chefs of France*, by Anthony Blake and Quentin Crewe. I can't count the number of my American colleagues who were profoundly influenced by that book. Not necessarily by the food or recipes in it, but by the lives of the chefs it profiled, and the incredible commitment they gave to their work.

Generally speaking, fine dining in this country has had three phases: First, the early years, beginning with Delmonico's in the nineteenth century through the days of the Brown Derby and

Continental cuisine in the mid-twentieth century. Second, the days of French haute cuisine, which historians trace to New York's 1939 World's Fair and the success of Le Pavillon. (After the fair, Le Pavillon's owner, Henri Soulé, and chef Pierre Franey remained in the United States as war refugees. Soulé would run the restaurant, with Franey in the kitchen, until its demise in 1966.). And third, the phase that I call the cuisine of personality-specific styles of cooking, and attitude, unique to individual chefs, which began with Paul Bocuse in France in the 1960s and Jean-Louis in America in 1979. I honestly can't overstate Jean-Louis's impact on American dining.

The days of French haute cuisine gave us what comes to mind for many with the words "fine dining"—stuffy restaurants with intimidating captains, disdainful sommeliers, and heavy French food. These restaurants made you feel inferior if you didn't know the difference between a soup spoon and a sauce spoon. I went to those restaurants, and it wasn't a good feeling. I knew I wanted to be in this profession, I wanted to cook French haute cuisine, but I wanted to run a restaurant that made people feel good. I think my generation changed this, and that wouldn't have happened without Jean-Louis.

Jean-Louis was one of the first modern chefs to go out into the country to find farmers and fishermen who could give him great lamb and live scallops in the shell. He figured out how to get fresh foie gras in this country. He was the first chef sourcing the best eggs.

He brought Eric Ripert into the country, and Larbi Dahrouch. Jimmy Sneed brought his five years' experience under Jean-Louis to the Frog and the Redneck in Richmond, Virginia. Jean-Louis discovered Rod Browne Mitchell of now legendary purveyor Browne Trading Company and worked with him to bring in the best caviar and the finest fish from the waters off the coast of Maine. He asked John and Sukey Jamison if they would bring him one of their baby lambs to try, and when he saw the quality of these lambs, he thanked the Jamisons with tears in his eyes.

"He knew the age of that lamb to within three days," John Jamison, now famous for his lamb, recalls. "Without Jean-Louis, there would be no Jamison Farm."

At the same time, French chefs moved to America to open restaurants—Roger Vergé, the legendary raconteur and three-star chef of Le Moulin de Mougins, opened restaurants in New York City, San Francisco, and even Disney World; and Michel Richard opened Citrus in Los Angeles. Jean Banchet brought fine dining into the Midwestern heartland with Le Français in Wheeling, Illinois. Jean-Georges Vongerichten arrived in 1986 to create Lafayette at the Drake Hotel and took New York by storm with his juices and vinaigrettes. And importantly, in the mid-1980s, Patrice Boely and Daniel Boulud opened the Polo Lounge at Westbury Hotel in Manhattan, where I was a poissonier.

They were doing amazing things at the Polo Lounge. They took all the fancy out of French cuisine, began creating composed plates, and got rid of stuffy tableside service. We were all getting more casual. We like refinement (indeed, we've brought back tableside service at some of our more casual continental cuisine restaurants, TAK Room and The Surf Club Restaurant), but my generation wanted friendly restaurants that also served Michelin-caliber food. Jean-Georges had four stars at Lafayette, but when he opened his own restaurant, JoJo, it was a casual, if very refined, French bistro. And Sirio Maccioni, who hired Daniel Boulud, created Le Cirque, a restaurant that felt like a party every night.

In fact, I'd argue that Daniel, Jean-Georges, and Eric Ripert are more American chefs than French chefs. If they had stayed in France, they might not have become who they are today.

The intimidating French restaurant that defined fine dining? That all changed when young American and French chefs brought a whole new attitude to food and cooking. Look at that generation. Larry Forgione, Alfred Portale, Jonathan Waxman at Jams, Jeremiah Tower at Chez Panisse and then Stars. Susan Spicer in New Orleans and Judy Rodgers in San Francisco. This list only scratches the surface. What a generation. We went from cooking French food, French classics, to serving the food of Daniel, Jean-Georges, or my food at The French Laundry. It became a cuisine of interpretation, a cuisine of expressing personality. We weren't going to fine restaurants to have their version of blanquette de veau or poulet en vessie. We were going to Charlie Trotter's for Charlie's food, and we were going to Norman's for Norman Van Aken's food.

WHERE IS FINE DINING HEADED? What's the future?

More and better. We have increasingly better ingredients, tools, more refined techniques, education, and we have better teams, made up of true professionals in the kitchen and in the dining room.

I don't see the cuisine of personality changing. I believe that's here to stay. I'm part of the first generation. We're now two generations beyond me and my colleagues. Grant Achatz, Eric Ziebold, Lisa Nakamura, Jonathan Benno, Corey Lee, Timothy Hollingsworth, Shuna Fish Lydon, Kwame Onwuachi, Jordan Kahn—too many young chefs to name came up through my kitchens (along with countless other famous chefs who began as commis in my colleagues' kitchens), and they, in turn, have branched out and taught the current generation. Wylie Dufresne, Julia Sullivan, Daniel Humm, Gavin Kaysen, Edouardo Jordan, Enrique Olvera, Kaelin Ulrich Trilling—all of them came from other chefs' kitchens and are now inspiring yet another new generation.

What will change, beyond the quality of the food? We're already seeing it at places such as César Ramirez's Brooklyn Fare and James Knappett's Kitchen Table—serving this kind of food, fine-dining food, at counters, like a sushi bar. This idea started with Joël Robuchon, who loved sushi and subsequently built outposts of L'Atelier in Paris, Asia, and the United States. Of course, there is Masa Takayama, our first Michelin three-star sushi chef—sushi has come a long way fast in America. David Chang upped the game, doing the same, serving fine food at a counter rather than on a white tablecloth—cooks just cooking and serving what pleased them—at Momofuku Ko. This is an important part of the evolution of fine dining: involving the diner. Bringing the diner into the process of cooking—this is relatively new. It's all very exciting.

NONE OF THIS would have happened without Jean-Louis doing what he did for cuisine in America—at least, not the *way* it happened. He brought his big Gascon spirit to America—he found the farmers and the foragers, the gardeners and the fishermen, and made them integral to the cuisine, showing other chefs the bounty available in America. He brought an exuberance and excitement to the kitchen and the dining room that hadn't been seen in America before him.

Jean-Louis died of lung cancer in 2001, at age fifty-five. He was a true radical. We miss him.

CREAM OF BROCCOLI SOUP

Brioche Melbas, Marcona Almonds, and White Truffles

Makes 6 servings

BRIOCHE MELBAS

Clarified butter (page 53)

Kosher salt

1 frozen brioche Pullman loaf

BROCCOLI PUREE

1,600 grams broccoli (crowns and stalks)

50 grams stemmed spinach leaves

20 grams Agrumato lemon oil

6 grams kosher salt

BROCCOLI SOUP BASE

25 grams whole butter

25 grams thinly sliced shallots

25 grams thinly sliced Holland leek

190 grams heavy cream

625 grams sweet onion essence (page 288)

225 grams ½-inch-dice (1.25-centimeter) peeled Yukon Gold potatoes

25 grams grated Parmesan cheese

Kosher salt

TO COMPLETE

Sweet onion essence (page 288), as needed

30 grams roasted and salted Marcona almonds

Parmesan mousse (recipe follows)

Fresh white truffles (optional)

SPECIAL EQUIPMENT

Electric slicer

2¾-inch (7-centimeter) smooth round cutter

1-inch (2.5-centimeter) smooth round cutter

Six 4½-inch-wide (11.5-centimeter), 6-inch-deep (15.25-centimeter) bowls

iSi siphon

2 cream chargers

Truffle slicer (optional)

This is a classic from the American repertoire, one of the dishes they teach aspiring chefs in cooking school. I love the old-fashionedness of it. Broccoli stems, skin on, are sliced thinly and cooked with onions, cream, and sweet onion essence; potatoes are added and the soup is pureed. We fortify the soup base with a very intense puree of broccoli tops, and add crunch with crispy brioche and Marcona almonds. This homey soup is then finished with a slice of white truffle.

FOR THE BRIOCHE MELBAS

Preheat the oven to 300°F (150°C). Lay a nonstick silicone baking mat on an inverted half sheet pan. Using a pastry brush, apply a thin layer of clarified butter to the mat and sprinkle lightly with salt. Butter and salt a second mat.

Cut off the end crust from the frozen brioche, then use an electric slicer to cut the loaf into at least six 1- to 1.5-millimeter-thick slices (it's best to make extras in case of breakage). The outer slices of brioche are best for this application, as there are fewer air pockets.

Punch the slices with a 2¾-inch (7-centimeter) smooth round cutter. Cut out the center of each piece with a 1-inch (2.5-centimeter) smooth round cutter.

Place the sliced brioche on the prepared sheet pan. Position the second baking mat, buttered-side down, over the bread. We top the mat with stainless-steel press pans, which are very heavy. If you do not have press pans, top it with a second inverted sheet pan.

Place in the oven. Bake for 7 minutes, then check the color. The finished melbas should be light golden brown and crisp. Return to the oven and bake as needed, checking often. Remove from the oven and let cool.

The melbas can be stored in an airtight container at room temperature for up to 2 days.

FOR THE BROCCOLI PUREE

Bring a pot of salted water to a boil. Reserve 100 grams of the broccoli florets for garnish. Reserve 300 grams of the stalks for the soup. For

the most vividly colored puree, cut 250 grams of tips from the broccoli crowns and blanch the tips in the boiling water until tender, adding the spinach to the water for the final 10 seconds. Drain. While still hot, transfer the broccoli tips and spinach to a blender and blend until smooth; add the lemon oil and salt and blend briefly to incorporate. Strain into a bowl and nestle the bowl in an ice-water bath. Let cool, stirring often for even cooling and to prevent oxidation.

FOR THE BROCCOLI SOUP BASE

Thinly slice the reserved 300 grams of broccoli stalks. Melt the butter in a large saucepot over medium-low heat. Add the shallots, leek, and broccoli stalks and cook gently, stirring often, for 6 to 8 minutes, until the vegetables begin to soften.

Add the cream, 325 grams of the sweet onion essence, and the potatoes. Simmer over medium heat, adjusting the heat as necessary to maintain a simmer, for about 15 minutes, until all the vegetables are tender. Carefully transfer the soup base to a blender, add the Parmesan, and blend, pouring in the remaining 300 grams stock as you blend, until smooth. Season to taste with salt.

Strain the soup through a chinois into a bowl and nestle the bowl in an ice-water bath. Let cool, stirring often for even cooling and to prevent oxidation.

TO COMPLETE

Using a knife, shave off the very tips of the reserved 100 grams of broccoli florets. Pass them through a blanching basket into an airtight container. Refrigerate until ready to use.

For each 100 grams of finished soup, whisk in 30 grams of the broccoli puree. Gently reheat the soup in a saucepot. If the soup is too thick to pour easily, thin it with more sweet onion essence.

Slice the Marcona almonds lengthwise in half. Arrange 3 almond halves in the bottom of each bowl. Transfer the Parmesan mousse to a siphon and charge it with two cream chargers, shaking the siphon vigorously between charges and after charging to ensure it is fully aerated for use. Siphon the mousse to cover the bottom of each bowl and sprinkle with the broccoli buds. Rest the brioche melba on top of the buds. At the table, pour the soup into the center of the melba and, if desired, shave white truffle over the soup.

Parmesan Mousse

Makes 6 servings

150 grams whole milk	2 grams minced shallot, rinsed	66 grams Pre-Hy (page 109)
150 grams heavy cream	2 grams lemon juice	1 large egg
70 grams grated Parmesan cheese (grated on a rasp grater)	6 grams fleur de sel	

Combine the milk and cream in a 1-quart (1-liter) saucepot and bring just to a simmer. Transfer to a blender and add the Parmesan, shallot, lemon juice, fleur de sel, and Pre-Hy. Blend on medium-high speed for 1 minute.

With the blender running, add the egg. Increase the speed to high and blend to incorporate, about 20 seconds. Pass the mousse through a chinois. Keep in a warm spot for up to 4 hours before serving.

FRENCH ONION SOUP

Warm Jellied Consommé, Beef Cheek, Country Bread, and Comté Mousse

Makes 6 servings

BEEF CHEEK

1 beef cheek, cold

Sel gris

Freshly ground black
pepper

**FRENCH ONION
CONSOMMÉ**

60 grams clarified butter
(recipe follows)

600 grams ½-inch-dice
(1.25-centimeter)
Vidalia onions

10 grams kosher salt

600 grams mushroom
essence (page 289)

300 grams apple cider

250 grams water

50 grams tamari

6 grams black
peppercorns

2 thyme sprigs

2 bay leaves

100 grams egg whites

8 grams iota carrageenan

CROUTONS

25 grams ¼-inch-dice
(6-millimeter) crustless
bread, preferably pain
de campagne or other
rustic bread

COMTÉ MOUSSE

75 grams whole milk

75 grams heavy cream

35 grams grated Comté
or Parmesan cheese

5 grams sliced shallot

1 gram lemon juice

3 grams fleur de sel

33 grams Pre-Hy (page
109)

1 large egg

TO COMPLETE

40 grams black truffle

Canola oil, for sautéing

40 grams ½-inch-dice
(1.25-centimeter)
Vidalia onion

4 grams thyme leaves

About 5 grams crispy
shallots (recipe follows)

SPECIAL EQUIPMENT

Immersion circulator

Chamber vacuum sealer

iSi siphon

2 cream chargers

Six 100-gram glasses

A lot of our dishes are simply what we'd want for dinner. David loves French onion soup so much, he even appreciates a poorly made one. It represents the best humble bistro fare, always fun to turn into a high-end dish.

The consommé is a warm gelatin, thickened with carrageenan (see page 108) and seasoned with apple cider and thyme. But the backbone of this soup is the mushroom essence, which gives it a meaty umami flavor.

A key technique here is the flash-seared onion. The onion is cooked in a very hot pan, not slowly caramelized, so it gets the flavors of browned onion but also retains the fresh flavor of uncooked onion. Onions are amazing for the variety of flavors they offer depending on how you cook them. We use a beef cheek as part of the garnish, but any braised beef, like short rib or oxtail, will work. We can turn this into a vegetarian dish by omitting the beef. The Comté cheese, in the form of a mousse, is shot from a siphon to top the soup with a cheesy foam, and crispy shallots give it some crunch.

FOR THE BEEF CHEEK

Set an immersion circulator in a water bath and heat the water to 64°C (147.2°F). Trim the beef cheek of any excess fat or sinew. Season liberally on all sides with sel gris and black pepper. Place the beef in a sous vide bag. Place the bag in the sealer chamber and vacuum seal. Put the bag in the water bath, cover the water bath with plastic wrap, and braise for 48 hours.

Remove the bag and let it sit at room temperature for 30 minutes, then submerge the bag in an ice-water bath to chill. Refrigerate the beef cheek in the bag for up to 1 week.

FOR THE FRENCH ONION CONSOMMÉ

Heat the clarified butter in a high-sided 2-quart (2-liter) saucepot over high heat. Add the onions and salt and cook, stirring frequently and scraping the bottom of the pan, for 8 to 10 minutes, until the onions have caramelized to a golden brown. Add the mushroom essence, apple cider, water, tamari, peppercorns, thyme, and bay leaves to the pot and bring the liquid to a simmer. Remove from the heat, cover with a lid, and steep for 10 minutes.

(continued)

Strain the liquid through a chinois into a clean 2-quart (2-liter) sauce-pot, pressing lightly on the solids to extract the liquid. Reserve one-quarter of the strained broth in a separate container. Place the egg whites in a medium bowl and whisk lightly just to break them up. Whisk the reserved broth into the egg whites to temper them. Quickly whisk the tempered egg whites into the pot of broth.

Place the pot over medium-high heat and cook, dragging a flat-sided silicone spatula over the bottom of the pot frequently to prevent the egg whites from scorching, until the egg whites rise to the top of the broth and form a raft. Simmer gently, without stirring, for 10 minutes, monitoring the broth carefully and adjusting the heat as necessary to keep the raft in one piece. If the broth bubbles too aggressively, it will break the raft. The resulting consommé will become perfectly clear; check the consommé by spooning a bit from the side of the pot.

Line a colander or perforated pan with a dampened tea towel and set it over a larger container. (Dampening the towel will prevent it from absorbing the consommé.) Carefully pour the contents of the pot through the towel; the raft should come out in one piece. Discard the raft.

Pour 1,000 grams (1 quart/1 liter) of the consommé into a separate container; reserve the remainder for another use. Whisk the carrageenan into the warm consommé until fully dissolved.

Refrigerate in an airtight container for up to 3 days or freeze for longer storage.

FOR THE CROUTONS

Preheat the oven to 325°F (163°C).

Spread the diced bread on a sheet pan and toast in the oven for 12 to 15 minutes, rotating the pan once or twice, until golden brown and crunchy. The croutons can be kept in an airtight container at room temperature for up to 2 days.

FOR THE COMTÉ MOUSSE

Heat the milk and cream in a 2-quart (2-liter) saucepot over medium heat just until it begins to simmer. Pour the milk-cream mixture into a blender. Add the cheese, shallot, lemon juice, and fleur de sel and blend on medium-high speed for 1 minute. While blending, add the Pre-Hy and the egg, then increase the blender speed to high and blend for 2 minutes. Pass the mousse mixture through a chinois into a container. If using immediately, keep the mixture warm; otherwise, it can be covered and refrigerated for up to 1 day.

TO COMPLETE

Carefully brush the surface of the truffle with a soft-bristled brush, like a toothbrush, to remove any dirt or debris without damaging the truffle. Rinse the truffle in a small bowl of cool water. Repeat as needed until the truffle is clean. Dry the truffle and cut it into ¼-inch (6-millimeter) dice.

Heat a medium sauté pan over high heat and add enough canola oil to just cover the bottom of the pan. Add the onion and quickly sauté, as you would for a stir-fry, until the onion pieces are brown around the edges but still retain their shape. Drain the onions on paper towels.

Reheat the Comté mousse in a saucepot over low heat, if needed. Transfer the mousse to a siphon and charge with two cream chargers, shaking the siphon vigorously between charges and after charging to ensure it is fully aerated for use.

Rewarm the consommé.

Remove the beef cheek from the sous vide bag and wipe off any excess cooking liquid or juices. Cut the beef into ¼-inch (6-millimeter) dice. Heat a film of canola oil in a small sauté pan over medium-low heat, add the beef cheek, and warm through.

Mix the croutons, truffles, caramelized onions, beef cheek, and thyme leaves together in a large bowl and divide among six 100-gram glasses. Pour in enough of the consommé to cover. Siphon the Comté mousse over the consommé, filling the glass to the top. Sprinkle the crispy shallots over the mousse and serve immediately.

Clarified Butter

Makes about 280 grams

450 grams whole butter,
    cubed

Traditional method: Place the butter in a 1-quart (1-liter) saucepot and melt over low heat, without stirring. Once the butter has melted, it will separate into three layers. Skim off and discard the foamy layer of milk solids floating on top. The clear yellow butter beneath it is the clarified butter. Carefully pour it into a container, leaving the milky liquid at the bottom behind. Use immediately, or cover and refrigerate for up to 10 days or freeze for longer storage.

Refrigerator method: Bring a stockpot of water to a simmer. Place the butter cubes in a heavy-duty resealable kitchen bag and seal. Set the bag in the simmering water to melt the butter. Transfer the bag to an ice-water bath, positioning the bag at an angle with one bottom corner of the bag in the most downward position. Refrigerate until the butter has solidified.

Remove the bag from the refrigerator, hold it over a bowl, and snip the bottom corner to allow the liquid to drain into the bowl. What remains is a solid block of clarified butter. Rinse it under cool running water for a few seconds to remove any remaining milk solids, then dry. Store, well wrapped, in the refrigerator for up to 10 days or freeze for longer storage.

Crispy Shallots

Makes about 300 grams

150 grams panko
    breadcrumbs
Canola oil, for deep-
    frying
150 grams peeled
    shallots

100 grams Cup4Cup
    gluten-free flour or
    all-purpose flour
Kosher salt

SPECIAL EQUIPMENT
Japanese mandoline

Preheat the oven to 320°F (160°C) with the fan off. Line a sheet pan with parchment paper.

Spread the panko over the prepared sheet pan and toast it in the oven for 7 to 10 minutes, until golden brown.

Fill a small saucepot with 1½ inches (4 centimeters) of canola oil. Heat the oil to 350°F (180°C). Thinly slice the shallots on a Japanese mandoline. Put the flour in a medium bowl. Toss the shallots in the flour, separating the rings so they are evenly coated. Shake off any excess flour and place the shallots in the hot oil. Fry the shallots until they are light golden brown and crunchy, about 5 minutes. Remove from the oil, drain on paper towels, and sprinkle with salt. Let cool.

Put the shallots in a food processor and pulse until coarsely ground, without any large pieces remaining. Add the panko and pulse three or four times to incorporate. Store in an airtight container at room temperature for up to 1 day.

INSPIRATION VERSUS INFLUENCE

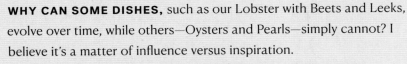

*Oysters and Pearls Versus
Lobster with Beets and Leeks*

WHY CAN SOME DISHES, such as our Lobster with Beets and Leeks, evolve over time, while others—Oysters and Pearls—simply cannot? I believe it's a matter of influence versus inspiration.

I know that Oysters and Pearls doesn't change. We *tried* to change it—we tried to do Oysters and Pearls 2.0, but it didn't work. When you can't figure out a way to improve a dish, and many of your guests come expecting to taste it for the first time, you simply have to do the best you can every day with each of its components, replicating the dish as it was first conceived.

When I began serving Oysters and Pearls, people were surprised, though to me, it's a completely logical combination. I was grocery shopping, and a purple box caught my eye. It was pearl tapioca for tapioca pudding, which my mother used to make—vanilla usually, but sometimes she'd put chocolate in it. I loved it; it was so comforting. I wondered what I could do with it now. The pearls in pearl tapioca bring to mind oysters. And caviar—which is typically served on a neutral base, such as blini. Sabayon made with the tapioca is another neutral base. So: a savory tapioca sabayon with oysters and caviar. I love pairing something as comforting as tapioca pudding with a very refined and luxurious ingredient like caviar. That the caviar itself mirrors the orbs of tapioca is a bonus. And it's delicious, of course. How could that not be excellent?

Unlike the enduring, unchangeable Oysters and Pearls, the felicitous pairing of two sweet, dynamic vegetables—beets and leeks—with lobster, on the other hand, predates The French Laundry and has evolved throughout my career. Lobster with Beets and Leeks began during my first days in New York, then at my restaurant Rakel in downtown Manhattan in the late 1980s. I think it was Daniel Boulud who brought me a jar of beet juice as a joke. Beets weren't the ingredient they are today; you rarely saw them back then. Jean-Louis Palladin knew it before most of us. In his book *Jean-Louis: Cooking with the Seasons,* he had a beet cream sauce he served with lobster. I don't think he paired them directly with the leeks, but he was definitely the chef from whom I got the idea to combine beets and leeks.

Initially, the beet sauce was splattered onto the plate with a spoon, à la Jackson Pollock. I'd serve it with crispy fried potatoes, sautéed leeks, and a tower of mashed potatoes.

By the time I'd opened The French Laundry, my plating had become extremely focused: I reduced beet juice to an intense red syrup and mounted it with butter. I would plate a spoonful of this, onto which I put leeks that had been blanched and reheated in beurre monté. On this base, I set a lobster tail and claw and topped it with a sheet of *pommes Maxim,* crispy browned potatoes. This was, I felt, the iteration of beets and leeks that came as close as possible to perfection.

Until Corey Lee became chef de cuisine. When Corey led the kitchen, he introduced a technique, learned during a cooking event we'd done in Australia, of dipping thin discs of potato in a cornstarch solution, then shingling them, for *pommes Maxim* far more crisp and elegant than the shards cooked en masse in a sheet pan. And I have no doubt that the dish will *continue* to evolve, because the buttery beets-leeks combination works so beautifully.

Now why does this dish take so well to reimagining and Oysters and Pearls doesn't?

I began to think about it after years of young chefs coming to me and telling me they were "inspired" by this or that preparation in *The French Laundry Cookbook.* I myself had stated this as one of my main goals in creating that book: I wanted it to inspire.

But I realize now that *influence* is more accurate than *inspire.* They are two different things. Inspiration involves combining two previously unrelated ideas and making something new out of them—a true aha moment. Oysters and Pearls combines two emotional opposites: the highly refined, sophisticated, adult pleasures we take in caviar, and the childhood pleasure of tapioca, two emotional worlds mediated by the primitive oyster.

Influence comes from countless sources around us—our colleagues' work, books, travel, and so on. I was not inspired by Jean-Louis's pairing of roasted beets. It was his influence that led me to pair beets and leeks with lobster.

Anything can inspire you. Inspiration comes from within. If inspiration comes to you three or four times in a lifetime, that's lucky.

CREAM OF MATSUTAKE MUSHROOM

Preserved Spruce Tips and Young Ginger

Makes 6 servings

VEGAN DASHI

5 grams kombu

490 grams water

18 grams peeled fresh
ginger, bruised and
thinly sliced

8 grams scallion, thinly
sliced

MATSUTAKE OIL

275 grams matsutake
mushroom trimmings
(see Note)

325 grams canola oil

20 grams kosher salt

MATSUTAKE
MUSHROOM SOUP

225 grams Koshihikari
rice

10 grams peeled fresh
ginger, bruised

100 grams matsutake
mushrooms, cleaned
and thinly sliced

900 grams water

Kosher salt

PRESERVED
SPRUCE TIPS

250 grams water

100 grams clover honey

60 grams lemon juice

18 grams sugar

5 grams kosher salt

200 grams spruce tips

PICKLED YOUNG
GINGER

450 grams young ginger

1,850 grams water

16 grams kosher salt

150 grams clover honey

100 grams lemon juice

100 grams grapefruit
juice

100 grams lime juice

100 grams orange juice

40 grams yuzu juice

60 grams mirin

TO COMPLETE

6 whole matsutake
mushrooms, cleaned

SPECIAL EQUIPMENT

Chamber vacuum sealer
(optional)

Japanese mandoline

This is another way to look at soup, a cream of mushroom with a dashi base that's thickened with Koshihikari rice, a premium Japanese short-grain rice distinguished by its aroma, sweet flavor, and texture. And like so many of our soups, the simpler it is, the better, as it has been since the restaurant's beginning. The main ingredient is cooked in the base liquid; then it's all pureed, seasoned, and garnished. While the dish is vegan, it has the complexity of a dish that has dairy fat.

FOR THE VEGAN DASHI

Submerge the kombu in a bowl of ice water for about 12 minutes to soften. Remove the kombu from the ice water and squeeze out any excess water.

Place the kombu, water, ginger, and scallion in a small saucepot. Bring to a boil, remove from the heat, cover with a lid, and set in a warm spot to steep for 1 hour.

Strain the dashi through a chinois into a bowl and nestle the bowl in an ice-water bath until cold. Refrigerate in an airtight container for up to 3 days.

FOR THE MATSUTAKE OIL

Place the mushroom trimmings in a food processor and process until broken down into small chunks, about ⅛ inch (3 millimeters). Transfer to a saucepot.

Add the canola oil to the pan and bring to a boil. Reduce the heat to low and cook for 30 minutes, or until the mushroom pieces are crisp. Season with the salt. Let cool, then cover and refrigerate for 8 hours or overnight. Strain the matsutake oil through a chinois into an airtight container.

The oil can be refrigerated for up to 3 weeks or frozen for up to 3 months.

FOR THE MATSUTAKE MUSHROOM SOUP

Place the rice, ginger, and sliced mushrooms in a rice cooker and add the water. Cook on the Porridge setting according to the manufacturer's instructions.

When the rice cooker cycle is done (about 1 hour), carefully remove and discard the ginger. This makes 1,000 to 1,200 grams of matsutake rice base.

Heat 350 grams of the vegan dashi in a small saucepot.

In two batches, blend the matsutake rice base with 300 grams of the vegan dashi and 75 grams of the matsutake oil (see Note). Adjust the consistency with additional hot dashi and more matsutake oil as needed, depending on the strength of the mushroom flavor.

As you finish each batch, pass the soup through a chinois into a bowl, then whisk together thoroughly to combine the batches. Season with salt to taste. Nestle the bowl in an ice-water bath to cool the soup rapidly.

The soup can be refrigerated in an airtight container for up to 3 days or frozen for up to 1 month.

FOR THE PRESERVED SPRUCE TIPS

Combine the water, honey, lemon juice, sugar, and salt in a small saucepot and bring to a boil. Pour the syrup into a bowl and nestle the bowl in an ice-water bath. Let cool. If you have a chamber vacuum sealer, pour the cooled syrup into a sous vide bag and add the spruce tips. Place the bag in the sealer chamber and vacuum seal. If you do not have a chamber vacuum sealer, pour the cooled syrup into a container, add the spruce tips, cover the container with plastic wrap, and refrigerate for at least 1 day before using.

The spruce tips can be refrigerated in the syrup for up to 1 month.

FOR THE PICKLED YOUNG GINGER

Peel the ginger (we use a spoon for this, as it removes just the outer skin cleanly and easily).

Warm 800 grams of the water and 8 grams of the salt in a small saucepot over medium-high heat just until the salt has dissolved. The water should not boil. Pour the salted water into a bowl and add the ginger. Cover the bowl with plastic wrap. Brine in the refrigerator for about 24 hours. Drain the ginger and cut it into brunoise (very fine dice).

Place the ginger in a medium saucepot with 800 grams of the water and the remaining 8 grams salt. Bring to a boil over medium-high heat, then drain the ginger.

Combine the remaining 250 grams water, honey, lemon juice, grapefruit juice, lime juice, orange juice, yuzu juice, and mirin in a large saucepot. Add the ginger. Cover with a cartouche and bring the liquid to a boil. Transfer the contents of the pot to a container and nestle the container in an ice-water bath to chill. Return the ginger and its cooking liquid to the saucepot and repeat the process twice more.

The ginger and its cooking liquid can be refrigerated in an airtight container for up to 1 month.

TO COMPLETE

Reheat the soup. Drain the spruce tips and gently pat dry with paper towels.

Just before serving, slice the matsutake mushrooms as thinly as possible (paper thin) on a Japanese mandoline.

Arrange the spruce tips and pickled ginger in the serving bowls and top with the freshly sliced matsutake mushrooms. Pour the soup into the bowls around the garnishes.

> ### NOTE
>
> Because we use so many matsutake mushrooms, we make the matsutake oil from the trimmings. If you do not have trimmings, substitute 75 grams extra-virgin olive oil in the matsutake mushroom soup.

SHRIMP BISQUE

French Leeks, Brioche Croutons, Garden Tarragon, and Regiis Ova Caviar

Makes 6 servings

SHRIMP STOCK

60 grams clarified butter (page 53)

1,000 grams shrimp shells (see Note), heads removed, rinsed in cold water

100 grams whole butter, cut into ½-inch (1.25-centimeter) dice

600 grams crushed San Marzano tomatoes, with their juices

240 grams ½-inch-thick (1.25-centimeter) carrot rounds

15 grams tarragon sprigs

4 quarts (4 liters) water

SHRIMP BISQUE

100 grams clarified butter (page 53)

625 grams shrimp shells (see Note), heads removed, rinsed in cold water

125 grams Armagnac, plus more to taste

210 grams ½-inch-dice (1.25-centimeter) yellow onion

125 grams thinly sliced sweet carrots

140 grams button mushrooms, washed and thinly sliced

90 grams leeks, rinsed, quartered lengthwise, and sliced

3 grams thyme sprigs

5 bay leaves

315 grams 1-inch-dice (2.5-centimeter) vine-ripe tomatoes

315 grams heavy cream

50 grams Koshihikari rice

50 grams whole butter, cut into ½-inch (1.25-centimeter) dice and chilled

5 grams lemon juice

17.5 grams Pre-Hy (page 109)

Kosher salt

20 grams tarragon sprigs

CRÈME FRAÎCHE

250 grams crème fraîche

5 grams lemon juice

4 grams kosher salt

BRIOCHE CROUTONS

100 grams clarified butter (page 53)

Fifty ½-inch (1.25-centimeter) cubes brioche

1 thyme sprig

1 garlic clove, skin on, smashed

1 gram kosher salt

FRENCH LEEKS

4 French leeks, white and light green portions only

Extra-virgin olive oil

TO COMPLETE

72 grams Regiis Ova caviar

Small tarragon leaves

Bisque is a great way to start a meal, and this shrimp bisque is simply made in the same way a lobster bisque is made: roasting the shells, adding tomato, deglazing with Armagnac. But this one is thickened with rice rather than flour, since Corey will try to make dishes gluten-free if doing so won't compromise the dish. He finishes the bisque with cream, a little lemon, and a drop more Armagnac.

FOR THE SHRIMP STOCK

Melt the clarified butter in a 12-quart (12-liter) rondeau over high heat. Add the shrimp shells and sauté, stirring often, for 5 minutes, or until a light-brown fond forms on the bottom of the rondeau. Reduce the heat to medium, add the whole butter, and cook for 3 minutes, or until the butter browns.

Push the shrimp shells to one side of the pot. Add the tomatoes to deglaze the pan and cook, stirring often, for 1 minute, then add the carrots and tarragon and cook for 3 to 4 minutes.

Add the water and bring to a boil, using a wooden spoon to scrape the fond from the surface of the rondeau. Reduce the heat to low and simmer gently until reduced by one-quarter, about 25 minutes.

Strain the stock through a china cap. Once the liquid has flowed through, use a wooden spoon to crush the solids in the china cap. The object is to extract as much of the natural shrimp essence as possible. Discard the crushed solids. Strain the shrimp stock through a chinois, swirling continuously to allow the liquid to flow through without forcing the solids through the chinois. Rinse the chinois and strain the stock through the chinois a second time into a 4-quart (4-liter) saucepot.

Cook the shrimp stock over high heat to rapidly reduce it, skimming the surface frequently to remove the impurities. After about 10 minutes, strain the stock into a smaller pot and continue reducing over high heat. When the stock has reduced to 1,500 grams (1½ quarts/1.5 liters), strain it into a bowl and nestle the bowl in an ice-water bath to chill it quickly. The shrimp stock can be refrigerated for up to 3 days or frozen for up to 3 months.

(continued)

FOR THE SHRIMP BISQUE

Heat the clarified butter in a 12-quart (12-liter) rondeau (you need a large, wide surface) over high heat until it is just about to smoke. Add the shrimp shells and cook, stirring, to caramelize them to a golden brown, about 8 minutes.

Turn off the heat and carefully deglaze the pan with the Armagnac, scraping the bottom of the pan to release the fond. Return the heat to medium. Add the onion, carrots, button mushrooms, and leeks to the pan. Add 1,500 grams of the shrimp stock, deglaze the pan, and bring to a boil. Add the thyme, bay leaves, tomatoes, and cream and simmer over low heat for 40 to 45 minutes, until the stock has reduced by about one-third.

Strain the contents of the pan through a china cap. Once the stock has flowed through, use a wooden spoon to crush the solids in the china cap. Discard the crushed solids. Strain the stock through a chinois, swirling continuously to allow the liquid to flow through without forcing the solids through the chinois.

Return the bisque to a 2-quart (2-liter) saucepot, add the rice, and cook over high heat, skimming the surface as needed, until the contents of the pan weigh 850 grams, about 30 minutes. Strain the soup into a blender and blend until smooth. Add the whole butter, lemon juice, Pre-Hy, and additional Armagnac to taste. Blend on high speed for about 30 seconds, or until the bisque is smooth. Season with salt to taste.

Strain the bisque through a chinois into a bowl. Bruise the tarragon by hitting it with the back of a knife and add it to the bisque. Nestle the bowl in an ice-water bath and chill until cold. Strain the bisque through a chinois into an airtight container.

The bisque can be refrigerated for up to 3 days or frozen for up to 3 months.

FOR THE CRÈME FRAÎCHE

In a bowl, whisk together the crème fraîche, lemon juice, and salt to combine. Transfer to a disposable pastry bag and pipe into a small squeeze bottle. Refrigerate for up to 1 day.

FOR THE BRIOCHE CROUTONS

Heat the clarified butter in a small sauté pan over medium-high heat. Add the brioche cubes, thyme, and garlic and toast the brioche, stirring continuously, for about 5 minutes, until golden brown. Drain the croutons on paper towels and season immediately with salt. Store in an airtight container at room temperature for up to 1 day.

FOR THE FRENCH LEEKS

Up to 4 hours before serving, bring a pot of salted water to a boil. Wash and dry the leeks; peel off any bruised outer layers. Cook the leeks in the boiling water for 5 minutes, or until tender. Transfer to an ice-water bath to cool. Dry on paper towels.

Slice the leeks into ¼-inch (6-millimeter) diamond-shaped pieces, cutting them at a 45-degree angle. You should be able to cut about 5 diamonds from each leek. Dress the leeks lightly with olive oil.

TO COMPLETE

Place a quenelle of caviar into each serving bowl. Evenly space the leeks around the caviar and add a dot of crème fraîche and a crouton between each leek. Carefully pour in the bisque. Garnish with the tarragon leaves.

> **NOTE**
> You can often purchase shrimp shells from your local fishmonger.

"CLAM CHOWDER"

New England Clams, Bacon Lardons, Celery Branch Salad, Sourdough Mousseline, and Chowder Sauce

Makes 6 servings

BACON LARDONS

500 grams slab bacon, preferably from Hobbs' Applewood Smoked Meats

30 grams clarified butter (page 53)

CHOWDER SAUCE

70 grams clarified butter (page 53)

275 grams ¼-inch-dice (6-millimeter) onion

125 grams ¼-inch-dice (6-millimeter) celery

125 grams ¼-inch-dice (6-millimeter) leeks (white and light green portions only)

170 grams white wine

170 grams Noilly Prat

335 grams clam stock (page 286)

675 grams heavy cream

3 grams thyme sprigs

1 small bay leaf

Zest of ⅔ lemon, removed with a vegetable peeler, pith trimmed off

Kosher salt

SOURDOUGH MOUSSELINE

100 grams ½-inch-dice (1.25-centimeter) crustless sourdough bread

15 grams sliced shallots

1 small bay leaf

190 grams heavy cream

190 grams whole milk

80 grams clam stock (page 286)

10 grams roasted garlic puree (recipe follows)

10 grams red wine vinegar

5 grams kosher salt

CLAMS

6 razor clams

18 littleneck clams

200 grams clarified butter (page 53), melted

TO COMPLETE

1 small celery stalk

Clarified butter (page 53)

12 chervil leaves

Extra-virgin olive oil

SPECIAL EQUIPMENT

Chamber vacuum sealer (optional)

Immersion circulator (optional)

Dehydrator

1 quart iSi siphon

2 cream chargers

Electric slicer (optional)

Childhood is a source of so many of my own inspirations for new dishes. This one is from Corey's childhood. When he was growing up in California, he and his dad would go to Fisherman's Wharf in San Francisco and eat clam chowder out of a sourdough bread bowl—which Corey says is a very touristy dish, but remains a powerful food memory. Here he combines the idea of chowder and sourdough by creating a sourdough mousseline, flavored and thickened with sourdough bread, then served from a siphon. It's brilliant.

FOR THE BACON LARDONS

If you have a chamber vacuum sealer, set an immersion circulator in a water bath and heat the water to 80°C (176°F). Place the slab of bacon in a sous vide bag. Place the bag in the sealer chamber and vacuum seal. Cook in the water bath for 6 hours. Remove the bag from the water bath and, while still warm, place it on a sheet pan with the meat side facing down. Cover with another sheet pan and add 4,000 grams of weight (such as cans of food). Refrigerate for 12 hours. Pressing the bacon will create an even surface for slicing and sautéing later. Remove the weight and sheet pan and cut the bacon into ⅛-inch-thick (3-millimeter) slices the length of the slab of bacon.

If you do not have a vacuum sealer or immersion circulator, cut ⅛-inch (3-millimeter) slices from the raw piece of slab bacon. Cut into chiffonade, as thinly as possible.

Heat a small sauté pan over medium-high heat and add the clarified butter. Add the bacon and cook until crisp. Remove from the pan and drain on paper towels. Keep in a warm spot for up to 4 hours before serving.

FOR THE CHOWDER SAUCE

Melt the clarified butter in a 6-quart (6-liter) rondeau over medium-low heat. Add the onion, celery, and leeks and spread them in a single layer over the bottom of the rondeau. Sweat the vegetables, scraping the sides and bottom of the pot often, until tender and translucent, without allowing them to take on any color (which would discolor the sauce), 6 to 8 minutes.

(continued)

Deglaze the pan with the white wine and reduce to au sec (nearly dry), 6 to 8 minutes. Add the Noilly Prat, increase the heat to medium, and reduce by about three-quarters, 12 to 14 minutes. Add the clam stock, increase the heat to medium-high, and cook until the stock has reduced by half, 8 to 10 minutes.

Add the cream and cook at a slow simmer for about 30 minutes, until the sauce has reduced by half, whisking every 2 minutes to make certain the sauce is not sticking to the sides or bottom of the pan (this is important in order to keep the sauce white).

Strain the sauce through a china cap, then strain through a chinois into a 4-quart (4-liter) saucepot and simmer over low heat for 10 minutes, until the sauce reaches nappe consistency. Remove the saucepot from the heat. Add the thyme, bay leaf, and lemon zest to the sauce, cover with a lid, and steep for about 30 minutes.

Strain the sauce through a chinois into a container and season with salt to taste. Lay a piece of plastic wrap directly against the surface of the sauce, cover, and refrigerate for up to 3 days.

FOR THE SOURDOUGH MOUSSELINE

Preheat the oven to 300°F (150°C).

Spread the diced bread on a sheet pan and bake for 45 minutes, or until light golden brown. Transfer the bread to a dehydrator and dehydrate at 160°F (71°C) until completely dry, about 24 hours.

Place the bread in a 2-quart (2-liter) saucepot and add the shallots and bay leaf. Pour in the cream and milk. Bring the mixture to a boil, remove the saucepot from the heat, cover, and steep for about 1 hour. The aromatics will flavor the warm milk and cream, and the bread will absorb the liquid.

Remove the bay leaf. Transfer the mixture to a blender, add the clam stock, and blend on high for about 1 minute. Add the roasted garlic puree, vinegar, and salt and blend to incorporate. Strain through a chinois, pressing on the solids.

Keep in a warm spot for up to 4 hours before serving or refrigerate in an airtight container for up to 3 days.

FOR THE CLAMS

Rinse the razor clams under cold running water until the water runs clear, about 30 minutes. Repeat with the littleneck clams. Set an immersion circulator in a water bath and heat the water to 80°C (176°F).

Shuck the razor clams and place the clam meat and 100 grams of the melted clarified butter in a sous vide bag. Shuck the littleneck clams and place in a second sous vide bag with the remaining 100 grams melted clarified butter. Place each bag in the sealer chamber and vacuum seal.

Place the bag with the littleneck clams in the water bath and cook for 2 minutes. Add the bag with the razor clams and cook for 1 minute more. Transfer both bags to an ice-water bath and chill the clams. Once cold, remove the clams from the bags. Cut away and reserve the finger portion of the razor clams.

TO COMPLETE

No more than 4 hours before serving, warm the mousseline, if necessary. Transfer it to a 1-quart siphon and charge with two cream chargers, shaking the siphon vigorously between charges and after charging to ensure it is fully aerated for use. Keep in a warm spot until serving.

Cut the celery stalk on the bias into eight ⅛-inch-thick (3-millimeter) slices. Transfer to a bowl of ice water to chill. Drain and dry on paper towels.

Reheat the bacon lardons and clarified butter in a small sauté pan. Keep warm.

Heat a plancha over a gas flame on high. Once hot, brush the surface with clarified butter and cook the razor clams, turning them as needed, until they are warm and take on a little color. Slice each razor clam on the bias into four or five ¾-inch (2-centimeter) diamond-shaped pieces.

Peel the outer muscles from each littleneck clam. Cut off the bottom half of the body (which won't be used). Reheat the littleneck clams in a small pot with a little clarified butter.

Reheat 250 grams of the chowder sauce. Lightly dress the chervil leaves with olive oil.

Divide the chowder sauce among the serving bowls. Arrange the clams, celery, and bacon lardons over the chowder. Siphon the mousseline in small mounds between the other components and garnish with the chervil leaves.

CAVIAR

Caviar has evolved along with everything else. We first bought only the caviar from wild fish. Caviar from farmed fish used to be terrible. But overfishing and restrictions in the main caviar-producing countries have made wild caviar all but impossible to get. However, as demand increased, and the wild sturgeon grew scarce, the sustainable farmed caviar got better and better. So much better than it was twenty years ago. Farmed caviar is excellent now. It may be a little more two-dimensional compared with really fine wild caviar, but it's consistent.

All our restaurants combined order about 32 kilograms of caviar a week—nearly 3,500 pounds each year. That's a lot of caviar. So we've partnered with Shaoching Bishop, a businesswoman with a passion for caviar, in our venture Regiis Ova, or "Royal Egg." Shaoching has been able to source farmed caviar of extraordinary quality. And so caviar remains one of the great luxuries of life.

ROYAL OSSETRA CAVIAR WITH CHOCOLATE-HAZELNUT EMULSION

Feuille de Brick, Celery, and Onion Oil

Makes 6 servings

CARAMELIZED ONION OIL

500 grams peeled yellow onions

185 grams canola oil

20 grams kosher salt

CHOCOLATE-HAZELNUT EMULSION

45 grams blanched hazelnuts

138 grams heavy cream

108 grams full-fat coconut milk

32 grams white chocolate, preferably Valrhona Opalys

13 grams dehydrated caramelized onions (page 193), before blending

6 grams Pre-Hy (page 109)

25 grams water

6 grams lemon juice

4 grams kosher salt

FEUILLE DE BRICK SPIRALS

Canola oil, for frying

1 sheet feuille de brick, about 12 inches (30 centimeters) in diameter

Cornstarch–egg white paste (page 235)

Dehydrated caramelized onions (page 193), ground to a powder

TO COMPLETE

12 celery leaves

70 grams Regiis Ova caviar, preferably Royal Ossetra

SPECIAL EQUIPMENT

Japanese mandoline

Six 5-inch-long (13-centimeter) metal rods, ⅜ inch (1 centimeter) in diameter (see Note)

Kitchen gloves

In the middle of service, while helping plate a special dish at the canapé station, Corey took a moment to snack on one of his favorite cookies, the classic Girl Scout cookie called Samoas. The crunchy, nutty flavors would go really well with caviar, he thought, and he put a little caviar on the cookie. It was delicious and inspired this dish, finished with a sweet-savory tuile as the crunchy cookie.

FOR THE CARAMELIZED ONION OIL

Julienne the onions as finely as possible on a Japanese mandoline. Put the onions and canola oil in a medium saucepot and bring to a boil over medium-high heat. Reduce the heat to low, add the salt, and caramelize the onions, stirring often, until golden brown, about 45 minutes.

Transfer to a container and let cool. Cover and refrigerate for at least 8 hours. Place a large dampened coffee filter in a strainer set over a container. Pour in the caramelized onions and oil and refrigerate for 8 hours to extract the oil. The oil can be refrigerated for up to 3 weeks or frozen for up to 3 months; discard the onions.

FOR THE CHOCOLATE-HAZELNUT EMULSION

The emulsion should be made and held at room temperature within 4 hours of serving. Preheat the oven to 350°F (180°C). Line a quarter sheet pan with a piece of parchment paper and spread the hazelnuts on the pan. Toast the nuts in the oven until golden brown, 12 to 15 minutes. Remove from the heat and let cool, then coarsely chop.

Combine the hazelnuts, cream, coconut milk, chocolate, and dehydrated caramelized onions in a 2-quart (2-liter) saucepot. Bring to a boil over medium-high heat, stirring continuously to avoid anything scorching on the bottom of the saucepot. Reduce the heat to medium and simmer, stirring continuously, for about 10 minutes, until the mixture has reduced by about two-thirds and looks as though it is about to break.

Pour the contents of the saucepot into a blender. Add the Pre-Hy and blend on high speed, using the tamper to stir the contents. The emulsion

will become very thick. Blend for 4 to 5 minutes, until smooth, adding just as much of the water as needed to help the emulsion blend.

Add the lemon juice and salt and blend briefly to incorporate. Strain the emulsion into a container and store at room temperature for up to 4 hours.

FOR THE FEUILLE DE BRICK SPIRALS

Make the spirals the same day you will serve them. Fill a tall saucepot with enough canola oil to completely submerge the rods once they are placed in the oil to fry. Heat the oil to 350°F (180°C). Place a cooling rack on a half sheet pan.

It is very important that the feuille de brick does not dry out as you work, so keep any pieces you aren't working with under a lightly dampened paper towel. Trim the edges to square and cut the feuille de brick into ¼-inch-wide (6-millimeter) strips at least 9 inches (23 centimeters) long.

Spray a metal rod, about 5 inches (12.5 centimeters) long and ⅜ inch (1 centimeter) in diameter, with enough nonstick spray that it is dripping with spray. Wrap one end of a strip of feuille de brick around the rod once, securing the first overlap with a dot of the cornstarch paste; if the feuille de brick is not sealed in this way, the spiral will unfurl when fried. Continue to wrap the feuille de brick strip around the rod in an evenly spaced spiral. Seal the final overlap of feuille de brick with a dot of the cornstarch paste. Set the feuille de brick–wrapped rod on the rack and wrap the remaining rods.

Carefully put the feuille de brick–wrapped rods in the hot oil and deep-fry for about 3 minutes, until golden brown. Return the rods to the rack (reserve the hot oil in the pot). Using gloved hands, shake off any excess oil and immediately and gently remove the feuille de brick spirals from the rods. The spirals will still be pliable when hot, but will become very fragile once cool. If they cool too much to remove from the rods, return them to the hot oil for a few seconds. Once the spirals have been removed from the rods, immediately sprinkle them with the dehydrated onion powder and let cool, then cut off the ends using a small pair of scissors.

TO COMPLETE

Reheat the frying oil to 350°F (180°C), if necessary. Drop the celery leaves into the oil and fry until the leaves are crisp; they are ready when the oil stops bubbling and the moisture has evaporated. Remove the leaves with a spider and drain them on paper towels.

Spoon a quenelle of the chocolate-hazelnut emulsion (about 10 grams) onto each serving plate. Place a quenelle of caviar (about 10 grams) next to the puree and lightly drizzle onion oil over the emulsion and the caviar. Rest a feuille de brick spiral on the caviar and arrange a few fried celery leaves on top.

> **NOTE**
>
> The feuille de brick spirals are made by wrapping metal rods in strips of feuille de brick and frying them. If you do not have six rods, you can fry the spirals in batches—just let the rods cool completely before wrapping them in feuille de brick for the next batch.

"FISH AND CHIPS"

Ale-Battered Blowfish with Malt Vinegar Jam

Makes 6 servings

MALT VINEGAR JAM

7 grams caraway seeds

225 grams malt vinegar, preferably Sarson's

225 grams water

50 grams light brown sugar

1 gram fleur de sel

7 grams agar-agar

SPLIT PEA AND ALE BATTER

30 grams dried split peas

250 grams Cup4Cup gluten-free flour

8 grams kosher salt

300 grams dark ale, plus more if needed

TO COMPLETE

Canola oil, for deep-frying

6 cleaned blowfish tails, 2 to 3 ounces (55 to 85 grams) each

Kosher salt

All-purpose flour, for dusting the fish

Freeze-dried peas, crushed between your fingers

Blanched fresh peas, warmed, for garnish

Mint leaves, preferably nepitella

SPECIAL EQUIPMENT

Chamber vacuum sealer (optional)

Cast-iron deep-fry pan (optional)

Infrared thermometer gun (optional)

We have fun serving common dishes, such as this British middle-class staple—fish and chips with mushy peas—in unusual ways. This one is very straightforward: ale-battered fish, deep-fried, with a sweet-sour malt vinegar jam and a garnish of peas and fresh herbs. We get blowfish, caught off Georges Bank, from Wulf's Fish, but you can use any firm white fish—cod, of course, is traditional and excellent. The tempura batter uses freeze-dried peas and gluten-free Cup4Cup flour, which creates a very crisp crust and holds that crispness longer. It's a great flour for all such crispy batters. The vinegar jam is gelled with agar, and we like to finish the dish with nepitella, an Italian mint with a flavor that's almost a cross between oregano and mint.

FOR THE MALT VINEGAR JAM

Lightly toast the caraway seeds in a small sauté pan over medium-low heat, continuously swirling the pan to ensure that the seeds are toasting evenly without burning, until fragrant. Let cool, then grind the toasted caraway seeds in a spice grinder until they are cracked but not ground to dust.

In a 1-quart (1-liter) saucepot, bring the vinegar, water, brown sugar, and fleur de sel to a boil over medium heat. Whisk in the agar-agar and boil gently, whisking continuously, for 1 minute to activate the agar-agar. Transfer to a bowl and nestle the bowl in an ice-water bath. Chill, undisturbed, until the jam base is completely firm and set.

Coarsely chop the jam base and transfer it to a blender. Beginning on low speed and gradually increasing to high, blend the jam until it is completely smooth, using the tamper to keep the jam moving. Pass the jam through a chinois into a container and season with the ground caraway.

If you have a chamber vacuum sealer, place the container, uncovered, in the sealer chamber. Run a complete cycle on full pressure to remove any air bubbles incorporated during blending. This will give the jam clarity and shine.

The jam can be refrigerated in an airtight container for up to 3 weeks.

(continued)

FOR THE SPLIT PEA AND ALE BATTER

Grind the split peas to a fine powder in a spice grinder. Transfer the pea powder to a bowl, add the flour and salt, and mix thoroughly. Whisk the ale into the dry mixture. If the batter is too thick, thin it with a bit more ale. The batter can be held at room temperature for up to 1 hour before frying the fish.

TO COMPLETE

Fill a cast-iron deep-fry pot with about 4 inches (10 centimeters) of canola oil. (If you do not have a cast-iron deep-fry pot, use another heavy pot with sides at least 8 inches/20 centimeters high.) Heat the oil to 350°F (180°C).

Season the blowfish with salt and lightly coat with the flour. Holding the blowfish by the tail, dip it in the batter to fully coat the flesh, leaving the tail exposed. Carefully lower the blowfish into the hot oil and fry for 3 to 5 minutes, turning the fish once or twice, until the batter is evenly colored and crisp and the fish is just cooked through. Transfer the fish to a paper towel to drain.

Fill a disposable piping bag with the malt vinegar jam and pipe the jam into a small squeeze bottle.

Arrange the fried blowfish on serving plates and sprinkle with the crushed freeze-dried peas. Garnish the plate with beads of the malt vinegar jam, blanched fresh peas, and mint.

TOOLS OF REFINEMENT, REVISITED

When we wrote *The French Laundry Cookbook* more than twenty years ago, our tools of refinement were the tamis (a drum sieve) and the chinois (a conical fine-mesh sieve). And they still are. We use them for countless preparations.

Almost every liquid and every puree is "passed," meaning passed through a sieve of some sort to achieve the finest possible texture. We pass long-simmered stocks through a chinois, gently swirling the sieve to encourage the stock to flow through, catching the solids in the sieve. We repeat this action again and again until the stock passes through and nothing is left in the chinois.

We press all purees, from cooked foie gras to vegetable puree, through a tamis using a plastic bench scraper, itself one of our most valuable kitchen tools.

Back then, we didn't have the tools for sous vide cooking—an immersion circulator or chamber vacuum sealer—but we still used the idea of precise-temperature cooking of proteins sealed in plastic. Have a look at the duck roulade in *The French Laundry Cookbook*. We wrapped duck breast in blanched chard leaves and rolled them in plastic, then poached them in barely simmering water, 200°F (93°C) or so, for 6 minutes. Perfect medium-rare duck using what would eventually be called sous vide.

Technology has evolved over the last two decades. Immersion circulators are now common in both restaurant and home kitchens. These devices heat water to an exact temperature and hold it there indefinitely, allowing us to cook anything to, say, 140°F (60°C), meaning we can serve medium-rare short ribs that are also incredibly tender.

Vacuum chamber sealers likewise became affordable to restaurants. They allow us to seal the food without air pockets (which would otherwise cause the package to float in the precisely heated water), maintain perfect compact shapes, vacuum seal liquids, and even compress fruits and vegetables.

The modernist cuisine movement developed and commercialized useful powders for new textures and processes, such as agar-agar, carrageenan, and transglutaminase ("meat glue," now sold under the brand name Activa), which allows us to combine bacon and rabbit flanks into what is, in effect, a single piece of meat that can be sealed and cooked sous vide till tender, then sliced for a great preparation (see *Under Pressure*, page 134). Many of these powders require a powerful blender, the Vitamix (or Vita-Prep, in professional kitchens), to ensure that they are adequately "sheared" into the liquid or puree.

As with our duck roulade, at The French Laundry, we had achieved similar effects the old-fashioned way, wrapping rabbit saddle in bacon (see page 207 of *The French Laundry Cookbook*). But ten years later, we had Activa and the immersion circulator, an excellent example of how the evolution of cooking leads not to new preparations but rather to more refined versions of classic preparations.

Perhaps the most game-changing appliance development of them all is what we refer to as the combi oven, which is a conventional oven, a convection oven, and a steam oven. It allows us to use any or all of them to create the precise environment (temperature and humidity) that we need. These ovens are truly exceptional machines and are used extensively throughout our kitchens (where we use Rational brand combi ovens).

So to the classic tamis and chinois, I'd add the immersion circulator, the chamber vacuum sealer, the Vitamix, and the combi oven as tools of refinement, all appliances that help refine the cuisine we make.

But I've realized that of all the tools of refinement, time is the greatest—having the time to refine and refine and refine. I've managed to create more time by opening the kitchen up and adding more chefs. When you're rushing to be ready for service, the final refinements sometimes get lost.

Time is the ultimate tool.

CHARCOAL-GRILLED JAPANESE EEL

Preserved Society Garlic Flowers and Sweet Vinegar

Makes 6 servings

OLIVE OIL-BRAISED JAPANESE EEL

1 dressed Japanese eel (about 2,000 grams)

250 grams extra-virgin olive oil

10 grams kosher salt

5 grams sliced peeled fresh ginger

5 grams lemon zest

1 sprig Genovese basil

1 garlic clove, smashed

1 gram chili flakes

PRESERVED SOCIETY GARLIC FLOWERS

300 grams water

150 grams champagne vinegar

150 grams sugar

10 grams kosher salt

50 small society garlic flowers

SWEET VINEGAR PUREE

6 grams agar-agar

TO COMPLETE

Canola oil

Nigella seeds

Maldon salt

SPECIAL EQUIPMENT

Immersion circulator

Chamber vacuum sealer

David likes to prepare eel because he knows I always smile when I get an eel dish. It's an underused fish here in America, where we're most familiar with it in sushi form, sweetened with molasses. We try not to obscure the earthy flavors of the eel, offsetting them by poaching the eel in olive oil, then passing it over a charcoal fire and serving it with sweet vinegar gelled with agar, and garnished with pickled society garlic flowers, which are lovely purple blossoms with a garlicky flavor, though not from the same genus as garlic.

The key technique to learn here is the eel preparation and the snipping of the eel bones. Three lines of small overlapping bones run the length of the eel. Moving from the head toward the tail, make small snips down the length of each row of bones; this makes them edible. In this preparation, the skin is left on, the eel is grilled skin-side down, and the blackened skin is removed after it's grilled, giving the eel a nice charred aroma.

FOR THE BRAISED EEL

If the eel is not totally dressed and the organs are still present, make a shallow slit along the underside of the eel, beginning at the head, until the knife reaches the urinogenital opening. Carefully deepen the slit just until the eel's organs are exposed. Be careful not to cut the organs. Using your fingers, remove the organs. With a paper towel, wipe the cavity clean. Continue the cut to reach the tail.

Keeping the knife lightly pressed down against the backbone, deepen the slit with shallow cuts along the length of the eel until the top fillet has been removed.

With the eel on the cutting board and its backbone facing up, make a slit along the length of the eel between the backbone and the bottom fillet, keeping the knife lightly pressed up against the backbone, using the length of your hand to press down on the backbone. Deepen the slit along the length of the eel until the backbone has been removed.

Trim the sides of the fillets to straighten them and remove their thinner edges. Each fillet has three rows of pin bones along its length. Run your fingers down the flesh against the grain of the fish to locate the rows of bones. Using very sharp small kitchen scissors held at a 45-degree angle

to the surface of the cutting board, snip ⅛-inch (3-millimeter) cuts into the flesh where the pin bones are located. Work on one row of pin bones at a time. The bones will not be removed, but snipping them will keep them from protruding from the surface of the fillet.

In a 1-quart (1-liter) saucepot, warm the olive oil, salt, ginger, lemon zest, basil, garlic, and chili flakes over medium-low heat to 185°F (85°C). Remove from the heat, cover with a lid, and steep for 10 minutes. Strain the oil into a bowl and nestle the bowl in an ice-water bath. Chill the oil completely.

Set an immersion circulator in a water bath and heat the water to 70°C (158°F). Cut each eel fillet into 3 equal pieces. Place the fillets and the chilled olive oil in a sous vide bag. Place the bag in a chamber vacuum sealer and vacuum seal. Cook in the water bath for 20 minutes.

Remove the bag and let cool on the counter to room temperature, then chill completely in an ice-water bath and refrigerate for up to 3 days.

FOR THE PRESERVED SOCIETY GARLIC FLOWERS

In a 1-quart (1-liter) saucepot, combine the water, vinegar, sugar, and salt. Bring to a simmer and stir to dissolve the sugar. Pour this pickling liquid into a bowl, nestle the bowl in an ice-water bath, and chill completely.

Pick the garlic flowers from the stalks and put them in a sous vide bag; add the cooled pickling liquid. Place the bag in the chamber vacuum sealer and vacuum seal just enough to remove the air in the bag and submerge the flowers in the liquid. Refrigerate for up to 1 month.

FOR THE SWEET VINEGAR PUREE

Strain 360 grams of the pickling liquid from the preserved society garlic into a small saucepot (reserving the pickled garlic flowers for garnishing). Bring the liquid to a boil over medium heat. Whisk in the agar-agar and, while whisking continuously, boil for 1 minute to activate the agar-agar. Transfer to a bowl and nestle the bowl in an ice-water bath. Chill, undisturbed, until the vinegar puree base is completely firm and set.

Cut the vinegar puree base into smaller pieces and transfer to a blender. Beginning on low speed and gradually increasing to high, blend until completely smooth, using the tamper to keep the puree moving. Pass the puree through a chinois into a container.

Place the container, uncovered, in the chamber vacuum sealer. Run a complete cycle on full pressure to remove any air bubbles incorporated during blending. This will give the puree clarity and shine.

Fill a disposable piping bag with the puree and pipe the puree into a small squeeze bottle. The puree can be refrigerated for up to 1 day.

TO COMPLETE

Prepare a fire (see page 270).

Drain the pickled garlic blossoms on a paper towel.

Remove the eel from the olive oil and gently wipe away any excess oil. Place the eel skin-side down on the work surface. Use one palm to gently hold the eel against the work surface while using the other to skewer the eel with two parallel skewers, inserting the skewers into the fattest part of the fillet, just to either side of the center. You will be able to feel the progress of the skewers; do not let them poke through the surface of the eel. Brush the eel with canola oil to prevent sticking.

Quickly roast the eel over very hot coals to lightly caramelize the flesh on both sides without overcooking, which would compromise the integrity of the eel. This should take 2 to 3 minutes total.

Remove the skewers and gently peel away the skins. Place the eel on the serving plates. Garnish the eel with several beads of vinegar puree, the preserved garlic blossoms, a light sprinkling of nigella seeds, and Maldon salt.

FIRSTS

THE EVOLUTION OF SERVICE

Developing Relationships with Our Guests

WHEN I OPENED THE FRENCH LAUNDRY twenty-six years ago, it was clear that the food demanded a new kind of service, something very different from the traditional fine-dining (usually French) approach, in which a formal waitstaff exuded an air of superiority, making all but the most well-known customers feel intimidated. From the opening cornet, through dishes such as Oysters and Pearls, Mac and Cheese, and Tongue in Cheek, my playful and unexpected food needed servers who could explain it with comfort and confidence. If they felt comfortable with this type of cuisine, the diners would, too.

The dining world was already on the brink of change. In Manhattan, the restaurateur Danny Meyer had introduced an enlightened service of warmth and grace at his Union Square Cafe, which opened in 1985. I wanted to offer my own version, but I was the chef; I couldn't be in the kitchen *and* the dining room. Believe me, if I could have personally delivered every plate to every diner, I would have.

So it was incredibly lucky, providential even, that a twenty-five-year-old Napa Valley native, Laura Cunningham, surprised me one day in 1994 when she knocked on my front door with wet hair. I opened the door, warily I'll admit, and she slipped her resume through the narrow gap. Laura would eventually become my partner in business and in life, but back then, I was slow to hire her.

She had deep knowledge of who lived and worked in Napa Valley, so the first thing I asked her to do was to take the guest list Don and Sally Schmitt had given me and mark all the VIPs. Even then I was slow to bring her on (though fortunately I eventually wised up). It wasn't until general manager Arthur Neola moved on, in December 1995, that she took the lead in all things operations.

When we opened in 1994, we were a scrappy small team with grand ambitions, and the fact that Laura knew half the people who came to the restaurant in its first year almost necessitated a casual welcome, one that was personal yet refined. In addition, the nature of the place was different, this old river-rock and timber building that had once been a brothel and a saloon in the late 1800s. From the beginning, Laura set the tone. She understood my perfectionism, intensity, and ambition, and brought this to service along with her highly intuitive sense of warmth and ease and ability to listen.

In the beginning, we didn't serve a lot of people; twenty or thirty diners a night was not uncommon. We had designated roles—captain, back waiter, runner and busser—but at first, everyone did everything. Laura led a small staff and soon hired Larry Nadeau, with whom she'd worked at Jonathan Waxman's Table 29 in Napa.

As the restaurant became more popular and diners responded with unusual enthusiasm, it was clear service needed to grow. Servers recognized the place was special and that the food they were in charge of serving really *was* different. Just as the chefs took great care to prepare and present the finest ingredients, the dining room staff deeply respected the food and shared the same enthusiasm and dedication toward the delivery and experience.

By the time Ruth Reichl called us the most exciting restaurant in the United States, the phones were ringing off the hook. This gave us something we needed to grow—the ability to forecast guest count. We could hire and round out our teams. In 1999, Laura promoted Larry to maître d', a position we'd never really had. Now Laura had more time to espouse her training standards and transform service as we know it today. But she was still overworked, effectively serving as the general manager and the beverage director and mentoring the next generation of managers.

An added layer was the fact that the restaurant is in Yountville, California, a small agricultural community, and Laura had to train ambitious youth coming to work to serve a sophisticated clientele—accustomed to Taillevent, Michel Bras, and Le Cirque—along with the highly experienced career servers. But Laura didn't hire people based on their resumes; she hired based on the human qualities in a server, young or old, experienced or not. Were they curious? Did they show empathy? Laura loved to interview, which was evident in our diverse teams and talent. I remember asking her about a young gentleman she had recently hired named Zion Curiel and what experience he had. She casually said, "None. He's currently working at Napa Auto Parts, but his charisma is sincere." This was typical of her style. Sure enough, Zion moved through every position to become a manager years later. Laura was curious about people and what they could offer to our collective efforts in this pursuit of reaching one's potential.

And she also asked . . . could they move well? The French Laundry is tiny and divided into several small spaces—on the ground floor, the dining room and its small alcove, and up a creaky wooden staircase, two more rooms. Tables were tight, and moving well in that space—efficiently and gracefully—was something we had to practice. Laura became so attuned to the importance of the servers' movements, both their own and in concert, that when we opened per se, she hired a ballet dancer to train the staff in spatial awareness.

A meal at either of our restaurants can last more than three hours, with multiple courses and multiple wines. The server's job is not just dropping plates and refilling water. Our servers need to develop a relationship with our guests. This requires intuition, genuine interest in the guest, and intelligence about what they are serving and why, as well as an awareness of the world around them. Laura made them aware.

This doesn't mean every server should be an extrovert. The woman who has served more guests than anyone in our history is Laura, and she is a great introvert. It does mean that servers must have a keen awareness of the room, of the guests, and embrace a spirit of generosity. They have to anticipate what the guest will need before they realize they need it. They must embody an intuitive nature. To me, that's the essence of fine-dining service.

For the first few years, we had a poorly organized cellar of about three hundred California wines we'd inherited from the Schmitts—heavily concentrated in the Napa Valley and reflecting the Schmitts' personal relationships. In our early, financially tight years, we worked our way through these wines. The year after the creation of the maître d' position, with our list growing thinner and us wanting to broaden its reach to "All World Wines," we hired a young wine director named Bobby Stuckey, who would go on to become a Master Sommelier. Bobby was charged with creating a list of wines from around the world commensurate with both the food and the clientele of The French Laundry, which was now more worldly than ever. Few restaurants in the valley served anything but California wines (it was even controversial to serve Sonoma wines in a Napa Valley restaurant).

But why shouldn't we have great world wines along with California and French wines?

Bobby created that list—and more. He was open, honest, and enthusiastic—without any pretense—and brought this tone to the wine service; the perfect complement to Laura and Larry. They were a dream team. It was about the wine and the food, not about the profit margins. He would spend just as much time expounding on the virtues of $30 Spotswood Sauvignon Blanc to a table of two as he would with a big table drinking bottles of $300 Diamond Creek Cabernet Sauvignon.

With these new positions—maître d' and sommelier—in place and thriving, Laura had the time to refine service further. While keeping the feel of the service casual and warm, exuding at all times generosity, heart, and a true desire to serve, she focused on educating and empowering the servers, ensuring that our version of fine-dining service continues to improve, evolve, and stay vital.

Another benchmark in service was our decision to include gratuity in the cost of the meal—that is, to eliminate tips altogether by including a service charge on each check. We weren't the first to do this, of course, as service compris is the standard in France and many other countries. And important American restaurateurs such as Alice Waters and Charlie Trotter also had made the move. Tips had always been their livelihood, and here we were replacing them with an unfamiliar system. But I knew a salaried position would give some certainty to their year and bring other benefits.

Over time, everyone saw how the benefits outweighed whatever drawbacks they may have expected. The service staff saw how the new system was an advantage to the kitchen staff, who typically earn much less than the servers but who now shared in the overall health benefits. Salaried servers equalized the pay benefits for all. It allowed us to give everyone health insurance and paid vacations.

This rich spirit of genuine service, and the experience that it defines for our diners, is what Laura Cunningham has established. She has truly transformed fine-dining service, not by making it less formal—it's still formal—but by making it more fun, combining ease and warmth with finesse, creating a spell of seduction under which our guests are happy to fall. Her work over the past twenty-six years has revolutionized service throughout the country, and she has freely served as a mentor and shared her wisdom with many, including the subsequent general managers of The French Laundry, Nicolas Fanucci and Michael Minnillo; per se's general manager, Sandra Schaeuffele; and many members of the dining room who have moved on.

SALADE VERTE

Cured Cucumber, Avocado Mousse, Sunflower Sprouts, and Black Yuzu Powder

Makes 6 servings

BLACK YUZU POWDER

2 whole yuzu

CURED CELTUCE AND CUCUMBER

1 (6- to 8-inch/15- to 20-centimeter) piece celtuce

400 grams prepared veg blanc (see page 185)

2 (8-inch/20-centimeter) serpentine cucumbers, peeled, if desired (see Note)

KIWI-YUZU CONDIMENT

275 grams ¼-inch-dice (6-millimeter) peeled kiwi

15 grams coarsely chopped lemongrass

50 grams bottled yuzu juice

250 grams water

10 grams kosher salt, plus more to taste

50 grams sugar

5.5 grams agar-agar

Fresh yuzu juice (optional)

AVOCADO MOUSSE

300 grams ripe avocado

20 grams coarsely chopped fresh cilantro leaves

14 grams pistachio oil

8 grams lime juice

6 grams fleur de sel

6 grams Pre-Hy (page 109)

4 grams shallot

0.5 grams ascorbic acid

100 grams crème fraîche

TO COMPLETE

1 medium kiwi, peeled

1 large ripe avocado

Extra-virgin olive oil

Fleur de sel

15 to 20 sunflower sprouts

SPECIAL EQUIPMENT

Immersion circulator

Chamber vacuum sealer

Dehydrator

#804 (⅜-inch/ 10-millimeter) plain piping tip

This "green salad" was our first uni-colored plate. It just made sense. It's by far David's favorite salad and can change to accommodate whatever is best of the season. If the avocados are at their peak, then that's what will be featured. In early spring, the asparagus are especially beautiful. Here it's diced kiwi, with a kiwi-yuzu condiment flavored with lemongrass. Avocado mousse goes down first and serves to anchor the avocado and cucumber. Sunflower sprouts and a black yuzu powder finish the dish.

To make the black yuzu, the yuzu are vacuum sealed and cooked in very hot water for 45 minutes, a process that also pasteurizes them. We put them in the dehydrator, still sealed, for two weeks, essentially aging them in a sterile environment, a process that turns them black. It's almost like hypercaramelization—the way black garlic is made. We remove them from the bag, fully dehydrate them, then pulverize them. The powder adds color to the plate, as well as intense acidity with a depth of flavor and umami from the aging process.

David recalls the initial inspiration: "During a dinner at Pierre Gagnaire in Paris, I was served a dish that was entirely red, rouget with beets and raspberries. I'd never had a dish in which all the components were the same color. It had never occurred to any of us to do a uni-colored dish. One day when we were having a menu meeting in spring, I said maybe we should do a dish that's entirely green, which sounded so goofy, we all laughed. But then we decided to try it. It was *stunning*. Now we have one for each season."

FOR THE BLACK YUZU POWDER

Set an immersion circulator in a water bath and heat the water to 100°C (212°F). Cut off the top and bottom of the yuzu and cut into ½-inch-thick (1.25-centimeter) slices. Use tweezers to remove and discard any seeds. Place the yuzu slices in a sous vide bag. Place the bag in a chamber vacuum sealer and vacuum seal. Cook in the water bath for 45 minutes. Immediately submerge the bag in an ice-water bath to chill. Remove from the ice-water bath and dry the outside of the bag.

Place the sealed bag in a dehydrator and dehydrate at 131°F (55°C) for 2 weeks. The yuzu slices will become completely black, break down, and soften somewhat. Remove the yuzu from the bag, spread the slices in a single layer on a dehydrating rack, and return to the dehydrator for

5 more days, until they are completely dry. Grind the dried yuzu in a spice grinder and store in an airtight container at room temperature for up to 6 months.

FOR THE CURED CELTUCE AND CUCUMBER

Peel the celtuce. Place it in a sous vide bag and add 150 grams of the veg blanc. Place the bag in the sealer chamber and vacuum seal. Place the cucumbers in a separate sous vide bag with the remaining 250 grams veg blanc and vacuum seal. The celtuce and cucumbers can be used immediately or refrigerated in their bags for up to 2 days.

FOR THE KIWI-YUZU CONDIMENT

Combine the kiwi, lemongrass, yuzu juice, water, salt, and sugar. Bring to a simmer over high heat, then reduce the heat to maintain a simmer and cook for about 5 minutes, until the kiwi is completely tender. Whisk in the agar-agar. While whisking continuously, boil for 1 minute to activate the agar-agar. Transfer to a bowl and nestle the bowl in an ice-water bath. Chill, undisturbed, until the kiwi-yuzu base is completely firm and set.

Coarsely chop the kiwi-yuzu base and transfer to a blender. Beginning on low speed and gradually increasing to high, puree until completely smooth, using the tamper to keep the puree moving. Season to taste with additional salt and a squeeze of fresh yuzu juice.

Strain the puree into a container and place the container, uncovered, in the chamber vacuum sealer. Run a complete cycle on full pressure to remove any air bubbles incorporated during blending. This will give the puree clarity and shine.

Fill a disposable piping bag with the puree and pipe the puree into a small squeeze bottle. Refrigerate for up to 3 days.

FOR THE AVOCADO MOUSSE

Cut the avocados in half, remove the pits, and scoop the flesh into a blender. Add the cilantro leaves, pistachio oil, lime juice, fleur de sel, Pre-Hy, shallot, and ascorbic acid and blend until perfectly smooth.

Add the crème fraîche and blend on medium-high speed just to incorporate. (If you overblend the puree at this point, it will split.) Pass the puree through a chinois. Transfer to a disposable piping bag fitted with a #804 (⅜-inch/10-millimeter) plain piping tip. Be sure to remove all the air from the piping bag so the avocado mousse does not oxidize.

TO COMPLETE

Remove the cucumber and celtuce from the brine and discard the brine. Slice 24 thin rounds each of the celtuce and the cucumber. Cut a piece of cucumber 3 inches (7.5 centimeters) long, and slice it lengthwise into 6 pieces. Cut the remaining cucumber and the celtuce into small bite-size pieces. They should be organic cuts and vary in size.

Halve the kiwi lengthwise, then slice one half crosswise into 6 half circles about ¼ inch (6 millimeters) thick. Cut the remaining kiwi half into ¼-inch (6-millimeter) dice.

Cut the avocado in half and remove the pit. Cut each half into 3 wedges and gently peel by pulling the skin back from the flesh. Lightly dress all the prepared vegetables with olive oil and fleur de sel.

Pipe avocado mousse onto each serving plate and use the mousse to anchor a wedge of avocado, some of the vegetables, and some kiwi slices. Squeeze several dots of the kiwi-yuzu condiment around the plate. Arrange the remaining cucumber, celtuce, and kiwi pieces on the dish. Garnish with the sunflower sprouts and a sprinkle of the black yuzu powder.

NOTE

We use cucumbers fresh from the garden, so their skins are very tender. If you're using store-bought cucumbers with thicker skins, you may want to peel them for this recipe.

SALADE ROUGE

Ruby Beets, Purple Brussels Sprouts, Pink Pearl Apples, Red Onion, and Pickled Beet Puree

Makes 6 servings

RUBY BEETS

4 ruby beets, about
  2 inches
  (5 centimeters) in
  diameter

½ navel orange

50 grams shallots

5 thyme sprigs

8 black peppercorns

Kosher salt

PICKLED BEET PUREE

4 grams allspice berries

4 grams black
  peppercorns

6 grams lemon zest
  (removed with a
  vegetable peeler)

335 grams strained red
  beet juice

165 grams champagne
  vinegar, plus more to
  taste

80 grams sugar

5 grams fleur de sel, plus
  more to taste

6 grams agar-agar

7 grams Ultra-Tex 8

PINK PEARL APPLES

200 grams red verjus

20 grams dried hibiscus
  flowers

55 grams sugar

2 Pink Pearl apples

5 grams Pre-Hy (page
  109)

**HONEY-POACHED
CRANBERRIES**

125 grams honey

30 grams water

10 grams fleur de sel

10 grams sherry vinegar

24 fresh cranberries, at
  room temperature

TO COMPLETE

18 baby purple Brussels
  sprouts

Canola oil, for sautéing

Fleur de sel

Lemon juice

8 red pearl onions, sliced
  into rings and pickled
  (see page 184)

Burgundy amaranth

Rosemary flowers

SPECIAL EQUIPMENT

Chamber vacuum sealer
  (optional)

Immersion circulator
  (optional)

In the fall, when beets are in season, the apple tree beside the restaurant—a gift from Don and Sally Schmitt, the original owners of The French Laundry—bears the most delicious pink apples with pink flesh. We love using the apples from our trees for this dish. They're gently cooked in a sweet-sour cuisson till they're perfectly tender. Red onions are made into the simplest of pickles. The cranberries are cooked in honey, and the dish is finished with tiny red leaves and herbs and pink apple puree. For the puree, we use agar to get the desired consistency and Ultra-Tex to prevent the sauce from bleeding (see The Liaisons, page 108), ensuring a flawless appearance.

The onions are fabulous compressed, becoming a vibrant pink, but they'll lose that intensity of color after a few hours.

FOR THE RUBY BEETS

Thoroughly wash the beets under cold running water and trim them of any root or stem. Place the beets, orange, shallots, thyme, and peppercorns in a 2-quart (2-liter) saucepot. Add water to cover the beets generously and season the water aggressively with salt. Bring the water to a simmer over medium-high heat. Reduce the heat to medium-low and cover with a lid. Simmer for 25 minutes, then check the beets by piercing them with a cake tester. They should be tender throughout. If not, continue to simmer them, checking with the cake tester every 5 minutes, until tender. Transfer the beets and their cooking liquid to a bowl and nestle the bowl in an ice-water bath to cool. Peel and dice 100 grams of the beets and reserve for the puree. Peel the remaining beets and cut into 6 wedges each.

FOR THE PICKLED BEET PUREE

Tie the allspice, peppercorns, and lemon zest in cheesecloth to make a sachet. Place the reserved 100 grams diced beets, beet juice, vinegar, sugar, fleur de sel, and sachet of spices in a 1-quart (1-liter) saucepot. Bring the liquid to a simmer over medium heat. Immediately remove from the heat, cover with a lid, and steep for 20 minutes.

Discard the sachet and return the pot to medium-high heat. Bring to a boil and whisk in the agar-agar. While whisking continuously, boil vigorously for 1 minute to activate the agar-agar. Transfer to a bowl and nestle the bowl in an ice-water bath. Chill, undisturbed, until the beet puree base is completely firm and set.

Cut the beet puree base into smaller pieces and transfer to a blender. Beginning on low speed and gradually increasing to high, blend until completely smooth, using the tamper to keep the puree moving. Stop the blender and scrape the sides of the container with a silicone spatula.

Blend again and with the motor running, shear the Ultra-Tex into the puree until completely hydrated, using the tamper to help incorporate. The puree will be very thick. Adjust the seasoning to taste with vinegar and fleur de sel.

If you have a chamber vacuum sealer, transfer the puree to a container and place the container, uncovered, in the sealer chamber. Run a complete cycle on full pressure to remove any air bubbles incorporated during blending. This will give the puree clarity and shine.

Fill a disposable piping bag with the puree and pipe the puree into a small squeeze bottle. The puree can be refrigerated for up to 2 days, but should be brought to room temperature before using.

FOR THE PINK PEARL APPLES

Combine the red verjus, hibiscus, and sugar in a 1-quart (1-liter) saucepot and bring to a simmer over medium heat, whisking gently to ensure the sugar is dissolved. Remove from the heat, cover with a lid, and steep for 20 minutes. Strain the poaching liquid into a bowl and nestle the bowl in an ice-water bath to chill.

If you have a chamber vacuum sealer, set an immersion circulator in a water bath and heat the water to 88°C (190.4°F). Once the poaching liquid is cold, transfer it to a sous vide bag. Peel the apples and cut each into 8 wedges. Trim the core from each wedge and immediately place the wedges into the bag with the poaching liquid to prevent oxidation. Place the bag in the sealer chamber and vacuum seal. Cook in the water bath for 20 minutes, until the apples are fully tender but still hold their shape. Immediately submerge the bag in an ice-water bath to chill.

If you don't have a chamber vacuum sealer, place the apple wedges and poaching liquid in a small saucepot that will hold them in a single layer. Gently bring the liquid to a simmer over medium-low heat. Cover the pot with a cartouche, and place in a 325°F (163°C) oven to cook for 15 to

20 minutes, until the apples are tender. Transfer the apples and syrup to a bowl and nestle the bowl in an ice-water bath to chill.

Once chilled, strain the liquid into a medium bowl and put the apples in a separate medium bowl. Whisk the Pre-Hy into the liquid and strain the liquid back over the apples. The Pre-Hy will give the poaching liquid added body and make a better glaze for the apples. Refrigerate for up to 1 day.

FOR THE HONEY-POACHED CRANBERRIES

Combine the honey, water, fleur de sel, and vinegar in a small saucepot and bring the mixture to a simmer over medium-low heat. Stir in the cranberries. Remove from the heat, cover with a lid, and let cool to warm room temperature. The cranberries can be used immediately or refrigerated for up to 1 day; return to room temperature before using.

TO COMPLETE

Bring a large pot of salted water to a boil. Trim the outer 3 or 4 leaves of each Brussels sprout. Submerge the leaves in the boiling water for 10 to 15 seconds to soften and cook them slightly but still allow them to retain their shape. Using a skimmer, remove the leaves from the water and drain on paper towels.

Add the whole Brussels sprouts to the pot and blanch for 2 to 3 minutes, until tender. Transfer to an ice-water bath and let cool for 2 to 3 minutes, then drain and transfer to paper towels to dry.

Heat a medium sauté pan over medium heat. Add enough canola oil to just coat the bottom of the pan. Add the whole Brussels sprouts and season with a pinch of fleur de sel. Cook, rolling the Brussels sprouts around in the pan, until they are evenly golden brown, about 3 minutes. Remove from the pan and hold on a tray at room temperature.

All the salad ingredients should be at room temperature. To build the salad, pipe a few mounds of beet puree in the center of each plate and arrange the apple wedges, beet wedges, cranberries, and larger onion rings on the plates. Garnish with the whole Brussels sprouts, Brussels sprout leaves, burgundy amaranth, and rosemary flowers.

SALADE BLANCHE

Parsnip, Pear, Endive, Roasted Walnut Crème Fraîche, and White Truffle

Makes 6 servings

ROASTED WALNUT CRÈME FRAÎCHE

250 grams crème fraîche

5 grams walnut oil

5 grams champagne vinegar, plus more to taste

5 grams kosher salt, plus more to taste

2 grams sugar

25 grams English walnuts, toasted and finely chopped

TO COMPLETE

1 medium parsnip, about 2 inches (5 centimeters) in diameter

1 (50- to 60-gram) white truffle, thinly sliced

4 heads white Belgian endive

1 ripe Bosc pear

Extra-virgin olive oil

Fleur de sel

6 English walnuts, toasted

SPECIAL EQUIPMENT

Japanese mandoline

½-inch (13-millimeter) plain round cutter

#803 (⁵⁄₁₆-inch/ 8-millimeter) plain piping tip

When we're preparing our white truffle menu in the fall, this is the first course, a classic combination of parsnip, pear, endive, and walnut. All the components are raw—I like that David shaves the walnuts—and we make the roasted walnut crème fraîche. It's not unlike the walnut cream soup, come to think of it, that Stephen Durfee, the original pastry chef at The French Laundry, served for dessert.

FOR THE ROASTED WALNUT CRÈME FRAÎCHE

In a bowl, whisk together the crème fraîche, walnut oil, vinegar, salt, and sugar. Stir in the walnuts.

TO COMPLETE

Bring a large pot of salted water to a boil. Peel the parsnip and slice on a Japanese mandoline into ⅛-inch-thick (3-millimeter) rounds. Blanch in the boiling water until tender, 30 to 45 seconds. Transfer to an ice-water bath and chill for about 30 seconds, until cold. Drain and dry on paper towels.

Using a ½-inch (13-millimeter) plain round cutter, punch 48 rounds from the truffle slices. Mince the truffle trimmings and fold them into the walnut crème fraîche. Transfer the crème fraîche to a disposable piping bag fitted with a #803 (⁵⁄₁₆-inch/8-millimeter) plain piping tip.

Cut off the bottom of the endives to remove the leaves. Cut the base of each leaf on a bias.

The crème fraîche will anchor the endive leaves. Pipe a strip of crème fraîche (about 30 grams) just off-center on each serving plate. Using a small offset spatula, spread the crème fraîche into a ⅛-inch-thick (3-millimeter) layer.

Peel and core the pear and cut it into brunoise. Lightly season the endive with olive oil and fleur de sel. Beginning at the top of the plate, anchor the bottom of a leaf in the crème fraîche. Begin adding leaves, alternating sides to create a shingled effect. Garnish the endive with the parsnip slices, additional crème fraîche, and the pear brunoise. Finish with the truffle rounds and shavings of roasted walnut.

SUMMER CORN PARFAIT

Chilled Corn, Corn Puree, Romaine, and Buttered Corn Mousse

Makes 6 servings

CURED CELTUCE

40 grams peeled celtuce

100 grams prepared veg blanc (see page 185)

CORN PUREE

225 grams corn juice

25 grams whole butter

3 grams kosher salt, plus more to taste

5 grams sugar

3 grams agar-agar

Lemon juice

ROMAINE-SPINACH GELÉE

1 sheet silver leaf gelatin

15 grams kosher salt

100 grams romaine lettuce heart

50 grams stemmed arrowleaf spinach leaves

CORN MOUSSE

1 sheet silver leaf gelatin

125 grams corn juice

100 grams water

13 grams whole butter

3 grams kosher salt, plus more to taste

3 grams sugar

10 grams Pre-Hy (page 109)

Lemon juice

TO COMPLETE

Canola oil, for deep-frying

4 grams sorghum kernels

15 grams romaine lettuce heart

90 grams corn kernels, blanched

4 grams freeze-dried corn kernels

SPECIAL EQUIPMENT

Chamber vacuum sealer (optional)

Immersion circulator (optional)

iSi siphon, cold

2 cream chargers

Six 185-gram glasses

We wanted to serve a corn canapé that wasn't corn soup (see page 38). David thought, why not a parfait? Then he considered what goes with corn and thought lettuce, one with some bitterness to contrast with the sweetness of the corn. We get such beautiful lettuces from the garden. He makes a romaine gelée, and mixes corn kernels with diced romaine and celtuce, sometimes called stem lettuce. We use it for its trunk, which has an intense lettuce flavor, and its bite; when sliced or diced, it has the texture of a water chestnut. He finishes the dish with a corn mousse dispensed from a siphon, like whipped cream on a parfait, and puffed sorghum, a little-used grain that puffs like tiny pieces of popcorn when fried.

FOR THE CURED CELTUCE

Cut the celtuce into cubes the size of corn kernels. If you have a chamber vacuum sealer, place the celtuce and veg blanc in a sous vide bag. Place the bag in the sealer chamber and vacuum seal. The celtuce is ready to use immediately. If you do not have a chamber vacuum sealer, combine the celtuce and veg blanc in a container, cover, and brine in the refrigerator for at least 2 hours.

The celtuce can be refrigerated in the veg blanc for up to 2 days.

FOR THE CORN PUREE

Combine the corn juice, butter, salt, sugar, and agar-agar in a sabayon pot or other thick-bottomed saucepot. Bring to a boil over medium heat, whisking continuously to keep the mixture from scorching, to thicken. Boil vigorously for 1 minute to fully activate the agar-agar. Transfer to a bowl and nestle the bowl in an ice-water bath. Chill the corn puree base until completely firm and set.

Cut the corn puree base into smaller pieces and transfer to a blender. Beginning on low speed and gradually increasing to high, blend until completely smooth, using the tamper to keep the puree moving. Strain through a chinois and season to taste with lemon juice and additional salt.

Transfer the puree to a disposable piping bag. Pipe 30 grams of the puree into the bottom of each of six 185-gram glasses, holding the bag against the bottom of the glass and moving the bag upward as you pipe. Refrigerate the glasses while you make the romaine-spinach gelée.

(continued)

FOR THE ROMAINE-SPINACH GELÉE

Submerge the gelatin in a bowl of ice water to bloom (soften) for about 5 minutes.

Bring 1,000 grams (1 quart/1 liter) water and the salt to a boil in a 2-quart (2-liter) saucepot. Add the romaine and spinach to the pot and boil vigorously for 3 to 4 minutes, until the greens are tender. Ladle out and reserve 75 grams of the cooking liquid. Drain the greens and spread on a clean kitchen towel. When cool enough to handle, wring out any excess liquid from the greens.

Place the greens and reserved cooking liquid in the blender and puree until completely smooth, scraping down the sides as necessary. Remove the softened gelatin from the ice water and squeeze out any excess water. Add the gelatin to the blender and puree until smooth. Pass through a chinois into a spouted container (discard the pulp in the chinois).

Pour 10 grams of the gelée over the corn puree in each glass and refrigerate to set the gelée.

FOR THE CORN MOUSSE

Submerge the gelatin in a bowl of ice water to bloom (soften) for about 5 minutes.

Place the corn juice, water, butter, salt, and sugar in a sabayon pot or saucepot and whisk over medium heat until it reaches a boil. While whisking continuously, boil vigorously for about 4 minutes to thicken and fully activate the natural starch in the corn juice.

Transfer the contents of the pot to a blender and blend on high speed for 1 to 2 minutes, until perfectly smooth. Remove the softened gelatin from the ice water (reserve the ice water) and squeeze out any excess water. Add the gelatin and the Pre-Hy to the blender and blend to fully incorporate. Season to taste with lemon juice and additional salt.

Pass the mixture through a chinois into a bowl and nestle the bowl in the ice-water bath. Chill completely, stirring occasionally. Once the corn mixture is fully chilled, remove the siphon from the refrigerator and fill it with the corn mousse. Charge the siphon with two cream chargers, shaking the siphon vigorously between charges and after charging, to ensure it is fully aerated for use. Return the siphon to the refrigerator until ready to complete the dish.

TO COMPLETE

Fill a small saucepot with at least 4-inch-high (10-centimeter) sides with about 1 inch (2.5 centimeters) of canola oil. Heat the oil to 400°F (204°C). Add the sorghum kernels and fry, removing them as they puff (like popcorn). Drain on paper towels.

Dice the center, lightest, and most tender parts of the romaine to match the size of the celtuce and corn. Drain and dry the celtuce and mix it with the blanched corn kernels and romaine.

Divide the vegetables among the glasses, forming an even layer over the gelée. Siphon the corn mousse into the glasses, filling them about two-thirds of the way to the top. Sprinkle with the freeze-dried corn kernels and puffed sorghum.

CRUDITÉS

Compressed Young Fennel, Nantes Carrots, Armenian Cucumbers, Radishes, Pickled Fennel Bulb, and Fermented Parsnip "Cream"

Makes 6 servings

FERMENTED PARSNIP "CREAM"

125 grams Koshihikari rice

400 grams water

100 grams buttermilk

125 grams fermented parsnips (page 186)

20 grams extra-virgin olive oil

Kosher salt

SEASONAL VEGETABLES

Nantes carrots

Radishes

Armenian cucumbers

Young fennel bulbs

TO COMPLETE

Pickled fennel bulb (page 184)

Extra-virgin olive oil

Fleur de sel

Cucamelon flowers (optional)

Oxalis (optional)

SPECIAL EQUIPMENT

Chamber vacuum sealer

Japanese mandoline (optional)

This dish shows off all the vegetables, but the real star is the fermented parsnip peels. Corey loves to use what we typically discard, such as parsnip peels. They're loaded with flavor, so he ferments them; then he cooks them with whey and rice to create a creamlike sauce.

FOR THE FERMENTED PARSNIP "CREAM"

Place rice, water, buttermilk, and parsnips in a rice cooker. Cook on the Porridge setting according to the manufacturer's instructions.

When the cooker cycle is done (about 1 hour), transfer mixture to a blender and blend on medium-high speed until smooth, about 2 minutes. With the blender running, stream in the oil and season with salt to taste. Strain into an airtight container. Refrigerate for up to 2 days.

FOR THE SEASONAL VEGETABLES

Rub the carrots with a new scouring pad to remove the peel while keeping their shape as round as possible. Leave a small portion of the stems attached. Depending on the shape of the carrots, cut them lengthwise on a mandoline or halve or quarter them on the bias. Depending on the shape of the radishes, clean and leave whole, halved, or quartered, leaving some of the stems attached. Cut cucumbers into thick slices or wedges and cut the young fennel bulbs in half.

Place the vegetables in a sous vide bag and add enough ice water to cover them. Place the bag in the chamber vacuum sealer and vacuum seal. Refrigerate for up to 1 day.

TO COMPLETE

Drain the pickled fennel and dry on paper towels, then slice. Drain the compressed vegetables and dry on paper towels. Season all the vegetables to taste with olive oil and fleur de sel. Bring the parsnip cream to room temperature, if necessary, transfer to a bowl, and dot the surface with olive oil. Arrange the compressed vegetables and pickled fennel over a bed of ice, garnish with cucamelon flowers and oxalis, if desired, and serve the parsnip cream on the side.

LEEKS VINAIGRETTE

Pain de Campagne and Black Winter Truffle Ravigote

Makes 6 servings

HEN EGG TERRINE

250 grams egg whites

6 grams kosher salt

175 grams egg yolks

LEEKS

150 grams Holland leeks (white portions only)

200 grams prepared veg blanc (see page 185)

BLACK WINTER TRUFFLE RAVIGOTE

375 grams water

40 grams champagne vinegar

43 grams sugar

10 grams kosher salt

4 grams Pre-Hy (page 109)

18 grams extra-virgin olive oil

30 grams minced black winter truffle

PAIN DE CAMPAGNE CROUTONS

100 grams extra-virgin olive oil

30 grams ¼-inch-dice (6-millimeter) crustless pain de campagne (crusts removed before cutting)

1 thyme sprig

1 garlic clove

3 grams kosher salt, plus more to taste

TO COMPLETE

2 French leeks, green portions only

Extra-virgin olive oil

Fleur de sel

18 thin slices black winter truffle, at least ⅝ inch (16 millimeters) in diameter each (optional)

SPECIAL EQUIPMENT

Combi oven

Chamber vacuum sealer

½-inch (13-millimeter) round cutter

½-inch (13-millimeter) flower-shaped cutter

This is a bistro classic we all love, one of our favorite salads. At Bouchon, we serve a classic leeks vinaigrette with egg and a red wine vinaigrette. At per se, Corey has refined the dish for four-star service. The leeks are cooked in veg blanc till they're very tender, then cut into diamonds. Corey creates a terrine with alternating layers of egg white and egg yolk, and makes a great ravigote sauce with truffles and champagne vinegar. He finishes the dish with pain de campagne croutons.

FOR THE HEN EGG TERRINE

Preheat a combi oven to 85°C (185°F).

In a blender, blend the egg whites and 2.5 grams of the salt on high speed for 8 to 10 seconds, until the whites are broken up. Strain the egg whites through a chinois into a container. Place the container, uncovered, in a chamber vacuum sealer. Run a complete cycle on full pressure to remove any air bubbles incorporated during blending. Stay at the machine, and if the egg whites begin to bubble over, stop the machine.

Blend the egg yolks and the remaining 3.5 grams salt on high speed for about 10 seconds, until smooth. Strain through a chinois into a deli container.

Place an eighth sheet pan into a 12 by 15-inch (30 by 40-centimeter) sous vide bag, leaving a 1-inch (2.5-centimeter) border between the pan and the bag. Place in the sealer chamber and vacuum seal to line the pan. Place the lined pan in a container with a lid.

Gently pour 85 grams of the egg whites into a small deli container or other plastic container. Slowly pour the egg whites onto the lined pan, holding the container close to the pan to avoid creating any bubbles. Use a small silicone spatula to move the whites into any areas or corners that are not filled. Cover the pan container with its lid and steam in the combi oven for about 10 minutes. Remove the container from the oven and uncover; the whites as well as all subsequent layers should feel firm to the touch after steaming.

Pour in 150 grams of the egg yolks, tilting the pan in each direction to form an even layer. Cover the container, return it to the combi oven, and steam for about 10 minutes. Remove the container from the oven, add another 85 grams of the egg whites (again being careful not to create bubbles when you pour them), cover, and steam for about 10 minutes. Uncover the container and cool the egg terrine in the refrigerator. It must be completely cold before portioning.

The hen egg terrine can be wrapped in plastic wrap and refrigerated for up to 3 days.

FOR THE LEEKS

Preheat the combi oven to 88°C (190°F).

Remove the outer layer of the leeks, cut them in half lengthwise, and rinse to remove any dirt. Place the leeks in a sous vide bag with the veg blanc. Place the bag in the sealer chamber and vacuum seal. Steam in the combi oven until tender when pinched with your fingers, about 20 minutes. Submerge the bag of leeks in an ice-water bath to chill. Refrigerate in the bag for up to 3 days before cutting.

FOR THE BLACK WINTER TRUFFLE RAVIGOTE

In the blender, blend the water, vinegar, sugar, and salt on low speed for 15 to 30 seconds, until the sugar and salt have dissolved. With the blender running on low speed, add the Pre-Hy and blend to combine, gradually increasing the speed to high.

With the blender running on medium speed, very slowly drizzle in the olive oil, maintaining the emulsion throughout the process.

Refrigerate in an airtight container for up to 3 days. Stir in the black truffle just before serving the dish.

FOR THE PAIN DE CAMPAGNE CROUTONS

Heat a medium sauté pan over medium-high heat. Add the olive oil, then the diced bread, thyme, and garlic and toast the croutons, stirring continuously, for about 2 minutes, or until golden brown. Drain the croutons on paper towels and immediately sprinkle with the salt. Discard the thyme and garlic and let cool.

The croutons can be stored in an airtight container overnight.

TO COMPLETE

Bring a large pot of salted water to a boil. Blanch the French leek greens for 2 minutes and chill in an ice-water bath. Dry on paper towels and cut into ½-inch (1.25-centimeter) pieces. Toss with olive oil and season with fleur de sel.

Drain the cold Holland leeks and dry on paper towels. Working toward the root end, slice them on a 45-degree angle into diamond-shaped pieces about ¾ inch (2 centimeters) wide.

Punch rounds from each slice of truffle (if using) with a ½-inch (13-millimeter) round cutter.

All components of the finished dish should rest at room temperature for about 20 minutes before plating.

Spoon 30 grams of the black truffle ravigote into each serving bowl. Using a small offset spatula, arrange 3 pieces of Holland leek facing different directions in a triangular formation at the bottom of each bowl. Arrange 3 pieces of the French leeks around the bowl. Cut and remove a small corner of the terrine to enable you to lift out pieces of the terrine more easily. Punch the hen egg terrine with a ½-inch (13-millimeter) flower-shaped cutter and arrange the terrine cutouts in the spaces between the leeks. Just before serving, sprinkle the croutons on top and arrange a truffle round (if using) over each Holland leek.

CLASSIC ROUX AND THE EVOLUTION OF THE LIAISONS

THE FIRST ADDED THICKENER, or liaison, was likely roux—flour cooked in butter, or any kind of fat, such as rendered beef fat. The fat separates the granules of flour so they don't combine and form clumps. When the roux is combined with liquid and heated, the flour granules absorb the liquid and expand, thickening the sauce. This has been used as a classical thickening device at least since Antonin Carême, born in Paris in the eighteenth century, wrote about it.

By the time I started cooking, in the 1970s, roux had become so common that we allowed it to become debased. My brother Joseph first showed me how to make a roux when I became chef of the Palm Beach Yacht Club. He told me that at his restaurant, they'd make a one-sixth pan full of blond roux—butter and flour—and stick it under a worktable, then just add some into whatever needed thickening, a gravy or a classic Bordelaise. It could be under the stove for a week getting rancid. Roux was just an all-purpose thickener we'd read about in Escoffier—it wasn't something we *thought* about. No one appreciated it or took much care when making it, and it became associated with heavy French food.

Then nouvelle cuisine entered the picture, with its emphasis on lighter cooking, and we discovered the cornstarch slurry. But like the last-minute thickener beurre manié, we considered that a "shoemaker" shortcut, something I'd hide if I had to use it.

By the time I opened The French Laundry in 1994, I didn't use roux at all and rarely used any kind of starch thickener. All the sauces we served achieved their viscosity through reduction.

In the late 1990s, Ferran Adrià came along and upended the culinary world with new thickeners, such as agar-agar, and "spherification" chemicals (alginates mixed with calcium chloride), ushering in the era of modernist cuisine. Thickeners took on an impressive if obfuscating name: "hydrocolloids." That word—technically denoting "forms a gel"—collectively in the kitchen means thickener. Flour is a so-called hydrocolloid. We prefer the classical name: "liaisons."

Twenty years later, we're back to using flour-thickening! In a big way, and mainly led by David Breeden, who respects our modern techniques but also reveres and continues to learn from the classics. If you take care to cook it properly (the flour needs to be cooked both in the roux and in the finished sauce), and store it properly, and learn how to use it properly, it's a superlative thickener. For roux-thickened sauces, once you achieve the right flavor, then reduce it to the right texture (too much reduction can make stock feel gluey on the palate), you thicken it with roux or sometimes a cornstarch slurry. The result is better because you haven't had to overcook your stock to achieve the texture you want. Presently we mainly use a version of this called beurre manié, "kneaded butter," equal parts flour and room-temperature butter mixed to a uniform paste (this can be added directly to a liquid, but the flour must be cooked).

We've gone from classical roux-thickened French sauces to reduction sauces to molecular gastronomy–thickened sauces and back again to Carême's flour-thickened sauces. So now we have many, many techniques, spanning all eras, to choose from. Who knows where we'll be twenty years from now!

In this section, we discuss the variety of old and new liaisons as they are used in the French Laundry and per se kitchens, from flour to Ultra-Tex (remember that despite their chemical-sounding names, they are all—save for gelatin—plant-based).

THE LIAISONS

Once we know how to achieve the perfect flavor in a sauce, a stock, or a glaze, we have to give it the optimal texture, because texture, of course, is one of the key facets of deliciousness. To do this, we usually have to increase the viscosity, and we now have a variety of thickeners, gelling agents, and emulsifiers at our disposal beyond the classic starches and eggs that we know from traditional techniques. We call these texture-modifying ingredients "liaisons."

When the modernist movement, popularized by Ferran Adrià, swept through the culinary world, it left behind several useful liaisons. These little helpers hadn't been common in conventional high-end kitchens before.

The simplest ones that most everyone has in their pantry are flour, cornstarch, and gelatin. The less familiar ones that Chef Ferran introduced to the kitchen are agar-agar (derived from seaweed), xanthan gum (a carbohydrate created by bacterial fermentation), Ultra-Tex (the brand name of a modified tapioca starch), and iota carrageenan (derived from Irish moss). Each has a specific function.

Flour and **cornstarch** swell and thicken the liquid as they are heated.

Gelatin is firm when cold but melts when warm or hot and releases flavor as it melts on the palate.

Agar-agar allows us to make firm gels from liquids, which can then be blended to a coulis texture.

Xanthan gum both thickens and fortifies emulsions. (The smallest amount in a classic mayonnaise will make it as thick as spackle, which is the way we believe mayonnaise should be served.)

Ultra-Tex is also cold-soluble but does not need heat to activate, so it's a great addition to stabilize whipped cream or to thicken a vegetable juice meant to be served with a natural raw flavor, such as carrot or tomato. It also helps control the moisture in a puree or relish, preventing the puree or relish from weeping.

Iota carrageenan creates a great custardlike consistency and gels when warm. We love the warm gelée effect it gives our playful rendition of French onion soup (see page 50).

The following are the general percentages of the liaisons used in the per se and French Laundry kitchens and the resulting consistencies.

BEURRE MANIÉ

5%: Lightly creamed soups or veloutés
10%: Meat-based sauces or jus
15%: Classic blanquettes or cream sauces
30%: Fully thickened béchamel or binders

Beurre manié, equal parts (by weight) flour and butter, kneaded or paddled to a paste, is perhaps the most broadly used thickener at The French Laundry. It's an old-school liaison, and it still works beautifully. It's used to thicken various preparations, from lightly creamed cauliflower soup to intensely flavored cabbage jus; to make "sou-béch" (béchamel flavored with onions, one of our most-used sauces; see page 111); and as a binder for cooked barley. Our basic ratio for the béchamel is 100% dairy and 15% beurre manié (7.5% butter; 7.5% flour), though we can go as high as 20%. David even makes a *boeuf manié*, beef fat mixed with flour, to thicken beef sauces. As with most of the liaisons, the key words here are "proper hydration." The flour must be cooked in the liquid, completely, with attention and care. The granules must fully hydrolyze and swell in the liquid, which is what gives the liquid body. One of the positive attributes of beurre manié is that it is 50% butter or other fat, so in addition to body, it also adds great flavor and richness to the preparation. Adding this liaison to meat-based sauces does not negate the absolute necessity of properly cleaning the flavorful stock or jus by passing it back and forth through a chinois or passoire. There are no shortcuts. The liaison is added to these sauces to capture the flavor when that flavor is brightest and might be compromised by further reduction.

CORNSTARCH

3%: Bouillon (fluid but with body)
6%: Nappé or glaze
10%: Firm gel

Cornstarch is cold-soluble and disperses easily in liquids. I really like it when it's used to lié, or thicken, clear soups or consommés. At 3%, it adds just enough body to nicely coat the palate and helps to keep the meticulously cut garnish suspended. At 6%, these broths become sauces that can be spooned over noisettes of lamb or fillets of fish. A 10% concentration will give you a firmer gel, great for a broth-based ravioli filling or for something you want to coat and deep-fry, such as a warm head cheese or a Hawaiian coconut haupia.

PRE-HY (PREHYDRATED XANTHAN GUM)

We'd like to call special attention to one liaison that we find profoundly useful when it's properly diluted: xanthan gum. Xanthan gum is one of the most often used and versatile liaisons, but it is severely potent. Just a little bit can achieve dramatic results. Add too much, however, and it's time to "begin again," as David says. It's so powerful in powdered form that it's easily mismeasured. If you're off by a tenth of a gram, you can ruin a whole sauce. To solve this problem, David developed what we call prehydrated xanthan gum, or Pre-Hy, as it's known in both kitchens, in effect diluting the powdered xanthan gum and making it much easier to use, a real game changer for us.

1%: Emulsification
2%: All-purpose Pre-Hy
3%: Bouillon consistency
5%: Velouté consistency
15%: Fruit or vegetable glaze (with 1% Ultra-Tex)

To make our all-purpose Pre-Hy, which is used throughout the book, put 1,000 grams of water into a blender. With the blender running on low speed, shear in 20 grams of xanthan gum while slowly increasing the speed to high. The xanthan gum should completely hydrate in the water. If you have a chamber vacuum sealer, pass the mixture through a chinois into a container and place the container, uncovered, in the sealer chamber. Run a complete cycle on full pressure to remove any air bubbles incorporated during blending. It will produce a clear gel, which will contribute to the clarity of the sauce or puree it will eventually be used in.

Pre-Hy is cold-soluble, so it can be mixed directly into liquid in a Vita-Prep (or Vitamix) to add viscosity. At 1%, the Pre-Hy is the perfect aid in a powerfully bound mayonnaise and a useful stabilizer of simple emulsified oil-and-vinegar-based vinaigrettes. At 3%, it adds just a hint of body to an otherwise thin juice or broth. That's all it needs to hang on the palate a little longer and therefore add to the perception of depth of flavor and satiety. When 3% is added to a beurre blanc or beurre monté, it becomes a stable butter glaze resembling a beurre fondue. At 5%, added to our classic creamy lobster broth or other creamy broths, it keeps the cream and stock perfectly emulsified and holds the frothy bubbles that we like so much. And finally, at the highest concentration, 15%, in tandem with a small amount of Ultra-Tex, marinades or poaching liquids can be thickened to coat fruits and vegetables in a shiny glaze.

GELATIN SHEETS

3 sheets: Soft-stirred gel
5 sheets: Tender, diceable gel (with 1 gram agar-agar)
15 sheets: Firm set, for slicing, such as a vegetable terrine (with 1 gram of agar-agar)

We love gelatin. It's one of the most versatile helpers for the garde manger station. We use silver-strength gelatin sheets, and the above numbers are all per 500 grams of liquid.

When we use 3 sheets, the gel strength is very light. Less than a typical Jell-O. This texture is wonderful simply stirred with a spoon and served over a light panna cotta for caviar. At 5 sheets per 500 grams, with the addition of a little agar, we achieve a somewhat firm gel that can be sliced, diced, or scooped. We do a version of melon and ham with scoops of a ham gelée and Parisiennes of compressed melon. It makes a beautiful salad. And finally, at the firmest set, we make a super-concentrated gelée that is used for making multilayered vegetable terrines, such as our "ratatouille" terrine that we serve in the height of summer when the garden is full of beautiful tomatoes, peppers, and eggplant.

AGAR-AGAR

0.75%: Coulis consistency
1%: Soft gel consistency
1.5%: Appareil or binder

Agar-agar is activated by heat, so whatever you want thickened must be boiled after the agar has been added. We have a standard protocol for this kind of thickening: boil everything together to activate the agar, chill the liquid, dice it, then blend it in a Vitamix until it's a smooth puree. The blending introduces a lot of air, however, so to remove the air, we compress the puree in a chamber vacuum sealer, which removes the air bubbles and results in a more intensely colored puree with excellent clarity. Agar has revolutionized our ability to make classic gastriques with vibrant, fresh flavor, which was previously lost during prolonged cooking to get the texture right. Fruit and vegetable purees are amazing when made with agar. It adds body without having to add too much cream or overcooking it for consistency's sake. Agar gels set at 1.5% also work as excellent binders, as in the pickled onion relish on page 126.

As with the Pre-Hy, we make a 2% agar base for more precise measuring and use it for light sauces, blending the gel in equal parts with, say, yogurt or an herb puree. At The French Laundry and per se, we use high-powered Vitamix blenders. To save a step, we simply boil 300 grams of water, put it in the blender, and shear in 6 grams of agar; the power of the blender maintains the heat required to activate. We then strain and chill.

ULTRA-TEX

0.5% to 1%, depending on the application

Ultra-Tex will thicken a cold liquid. When blended, it helps keep all things from weeping, such as preventing tinted water from falling out of a ratatouille or a spinach puree. The word for this is "syneresis"—when a gel contracts, it squeezes out water. Ultra-Tex absorbs this water. As it swells, it thickens. It's fabulous for creamed vegetable preparations. Even adding 0.5% keeps sauces from breaking. We rarely need to add more than 1%. The tapioca, the source of Ultra-Tex, swells to give purees, gels, and emulsions a great sheen. Added to crème fraîche and whipped cream, it will hold them for hours—they won't break—a great convenience.

IOTA CARRAGEENAN

0.75%: Tender warm gelées
1%: Custard consistency

Iota carrageenan is less often used but is very valuable when you need it. We use it at 0.75% for very tender and trembling gelées, typically meat-based ones meant to be served warm. We mix it at 1% with organic soy milk to make à la minute vegan custards, or add 1% to creamy cauliflower soup to make a warm cauliflower custard that is served with caviar as an updated version of our cauliflower panna cotta. When you're eating a dish made with carrageenan, you may have the sense that you're familiar with the texture, but can't place how. (It's used to make the kind of pudding you buy in little packets at the grocery store, an occasional guilty snack for some of us!)

BÉCHAMEL

I want to share béchamel sauce and its many uses with you because it truly embodies the ideal simplicity and efficiency of preparing a meal. The sauce is one of the oldest preparations there is, and we use it in all kinds of ways, though you may not recognize it.

Béchamel, in its simplest form, is milk thickened with flour and then seasoned. Dairy and flour—that's it. For ours we use 100% liquid (usually half milk and half cream) with 7.5% flour combined with 7.5% butter. For example, 500 grams milk, 500 grams cream, 75 grams flour, and 75 grams butter. The flour and butter can be added at the beginning of cooking (in which case it's called a roux; see page 107 for more on this classical, often misunderstood, useful tool); then you whisk in the dairy and simmer until the mixture thickens. Or you can knead together the flour and butter to create a beurre manié (see page 108), boil the dairy, then whisk in the beurre manié and gently simmer it for 10 minutes or so.

The two important steps in the béchamel process are simmering and blending. The sauce is best simmered over indirect heat, preferably on a heat diffuser, and covered with a lid; this avoids the risk of scorching and also developing a skin on the surface of the sauce. Using an appropriate-size pot is also important. The pot should be straight-sided and should be filled past the halfway mark (we use a 2-quart/2-liter saucepot for the amounts mentioned above). Bring the sauce to a simmer—it should have large bubbles going at a leisurely pace. After 10 minutes, the starch granules will have fully swelled in the dairy and the sauce will be shiny. At this point, you can season with salt and acid as you wish.

The sauce is then transferred to a Vitamix blender and blended, starting on low speed and slowly increasing the speed to high, until it's completely smooth and homogenous. We strain it through a chinois and store it in a covered container with plastic wrap pressed directly against the surface to prevent a skin from forming. It's the perfect sauce base.

The viscosity of the basic béchamel can be adjusted by upping or lowering the fat and flour percentages to make it thicker or thinner. We use a range of consistencies, from a velvety velouté (10% beurre manié) to nappé blanquettes and creamy sauces (15% beurre manié), and, using 30% beurre manié, a fully thickened binder such as the one used in Corey's creamed fava leaves on the suckling pig (see page 262).

The basic sauce is just as flexible in terms of its flavoring, which can be modified by changing the liquid or the fat. The milk can be replaced with a rich chicken stock (technically making it a velouté) for a classic sauce suprême, or with brown veal stock for a rich meat gravy. The butter is also easily replaced by rendered fats, such as beef fat (*boeuf manié*). Even lamb and chicken fats are good substitutes, or olive oil for a Mediterranean-inspired sauce.

At The French Laundry, David makes any number of béchamel-style sauces by changing the vegetable used in the base and then pureeing the whole mixture: mushroom, bell pepper, spinach, pea, coconut, white asparagus, walnut, green asparagus, even a browned butter béchamel. We do a cauliflower béchamel for our Green Bean Casserole in the height of the summer season, as well as a white truffle version for our Mac and Cheese in the winter. We make an eggplant béchamel for Eggplant Parmesan (page 176). And a béchamel with onion (which makes it a soubise), the most versatile version of all, is used as the base for so many preparations that they refer to it as "sou-béch" (see recipe this page). All have become staples in our kitchens.

Even with all the new ways we have to manipulate the texture of a sauce—Pre-Hy (page 109) and agar-agar and Ultra-Tex (page 110)—more often than not, the classic technique remains superior. It's a classic for a reason.

Sweet Onion Béchamel, *aka* Sou-Béch

Makes about 1,000 grams

4 thyme sprigs	15 grams fleur de sel, plus more to taste
½ bay leaf	
100 grams whole butter	100 grams all-purpose flour
300 grams ¼-inch-dice (6-millimeter) Vidalia onion	500 grams whole milk
	500 grams heavy cream
	Lemon juice

A béchamel is a so-called mother sauce because it changes when different flavors are added. A béchamel enriched with Gruyère is a Mornay sauce; a béchamel flavored with shellfish butter is a Nantua sauce; a béchamel flavored with onion is a soubise sauce.

But we've found that the béchamel flavored with the sweetness of onion is uncommonly versatile, so much so that, as often as not, it replaces the basic béchamel. It's become so ubiquitous that it took on its own name in the kitchen: sou-béch.

Lay a piece of cheesecloth on the work surface. Put the thyme sprigs and bay leaf on the cheesecloth, fold in the two ends, and roll it into a sachet. Tie both ends with butcher's twine.

Melt the butter in a 2-quart (2-liter) saucepot over medium-low heat. Add the onion and fleur de sel and cook gently for 5 to 7 minutes, until they are tender and fragrant. Stir in the flour to combine. While whisking continuously, add the milk and cream and bring to a simmer, taking care that the flour is thoroughly incorporated in the liquid. Add the sachet and reduce the heat to low.

Simmer the sauce gently for 10 minutes, stirring frequently to ensure it does not stick to the pan. Discard the sachet. Transfer the contents of the pot to a blender and blend, beginning on low speed to release the steam and gradually increasing the speed, until the sauce is very smooth. Adjust the seasoning to taste with lemon juice and additional fleur de sel, then strain through a chinois into an airtight container. Press a piece of plastic wrap directly against the surface of the béchamel and let cool.

Once cool, cover the container and store in the refrigerator for up to 3 days.

HIRAMASA WITH APPLE VIERGE

Pickled Kumquats and Marcona Almonds

Makes 6 servings

CITRUS-CURED HIRAMASA

Citrus Cure

240 grams sugar

160 grams kosher salt

Zest of ⅓ orange, grated on a rasp grater

Zest of ½ lemon, grated on a rasp grater

Zest of 1 lime, grated on a rasp grater

Hiramasa

180 grams cleaned hiramasa fillet (skin and bones removed), brined (see page 187)

DILL OIL

30 grams stemmed spinach leaves

130 grams dill fronds

375 grams canola oil

6 grams kosher salt

PINK PEARL APPLE PARISIENNES

200 grams strained Pink Pearl apple juice (from peeled Pink Pearl apples)

1 gram ascorbic acid

1 Pink Pearl apple

GRANNY SMITH APPLE VIERGE

300 grams Granny Smith apple juice (from unpeeled Granny Smith apples)

1.5 grams ascorbic acid

14 grams champagne vinegar

11 grams sugar

5 grams kosher salt

6 grams Pre-Hy (page 109)

PICKLED KUMQUATS

Rice Wine Vinegar Pickle

200 grams rice wine vinegar

130 grams mirin

20 grams sugar

20 grams thinly sliced peeled fresh ginger

5 grams kosher salt

5 grams white soy sauce

Kumquats

15 kumquats

TO COMPLETE

Extra-virgin olive oil

9 roasted and salted blanched Marcona almonds, cut into 2 cubes each

18 dill fronds

SPECIAL EQUIPMENT

Parisienne scoop (melon baller), about ½ inch (13 millimeters) in diameter

Chamber vacuum sealer (optional)

In the fall in New York City, Corey likes to serve this sashimi-like preparation of hiramasa, balanced by the sweet acidity of apples, especially the Pink Pearl apples from The French Laundry's courtyard, used here in the garnish, along with kumquat and almond.

This fish, like most of our fish, is not only brined but lightly cured before being served, which seasons the fish and makes the texture more firm, much like gravlax.

FOR THE CITRUS-CURED HIRAMASA

Make the citrus cure: In a large bowl, whisk the sugar and salt to combine. Place the orange, lemon, and lime zests in a food processor. Add 150 grams of the sugar-salt mixture and process for about 30 seconds, until the zest is ground and the mixture resembles wet yellow sand. Transfer to the bowl with the remaining sugar-salt mixture and mix thoroughly.

Cure the hiramasa: Spread one-third of the citrus cure over the bottom of a deep container. Place the hiramasa on top of the cure. Apply the remaining cure liberally, packing it over the entire surface of the hiramasa. Refrigerate, uncovered, for 30 minutes to cure.

While the fish cures, set a cooling rack on a sheet pan and top it with a piece of parchment paper and then a clean kitchen towel.

Rinse the cure from the fish with cold running water and place the fish on the towel. Refrigerate, uncovered, for about 8 hours or overnight to dry, then store the fish in an airtight container for up to 3 days.

FOR THE DILL OIL

Cut the spinach into very fine chiffonade and place in a blender with the dill, canola oil, and salt. Blend on high speed for at least 5 minutes, or until the greens warm and "cook," to remove their raw, spicy flavor.

Pour the mixture into a large bowl and nestle the bowl in an ice-water bath. Chill, stirring from time to time, until completely cool. Place a large dampened coffee filter in a strainer set over a container. Pour in the chilled mixture and refrigerate overnight to extract the oil. Transfer the oil to a small squeeze bottle.

Refrigerate the oil for up to 3 weeks or freeze for up to 3 months.

FOR THE PINK PEARL APPLE PARISIENNES

Pour the Pink Pearl apple juice into a bowl and stir in the ascorbic acid (this will help keep the apple from oxidizing).

Peel the apple, then peel away any bruised or discolored flesh. Using a Parisienne scoop (melon baller) about ½ inch (13 millimeters) in diameter, scoop deeply into the flesh of the apple. Rotate the scoop one-quarter of the way counterclockwise, then rotate back clockwise to form a perfectly round ball. Tap the handle of the scoop on the edge of the bowl to release the apple into the apple juice. Repeat to scoop as many balls from the apple as you can.

If you have a chamber vacuum sealer, transfer the apples and apple juice to a sous vide bag. Place the bag in the sealer chamber and vacuum seal. Refrigerate for up to 3 days. If you do not have a chamber vacuum sealer, press a piece of plastic wrap against the apples to keep them below the surface of the juice, cover the bowl, and refrigerate for up to 24 hours (any longer and the apples could oxidize).

FOR THE GRANNY SMITH APPLE VIERGE

Place the Granny Smith apple juice, ascorbic acid, vinegar, sugar, and salt in the blender and blend on medium speed until incorporated, 10 to 15 seconds. With the blender running on medium speed, add the Pre-Hy and blend for 1 to 2 minutes, then drizzle in 17 grams of the dill oil and blend to emulsify. Strain the vierge into an airtight container, cover, and refrigerate for up to 3 days.

FOR THE PICKLED KUMQUATS

Make the rice wine vinegar pickle: Combine the vinegar, mirin, sugar, ginger, salt, and soy sauce in a small saucepot and bring to a boil. Transfer to a bowl and nestle the bowl in an ice-water bath to chill.

Pickle the kumquat peels: Quarter the kumquats through the root end. Cut away the flesh and discard it, then use a paring knife to trim as much of the pith from the peels as possible. Put the kumquat peels in a small saucepot and cover with cold water. Bring the water to a boil, then drain the peels and return them to the saucepot. Cover with cold water and repeat twice more. Place the blanched kumquat peels in an airtight container and pour over the chilled pickling liquid. Refrigerate for up to 3 months.

TO COMPLETE

Trim the hiramasa fillet to straighten the sides and cut it into 6 equal pieces, about 30 grams each. Temper at room temperature for about 15 minutes. Lightly coat the fish with olive oil.

Heat a plancha over a gas flame on high. Once hot, sear the pieces of fish on all 6 sides, about 3 seconds per side or until the surface becomes opaque. The fish will still be raw inside. Remove the hiramasa from the plancha and let it rest for 3 to 4 minutes, then slice each piece in half lengthwise.

Arrange 2 slices of hiramasa at the bottom of each serving bowl. Pour about 20 grams (or enough to cover the bottom of the bowl) of the Granny Smith vierge around the hiramasa. Garnish with the kumquat peel, apple Parisiennes, Marcona almonds, and dill fronds. Drizzle droplets of dill oil on the vierge.

ICED OPAH CRUDO

Harmonie Cucumber Gazpacho, Pickled Lemon, and Cucamelon Blossoms

Makes 6 servings

HARMONIE CUCUMBER GAZPACHO

750 grams Harmonie cucumbers

25 grams peeled shallots

8 grams peeled garlic

2 grams cleaned jalapeño (seeds and pith removed)

20 grams cilantro leaves

5 grams sea salt, plus more to taste

13 grams Pre-Hy (page 109)

10 grams lime juice

PICKLED MEYER LEMON

100 grams tomato water (page 289)

50 grams champagne vinegar

50 grams sugar

6 grams kosher salt

2 grams fennel seed

1 gram saffron

1 Meyer lemon

COMPRESSED CUCAMELONS

10 cucamelons

100 grams water

50 grams sugar

50 grams champagne vinegar

OPAH

400 grams cleaned center-cut opah fillet, brined for 30 minutes (see page 187)

TO COMPLETE

Maldon salt

Cucamelon with blossoms

Nasturtium leaves

SPECIAL EQUIPMENT

Japanese mandoline

Chamber vacuum sealer (optional)

Masticating juicer

6 serving bowls, frozen

Opah, also called moonfish, is a huge round fish caught in the Pacific that has great flavor and texture when served raw and very cold. The top loin of the fish is very lean, while the bottom is as fatty as tuna belly. We dice the lean sections and serve them with diamonds of the fatty section. We combine it with a gazpacho made from the very floral Harmonie cucumber, jalapeño, shallots, and garlic. All these ingredients are mixed with cilantro leaves and sea salt and allowed to macerate for a few hours before being juiced and then blended with a little Pre-Hy. At the last minute, we season the gazpacho with fresh-squeezed lime juice. Any organic, garden-fresh cucumber that's not bitter will be a good substitute for the Harmonie. The dish, however, must be served *ice* cold.

FOR THE HARMONIE CUCUMBER GAZPACHO

On a Japanese mandoline, thinly slice the cucumbers, shallots, and garlic to about ⅛ inch (3 millimeters) thick and place in a large bowl. Coarsely chop the jalapeño and add it to the bowl. Add the cilantro and salt and toss the ingredients together.

If you have a chamber vacuum sealer, transfer the vegetables to a large sous vide bag. Place the bag in the sealer chamber and vacuum seal. Refrigerate the vegetables for 3 hours to macerate. If you do not have a chamber vacuum sealer, transfer the vegetables to an airtight container and refrigerate overnight to macerate.

Using the masticating juicer, juice the vegetables into a bowl, whisk in the Pre-Hy, and strain the gazpacho into an airtight container. Season with the lime juice and additional salt to taste. Refrigerate for up to 1 day.

FOR THE PICKLED MEYER LEMON

In a 1-quart (1-liter) saucepot, combine the tomato water, vinegar, sugar, salt, fennel seed, and saffron. Bring to a boil, remove from the heat, cover with a lid, and steep for 15 minutes. Strain the pickling liquid into a bowl and nestle the bowl in an ice-water bath to chill.

Quarter the lemon through the stem end. Cut away the flesh and discard it, then use a paring knife to trim most of the pith away from the rinds, leaving about 1 millimeter of pith on the rinds. Cut the lemon rinds into ¼-inch (6-millimeter) diamond-shaped pieces and put them in a small saucepot. Cover with cold water and bring to a boil. Drain the rinds and return them to the saucepot. Repeat twice.

If you have a chamber vacuum sealer, place the lemon rinds in a sous vide bag and pour in the chilled pickling liquid. Place in the sealer chamber and vacuum seal. If you do not have a chamber vacuum sealer, add the lemon rinds to the bowl with the chilled pickling liquid and cover and refrigerate.

Refrigerate for up to 1 week.

FOR THE COMPRESSED CUCAMELONS
Rinse the cucamelons thoroughly and remove any stem still attached. Cut them in half lengthwise. If you have a chamber vacuum sealer, put them in a sous vide bag. If you do not have a chamber vacuum sealer, put them in a bowl.

Put the water, sugar, and vinegar in a small saucepot and bring to a simmer, stirring to dissolve the sugar and salt. If you have a chamber vacuum sealer, pour the brine into a bowl and nestle the bowl in an ice-water bath to chill. Pour the chilled brine into the sous vide bag with the cucamelons, place in the sealer chamber, and vacuum seal. Refrigerate

until serving. If you do not have a chamber vacuum sealer, pour the hot brine into the bowl over the cucamelons and nestle the bowl in an ice-water bath to chill, then cover and refrigerate.

Use within a few hours.

FOR THE OPAH
Cut the brined opah into bite-size cubes. Refrigerate, uncovered, for up to 1 day.

TO COMPLETE
Drain the cucamelons and pickled lemon and dry on paper towels.

Lightly season the opah with Maldon salt.

Arrange the pieces of opah in the serving bowls. Add the compressed cucamelons, cucamelons with blossoms, and pickled lemon. Carefully pour the gazpacho into the bowls and garnish with the nasturtium leaves.

TEMPURA-FRIED SOFT-SHELL CRAB

Gem Lettuce Chiffonade, Spicy Peanuts, and Sweet Carrot Aïoli

Makes 12 servings

CARROT OIL

375 grams coarsely chopped carrots

300 grams canola oil

38 grams kosher salt

CARROT AÏOLI

400 grams carrot juice

24 grams egg yolks

10 grams Burgundy mustard

4 grams minced shallot

16 grams lemon juice

5 grams kosher salt

SPICY PEANUTS

Canola oil, for deep-frying

150 grams water

150 grams sugar

100 grams Virginia peanuts

2.5 grams Espelette pepper or togarashi

Fleur de sel

GEM LETTUCE CHIFFONADE

60 grams Little Gem lettuce leaves

SOFT-SHELL CRABS

6 soft-shell crabs

TO COMPLETE

Canola oil, for deep-frying

250 grams Cup4Cup gluten-free flour

8 grams kosher salt, plus more as needed

300 grams sparkling water, plus more as needed

Extra-virgin olive oil

25 grams toasted white sesame seeds

SPECIAL EQUIPMENT

Chamber vacuum sealer (optional)

Immersion circulator (optional)

Latex gloves

This deep-fried crab with spicy candied nuts is a classic East Coast delicacy combined with Corey's Chinese heritage (think honey and walnut shrimp). Most important to Corey, though, is having found a way to use the trimmings. We use so many carrots at per se, we probably threw away pounds of carrot peelings every week. Corey now makes a carrot oil from these trimmings and uses this oil, along with reduced carrot juice, to make a fabulous carrot aïoli. Whole carrots are used here to get the small quantity of peels needed, but if you work in a kitchen that produces a lot of carrot peels, store them in an airtight container in the fridge until you have the amount you need.

FOR THE CARROT OIL

Place the carrots in a food processor and pulse until the carrots resemble those grated on a box grater.

If you have a chamber vacuum sealer, set an immersion circulator in a water bath and heat the water to 88°C (190.4°F). Place the carrots, canola oil, and salt in a sous vide bag. Place the bag in the sealer chamber and vacuum seal. Cook in the water bath for 30 minutes. The carrots should soften but still retain their shape. Immediately submerge the bag in an ice-water bath to chill.

If you do not have a chamber vacuum sealer, transfer the chopped carrots to a medium saucepot, add the oil, and bring to a boil over medium-high heat. Reduce the heat to low and cook the carrots for 30 minutes. Season with the salt. Transfer to a bowl and nestle the bowl in an ice-water bath to chill.

Cover and refrigerate for 8 hours or overnight. Place a large dampened coffee filter in a strainer set over a container. Pour in the carrots and oil and refrigerate for 8 to 12 hours to extract the oil. The carrot oil can be refrigerated in an airtight container for up to 3 weeks or frozen for up to 3 months; discard the carrots.

FOR THE CARROT AÏOLI

Bring the carrot juice to a boil in a medium saucepot over high heat. Reduce the juice to 40 grams, about 25 minutes. Pour the juice into a bowl and nestle the bowl in an ice-water bath to chill.

(continued)

Transfer the chilled carrot juice to a blender and add the egg yolks, mustard, shallot, lemon juice, and salt. With the blender running on medium-low speed, gradually begin to drizzle in 200 grams of the carrot oil, making certain that the emulsion is maintained. As the volume of the aïoli increases, you can increase the speed. Scrape down the sides and base of the blender container with a silicone spatula. Pass the aïoli through a chinois into an airtight container. Refrigerate for up to 3 days. Bring to room temperature before using.

FOR THE SPICY PEANUTS

Line a sheet pan with parchment paper. Have a pair of gloves on hand to protect your hands while separating the fried peanuts. Fill a medium saucepot no more than one-third full with canola oil. Heat the oil to 350°F (180°C).

Put the water and sugar in a small saucepot. Bring to a simmer over medium-high heat and add the nuts. Cook, stirring often, until most of the water has evaporated and the syrup has reduced to a thick nappe, coating the nuts, about 15 minutes. (The temperature of the syrup will be about 240°F/115°C.)

Drain the nuts in a basket strainer, allowing the excess syrup to drip off. Immediately stir the nuts into the hot oil. Fry, stirring continuously to prevent the nuts from sticking together and to create an even candy shell around each peanut, until the nuts are a light golden brown (they will continue to darken as they cool), 2 to 3 minutes.

Spread the nuts on the sheet pan in a single layer; season generously with the Espelette pepper and fleur de sel. Working quickly, use gloved hands to separate the nuts. Let cool completely. Store in an airtight container at room temperature for up to 3 days, or place a food-safe silica gel pack in the container to store for up to 5 days.

FOR THE GEM LETTUCE CHIFFONADE

Wash and dry the lettuce leaves and slice into fine chiffonade. Hold the cut lettuce in ice water for up to 2 hours to prevent it from discoloring.

FOR THE SOFT-SHELL CRABS

Cut off the face of each crab and discard. Cut off the two claws and set them aside. Cut off the legs and discard (at the restaurant, we save them for stock). Using scissors, cut off the spikes and sides of the crab. Lift the exoskeleton and, using scissors, trim away the feathery lungs, exposing the meat. If it is early in soft-shell crab season and the exoskeleton is soft, it can be left attached and eaten. If it is late in the season and the exoskeleton has toughened, it would be unpleasant to eat and should be pulled back and cut off. Pull away and discard the apron on the underside of the crabs. Cut each body in half and drain on paper towels.

The cleaned crabs and reserved claws can be covered and refrigerated for up to 1 day.

TO COMPLETE

Fill a Dutch oven or heavy-bottomed saucepot with about 2 inches (5 centimeters) of canola oil. The oil should be deep enough to allow the crabs to float freely. Heat the oil to 375°F (190°C).

Whisk the flour and salt together in a bowl. Coat the crab bodies and claws in the flour and set aside on a tray.

While whisking, slowly pour the sparkling water into the flour. The batter should have a consistency similar to a thin pancake batter. If the batter is too thick, it will not form a fine, even coating; add more sparkling water as needed. Pour the batter into a pint (500-milliliter) container or a small bowl deep enough for a crab to be submerged in the batter.

Dip the crab bodies and claws in the batter, allowing the excess batter to drip off. Add to the oil and fry for 3 to 4 minutes, adjusting the heat as necessary, until golden brown. Drain briefly on paper towels. Immediately toss the soft-shell crabs in enough carrot aïoli to coat.

Drain and dry the lettuce. Toss with a light coating of olive oil and season with salt.

Spread about 10 grams of lettuce chiffonade in the center of each serving plate. Top each with one piece of the aïoli-coated soft-shell crab and one claw. Sprinkle with the sesame seeds. Using a rasp grater, grate the spicy peanuts over the dish.

ON
FINE DINING

*It's All About
Precision*

WHAT IS FINE DINING? To many people, fine dining is defined by dress code and dollars spent. But that's far too simplistic. What about service? Ambience and attitude? Vision of culinary craft? Back when the estimable Ruth Reichl was reviewing restaurants for the *New York Times*, she was so enamored of a Manhattan noodle shop, she wanted to give it four stars, but the place was so casual, she wasn't allowed to give it more than three. In 1983, at a time when four-star ratings were usually reserved for high-end French restaurants, Mimi Sheraton gave four stars to a Japanese restaurant. The idea of fine dining was beginning to change.

So, what is fine dining?

I don't have a definition, but I've been around long enough to have read its obituary many times—but fine dining never dies. It evolves, pushed forward by new generations with new ideas.

In the 1960s, it was La Caravelle and La Côte Basque. Two decades ago, Michelin three-star chef Joël Robuchon was inspired by Japanese sushi and Spanish tapas and opened L'Atelier, where chefs in kitchen whites doubled as servers, delivering food from behind the counter. Today fine dining is César Ramirez over at Brooklyn Fare, a restaurant that is basically counter service.

Dress codes have evolved, too. The formal requirements of the fifties have long since given way to a culture where you can show up in blue jeans to a fancy degustation and no one blinks an eye.

Fast-forward to the mid-2000s. Alain Ducasse was moving his super-high-end restaurant out of the Essex House on Central Park West to the St. Regis, and opening Adour. He was still a Michelin three-star chef doing very high-end food, but he was attempting to make it more casual. My partner, Laura, and I made a reservation at Adour, and Laura called the restaurant to see if I could wear jeans. We had a no-jeans policy at The French Laundry, and I was curious about Ducasse's policy. Do you know what the maître d' said to her? Depends on the jacket. Echoes of Charles Masson Sr. And it makes so much sense. Everyone is seated in a restaurant, so all we see is your jacket. The maître d', the restaurant policy, at Adour was right. And so we changed our policy. Wear your jeans, if that's what you like.

Fine dining has to be flexible. There can't be any preordained policy about the way our guests look, the way they eat or drink, any of those things.

There has to be mutual respect between the restaurant and the diner.

But ultimately more than dress code, more than whether the food is French or Japanese or Spanish tapas, the definition of fine dining is in the mind of the consumer. And most consumers define it by the cost.

Elevated costs are, of course, a magnet for criticism. But fine dining is expensive because of service providing luxury in a time and place and because of the ingredients we're sourcing, which are often exquisite and extremely rare, and crafted by individuals who do an incredible job, farming or foraging or in their gardens or dairies, often by themselves or with very small staffs.

I don't know how much Diane St. Clair's butter costs to make; she makes 30 pounds of butter a week. But I'm there helping to support her, to support her vision and her métier. How much is it *worth*? I don't know. She wants to send her son to NYU, so she increases the price by 50 cents a pound—am I going to say no to that? No, I want to support her. But more important, it's not only *my* willingness to pay extra for extraordinary butter; it's the guests who are putting her son through school, by coming to the restaurant and enjoying a special meal. I don't think the guests realize how many lives they change simply by dining at our restaurants. Not just mine, but all restaurants throughout the country.

Is fine dining defined by how much work goes into the food? Because labor is another big expense. Part of what defines us is the precision of the work. Ultimately that's what I'd like fine dining to mean to people. Precision in the kitchen and in the service. Every step of the food prep is done with exactitude and a high level of craftsmanship. You can get a poached egg at Denny's, or you can come here and get one of Brent Wolfe's quail eggs, poached and served on its own spoon sauced with beurre monté and a *pluche* of chervil. They're not the same thing and, of course, they have different values.

Ultimately, value to me has nothing to do with the amount of money you spend; it has to do with the experience you have in spending that money.

Life experiences and the memories that only expand with time, memories of something that's both as ordinary and as extraordinary as a meal. That's what fine dining means to me.

SMOKED MONTANA RAINBOW TROUT CHAUD-FROID

Pickled Onion Relish and Caraway Lavash

Makes 6 servings

SMOKED MONTANA RAINBOW TROUT (SEE NOTE)

100 grams kosher salt

100 grams sugar

5 grams coriander seeds

4 grams black peppercorns

2 grams fennel seed

2 grams dill pollen

0.5 grams chili flakes

6 Montana rainbow trout fillets, 225 to 250 grams each

15 grams fresh dill

Applewood chips

PICKLED ONION RELISH

200 grams water

100 grams champagne vinegar

100 grams sugar

5 grams fleur de sel

350 grams Vidalia onion brunoise

4 grams agar-agar

8 grams pickled mustard seeds (page 186)

1 gram dill pollen

CARAWAY LAVASH

300 grams all-purpose flour

24 grams sugar

6 grams kosher salt

105 grams whole milk

70 grams eggs

40 grams whole butter, melted

50 grams egg yolks

10 grams water

30 grams ground caraway seeds

3 grams fleur de sel

WHITE ASPIC CHAUD-FROID

15 sheets silver leaf gelatin

250 grams heavy cream

250 grams whole milk

90 grams beurre manié (page 108)

8 grams fleur de sel

1 gram agar-agar

TO COMPLETE

25 grams preserved horseradish

Chervil leaves

Chive tips

SPECIAL EQUIPMENT

Smoker

Chamber vacuum sealer (optional)

Pasta machine

1¼-inch (30-millimeter) fluted round cutter

½-inch (13-millimeter) plain round cutter

Chaud-froid literally means "hot-cold," a reference to the cooked items being served cold, very old school. This type of preparation represents a style and level of craftsmanship that shouldn't be lost—we haven't served dishes this way in decades. They were typically reserved for the grand banquet halls and wedding parties of yesteryear. Yet it's still a great technique: a cooked sauce that's served cold, here as a kind of white aspic, which is simply béchamel set with gelatin and a small amount of agar. This is the "sauce" for trout that's lightly cured like a quick gravlax, rinsed, then dried overnight. The fish is then smoked over applewood, chilled, and glazed in the sauce. David credits his inspiration for this dish to master chef Seth Simmerman, one of his early mentors.

FOR THE SMOKED MONTANA RAINBOW TROUT

Mix the salt, sugar, coriander seeds, peppercorns, fennel seed, dill pollen, and chili flakes in a large bowl.

Line a half sheet pan with parchment paper. Lay the trout fillets on the pan, flesh-side up. Season the flesh side of the fillets liberally with about two-thirds of the cure; they should be completely covered. Lay the fresh dill on the flesh of the fish and cover with the remaining cure. Cover with cheesecloth and refrigerate for 3 hours to cure the fish.

Gently rinse the cure and dill from the trout and pat dry. With tweezers, remove any pin bones. Using applewood chips, smoke the trout (see page 239).

FOR THE PICKLED ONION RELISH

Combine the water, vinegar, sugar, and fleur de sel in a 1-quart (1-liter) saucepot and bring to a vigorous simmer. Add the onions and cook for 1 minute, or until the onions are tender but still retain their shape. Drain the onions, reserving the cooking liquid. You should have 400 grams of liquid. Spread the onions on a tray to cool, then refrigerate.

Return the liquid to a 1-quart (1-liter) saucepot and bring to a boil. Whisk in the agar-agar. While whisking continuously, boil for 2 minutes to activate the agar-agar. Pour the liquid into a bowl and nestle the bowl in an

ice-water bath. Chill, undisturbed, until the relish base is completely firm and set.

Cut the relish base into smaller pieces and transfer to a blender. Beginning on low speed and gradually increasing to high, blend until completely smooth, using the tamper to keep the puree moving. Pass the puree through a chinois into a container.

If you have a chamber vacuum sealer, place the container, uncovered, in the sealer chamber. Run a complete cycle on full pressure to remove any air bubbles incorporated during blending. This will give the puree clarity and shine.

Combine the onions, puree, pickled mustard seeds, and dill pollen in an airtight container. Refrigerate for up to 3 days.

FOR THE CARAWAY LAVASH

In the bowl of a stand mixer fitted with the paddle, combine the flour, sugar, and salt. Stir the milk and eggs together. With the mixer running on low speed, add the milk and eggs to the flour mixture, then add the melted butter. Mix on low speed until the dough forms a ball, then mix for 3 minutes more. Remove the dough from the bowl.

If you have a chamber vacuum sealer, place the dough in a sous vide bag, place the bag in the sealer chamber, and vacuum seal. If you do not have a chamber vacuum sealer, wrap the dough in plastic wrap. Refrigerate overnight to allow the dough to rest.

Preheat the oven to 320°F (160°C). Line a half sheet pan with a nonstick silicone baking mat.

Cut off a 60-gram piece of the dough and wrap the remaining dough in plastic wrap; 60 grams will make about 30 crackers; the remaining dough can be baked separately or frozen for another use. Press the piece of dough with your hands to flatten. Using a pasta machine, roll out the dough, beginning on the widest setting and lowering the setting on each pass through, until the dough is 1 millimeter thick. If the dough seems sticky, lightly flour it between each rolling. Roll the sheet as wide as possible and lay it in the prepared sheet pan. Cover the dough with a second baking mat and let rest for 10 minutes.

Meanwhile, mix the egg yolks with the water in a small bowl. Brush the dough with the egg yolk; the coating should be generous and coat the dough completely. Put the caraway in a passoire (a small fine strainer)

and dust the dough with the caraway by tapping the side of the passoire with a spoon, evenly covering the entire sheet. You will have more caraway than you need to dust the dough properly; the remainder can be reserved for another use. Sprinkle with the fleur de sel.

Parbake the dough for 3 to 4 minutes and remove from the oven (keep the oven on). The dough will look glossier and a deeper yellow. Using an offset spatula, transfer the dough to a cutting board and punch out crackers with a 1¼-inch (30-millimeter) fluted round cutter. You will need 18 crackers for this recipe, but bake extra, as there may be some breakage. Using a ½-inch (13-millimeter) plain round cutter, punch out the center of each cracker; the centers can be discarded or baked and enjoyed separately.

Using a small offset spatula, return the punched crackers to the lined sheet pan mat. Top with a second baking mat and a second sheet pan and bake for 7 minutes. Rotate the pan 180 degrees and bake for 7 minutes more, or until the crackers are a deep golden color, then bake, checking every 2 minutes, until the desired color is reached. Remove from the oven and let cool.

Store the lavash in an airtight container for up to 1 day, or place a food-safe silica gel pack in the container to store for up to 3 days.

FOR THE WHITE ASPIC CHAUD-FROID

Shortly before using, submerge the gelatin in a bowl of ice water to bloom (soften) for about 5 minutes.

Combine the cream, milk, beurre manié, and fleur de sel in a 1-quart (1-liter) saucepot. Bring to a simmer over medium heat, whisking from time to time to ensure the beurre manié fully incorporates and the mixture does not stick to the bottom of the pot, then reduce the heat to low.

Remove the softened gelatin from the ice water and squeeze out any excess water. Add the gelatin to the pot and whisk to dissolve and incorporate. Whisk in the agar-agar. Return to a simmer and cook, whisking continuously, for 1 minute to activate the agar-agar. Transfer to a blender and puree until smooth. Pass through a chinois into a tall microwavable flexible container or a liquid measuring cup with a wide spout. Press a piece of plastic wrap against the surface to keep a crust from forming and hold at room temperature.

The chaud-froid must be slightly warm for use. It should have a slightly thick and silky texture, similar to a béchamel sauce, but should run freely so it glazes the trout with a smooth, even coating. If the chaud-froid cools, becomes too thick, or begins to set up, it can be reheated in the microwave in 10-second intervals, stirring and checking the consistency after each interval, until it is warm and loosened.

GLAZE THE TROUT

Line a half sheet pan with two layers of plastic wrap (to help with cleanup) and top with a cooling rack. Gently peel the skin off each smoked trout fillet, pulling from the "tail" toward the "head" of the fillet at an acute angle (rather than pulling upward). To avoid tearing the flesh, it helps to lay one hand on the fillet from which you've removed the skin as you remove the rest. Lay the trout on the rack, skinned-side down. Pour the chaud-froid from the container in an even layer across the top of each fillet. Tap the pan against the counter to help remove any excess chaud-froid and create a more even coating.

Refrigerate the fish for 5 minutes, or until the chaud-froid is set. Test it by touching the edge of the chaud-froid; if your fingers do not leave an imprint, it is set. Transfer the glazed trout to a cutting board and keep at room temperature if serving within 30 minutes.

The glazed trout can be stored in an airtight container for up to 3 days (this includes any storage of the smoked trout before glazing).

TO COMPLETE

If necessary, place the glazed trout on a cutting board. Warm the blade of a long, thin slicing knife in warm water. Trim the sides of each fillet to square them off.

Spoon about 35 grams of the onion relish in a line in the center of each plate. Carefully lay the trout over the relish. Spoon small dollops of the relish over the trout, along with small pinches of preserved horseradish. Garnish with the caraway lavash. Using the relish as a base, anchor the chervil and chive tips on the trout.

> **NOTE**
>
> If you aren't able to cure and smoke the trout yourself, you can omit the ingredients called for in the smoked Montana rainbow trout component and substitute 6 presmoked Montana trout fillets, 225 to 250 grams each.

CHAMPIGNON DE BOIS

Cèpes Mushroom Croquette, Creamed Watercress Puree, and Tiny Blooms

Makes 6 servings

WATERCRESS "TURF"

2 sheets silver leaf gelatin

85 grams whole butter, diced, at soft room temperature

125 grams watercress leaves

75 grams crustless brioche (crust removed before weighing)

5 grams roasted garlic puree (recipe follows)

MUSHROOM CROQUETTE

6 medium cèpes, with 2- to 2½-inch (5- to 6.25-centimeter) caps, preferably with larger stems

Rendered beef fat or clarified butter (page 53), for sautéing

30 grams whole butter

2 garlic cloves, skin on, smashed

4 thyme sprigs

100 grams mushroom essence (page 289)

50 grams veal stock (page 287)

5 grams minced shallot

5 grams flat-leaf parsley leaves, finely chopped

150 grams mousse base (page 253), made with veal or chicken

170 grams cornstarch–egg white paste (page 235)

100 grams dehydrated potato flakes, lightly crushed

CREAMED WATERCRESS PUREE

40 grams leek

40 grams whole butter

100 grams heavy cream

250 grams watercress leaves

4 grams Pre-Hy (page 109)

Kosher salt

TO COMPLETE

30 grams dried porcini mushrooms

Canola oil, for deep-frying

Clarified butter (page 53), for sautéing

Kosher salt

25 grams whole butter

3 thyme sprigs

2 garlic cloves, skin on, smashed

Fleur de sel

Eighteen 1- to 1½-inch (2.5- to 4-centimeter) chive tips

Watercress flowers

SPECIAL EQUIPMENT

Two 3-millimeter-thick confectionary rulers

2½-inch (64-millimeter) plain round cutter

Immersion circulator

We love the simple fun of this dish, which came about by accident. At per se we'd received a case of cèpes that were all broken—the stems had all separated from the tops. We couldn't serve them as we typically do, with the cap and stem sliced thick and seared, but we had to do something with them. Someone suggested making croquettes—which was a perfect idea. The mushrooms were chopped and mixed with a basic veal mousseline to make a "stem," then breaded and deep-fried. The tops were cooked in beef fat until set. They made "turf" from watercress, a plant that grows where the mushrooms grow. It's a good rule that David follows: "If it grows together, it goes together."

FOR THE WATERCRESS "TURF"

Submerge the gelatin in a bowl of ice water to bloom (soften) for about 5 minutes.

Melt 20 grams of the butter in a 2-quart (2-liter) saucepot over medium-low heat. Add the watercress leaves and wilt in the butter for 1 to 2 minutes. Drain the watercress on a clean kitchen towel and let cool slightly. Using the towel, wring out any excess moisture from the watercress.

Finely grind the brioche in a food processor and transfer it to a bowl. Put the watercress in the food processor and add the remaining 65 grams butter and the roasted garlic puree. Process until very smooth, 1 to 2 minutes, scraping the bowl as needed.

Return the brioche to the food processor and process, scraping the bowl as needed, until fully incorporated and homogenous. Scrape and process a final time.

Remove the softened gelatin from the ice water and squeeze out the excess water. Melt it completely in a small pot over low heat or in a small bowl in the microwave. With the food processor running, pour in the melted gelatin. Blend for 1 minute more, until the gelatin is fully incorporated into the panade.

Lay a piece of parchment paper on the counter and place one 3-millimeter-thick confectionery ruler on each side. Transfer the panade to the parchment and cover with a second piece of parchment. Gently press down on the panade to flatten it. Using a rolling pin resting on the rulers, roll out the panade. Toward the end of rolling, lift the top piece of parchment and lay it back down, then roll again to eliminate any wrinkles. Remove the rulers and slide the panade on the sheet of parchment onto an inverted half sheet pan and freeze for at least 1 hour, until solid.

Working quickly to keep the panade from thawing, punch 6 discs from the panade with a 2½-inch (64-millimeter) plain round cutter, twisting the cutter as you remove it and wiping it clean with a damp towel between cuts. Transfer the discs to a container, separating each of the pieces with parchment, and refrigerate for up to 1 day.

FOR THE MUSHROOM CROQUETTE

Using a tourné knife, make a cut around each mushroom stem where it meets the cap, then twist the stem to remove it. Using a cloth or small knife, gently remove any dirt or debris from the mushrooms. Coarsely chop 150 grams of the stems (reserve the caps).

Heat a film of rendered beef fat in a medium sauté pan over medium heat. Add the chopped mushroom stems, reduce the heat to low, and cook, stirring often and gradually increasing the heat as the moisture in the mushrooms dissipates, until the mushrooms have caramelized to a golden brown, 2 to 3 minutes. Add the butter. Once the butter foams, add the garlic and thyme. Reduce the heat to low and cook for 2 to 3 minutes, until the butter just turns brown. Remove from the pan and drain on paper towels. Discard the garlic and thyme and return the mushrooms to the pan.

Add the mushroom essence and veal stock and cook over medium heat until the liquid becomes quite thick and glazes the mushrooms, 5 to 8 minutes. Remove from the heat and add the shallot and parsley. Spread the mushroom mixture over a tray and let cool in the refrigerator.

Transfer the mushroom mixture to the bowl of a stand mixer fitted with the paddle and add the mousse base. Mix on medium speed until homogenous. Transfer the mushroom farce to a disposable piping bag.

Set an immersion circulator in a water bath and heat the water to 64°C (147.2°F).

Wipe the work surface with a dampened towel. Place a 12-inch (30-centimeter) square of plastic wrap on the surface. Top with a sec-ond square of plastic wrap of the same size. Weigh a 40-gram portion of the farce and center it on the square of plastic. Bring the corners of the plastic together and twist until the farce forms a very tight ball. As you twist and form the ball, use a cake tester to pierce the plastic to release any air pockets in the farce.

Loop a length of butcher's twine around your index finger and hold it about ¼ inch (6 millimeters) up the plastic from the farce. Wrap the twine around the twisted plastic four or five times, with the last wrap pushing against the farce to compress it into a tight ball. Thread the twine through the loop and pull on the two ends of the twine to tighten. Knot twice to secure and trim the excess twine. Pierce any remaining air pockets with a cake tester. Repeat with the remaining farce.

Cook the balls of farce in the water bath for 12 to 15 minutes, until they are firm to the touch and hot throughout. To test, poke a cake tester into the center of a ball, then hold it to your lip; it should be hot. Submerge in an ice-water bath to chill.

Place the cornstarch paste in a bowl and the potato flakes in a second bowl. Spread a layer of potato flakes over the bottom of an airtight container large enough to hold the croquettes in one layer.

Remove the balls from the ice bath and remove the plastic. Dry them on paper towels, then place in the cornstarch paste and turn to fully coat. One at a time, remove the balls from the paste, allowing any excess to drip off, and coat in the potato flakes, patting with your hands to coat them completely. Arrange the balls in the container, cover, and refrigerate for up to 2 hours.

FOR THE CREAMED WATERCRESS PUREE

Cut the leek into ¼-inch (6-millimeter) dice and rinse in tepid water to remove any dirt. Brown the butter in a 1-quart (1-liter) saucepot over medium heat. Add the leek and cook gently until tender, about 3 minutes. Add the cream and reduce to a glaze, about 6 minutes. Cover the pot and set aside in a warm spot.

Bring a pot of salted water to a boil. Blanch the watercress leaves in the boiling water for 2 to 3 minutes, until very tender. Drain the watercress and spread on a clean kitchen towel. Let cool slightly, then wring out any excess water.

While still hot, place the leek mixture and blanched watercress in a blender and blend until smooth. With the blender running on medium-high speed, add the Pre-Hy and blend for 1 minute more to incorporate. Season with salt to taste. Fill a disposable piping bag with the puree and pipe the puree into a small squeeze bottle. Keep in a warm spot for up to 4 hours before serving.

TO COMPLETE

Grind the porcinis to a powder in a spice grinder (it is all right if there are a few larger pieces). Cut a piece of cheesecloth about 6 inches (15 centimeters) square and spoon the ground porcinis into the center. Pull the corners of the cheesecloth together, forming a small pouch that isn't tight around the powder. Secure the top with a piece of butcher's twine or a rubber band.

Fill a medium saucepot with 3 inches (7.5 centimeters) of canola oil. Heat the oil to 350°F (180°C).

Heat a film of clarified butter in a medium sauté pan over medium heat. Add the reserved mushroom caps to the pan, stem-side up, and season lightly with salt. Sauté for 1 minute, then add the whole butter, thyme, and garlic to the pan. Baste the mushroom caps with the butter until they are cooked through and hot. They should not take too much color. Keep warm.

Remove the croquettes from the refrigerator about 5 minutes before frying. Fry the croquettes in the hot oil until golden brown and hot in the center, 3 to 4 minutes. Remove from the oil and drain on paper towels for about 1 minute.

Carefully place one round of the panade on each serving plate. Pipe the watercress puree in a mound in the center of the panade and stand a croquette on top, using the puree to hold it in place. Top with a mushroom cap, stem-side down. Sprinkle with fleur de sel. Garnish with additional watercress puree, chive tips, and watercress flowers. Lightly dust the plate with the porcini powder by gently shaking the cheesecloth pouch over the plate.

Roasted Garlic Puree

Makes 250 grams

10 large heads garlic	Kosher salt	15 grams extra-virgin olive oil

While this may seem like a lot of puree, it has many uses. It can be used to make roasted garlic bread (added to the dough itself), roasted garlic aïoli, garlic hummus, and garlic butter. It imparts a garlic flavor to items such as pasta sauce without adding the strong, pungent flavor of raw garlic.

Preheat the oven to 325°F (163°C). Place a baking rack over a sheet pan. Slice off just enough from the top of each head of garlic to expose the tops of the cloves. Place the heads of garlic in a medium saucepot and add water to cover. Bring the water to a boil over medium-high heat. Turn off the heat and remove the garlic. Lightly season the garlic with salt.

Place the heads of garlic in the center of a 12-inch (30-centimeter) square of aluminum foil and fold up the sides to form a foil tray. Drizzle the olive oil over the garlic and cover with a second piece of foil, crimping the foil along the edges to seal the two pieces together. The sealed pouch will steam and roast the garlic at the same time.

Place the pouch on the baking rack and bake for 1 to 1½ hours, until the garlic is cooked through and light golden brown in color. Remove the garlic from the foil and let sit until cool enough to handle.

Place a fine-mesh strainer or tamis over a bowl. While the garlic is still warm, push the whole heads of garlic, cut-side down, against the strainer, pressing the garlic cloves through; discard the skins. Let the roasted garlic puree cool to room temperature. Refrigerate in an airtight container for up to 7 days.

CHARCUTERIE

Though charcuterie—pâtés, sausages, rillettes—is typically considered to be a more rustic style of cooking than one expects in a fine-dining restaurant, it has a place at The French Laundry and per se. Jonathan Benno introduced a *pâté en croûte* and a *fromage de tête* to the menu years ago when he was the chef of per se, and David carries that on with the dishes featured here: Tourte de Gibier with Wild Napa Watershed Duck, Jefferson Street Persimmons, Bitter K+M Chocolate Gelée, and Foie Gras Mousse (below) and Liver and Onions (page 136).

He also makes the best kielbasa I've ever tasted. We use it as a garnish for a meat course, or sometimes we wrap it in dough and serve it as a "Pigs in a Blanket" canapé.

LIVER AND ONIONS

Devil's Gulch Ranch Rabbit Liver Pâté, Caramelized Onion Compote, Crispy Onion Rings, and Whole-Grain Mustard Béchamel

MUSTARD BÉCHAMEL

A straightforward, rich béchamel, equal parts milk and cream thickened with beurre manié, seasoned with mustard, horseradish, lemon, and Tabasco.

RABBIT LIVER PÂTÉ

As old-fashioned as the béchamel: pâté cooked in a terrine mold lined with bacon. 300 grams rabbit, 200 grams pork back fat, 350 grams rabbit liver, a panade of brioche and milk (200 grams each), and an egg. We also add 50 grams of brandy and 20 grams of salt, along with other aromatics (black pepper, thyme, nutmeg).

After it's ground, it's mixed with hand and fingers, "tiger-style," to make it sticky. Pack it in the terrine mold lined with bacon, cover, and bake in a water bath at 300°F (150°C) to an internal temperature of 135°F (57°C), about an hour. Or you can steam it at 250°F (121°C) for 40 minutes in a combi oven.

ONION RINGS

As simple as their name. We dip rings in our standard cornstarch–egg white mixture (page 235), coat them in potato flakes, then deep-fry them at service.

CARAMELIZED ONION COMPOTE

Deeply caramelized onions are chopped, combined with veal stock, seasoned, and thickened with some Pre-Hy. Final seasonings: salt, pepper, and Worcestershire sauce.

This is a straightforward liver-and-pork pâté recipe from my Rakel days, back then done with chicken liver (instead of rabbit), pork, fat, a panade of brioche and milk, and egg. We serve this current version with some crispy onion rings, a mustard béchamel, and an onion compote.

SOFT-BOILED BANTAM HEN EGG WITH SHAVED WHITE TRUFFLES

Creamed Arrowleaf Spinach and Sauce Soubise

Makes 6 servings

SAUCE SOUBISE

1 sheet silver leaf gelatin

35 grams ½-inch-dice (1.25-centimeter) bacon

65 grams peeled Vidalia onion

12 grams whole butter

5 grams kosher salt

5 grams sugar

70 grams water

70 grams heavy cream

15 grams crème fraîche

6 grams beurre manié (page 108)

7 grams Pre-Hy (page 109)

CREAMED SPINACH BÉCHAMEL

30 grams leek (white and light green portions only)

20 grams whole butter

125 grams heavy cream

25 grams beurre manié (page 108)

200 grams stemmed arrowleaf spinach leaves

Kosher salt

WILTED SPINACH

40 grams onion

35 grams whole butter

3 grams kosher salt

325 grams stemmed arrowleaf spinach leaves

TO COMPLETE

60 grams fresh white truffles (optional)

6 large Bantam hen eggs

340 grams beurre monté (page 220; optional)

2 grams lemon juice

Fleur de sel

SPECIAL EQUIPMENT

Milk frother

Truffle slicer

In a world of simultaneously gelatinous and gummy sous vide eggs, we believe you can't beat the texture and flavor of a traditionally soft-boiled egg. The soft-boiled egg has many faces at The French Laundry. The one we include here is an austere presentation with white truffles and sauce soubise. It's very simple and decadent. We cook the eggs, then hold them in beurre monté to keep them warm. The beurre monté also gives the eggs a beautiful sheen and additional flavor.

FOR THE SAUCE SOUBISE

Submerge the gelatin in a bowl of ice water to bloom (soften) for about 5 minutes.

Lightly caramelize the bacon in a 1-quart (1-liter) saucepot over medium heat for 3 to 4 minutes, until the fat has rendered and the bacon is golden brown.

Cut the onion in half through the root end, remove the root, and slice the onion lengthwise about ⅛ inch (3 millimeters) thick. Add the onion, butter, salt, and sugar to the saucepot with the bacon and cook gently to sweat the onion until translucent. Add the water, cream, and crème fraîche. Bring to a simmer and cover with a lid to prevent oxidation. Simmer gently over low heat, without reducing the liquid, for 10 minutes. Remove the pieces of bacon from the sauce and discard. Transfer the sauce to a blender.

Remove the softened gelatin from the ice water and squeeze out the excess water. Add the gelatin to the blender, then add the beurre manié and Pre-Hy. Beginning on low speed and gradually increasing to high, blend for 3 to 4 minutes, until the sauce has thickened and is very smooth. Pass through a chinois into a small pot; keep covered until serving.

FOR THE CREAMED SPINACH BÉCHAMEL

Cut the leek into ¼-inch (6-millimeter) dice and rinse in tepid water to remove any dirt. Brown the butter in a 2-quart (2-liter) saucepot over medium heat. Add the leeks and cook gently until tender, about 3 minutes. Add the cream and bring to a boil. Remove from the heat and

whisk in the beurre manié. Return to the heat and cook, whisking continuously, for about 1 minute, until the cream has thickened. It will be very thick, as if it is about to break. Keep warm.

Bring a pot of salted water to a boil. Blanch the spinach in the boiling water for 2 to 3 minutes, until very tender. Drain the spinach and spread it on a clean kitchen towel. When it has cooled enough to touch, wring out any excess water. While still hot, place the thickened cream and blanched spinach in the blender and puree until smooth. Season with salt to taste and set aside.

FOR THE WILTED SPINACH

Chop the onion very finely, until it resembles a paste. Melt the butter in a large sauté pan over medium-low heat. Add the onion and salt and cook gently, stirring continuously, for 2 to 3 minutes, until the onion is soft and fragrant but without letting it take on any color.

Add the spinach and increase the heat to medium-high. Quickly cook the spinach until tender. Drain the spinach and spread it on a clean kitchen towel. When it has cooled enough to touch, wring out any excess water and coarsely chop. Mix the wilted spinach and creamed spinach béchamel together in a small pot and keep warm.

TO COMPLETE

Using a soft bristled brush, like a toothbrush, carefully brush the surface of the truffles (if using) to remove any dirt or debris, without damaging them. Rinse the truffles in a small cup of cool water; repeat as needed until the truffles are clean of any dirt.

Bring a large pot of water to a boil. The pot should be large enough and the water should be boiling hard enough that it remains at a boil when the eggs are added. Gently add the hen eggs to the pot and boil for 6 minutes. Transfer the eggs to a colander and run warm water over them until they are cool enough to handle. Peel the eggs and keep warm (the eggs can be held in a pot of just-warm beurre monté for 30 to 40 minutes before serving).

Bring the soubise to a simmer over medium-low heat and season with the lemon juice. Transfer to a narrow, high container. Holding a milk frother between the edge of the container and a spoon, foam the soubise until it is very bubbly.

Divide the creamed spinach among the serving bowls and cover with the frothy soubise. Season the eggs with fleur de sel and place them on top of the soubise. Garnish with shavings of white truffle, if desired.

"PEAS AND CARROTS"

Spicy Lamb Merguez, Sweet Carrot Crepe, Chickpea Yogurt, and Garden Pea Tendrils

Makes 6 servings

MERGUEZ SPICE

7.5 grams kosher salt

1.5 grams pink salt

1.5 grams Aleppo pepper

1 gram cumin seed

1 gram fennel seed

1 gram garlic powder

0.5 grams Hungarian paprika

0.5 grams coriander seeds

0.5 grams ground chipotle chile

SPICY LAMB MERGUEZ

250 grams lamb, equal parts fat and meat

2 grams polyphosphate

35 grams crushed ice

5 grams cilantro leaves

2 grams mint leaves

CURED CARROTS

2 small purple carrots

7 small sweet carrots, about 6 inches (15 centimeters) long

300 grams prepared veg blanc (see page 185)

CHICKPEA YOGURT

80 grams dried chickpeas

1 medium carrot

1 celery stalk

25 grams baking soda

1 garlic clove, peeled

250 grams plain whole-milk yogurt

40 grams extra-virgin olive oil

15 grams lemon juice, plus more to taste

15 grams roasted garlic puree (page 133)

12 grams fleur de sel

2 grams ground cumin

2 grams ground coriander

Kosher salt

SWEET CARROT CREPES

350 grams strained carrot juice (from fresh bunch carrots)

90 grams whole milk

6 large eggs

175 grams all-purpose flour

45 grams whole butter, melted

7 grams kosher salt

TO COMPLETE

Canola oil, for sautéing

Extra-virgin olive oil

Fleur de sel

Green and yellow pea tendrils

SPECIAL EQUIPMENT

Small meat grinder with small and medium dies, chilled

Chamber vacuum sealer (optional)

Immersion circulator (optional)

Japanese mandoline

#805 (⁷⁄₁₆-inch/ 11-millimeter) plain piping tip

3½-inch (90-millimeter) plain round cutter

The "Peas and Carrots" dish from *The French Laundry Cookbook* became one of the iconic dishes for us. It was originally conceived and developed by Jonathan Benno back in the early days of The French Laundry. The dish, a crepe filled with diced lobster meat and served with a carrot-ginger emulsion and pea tendrils, was really just a way to serve inelegant lobster knuckles (conceal them within a crepe), but the peas-and-carrots combo used to garnish it would find many forms throughout the years. The original "Peas and Carrots" was one of the first dishes David had at The French Laundry before he began working at the restaurant. Here he takes the idea in a Mediterranean direction, making that same crepe but using carrot juice as the base rather than the traditional dairy. (Note the shape of the carrots—these have been dubbed "carokras" because they're shaped like okra, the result of a very short and fat variety of carrot called Chantenay that we grow in the garden.)

FOR THE MERGUEZ SPICE

Combine all the ingredients for the merguez spice in a spice grinder and grind to a powder. The spice mix can be stored in an airtight container for up to 1 month.

FOR THE SPICY LAMB MERGUEZ

Dice the lamb into 1-inch (2.5-centimeter) cubes and mix with the merguez spice and polyphosphate. Cover and refrigerate overnight.

Grind the lamb once through the medium die of the grinder into a bowl. Mix in the ice, cilantro, and mint and grind again through the medium die. Grind once more through the small die. Mix the sausage together by hand until it is homogenous and feels tacky. The merguez mixture can be refrigerated in an airtight container for up to 2 days.

FOR THE CURED CARROTS

If you have a chamber vacuum sealer, set an immersion circulator in a water bath and heat the water to 88°C (190.4°F).

Rub the purple carrots and one of the sweet carrots with a new scouring pad to remove the peel while keeping their shape as round as possible. Thinly slice the carrots into 2- to 3-millimeter-thick rounds on a Japanese mandoline. Place the carrot rounds and 100 grams of the veg blanc

in a sous vide bag. Place the bag in the sealer chamber and vacuum seal. The carrots can be used immediately or refrigerated for up to 2 days.

If you don't have a chamber vacuum sealer, combine the carrot rounds and the veg blanc in a container, cover, and refrigerate for at least 2 hours or up to 2 days.

Wash the remaining 6 sweet carrots and cut them into pieces about 2 inches (5 centimeters) long. You will need a total of 18 pieces.

To turn the pieces into carokras (cone shape), use a tourné knife to bevel one end of the carrot. Pull the tourné knife from the edge of the bevel to the center of the opposite end to create a straight cut that angles inward. Rotate the carrot slightly and repeat the same cut, at the same angle, until you have gone around the entire carrot. Repeat with the remaining pieces.

Place the carrot pieces and the remaining 200 grams veg blanc in a sous vide bag. Place the bag in the sealer chamber and vacuum seal. Cook in the water bath for 1 hour, until the carrots are completely tender.

If you don't have a chamber vacuum sealer, bring a pot of salted water to a boil and blanch the carrots for 3 to 4 minutes, until tender. Chill the carokra carrots in an ice-water bath. The carokra carrots can be refrigerated in the sous vide bag or ice-water bath for up to 1 day.

FOR THE CHICKPEA YOGURT

Soak the chickpeas in 300 grams water overnight, then drain.

Peel the carrot and cut it into large pieces, about 2 inches (5 centimeters) long. Cut the celery to roughly the same size. Put the chickpeas, carrot, celery, 1,000 grams (1 quart/1 liter) water, the baking soda, and garlic in a 2-quart (2-liter) saucepot, cover, and simmer over medium-low heat until the chickpeas are fully tender, 1½ to 1¾ hours; add more water as needed. Remove and discard the carrot, celery, and garlic.

Drain the chickpeas and transfer to a blender. Add the yogurt, olive oil, lemon juice, roasted garlic puree, fleur de sel, cumin, and coriander. Beginning on low speed and gradually increasing to high, blend until completely smooth, using the tamper to keep the puree moving. Add additional lemon juice and salt to taste. Transfer to a disposable piping bag fitted with a #805 (7/16-inch/11-millimeter) plain piping tip. Keep in a warm spot for up to 4 hours before serving.

FOR THE SWEET CARROT CREPES

Put the carrot juice, milk, and eggs in a blender and blend on low speed to combine. Add the flour, melted butter, and salt and blend until smooth. Pass through a chinois.

Place a piece of parchment paper on a sheet pan. Heat an 8-inch (20-centimeter) nonstick pan over medium heat. To ensure the crepe does not stick, spray the pan lightly with nonstick spray and wipe with a paper towel. Pour 60 grams of the batter into the pan, swirling the pan until the batter coats the bottom evenly. Cook until the surface of the crepe is set. Invert the pan, holding it about 3 inches (7.5 centimeters) over the parchment paper, and let the crepe fall from the pan.

Top the crepe with a piece of parchment and repeat, cooking and layering the crepes to make a stack of 12 crepes. The crepes can be wrapped in plastic wrap and kept in a warm place.

TO COMPLETE

Preheat oven to 350°F (180°C). Bring the carrots to room temperature.

Divide the merguez into 12 small oval-shaped patties. Place one piece of merguez slightly off-center on a crepe and gently fold the crepe over, enclosing the sausage (the crepe will not stick together or close completely at the corners). Use a 3½-inch (90-millimeter) plain round cutter to punch the crepe around the merguez. Repeat with the remaining crepes and merguez.

Heat a large nonstick sauté pan over medium heat and lightly coat the bottom with canola oil. Add the filled crepes to the pan and sauté to lightly brown the bottom. Transfer the pan to the oven and cook for 6 to 8 minutes, until the merguez is fully cooked. Remove from the pan and drain on paper towels for about 3 minutes.

Dry the pickled carrots and carokra carrots on paper towels and place them in separate bowls. Toss with olive oil and season with fleur de sel.

Pipe two mounds of chickpea yogurt onto each serving plate. Top each mound with a crepe, pressing lightly to anchor. Pipe dots of chickpea yogurt around the plate, topping each with a slice of pickled carrot. Garnish with more pickled carrots, the carokra carrots, and pea tendrils.

PB&J

Slow-Poached Hudson Valley Foie Gras,
Concord Grape Gelée, Peanut Brittle,
Celery Branch, and Kendall Farms Crème Fraîche

**THE
GARNISHES**
Concord grape
gelée and crème
fraîche.

**THE GENOISE
"BREAD"**
We make two types
of genoise—a white
crème fraîche and a
purple Concord
grape—using a little
foie fat in the
batters. To create
the cake's
herringbone
pattern, we first
spread white batter
on a Silpat, draw a
square-toothed
trowel across it,
freeze it, then
spread purple
batter, filling in the
grooves, and finish
by steaming for
15 minutes.

We then cut the
genoise in 2-inch
strips and reverse
every other one as
we lay them onto a
sheet of plastic
wrap, matching up
the stripes. We wrap
the foie in the cake,
holding everything
together by Activa.
Vacuum sealed, this
will keep for up to
2 weeks.

EVEN MORE TEXTURE

Chilled celery curls and peanut brittle. Skippy natural peanut butter and hot caramel are mixed together, poured onto a Silpat, then folded and folded as it cools. Once hardened, the brittle is grated over the celery.

THE FOIE GRAS

We cure the whole foie in a 5% brine (with a pinch of pink curing salt). We then vacuum seal with a quartered vanilla bean, 50 grams Sauternes, 10 grams water, and a pinch of sugar and cook in a 30°C (86°F) water bath for 3 hours. We chill it in an ice bath, devein each lobe, shape into roulades, then vacuum seal to compress and shape them.

This is an extraordinary way to serve foie gras in the classic "au torchon" style, but here, it's wrapped in a striped genoise—the "bread" for the PB&J. Great craftsmanship and finesse are needed to accomplish this, and the finished dish shows it. The genoise-wrapped slice of foie gras is accompanied by diced Concord grape gelée, a crème fraîche puree, ribbons of chilled celery for crunch, and peanut brittle—Corey's favorite—that's grated over the plate tableside.

VEGETABLES

TOUT ARTICHAUT

Braised Artichoke Heart, Caramelized Artichoke Puree, and Artichoke Soup

Makes 6 servings

ARTICHOKES AND ARTICHOKE ESSENCE

2 lemons, halved

9 Violet de Provence artichokes, about 2½ inches (6.5 centimeters) in diameter

500 grams prepared veg blanc (see page 185)

2 strips orange zest (removed with a vegetable peeler)

100 grams extra-virgin olive oil

6 large globe artichokes, about 3½ inches (9 centimeters) in diameter

CARAMELIZED ARTICHOKE PUREE

65 grams sunchokes

75 grams Vidalia onion

25 grams clarified butter (page 53)

265 grams water

135 grams heavy cream

55 grams whole butter

3 grams kosher salt

Fleur de sel

Lemon juice

CRÈME DE ARTICHAUT

2 sheets silver leaf gelatin

150 grams heavy cream

25 grams whole butter

15 grams beurre manié (page 108)

Fleur de sel

Lemon juice

TO COMPLETE

Canola oil

15 grams whole butter

18 small nasturtium leaves

SPECIAL EQUIPMENT

Immersion circulator

Chamber vacuum sealer

Milk frother

"All artichoke"—David wanted to present all the flavors and textures of the artichoke, one of my favorite vegetables. He even found a way to use the leaves, which we once discarded, cooking them with water for 12 hours to make an artichoke "essence." The liquid is very bitter, so he sweetens it with cream and adds body with beurre manié; incorporating some gelatin keeps the bubbles in the froth stable. The artichokes that will be served whole are cooked in veg blanc with additional lemon, orange, and olive oil.

FOR THE ARTICHOKES AND ARTICHOKE ESSENCE

Fill a large bowl with water (enough to submerge the artichokes). Squeeze the juice from the lemons into the water and add the juiced lemon halves as well.

To clean the violet artichokes, hold an artichoke with the stem end toward you. Pull off the very small bottom leaves. Break off the larger leaves by pushing with your thumb against the bottom of each leaf as you snap it off, about ½ inch (1.25 centimeters) above its base, so you are well above the meaty portion (which will become part of the heart), and pulling it down toward the stem. A small portion of the bottom of the artichoke leaves should be left anchored to the base. Continue removing the outer leaves, reserving them in a separate large bowl for the artichoke essence, until you reach leaves that are tender and yellow. Remove 4 or 5 of these tender yellow leaves and drop them into the acidulated water.

Trim off the top of the artichoke to about 1 inch (2.5 centimeters) above the heart. Using a paring knife, cut around the bottom of the artichoke in a strip to cut away the tough dark green parts of the leaves and expose the tender heart. Then, holding the knife at a 45-degree angle, trim the base of the artichoke next to the stem. Trim the stems to about ¾ inch (2 centimeters) long. Drop the trimmed violet artichoke heart into the acidulated water, cover the bowl with a damp towel to keep it submerged, and repeat to trim the remaining violet artichokes.

Set an immersion circulator in a water bath and heat the water to 88°C (190.4°F).

(continued)

Remove the violet artichoke hearts from the acidulated water (reserve the water for the globe artichokes) and transfer them to a sous vide bag. Add 400 grams of the veg blanc, the orange zest, and the olive oil to the bag. Place in a chamber vacuum sealer and vacuum seal. Place the reserved tender yellow leaves and remaining 100 grams veg blanc in a separate sous vide bag. Place in the sealer chamber and vacuum seal. Place both bags in the water bath. Remove the leaves after 13 minutes and immediately submerge in an ice-water bath to cool. Cook the hearts for a total of 30 to 60 minutes, until tender but still holding their shape. When the hearts are done, submerge the bag in the ice-water bath to cool. Keep the water bath at 88°C (190.4°F) for the artichoke essence. The violet artichokes and leaves can be refrigerated in their bags for up to 3 days.

To clean the globe artichokes, remove the outer green leaves as you did with the violet artichokes and reserve them for the artichoke essence. When you reach leaves that are tender and yellow, trim off the top two-thirds of the artichoke to where the meaty heart begins and drop the trimmed artichokes into the acidulated water. Remove the chokes and stems and discard. Reserve the globe artichokes in acidulated water for the caramelized artichoke puree.

To make the artichoke essence, weigh the reserved outer leaves from the violet and globe artichokes, place them in a sous vide bag, and add half as much water by weight. Place in the sealer chamber and vacuum seal. Cook in the water bath for 8 hours. Submerge the bag in an ice-water bath to chill. Strain the liquid through a china cap, gently pushing on the solids with a ladle to extract as much flavor as possible. Strain the artichoke essence once more through a chinois and refrigerate in an airtight container for up to 3 days.

FOR THE CARAMELIZED ARTICHOKE PUREE

Thoroughly wash the sunchokes in cold water. Cut the sunchokes, globe artichoke hearts, and onion into about ½-inch (1.25-centimeter) dice. Heat a medium pot or small rondeau over medium-high heat. Reduce the heat to medium and add the clarified butter, sunchokes, artichoke hearts, and onion. Cook, stirring and scraping the bottom and sides of the pot continuously to prevent the vegetables from sticking, for 5 to 8 minutes to caramelize the vegetables. Add the water, cream, whole butter, and salt and bring to a gentle boil, stirring with a silicone spatula as it thickens to prevent it from burning. Reduce the liquid until it thickens and glazes the vegetables, 8 to 12 minutes.

Transfer to a blender. Beginning on low speed and gradually increasing to high, blend until the puree is perfectly smooth and very thick, using the tamper to keep the puree moving. Adjust the seasoning with fleur de sel and lemon juice to taste, then pass the puree through a chinois into a small container, such as a deli container. Press a piece of plastic wrap directly against the entire surface of the puree and cover with a lid. Refrigerate for up to 3 days.

FOR THE CRÈME DE ARTICHAUT

Submerge the gelatin in a bowl of ice water to bloom (soften) for about 5 minutes. (If you have more than 200 grams artichoke essence, bring it to a boil over medium heat and cook until reduced to 200 grams.)

Add the cream, butter, and beurre manié and return to a boil. Whisk continuously until the beurre manié is completely incorporated and the sauce is slightly thickened, 2 to 3 minutes. Remove the softened gelatin from the ice water and squeeze out the excess water. Whisk the gelatin into the crème.

Transfer to a blender. Beginning on low speed and gradually increasing to high, blend the crème until perfectly smooth. Season to taste with fleur de sel and lemon juice. Strain through a chinois into a covered container and keep in a warm spot until serving or refrigerate for up to 3 days.

TO COMPLETE

Reheat the artichoke puree and crème de artichaut as needed.

Drain the violet artichokes, cut each in half lengthwise, and pat dry. Carefully dry the fragile artichoke leaves on paper towels.

Heat a medium sauté pan over medium heat. Add enough canola oil to coat the bottom of the pan. Add the violet artichokes, cut-side down, and cook for 3 to 5 minutes, until golden brown and caramelized. Add the butter and swirl to melt. Reduce the heat to low, add the artichoke leaves, and gently warm for about a minute. Remove the artichokes and leaves and drain on paper towels.

Place a spoonful of the artichoke puree in the bottom of each serving bowl. Arrange the leaves around the puree and place 3 artichoke halves over the puree. Use a frother to foam the crème de artichaut by holding the frother between the side of the container and a spoon. Skim the foam from the surface of the crème with a spoon and place it on top of the dish. Garnish with the nasturtium leaves.

PATIENCE AND PERSISTENCE

*It's All About
Balance*

FROM 1978, WHEN I WAS THE CHEF AND OWNER of the Cobbly Nob (which failed out of my general ignorance, at age twenty-three, of the restaurant business), through to my opening of The French Laundry sixteen years later, I worked really hard but had very little to show for it, beyond many critical successes and a reputation for having a temper in the kitchen. But as The French Laundry's success grew, and allowed me and my team to develop a group of restaurants and ancillary businesses, it's given me a perspective on what the useful qualities are in a chef that allows her, him, or them to grow.

It's not enough simply to recognize the six basic "dishwasher disciplines"—organization, efficiency, critical feedback, routine, repetition, teamwork—those key attributes I learned as a teenager that continue to guide me through my work to this day (see page 222). There are two other personality qualities that are critical catalysts for making these six gears engage meaningfully: patience and persistence. These are common qualities that the leadership of any organized group—a kitchen, a sports franchise, a military unit—will benefit from.

Patience, which it took me a long time to develop, is the first quality a young chef, or any young aspirant in any field, must embrace. The counterpart to patience is ambition, and while ambition is important—we need to have goals—too much ambition can be harmful.

I've made critical mistakes in my life, in my career, because I was too impatient, and perhaps too ambitious. I became a chef before I'd even learned to cook. This had more to do with my mom, and our circumstances, but I'd never been a chef de partie, a beginning cook, an assistant. I didn't even know what a "chef de partie" was when I became the chef of the Palm Beach Yacht Club.

Patience should temper ambitions. Not standards, mind you—standards should always be moving up. But ambition is always wanting to push yourself forward—push, push, push—regardless of whether you're ready. Patience forces you to wait.

Ambition can be so strong as to be blinding, whereas a third quality, aspiration, is like ambition but more planned, shorter in scope, and is a good stepping-stone toward one's goals. It may be a chef's *ambition* to own his or her own restaurant one day, but for now, the young chef *aspires* to move from, say, garde manger to the fish station.

One of my chefs, a terrific cook and leader, wanted to own his own restaurant, and he thought that because he was chef de cuisine at one of my restaurants, he could simply quit and open his own place. But he was impatient and made a move without understanding all the steps that were needed to reach that goal, and he was forced to return to cooking for someone else. Because he is so talented, I see this as a missed opportunity; we're missing the personal vision of a talented chef. He had too much ambition and not enough patience.

Corey Lee, who led the French Laundry kitchen for several years, slowly gathered all the information he needed while working at the restaurant; he aspired to complete each small step before fulfilling his ambition and venturing out on his own to open the very successful Benu in San Francisco—and earning three Michelin stars.

Me, I had no patience at all when I was young. I wanted everything fast. I became a yacht club chef with zero cooking experience, then a restaurant chef at the Cobbly Nob before I knew what I was doing. The restaurant failed, and I kept leapfrogging forward.

I needed to learn the fundamentals of cooking, of being a manager, of being a businessman, before I could succeed. And it took two decades of failing and, fortunately, of *learning* from those mistakes before it all came together.

Which brings me to a fourth quality, a quality I did have, one that saved me from fatal ambition—persistence. Having too much ambition and not enough patience, I was destined to fail. But I had the persistence to survive those failures. I kept working.

Thrust forward by my ambitions, I initially couldn't succeed because I hadn't put in the work I needed to do in order to become the person I wanted and needed to be. But I persisted. I never relinquished my standards. And that's how The French Laundry, and all that would come from its success, came to be. Ambition, yes, but tempered by patience and persistence.

CROQUETTE DE LEGUMES D'HIVER

Cauliflower "Tabbouleh," Pickled Ají Dulce, and Lacinato Kale Aïoli

Makes 6 servings

KALE AÏOLI

130 grams stemmed
   lacinato kale leaves

30 grams stemmed baby
   spinach leaves

375 grams canola oil

6 grams kosher salt, plus
   more to taste

2 large egg yolks

25 grams Burgundy
   mustard

3 grams minced shallot

36 grams whole-milk
   Greek yogurt

Kosher salt

**CROQUETTES DE
LEGUMES D'HIVER**

30 grams bulgur wheat

60 grams peeled celery
   root

60 grams peeled
   rutabaga

60 grams peeled turnip

60 grams peeled carrots

50 grams peeled onion

5 grams minced garlic

1 gram ground coriander

1 gram ground cumin

1 gram white sesame
   seeds

2 grams flat-leaf parsley
   leaves, coarsely
   chopped

2 grams mint leaves,
   coarsely chopped

2 grams cilantro leaves,
   coarsely chopped

65 grams chickpea flour

2 grams baking soda

2 grams lemon zest

2 grams Agrumato
   lemon oil

Kosher salt

TO COMPLETE

Canola oil, for deep-
   frying

1 small head cauliflower
   (at least 200 grams)

25 grams chiffonade of
   flat-leaf parsley

12 grams chiffonade of
   Little Gem lettuce

20 grams tomato
   concasse

20 grams brunoise of
   pickled red pearl onions
   (page 184)

15 grams extra-virgin
   olive oil

6 grams lemon juice

Kosher salt

Espelette pepper

Ground sumac

Flat-leaf parsley leaves,
   washed and dried

Pickled ají dulce peppers
   (see page 183),
   quartered and seeded

SPECIAL EQUIPMENT

Meat grinder with a
   medium die

This dish is a nod to former per se chef de cuisine Eli Kaimeh, born in New York to Syrian parents, who grew up eating Middle Eastern food. He created this "tabbouleh" of cauliflower as well as the croquettes, a kind of "falafel" made with ground winter vegetables seasoned with coriander, garlic, and parsley. They're bound with chickpea flour, shaped into a quenelle, and fried till super crispy. Corey also makes these croquettes with only cauliflower, utilizing the entire vegetable, stem and all.

FOR THE KALE AÏOLI

Cut the kale leaves and the baby spinach into a very fine chiffonade and place in a blender with the canola oil and salt. Blend on high speed for at least 5 minutes, until the greens warm and "cook," to remove their raw, spicy flavor.

Pour the mixture into a large bowl and nestle the bowl in an ice-water bath. Chill, stirring from time to time, until cool. Place a large dampened coffee filter in a strainer set over a container. Pour in the kale oil and refrigerate overnight to extract the oil. (The kale oil can be refrigerated in an airtight container for up to 3 weeks or frozen for up to 3 months.)

Place the egg yolks, mustard, and shallot in the blender and blend on high speed. With the blender running on high speed, slowly stream in 200 grams of the kale oil and blend until the aïoli is completely emulsified and thickened. Transfer the aïoli to a bowl and fold in the yogurt to prevent the emulsion from breaking. Season with salt to taste. Pass the aïoli through a chinois. Fill a disposable piping bag with the aïoli and pipe the aïoli into a small squeeze bottle.

Refrigerate for up to 3 days.

FOR THE CROQUETTES DE LEGUMES D'HIVER

Soak the bulgur wheat in water to cover for 1 hour to soften. Drain the bulgur, transfer to a clean kitchen towel, and squeeze out any excess moisture. Cut the celery root, rutabaga, turnip, carrots, and onion into ½-inch (1.25-centimeter) dice. Grind all the root vegetables through the medium die of a meat grinder into a bowl. Mix in the garlic and bulgur wheat to combine.

(continued)

Heat an 8-quart (8-liter) rondeau over medium heat. Add the ground vegetable farce and cook gently (sweat) for 5 to 10 minutes, until the mixture is dry but without letting it take on any color. Transfer the farce to a bowl and let cool to room temperature. Stir in the coriander, cumin, sesame seeds, parsley, mint, cilantro, chickpea flour, and baking soda. Stir in the lemon zest and lemon oil. Season with salt to taste. Cover and refrigerate the vegetable farce for at least 2 hours, until completely cold.

TO COMPLETE

Fill a Dutch oven or a heavy-bottomed saucepot with at least 9-inch-high (23-centimeter) sides with 3 inches (7.5 centimeters) of canola oil; ideally, the oil should come no more than one-third up the sides of the pot. Heat the oil to 350°F (180°C). Set a cooling rack on a sheet pan.

While the oil heats, using a box grater, grate 200 grams of cauliflower from the top of the head. Put the cauliflower in a large bowl and add the chiffonaded parsley, lettuce, tomato concasse, pickled red onion, olive oil, and lemon juice. Season with salt, Espelette pepper, and sumac to taste.

Working in batches, use a spider to carefully place the parsley leaves in the oil and fry until there are no longer bubbles forming around the leaves, about 15 seconds. Transfer to the rack and repeat with the remaining parsley. Reduce the heat and let the oil cool to 280°F (138°C) to fry the croquettes.

Line a sheet pan with parchment paper. As the oil cools, shape the vegetable farce for the croquettes into 12 quenelles, about 25 grams each, and place them on the prepared pan. Fry the croquettes in two batches. Using a spider, stir the oil to be certain that the croquettes do not stick together or to the bottom of the pan, but try not to touch the croquettes, as they could lose their shape. Fry for about 5 minutes, until the croquettes have a rich brown color, flipping them halfway through cooking for even coloring. Transfer to the rack to drain and repeat to fry the remaining croquettes.

Arrange 2 croquettes and 2 quenelles of the cauliflower tabbouleh on each serving plate. Garnish them with the fried parsley leaves. Garnish the plate with pickled pepper pieces and the kale aïoli.

SUNCHOKE CUSTARD

Egg Flower Soup and Sunchoke Beignets

Makes 6 servings

SUNCHOKE-INFUSED CREAM AND HEARTH-ROASTED SUNCHOKES

150 grams sunchokes

270 grams heavy cream

270 grams whole milk

8 grams fleur de sel

SUNCHOKE ESSENCE

500 grams sunchokes

750 grams prepared veg blanc (see page 185)

BLACK TRUFFLE COULIS

200 grams fresh black truffles

45 grams button mushrooms

40 grams peeled Yukon Gold potato

200 grams mushroom essence (page 289)

250 grams water

5 grams fleur de sel, plus more to taste

Sherry vinegar

SUNCHOKE BEIGNETS

40 grams toasted sunflower seeds

100 grams water

40 grams whole butter

5 grams kosher salt

60 grams all-purpose flour

1 large egg

SUNCHOKE CUSTARD

130 grams eggs

4 grams Pre-Hy (page 109)

4 grams fleur de sel

4 grams lemon juice

TO COMPLETE

7.5 grams cornstarch

Canola oil, for deep-frying

Fleur de sel

1 large egg

Sunflower sprouts

SPECIAL EQUIPMENT

Meat grinder with a small die

Combi oven (optional)

6 serving bowls, about 4½ inches (12 centimeters) in diameter by 1½ inches (4 centimeters) deep

This is kind of a like a *chawanmushi*, a Japanese steamed custard. We make a sunchoke consommé, swirl in egg from a dropper to create ribbons of egg, and add shaved truffle. It's a take on a classical consommé with custard royale, a plain egg custard diced and used as garnish. But in a way, this also reflects a French Laundry staple: truffle custard, served in an eggshell, onto which we drizzle a veal-truffle sauce before adding a chive chip. I love how interwoven these preparations are, all of them connected to the central ideas of The French Laundry twenty-six years ago.

To add crunch, we make sunchoke beignets, roasting the reserved sunchokes from the custard infusion till they're dried and condensed, then passing them through a meat grinder and adding them to a straightforward pâte à choux, which is dropped into hot oil and fried into a nutty, crispy accompaniment to the custardy soup. The beignets are delicious on their own. In the spring, we like to change this to a pea custard and pea beignets, which also work beautifully.

FOR THE SUNCHOKE-INFUSED CREAM AND HEARTH-ROASTED SUNCHOKES

Thoroughly wash the sunchokes in cold water and brush to remove any dirt. Cut into ½-inch (1.25-centimeter) dice and place in a 1-quart (1-liter) saucepot. Add the cream, milk, and fleur de sel and bring to a boil over medium heat. Transfer to a container and let cool to room temperature. Cover and refrigerate overnight.

Strain the sunchoke-infused cream through a chinois, lightly pressing on the sunchokes to extract as much cream as possible. Dry the sunchokes on paper towels and reserve 150 grams for hearth-roasting. The cream can be refrigerated for up to 1 day.

Prepare a fire (see page 270) or preheat an oven to 375°F (190°C).

Place the reserved 150 grams sunchokes in a cast-iron pan and position the pan about 6 inches (15 centimeters) above the open flame or place in the oven. Roast them slowly, turning often, for about 20 minutes over the flame or about 1 hour in the oven, until they are golden brown. Remove and set aside at room temperature for the sunchoke beignets, or transfer to an airtight container and refrigerate for up to 1 day.

(continued)

Thoroughly wash the sunchokes in cold water and brush to remove any dirt. Dry on paper towels. Cut the sunchokes into pieces small enough to fit into the feed tube of a meat grinder. Grind the sunchokes through the small die of the grinder into a bowl. Place the sunchokes and veg blanc in a pot and bring to a simmer over medium heat. Transfer the sunchokes and veg blanc to a storage container, cover, and refrigerate overnight. Strain the sunchoke essence through a chinois.

FOR THE BLACK TRUFFLE COULIS

Carefully brush the surface of the truffles with a soft-bristled brush, like a toothbrush, to remove any dirt or debris without damaging the truffles. Rinse the truffles in a small cup of cool water and repeat as needed until the truffles are cleaned of any dirt. Dry the truffles. Finely chop 25 grams of truffle and reserve it for the soup.

Cut the remaining 175 grams truffles, the mushrooms, and the potato into ½-inch (1.25-centimeter) dice and place in a 2-quart (2-liter) sauce-pot. Add the mushroom essence, water, and fleur de sel. Simmer over medium-low heat for 25 to 30 minutes, until the vegetables are completely tender. Increase the heat and reduce the liquid to 150 grams.

Transfer the vegetables to a blender with half the liquid. Blend, beginning on low speed and gradually increasing to high, using the tamper to keep the ingredients moving and adding the remaining liquid as necessary to puree. If the coulis is still too thick once all the liquid has been added, add small amounts of water. Once the ingredients are moving on their own, blend for 2 minutes, until the coulis is perfectly smooth, hot, and steaming.

Pass the coulis through a chinois into a bowl, using the back of a ladle to push down on the solids. Nestle the bowl in an ice-water bath and chill completely, stirring from time to time. Season the coulis with vinegar and fleur de sel to taste and transfer 120 grams to a disposable piping bag. Keep in a warm spot until serving. The remaining truffle coulis can be transferred to an airtight container and frozen for up to 3 weeks.

FOR THE SUNCHOKE BEIGNETS

Grind the hearth-roasted sunchokes and the sunflower seeds through the small die of the meat grinder into a bowl.

Place the water, butter, and salt in a 1-quart (1-liter) saucepot. Bring to a boil over medium heat. Quickly stir in the flour with a stiff silicone spatula or wooden spoon until a ball forms and a thin film develops on the bottom of the pot. Transfer the dough ball to the bowl of a stand mixer fitted with the paddle. Mix on medium speed for about 1 minute, or until the steam dissipates.

Add the egg and mix until fully incorporated, scraping the sides of the bowl and the paddle with a spatula to ensure the dough is evenly mixed. Add the ground sunchoke-sunflower mixture to the dough and mix until homogenous.

The pâte à choux (beignet batter) can be refrigerated in an airtight container for up to 2 days. The beignets can be shaped right before frying, or they can be shaped, placed on a sheet pan sprayed with nonstick spray, covered, and refrigerated for up to 1 day.

FOR THE SUNCHOKE CUSTARD

Bring 165 grams of the sunchoke-infused cream to a boil in a small saucepot over medium heat.

Place the eggs, 165 grams of the sunchoke essence, and the Pre-Hy in a blender. Blend on low speed to avoid aerating the custard; high speeds would cause air bubbles and give the custard an inferior texture. With the blender running, slowly pour the hot sunchoke cream through the hole in the lid to temper the eggs. Season with the fleur de sel and lemon juice and pass through a chinois.

Preheat a combi oven to 83°C (181.4°F) or preheat a convection oven to 350°F (180°C) with the fan off.

Arrange the serving bowls in a deep pan (deep enough that you can cover the pan without the covering touching the bowls). Pipe a 10-gram mound (about 1 tablespoon) of the truffle coulis in the center of each bowl. Pouring to the side of the mound, pour in 70 grams of the custard, or enough to completely cover the truffle puree.

If you are using a combi oven, fill the pan with warm water to reach halfway up the sides of the bowls. If you are using a conventional oven, fill the pan with the hottest water your tap produces to reach the level of the custard. Cover the pan with aluminum foil and steam in the combi oven for 15 to 20 minutes or bake in the conventional oven for about 30 minutes, until the custard appears set (lift a corner of the foil to check). Once the custard appears set, remove a bowl and tilt it slightly. The custard can jiggle, but it shouldn't slide or move down the side of the bowl; if it does, cook for 2 minutes more, then check again, repeating as necessary until the custard is set. Remove the pan from the oven but leave the bowls in the water to keep warm while you finish the soup and beignets.

TO COMPLETE

Whisk together the cornstarch and 250 grams of the sunchoke essence in a 1-quart (1-liter) saucepot. Bring to a boil over medium heat. Reduce the heat and simmer for 2 to 3 minutes to thicken the sauce and cook the cornstarch. Stir the reserved 25 grams finely chopped black truffles into the soup and keep warm.

Fill a pot with at least 8-inch-high (20-centimeter) sides with 3 to 4 inches (7.5 to 10 centimeters) of canola oil. Heat the oil to 375°F (190°C). Add no more than half the beignets to the hot oil; they should not crowd the oil. Fry, turning them from time to time, for 4 to 5 minutes, until they are an even golden brown and the centers are hot. To test, poke a cake tester into the center of a beignet and hold the tester to your lip; it should be hot. Lift the beignets from the oil with a spider, drain on paper towels, and season with fleur de sel. Repeat with the remaining batch. If the beignets are held too long, they may soften. If that happens, return them to the hot oil to crisp just before serving and reseason with fleur de sel.

Meanwhile, complete the egg flower soup. Lightly beat the egg and pour through a small funnel into a small squeeze bottle. Bring the soup to a gentle simmer. Moving your hand in a circular motion, slowly drizzle in streams of the egg. There should be ribbons of egg throughout the soup; let the soup sit, without stirring, until the egg has set. Once the egg has set, very gently stir the soup with a silicone spatula.

Working carefully but quickly, gently spoon about 40 grams of the soup over the custard in each bowl, creating a layer about ½ inch (1.25 centimeters) deep. Serve the hot beignets in separate bowls on the side, garnished with sunflower sprouts.

THE FRENCH LAUNDRY GARDEN

Cultivating Flavor

THE FRENCH LAUNDRY has a three-acre garden directly across the street from our restaurant. It is a great source of pride for all of us, and a pleasure for visitors to Yountville and our neighbors here. And for our chefs, the garden is the ultimate luxury.

When I bought The French Laundry from Don and Sally Schmitt, the spot where the garden is now was just an overgrown field. Don and Sally had six raised beds at The French Laundry (which they had purchased in 1974), as well as an herb garden and a persimmon tree. And my chefs and I used those beds when I took over the restaurant.

In 2002, I bought the overgrown field across the street, and we began developing it, but slowly, with four 20 by 20-foot in-ground beds. That was it. Our very first gardener, Scotty Boggs, was a chef de partie at the time and took a strong interest in developing the first gardens on our new property. The garden changed his life—he now farms as a profession. Now we have twenty beds, two hoop houses, a chicken coop, colonies of bees, and a putting green designed by the golfer Johnny Miller!

We grow a thousand varieties of plants; 250 of them supply food to the restaurants, including over 1,400 pounds of tomatoes alone each season. Our garden chefs grow plants to be eaten, to be drunk, to be admired for their beauty and fragrance alone. They grow passion fruit vines in the parking lot; jasmine, violas, pansies, and lilies for infusions; and fresh herbs for distillations. And I've revived the honeysuckle in front of the restaurant that was so prominent when Don and Sally Schmitt owned The French Laundry.

We also have a small garden behind Ad Hoc, a half mile from The French Laundry, an acre at the nearby Trefethen vineyards, and a one-acre stone fruit orchard in Napa. And four beehives—three for honey (about thirty pounds per hive per year) and one just for the bees, kept in the hollow stump of a sycamore tree that had been in front of my dad's house next to the restaurant.

And the garden has in many ways determined the menu of The French Laundry more than the chefs. Sometimes it controls the chefs themselves.

We hired our first head gardener, Tucker Taylor, in 2007 and he really brought the garden to where it is today. Brett Ellis is now the head gardener.

Gardeners sense the world the way their plants do, feeling the growing warmth of the soil, the waning sunlight after the summer solstice, all the earthly signals that tell a plant when to grow, when to blossom, and when to put all its energy into its offspring: our food.

Because we don't need to grow for a farmers' market, we can cultivate our garden purely for flavor, for intermittent picking, and, of course, for what's on the menu. Not only is the harvest very, very fresh (in our case, the "farm-to-table" journey means walking across the street), but it's also specific to our chef's desires.

The French Laundry may take the very smallest sections of the heart of a certain lettuce, leaving lovely leaves behind for our more casual restaurants, Ad Hoc and Bouchon. Our Mexican restaurant, La Calenda, will use the special type of cilantro that our gardeners grow for them.

The garden team spends eight to twenty hours a day harvesting, picking peas early in the morning when they're at their sweetest, before the morning sun has turned sugars into carbohydrates; harvesting snowy heads of cauliflower just after a frost, when the brassicas generate abundant carbohydrates (see Frost-Kissed Garden Cauliflower, page 33).

Our gardeners know one thing for certain: everything on this earth wants to reproduce, and that, ultimately, is the source of their great daily harvest.

LA RATTE POTATO CULURGIONES

Black Winter Truffle Consommé, Parmesan Tuile, and Shaved Black Winter Truffles

Makes 6 servings

**BLACK WINTER
TRUFFLE BOUILLON**

50 grams peeled shallots

40 grams leek (white
portion only)

20 grams celery stalk

30 grams peeled
purple-top turnip

50 grams water

1 bay leaf

1 savory sprig

600 grams mushroom
essence (page 289)

50 grams minced black
truffle

10 grams sherry vinegar

7 grams kosher salt, or to
taste

PARMESAN TUILE

20 grams all-purpose
flour

7 grams sugar

2 grams kosher salt

45 grams whole butter, at
room temperature

23 grams egg whites

Block of Parmesan
cheese, for grating

**LA RATTE POTATO
FARCE**

250 grams peeled La
Ratte potatoes

75 grams heavy cream

63 grams whole milk

5 grams fleur de sel

55 grams whole butter, at
spreadable room
temperature

55 grams mascarpone
cheese, at room
temperature

38 grams grated
Parmesan cheese
(grated on a rasp
grater)

25 grams grated black
winter truffle (grated on
a rasp grater)

CULURGIONES

3 sheets basic pasta
dough (recipe follows)

Semolina, for dusting

TO COMPLETE

30 slices black winter
truffle

Extra-virgin olive oil

SPECIAL EQUIPMENT

Japanese mandoline

Immersion circulator
(optional)

Chamber vacuum sealer
(optional)

#806 (½-inch/
13-millimeter)
plain piping tip

2¾-inch (7-centimeter)
plain round cutter

15-millimeter flower-
shaped cutter

These are stuffed dumplings as they are shaped in Sardinia, served in a black truffle broth. If you have access to plenty of truffles, the truffle flavor doesn't get any better than this. It's very much like the Black Truffle Explosion developed and popularized by former French Laundry sous chef Grant Achatz at his Chicago restaurant Alinea.

FOR THE BLACK WINTER TRUFFLE BOUILLON

Slice the shallots, leek, celery, and turnip as thinly as possible on a Japanese mandoline and place them in a 2-quart (2-liter) saucepot. Add the water and bay leaf and sweat over low heat. (Adding water without any butter or oil will prevent the vegetables from caramelizing.) Cook gently for 5 to 8 minutes, until the vegetables are tender. Add the savory and the mushroom essence.

Simmer over medium heat for about 10 minutes. Remove from the heat, cover with a lid, and steep for 20 minutes. Strain the liquid through a small chinois into a clean 2-quart (2-liter) saucepot. Add the truffle and warm gently over low heat; do not allow the liquid to simmer. Remove from the heat, cover with a lid, and steep for about 5 minutes.

Line a strainer with a dampened tea towel and strain the bouillon through it into a container. Squeeze the tea towel to extract as much flavor from the truffle as possible. Reserve the truffle for the potato farce. Season the bouillon with the vinegar and salt.

Refrigerate in an airtight container for up to 3 days.

FOR THE PARMESAN TUILE

In a small bowl, mix together the flour, sugar, and salt. In a separate bowl, whisk the softened butter until it is completely smooth and mayonnaise-like in texture.

Whisk the egg whites into the dry ingredients until completely incorporated and smooth. Whisk in the softened butter one-third at a time, scraping the sides of the bowl as necessary and whisking until the batter is creamy and without any lumps. Transfer the batter to a smaller container (it will be easier to work with) and use within 1 hour.

(continued)

Preheat the oven to 300°F (150°C) with the fan off. Cut a 1-inch (2.5-centimeter) round from the lid of a plastic container to engineer a stencil.

Place a nonstick silicone baking mat on the work surface. Place the stencil in one corner of the mat and, holding the stencil flat against the mat, scoop about 3 grams of the batter onto the back of an offset spatula and spread it in an even layer over the stencil. Run the spatula over the entire stencil to remove any excess batter. Carefully lift the stencil, leaving behind an even round of batter, and repeat the process to fill the baking mat, leaving about 1½ inches (4 centimeters) between the tuiles (you will need at least 18 tuiles for this recipe). Using a rasp grater, generously grate Parmesan in a mounded layer over the surface of the tuiles.

Place the baking mat on a sheet pan and bake for 6 minutes. Rotate the sheet pan 180 degrees and bake for 3 to 5 minutes more, until the tuiles are golden brown and crisp. Let them cool on the baking mat.

Store the Parmesan tuiles in an airtight container with a food-safe silica gel pack at room temperature for up to 2 days.

FOR THE LA RATTE POTATO FARCE

If you have a chamber vacuum sealer, set an immersion circulator in a water bath and heat the water to 100°C (212°F). Place the potatoes in a sous vide bag. Place in the sealer chamber and vacuum seal. Cook in the water bath for 45 minutes. If you do not have a chamber vacuum sealer or immersion circulator, the potatoes can be cooked in salted boiling water for about 18 minutes, until tender when tested with a cake tester.

Working quickly, pass the hot potatoes through a fine-mesh tamis into a tall-sided 2-quart (2-liter) saucepot. "Cream" them with a silicone spatula, working them against the side of the pot, until they are perfectly smooth and homogenous.

Bring the cream and milk to a boil in a 2-quart (2-liter) saucepot. Stir small additions of the cream and milk into the potatoes to incorporate. As the mixture loosens, switch to a whisk and vigorously whisk in the remaining cream and milk. Season with the fleur de sel.

Whisk in the butter, then the mascarpone, and finish with the Parmesan. Pass through a chinois into a bowl. Stir in the reserved cooked truffle and the grated raw truffle, and nestle the bowl in an ice-water bath to cool. Transfer the cooled farce to a piping bag fitted with a #806 (½-inch/13-millimeter) plain piping tip.

FOR THE CULURGIONES

Work with one sheet of pasta at a time, keeping the remaining pasta covered by a damp kitchen towel and working quickly to prevent the pasta from drying out. Punch the pasta into discs with a 2¾-inch (7-centimeter) plain round cutter, about 12 discs per sheet. As they are cut, place the pasta discs under a damp kitchen towel to prevent them from drying out. Each disc should have a dull side and a shiny side.

Dust a sheet pan with a thin layer of semolina. Place a disc of pasta on the work surface, dull-side up. Pipe a line of the potato farce (about 8 grams of farce per disc) in the center of the disc, leaving about ¼ inch (6 millimeters) of pasta exposed on each end of the farce. Pick up the disc of pasta like an open taco. Make a very small pinch at the extreme right (if you are right-handed) of the pasta taco. Push this pinch inward, which will create two flaps of pasta. Pinch these two flaps together, creating a pleat, and tuck it into the farce to create two more flaps. Continue this pinching process, pushing each pinch into the farce, creating as many pleats as possible, along its length. Some of the farce may escape at the end of the culurgione. Remove and reuse the excess farce. Pinch once more to close the culurgione and twist the end 180 degrees for a final seal. Place the shaped culurgione on the semolina-dusted pan (the semolina will help prevent sticking). Repeat with the remaining pasta and farce. Don't let the culurgiones touch each other, as they may stick together.

The culurgiones can be cooked immediately, or they can be frozen on the sheet pan, then transferred to airtight freezer bags and stored in the freezer for up to 3 days. Cook the culurgiones from frozen.

TO COMPLETE

Punch the truffle slices with a 15-millimeter flower-shaped cutter and set aside until ready to plate.

Bring a large pot of lightly salted water to a boil. Add the culurgiones and cook for about 1½ minutes (or about 2½ minutes, if they are frozen). Drain and toss with a bit of extra-virgin olive oil.

Arrange 3 culurgiones in each serving bowl. Pour in the bouillon. Set a Parmesan tuile on top of each culurgione and garnish with the truffles.

Pasta Dough

Makes 300 grams (3 sheets)

Basic Pasta Dough
212 grams 00 flour, plus more as needed

3 large egg yolks

1 large egg

7 grams whole milk

7 grams extra-virgin olive oil

Red Pepper Pasta Dough
200 grams 00 flour, plus more as needed

3 large egg yolks

1 large egg

8 grams whole milk

7 grams extra-virgin olive oil

50 grams reduced red pepper juice (see Note)

SPECIAL EQUIPMENT
Pasta machine

Mound the flour on a board or other surface and create a well in the center. Make sure the well is wide enough and deep enough to hold all the eggs without spilling.

Place the egg yolks, egg, milk, and olive oil in the well (and add the reduced red pepper juice if making red pepper pasta dough). If the eggs are whole, use your fingers to break them up. Using your fingers, begin turning the eggs in a circular motion, keeping them within the well and not allowing them to spill over the sides. This circular motion allows the eggs to gradually pull in flour from the sides of the well; it is important that the flour not be incorporated too rapidly, or the dough will be lumpy. Keep moving the eggs while slowly incorporating the flour. Using a pastry scraper, occasionally push the flour toward the eggs; the flour should be moved only enough to maintain the gradual incorporation of the flour, and the eggs should continue to be contained within the well. The mixture will thicken and eventually get too tight to keep turning with your fingers.

When the dough begins thickening and starts lifting itself from the board, begin incorporating the remaining flour with the pastry scraper, lifting the flour up and over the dough that's beginning to form and cutting it into the dough. When the flour from the sides of the well has been cut into the dough, the dough will still look shaggy. Bring the dough together with the palms of your hands and form it into a ball. The dough will look flaky but will hold together.

Knead the dough by pressing it, bit by bit, in a forward motion with the heels of your hands rather than folding it over on itself as you would with a bread dough. Re-form the dough into a ball and repeat the process several times. The kneading process can take anywhere from 10 to 15 minutes. Even if you think you are finished kneading, knead it for an extra 10 minutes; you cannot overknead this dough. The dough should feel moist but not sticky. Let the dough rest for a few minutes while you clean the work surface.

Put the dough in a resealable plastic bag to ensure that it does not dry out. Let the dough rest for at least 30 minutes and up to 1 hour. The dough can also be put in a sous vide bag, vacuum sealed, and refrigerated for up to 1 day before proceeding.

Dust the work surface with 00 flour. Remove the pasta from the bag and flatten it. Divide it into three parts and cover with a damp kitchen towel to prevent the dough from drying out.

Set the rollers of the pasta machine to the widest setting. Take one-third of the dough, keeping the rest covered with the towel, and run it through the machine. Fold the dough in half end to end, turn it a quarter turn, and run it through the machine again on the same setting. Repeat this procedure two more times, but the last time, fold the pasta sheet in half lengthwise to give you a narrower piece of pasta and run it through the machine.

Set the opening of the rollers down one notch and run the pasta through twice. Do not fold it over. Continue decreasing the roller setting and running the dough through twice until the sheet of pasta is quite thin (there may be a recommended setting for your machine; if not, the next to the thinnest setting is usually best).

Keep the rolled pasta sheet covered with a damp kitchen towel as you roll the remaining two pieces of dough. Use the dough as directed in the recipe.

NOTE

Reduced Red Pepper Juice: Strain 500 grams red bell pepper juice into a 1-quart (1-liter) saucepot. Cook over medium-high heat for about 30 minutes, until the juice reduces to 50 grams and is bright red with a syrupy consistency. Strain the reduced red pepper juice into a bowl and nestle the bowl in an ice-water bath to cool, then stir in 1.5 grams Espelette pepper.

BIG-POT BLANCHING, REVISITED

In *The French Laundry Cookbook*, I explained big-pot blanching, my conviction that the best way to cook a green vegetable is in a giant pot with a lot of heavily salted water at a raging boil, so much water that the boil is not lost when you add the vegetable, and so much salt that the water tastes like the ocean. This will give you the greenest of green vegetables and adds salt to them as well.

And none of this has changed after all this time, except for the acknowledgment that everyone will salt the water a little differently, meaning inconsistently, and that all green vegetables are not the same.

And so our big-pot blanching has evolved. We've arrived at what to us are the perfect concentrations. We blanch soft green vegetables in a pot of water with 3% salt added. This is generally the concentration of seawater. We blanch hard vegetables, such as green beans, in a 6% salt solution, which is very salty.

A new element in our technique, however, is the use of timers, both while blanching and while shocking the vegetables—plunging them into ice water to stop the cooking. We are adamant about this. The general rule is that the vegetable should be in the ice-water bath almost as long as it was in the blanching water, but no longer. It's unnecessary to let a beautifully cooked vegetable soak indefinitely in an ice bath. The ice water will begin pulling out the seasoning imparted by the salted blanching water. This recognition led us to the standard practice of seasoning the ice-water bath with 3% salt as well. We border on obsessive with this, but it produces consistent results.

RED PEPPER FARFALLE

Ají Dulce Peppers, Summer Pole Beans, Fiore Sardo, and Minestrone

Makes 8 servings

MINESTRONE

600 grams cored, ½-inch-dice (1.25-centimeter) vine-ripened tomatoes

450 grams ½-inch-dice (1.25-centimeter) yellow onions

185 grams ½-inch-dice (1.25-centimeter) sweet carrots

165 grams ½-inch-dice (1.25-centimeter) celery

165 grams ½-inch-dice (1.25-centimeter) leeks (white portions only), rinsed to remove any dirt

1 (40-gram) piece Parmesan rind, or 40 grams grated Parmesan cheese

15 grams thyme sprigs

6 garlic cloves, skin on, smashed

2 grams chili flakes

1 bay leaf

1,250 grams sweet onion essence (page 288)

1,250 grams water

30 grams Pre-Hy (page 109), or less as needed

100 grams whole butter, cut into cubes and chilled

15 grams extra-virgin olive oil

Kosher salt

20 grams bruised basil leaves

RED PEPPER FARFALLE

3 sheets red pepper pasta dough (see page 169)

00 flour, for dusting

Semolina, for dusting

SUMMER BEANS

250 grams shelled fresh cranberry (borlotti) beans

450 grams sweet onion essence (page 288)

1 sweet carrot, peeled

½ small onion, root end attached, peeled

1 bay leaf

3 grams thyme sprigs

3 grams peeled garlic cloves, crushed

12 small yellow wax beans

12 haricots verts

12 romano beans

Extra-virgin olive oil

Kosher salt

TO COMPLETE

Extra-virgin olive oil, preferably Armando Manni, in a small squeeze bottle

18 small red basil leaves

18 small green basil leaves

6 small whole pickled ají dulce peppers (see page 183), quartered and seeded

Garden sprouts

Fiore Sardo cheese

SPECIAL EQUIPMENT

Large pressure cooker

1½-inch (38-millimeter) fluted round cutter

Corey developed this take on an Italian American classic having both experienced the minestrone at Olive Garden (soup, salad, breadsticks) and taken some time away from per se working with the innovative team at Torrisi Italian Specialties. First and foremost, we love this beautiful pasta, farfalle. We love a soup. We love the summer beans when they come in and all the amazing peppers we have access to at the same time and that are so abundant in the hot weather, especially our favorite pepper, the ají dulce. There's even reduced red pepper juice in the pasta dough, giving it a vibrant color. All these elements are held together by an intense sweet onion essence, and the dish is finished with gratings of a hard pecorino, which gives the dish some smokiness.

We use cranberry and wax beans here, but any kind of pole-bean-and-fresh-bean combination will work—choose what's best in season.

FOR THE MINESTRONE

Put the tomatoes, onions, carrots, celery, leeks, Parmesan, thyme, garlic, chili flakes, bay leaf, sweet onion essence, and water in a pressure cooker. Cook on the highest setting (stock setting) according to the manufacturer's instructions for 35 minutes. Once cool, transfer to a covered container and refrigerate overnight.

Transfer the minestrone to a 2-quart (2-liter) saucepot, cover, and cook over medium-high heat for 1 hour, reducing the heat as necessary to maintain an active simmer. Immediately strain through a china cap. If you have more than 1,000 grams (1 quart/1 liter) of liquid, return it to a clean pot and reduce to 1,000 grams (1 quart/1 liter). You will be adding 3 percent of the weight of the liquid in Pre-Hy, so if you have less than 1,000 grams (1 quart/1 liter) of liquid, adjust the amount accordingly.

Transfer the liquid to a blender. With the blender running on low speed, add the Pre-Hy, then add the cold butter one piece at a time. Add the oil and blend, gradually increasing the speed to high, for 1½ to 2 minutes, until emulsified. Season with salt to taste and strain through a chinois into a container. Add the basil, cover with a lid, and infuse for 15 minutes. Strain into a clean airtight container.

The minestrone can be refrigerated for up to 3 days or frozen for up to 1 month.

(continued)

FOR THE RED PEPPER FARFALLE

Work with one sheet of pasta at a time, keeping the remaining pasta covered by a damp kitchen towel and working quickly to prevent the pasta from drying out. Dust the work surface with 00 flour and top with one sheet of the pasta dough. Punch the pasta into discs using a 1½-inch (38-millimeter) fluted round cutter. You should be able to punch about 32 discs from each sheet of pasta. As they are cut, place the pasta discs under a damp kitchen towel to prevent them from drying out.

Fold one pasta disc in half without pressing. Holding the crease, fold back the fluted edges, reaching about halfway to the crease. Lay the farfalle on the work surface and pinch the center tightly to seal. Using your fingertips or a pair of tweezers, fluff out the layers to form the bow-tie shape.

Place the shaped farfalle on a nonstick sheet pan dusted with semolina, and repeat with the remaining pasta discs. For this recipe, you will need at least 64 farfalle.

Freeze the farfalle on the sheet pan. Once frozen, they can be stored in a resealable plastic bag in the freezer for up to 1 week. Cook them from frozen.

FOR THE SUMMER BEANS

Put the cranberry beans, sweet onion essence, carrot, and onion in a pressure cooker. Place the bay leaf, thyme, and garlic in a disposable tea bag to make a sachet; add it to the pressure cooker. Cook the beans on the bean (or simmer) setting according to the manufacturer's instructions for about 20 minutes. Remove the carrot, onion, and sachet.

Bring a large pot of salted water to a boil. Blanch the wax beans in the boiling water for about 2½ minutes, until tender. Immediately plunge into an ice-water bath. Dry on paper towels. Repeat to blanch the haricots verts, then the romano beans. Cut the wax beans in half lengthwise. Cut the haricots verts into an oblique cut and the romano beans on the bias to the approximate size of the cranberry beans. Combine all the beans in a bowl and toss with olive oil and salt to taste.

TO COMPLETE

Bring a large pot of lightly salted water to a boil. Add 64 of the frozen farfalle and cook for about 2½ minutes. Drain the pasta and toss in a light coating of olive oil.

Warm the minestrone in a saucepot.

Divide the beans and farfalle among the serving bowls. Ladle the minestrone over the top. Garnish with the basil leaves, pickled peppers, and sprouts. Squeeze drops of olive oil on the surface of the minestrone. Using a rasp grater, grate Fiore Sardo over the top.

SOYOUNG SCANLAN

Andante Dairy,
Petaluma, California

Soyoung Scanlan was born in Seoul, South Korea, in 1967. Her first and ongoing passion was music, and she was such a good pianist, she became a professional accompanist for Seoul's vocalists, cellists, and violinists—while she was still in college.

But she was a practical young woman and knew she needed a more reliable vocation, and so she studied biotechnology and food engineering (despite the fact that women didn't study such subjects in her country), earning her BA and a master's degree in Korea. Wanting to travel and learn English, she moved to Boston in 1994 to continue her science education. There she met her husband, an acoustical engineer working at Bose. When he was transferred to San Francisco, she joined him, but in her world of science education, she felt disconnected from life and needed to find "something that would use all my senses," she says, "and give me the feeling of being alive."

She and her husband spent close to a month in France, traveling widely in the Alsace and Loire regions. *The food markets!* she thought. *And the cheeses at the markets!* She'd never experienced this kind of cheese—American artisanal cheesemaking was in its infancy.

Soyoung read about a cheesemaker named Cindy Callahan, of Bellwether Farms, one of The French Laundry's first and finest cheesemakers (profiled in the first book), and learned from her about the master's program in dairy science at Cal Poly in central California. Soyoung received a scholarship from a California dairy research association and studied the chemistry of milk for two years.

With her education and dairy science knowledge, she found a job making cheese for Larry Peter, owner of Petaluma Creamery and Spring Hill Jersey Dairy in Petaluma, California, a job that led to finding Barbara Backus of Goat's Leap dairy in St. Helena, north of Yountville, who agreed to give Soyoung space to make her cheese. Soyoung wanted to make a cow's-milk cheese there, but the only person who would sell her small quantities of milk, 30 gallons at a time, was Mr. Peter. So she would drive an hour north from San Francisco to Petaluma at 4 a.m. to pick up the milk, then drive another hour to St. Helena to work on the cheeses. She began to experiment and learn. She mixed goat's milk and cow's milk, something rarely done here in America's burgeoning artisanal cheesemaking scene, though common in Europe.

When she was satisfied with her product, she brought some to the Oakville Grocery, a specialty store near The French Laundry where a lot of chefs would go to find new cheeses. There French Laundry sous chef Eric Ziebold found Soyoung on a tip from Sadie Kendall of Kendall Farms, from whom we bought our crème fraîche (those lids would become our first stencils for the cornets; see page 1). Eric invited Soyoung to The French Laundry and asked her to bring selections of her cheese.

"I'd never been in a professional kitchen before," Soyoung says. "I arrived in the afternoon and the kitchen was in the middle of chaotic prep. I'd heard stories about Chef Keller and I was very nervous. I heard he was scary. But when I arrived, he and Eric shut down prep, covered a steel table with a white tablecloth, and said, 'Everyone, stop, we're going to have a cheese tasting.' He asked all the chefs to put on clean aprons to taste the cheese. It was like a dream. I couldn't believe the respect they were showing me, and my cheese. I'd brought them Nocturne, cow's milk with ash. I name all my cheeses after musical terms, even my company, Andante. I also brought Mélange, a goat-cow mix with a white rind, and Rondo, also goat and cow but with herbs.

"They liked the cheese. I said I didn't have very much. Chef Keller said, 'I'll take everything you have.' I left realizing we hadn't talked price.

So I called Eric and he said, 'Charge us whatever you need in order to keep producing the cheese.'"

Months after we began buying from Soyoung, Goat's Leap had to ask her to leave for business reasons. But she had pounds and pounds of cheese that was in the middle of aging. When she told me, I said, "I'll buy them, and we'll age them here."

She's been with us now for twenty years. She currently sells us a few cheeses and sources European cheeses for us, but we feature her astonishing Etude in different ways in our single cheese course, the gougère.

Soyoung still plays the piano every day. When she's stressed and her mind feels muddled, she plays Bach's *Well-Tempered Clavier* to find balance. And she plays with her thirteen-year-old daughter, who attends a music conservatory. And so both her love of music and her deep knowledge of the sciences come forth in her beautiful cheeses.

EGGPLANT PARMESAN

Roasted Eggplant Galette, Charred Eggplant Béchamel, and Parmesan Mousse

Makes 6 servings

TOMATO RAISINS

30 cherry or Sungold
tomatoes

5 grams pickling lime
(calcium hydroxide)

1 gram kosher salt

500 grams water

100 grams extra-virgin
olive oil

1 garlic clove, skin on,
smashed

1 basil sprig

**CHARRED EGGPLANT
BÉCHAMEL**

375 grams Italian
eggplant

15 grams canola oil

3 grams kosher salt

45 grams whole milk

45 grams heavy cream

20 grams beurre manié
(page 108)

3 grams grated Parmesan
cheese (grated on a
rasp grater)

3 grams roasted garlic
puree (page 133)

3 grams fleur de sel, plus
more to taste

Red wine vinegar

EGGPLANT GALETTE

270 grams Italian
eggplant

20 grams canola oil

7 grams kosher salt

50 grams whole-milk
Greek yogurt

90 grams water

8 grams roasted garlic
puree (page 133)

5 grams sherry vinegar

75 grams all-purpose
flour, plus more for
breading the galette

1 large egg

130 grams egg yolks

100 grams panko
breadcrumbs

Fleur de sel

TO COMPLETE

Olive oil, for frying

Kosher salt

Parmesan mousse
(page 49)

3 or 4 purple basil sprigs
with buds

SPECIAL EQUIPMENT

Dehydrator

Combi oven (optional)

iSi siphon

2 cream chargers

This is David's interpretation of the ever-present Italian classic, with a few French techniques thrown in for good measure. Here David makes a galette, which is actually a roasted eggplant pâte à choux—a great meat substitute in general—which he breads and fries in olive oil. He serves it with a delicious charred eggplant béchamel, a Parmesan mousse, and dehydrated cherry tomatoes, aka "tomato raisins."

FOR THE TOMATO RAISINS

Bring a pot of salted water to a boil. Blanch the tomatoes in the boiling water until their skins just loosen, 3 to 5 seconds. Plunge the tomatoes into an ice-water bath, then drain and peel with a paring knife.

Whisk together the pickling lime, salt, and water in a bowl to dissolve. Add the tomatoes and soak for 1 minute. Drain the tomatoes in a strainer set over a bowl, reserving the lime solution, and thoroughly rinse the tomatoes.

Dry the tomatoes in a dehydrator set to 160°F (71°C) for 4 to 6 hours, until they shrivel and resemble raisins.

Slowly heat the oil in a 1-quart (1-liter) saucepot until just warm. Add the garlic and basil, remove from the heat, and steep for 5 to 10 minutes, until fragrant. Let cool, then add the dehydrated tomatoes.

Refrigerate in a covered container for up to 3 days.

FOR THE CHARRED EGGPLANT BÉCHAMEL

Preheat a salamander or broiler to high.

Pierce the skin of the eggplant several times with a fork. Coat the eggplant with the canola oil, season with the salt, and set on a half sheet pan. Place the eggplant under the salamander or broiler and broil, turning them often, until the skin is heavily charred and the flesh is cooked, 25 to 40 minutes. Transfer the eggplant to a bowl, cover with plastic wrap, and let stand at room temperature for 30 minutes. You will need 100 grams of the charred eggplant for the béchamel; reserve the remainder for the eggplant galette.

(continued)

Bring the milk and cream to a boil in a 1-quart (1-liter) saucepot. Whisk in the beurre manié and simmer for about 1 minute, whisking frequently so it does not stick to the pot.

Transfer to a blender and blend on low speed for 2 to 3 minutes, until homogenous. Add 100 grams of the charred eggplant, the Parmesan, roasted garlic puree, and fleur de sel. Blend on high until perfectly smooth. Adjust the seasoning with vinegar and additional fleur de sel to taste. If you will be using the béchamel within 1 hour, transfer it to a disposable piping bag and keep in a warm spot. The béchamel can be refrigerated in an airtight container with a piece of plastic wrap pressed directly against the surface for up to 2 days.

FOR THE EGGPLANT GALETTE

Preheat the oven to 350°F (180°C). Line a half sheet pan with parchment paper.

Peel the eggplant and cut into medium dice. Toss with the canola oil and 4 grams of the salt and spread on the prepared pan. Bake for 20 to 25 minutes, until just tender. Remove from the oven and set aside.

If you have a combi oven, preheat it to 100°C (212°F).

Place 35 grams of the reserved charred eggplant, the yogurt, 70 grams of the water, the roasted garlic puree, the vinegar, and the remaining 3 grams salt in a blender and blend until smooth. Transfer to a 2-quart (2-liter) saucepot and bring to a boil. Reduce the heat to medium-high. Quickly stir in the flour with a wooden spoon until a ball of dough forms. Reduce the heat to medium-low and stir until the dough easily pulls away from the sides of the pan and the bottom is lightly toasted, 2 to 4 minutes. The dough should no longer feel tacky.

Transfer the dough ball to the bowl of a stand mixer fitted with the paddle and mix on low speed until the steam dissipates. Increase the speed to medium, add the egg, and mix until fully incorporated. Scrape the sides of the bowl and the paddle. With the mixer on low speed, add the remaining charred eggplant and mix just to incorporate.

Lightly dampen a large cutting board and lay a piece of plastic wrap on it. Cut six 6-inch (15-centimeter) squares from the plastic wrap. Place about 65 grams of the galette mixture in the center of each plastic square. Fold in the edges of the plastic wrap and shape the galette mixture into small oval patties, just under ½ inch (1.25 centimeters) thick. Press the packets lightly to fill in any voids and place on a sheet pan.

Steam the patties in the combi oven, still wrapped in the plastic, for 15 minutes, until set and just firm to the touch. If you do not have a combi oven, set a basket steamer in a pot large enough for the basket to fit fully extended. Add water to the pot, keeping it at least 1½ inches (4 centimeters) below the basket, and bring to a boil over high heat. Lay the patties in the basket in a single layer, cover, and steam for 15 to 17 minutes, until set and just firm to the touch. Refrigerate the galettes, still wrapped in the plastic, until cold.

Whisk together the egg yolks and the remaining 20 grams water in a small bowl. Put some flour in a separate bowl. Crush the panko with your hands and place in a third bowl. Lightly dust each galette with flour, shaking off any excess, then dip in the egg wash. Lift from the egg wash, letting any excess run off, and transfer to the bowl of panko. Toss to coat completely, gently packing the panko against the galette to help it adhere. Arrange the patties in a container, cover with any excess panko, and refrigerate until ready to fry, up to 4 hours.

TO COMPLETE

Remove the eggplant galettes from the refrigerator about 30 minutes before frying to temper slightly.

Place the tomato raisins on a paper towel to drain.

If the béchamel was refrigerated, reheat it in a microwave in 15-second intervals, stirring after each interval, for 1 minute. Transfer the béchamel to a disposable piping bag. Keep in a warm spot until ready to plate.

Fill a skillet large enough to hold the galettes in one layer with ¼ inch (6 millimeters) of olive oil. Heat the oil over medium-high heat. Shake excess panko from the galettes and add them to the hot oil. Fry, adjusting heat as necessary, for about 3 minutes per side, until golden brown. Remove from the oil, drain on paper towels, and season with salt.

Transfer the Parmesan mousse to a siphon and charge it with two cream chargers, shaking the siphon vigorously between charges and after charging to ensure it is fully aerated for use.

Pipe a large dollop of the béchamel in the center of each serving plate and place a galette alongside it. Garnish with tomato raisins and basil leaves and buds. Siphon the Parmesan mousse into a bowl and spoon a dollop over the top at the table to finish.

PICKLES AND VEGETABLE PRESERVATION

PICKLES AND OTHER VEGETABLE cures are really important to us. The French Laundry garden has become so valued that David likes to remind us that the gardeners—not the chefs—run the kitchen. We simply utilize what they come in with. In California, we have a long growing season, so we have extraordinary bounty most of the year; yet there are periods where the gardeners simply have to pick all the turnips, all the cucumbers, all the peppers or the vegetables will go bad. And when they do pick them, it's our responsibility not to waste them. We don't make an extraordinary turnip chutney because it's great in itself; we develop a chutney so that we don't waste the turnips, and it's up to us to make it an extraordinary garnish. No one said, "Let's ferment parsnips and make a great cream for crudités." Fermentation is a way to preserve the vegetable and develop flavor. You have to move with the rhythm of the garden.

The following are just a few of our preservation methods for pickling and preserving vegetables.

Blue-Ribbon Pickle

Makes about 850 grams

375 grams water

225 grams distilled white vinegar

105 grams dill leaves and tender stems

90 grams sugar

55 grams kosher salt

9 grams sliced tender yellow celery leaves (⅛-inch-thick/ 3-millimeter slices)

6 grams thinly sliced garlic

3 grams mustard seeds

3 grams black peppercorns

0.5 grams allspice berries

0.5 grams coriander seeds

0.75 grams chili flakes

Pickled Ají Dulce Peppers

750 grams ají dulce peppers

Pickled Persian Cucumbers

3 (4- to 6-inch-long/ 10- to 15-centimeter) Persian cucumbers, cut into ⅛-inch-thick (3-millimeter) rounds

Pickled Yellow Celery

3 or 4 yellow celery heart stalks, sliced 2 millimeters thick

---

SPECIAL EQUIPMENT

Chamber vacuum sealer (optional)

This recipe comes from David Breeden's grandmother Betty Breeden, who helped to raise him and to whom he was devoted. It's our all-purpose pickle—anything that benefits from pickling can be used with this: onions, fennel, turnips. David more or less worked backward from taste memories to re-create it. He thinks the balance of salt and sugar and acid is exactly as he remembers it as a child. And the spices, he says, are just an old-fashioned Southern-style pickling mix: allspice, coriander, mustard seed, pepper, dill, chili flakes, garlic, and celery.

This pickle is brought to a boil on the stovetop. Depending on the vegetable, it is either poured hot over the vegetable or cooled first.

Place the water, vinegar, dill, sugar, salt, celery leaves, garlic, mustard seeds, peppercorns, allspice, coriander, and chili flakes in a 2-quart (2-liter) saucepot and bring the pickling liquid to a boil over high heat.

For Pickled Ají Dulce Peppers: Stem the peppers and leave them whole, or seed them and cut them into ¼-inch-thick (6-millimeter) slices. Place the whole or sliced peppers in a bowl large enough to hold them and the pickling liquid.

Pour the hot pickling liquid over the peppers and place a clean kitchen towel over them to ensure that they remain submerged in the liquid. Let cool to room temperature, then nestle the bowl in an ice-water bath to cool completely.

For Pickled Persian Cucumbers or Yellow Celery: Transfer the pickling liquid to a bowl and nestle the bowl in an ice-water bath to chill. Add the sliced cucumber or celery to the bowl with the chilled pickling liquid.

IF YOU HAVE A CHAMBER VACUUM SEALER

Transfer the vegetable and pickling liquid to a sous vide bag. Place in the sealer chamber and vacuum seal. The pickles can be used immediately or refrigerated in the bag for 3 months.

IF YOU DO NOT HAVE A CHAMBER VACUUM SEALER

Transfer the vegetable and pickling liquid to an airtight container and refrigerate for at least 3 days before using. The pickles can be refrigerated for up to 3 months.

Pickled Pearl Onions and the 2:1:1 Pickle

Yield varies (makes enough pickling liquid for 18 pearl onions)

50 grams champagne
    vinegar
50 grams sugar
100 grams water
2 grams kosher salt
Red pearl onions, peeled

SPECIAL EQUIPMENT
Japanese mandoline
    (optional)
Chamber vacuum sealer
    (optional)

This is used in the Smoked Sturgeon Rillettes on an Everything Bagel (page 23), but it's really a versatile garnish for just about anything that needs an acidic counterpoint. But the real purpose of this recipe is the ratio—it's a 2:1:1 pickle. That is, 2 parts water, 1 part vinegar, and 1 part sugar. It's a great ratio to pickle any vegetable. We usually just season with salt by eye, but if you wanted to be precise, you could go as high as adding up to 3% salt, which would preserve the onions further (here by adding 6 grams of salt). We use this simple pickle to season our vegetables and give them crunch by vacuum sealing them, which forces the pickle into the vegetable. We do this right before service, and they become super-crunchy. If you don't have a chamber vacuum sealer, be sure to pickle your vegetables for at least six hours before using.

Combine the vinegar, sugar, water, and salt in a 1-quart (1-liter) saucepot and heat over medium-high heat, whisking occasionally, until the sugar has dissolved. Pour the pickling liquid into a bowl and nestle the bowl in an ice-water bath to cool.

For Petals and Brunoise: Cut the pearl onions in half through the root end. Cut off the root and cut each half into 3 wedges. Peel away the outer leaves to create "petals." If making a brunoise, cut the petals into ⅛-inch (3-millimeter) cubes.

For Slices (Rings): Cut the pearl onions into 1- to 2-millimeter-thick rings using a Japanese mandoline.

If you have a chamber vacuum sealer, put the onions and pickling liquid in a sous vide bag. Place in the sealer chamber and vacuum seal. If you do not have a vacuum sealer, put the onions in the bowl with the pickling liquid and cover.

Refrigerate the onions for at least 2 hours or up to 1 day before using.

Pickled Fennel Bulb

Yield varies

Brined Fennel
1,800 grams water
18 grams kosher salt
1 fennel bulb

Pickle
120 grams Pernod
300 grams distilled white
    vinegar
30 grams kosher salt
30 grams sugar

1 head garlic, halved
4.5 grams fennel seed
1.5 grams star anise
1 gram coriander seeds
0.3 grams chili flakes

We use this pickle in our Crudités (page 100) to accompany fresh compressed fennel. It's another terrific all-purpose pickle.

BRINE THE FENNEL

Whisk together the water and salt in a medium saucepot and bring to a boil. Let cool.

Cut across the bottom of the fennel bulb to remove the root. Slice the bulb in half lengthwise and peel away the layers of fennel, keeping the pieces as large as possible. Pour the cooled brine into a small bowl, add the fennel to the bowl, and place a clean kitchen towel on the surface to ensure that the fennel pieces are completely submerged. Brine in the refrigerator for 24 hours.

MAKE THE PICKLE

Pour the Pernod into a 2-quart (2-liter) saucepot and bring to a boil over high heat, allowing it to flame and reduce by half, about 1 minute. Add the vinegar, salt, sugar, garlic, fennel seed, star anise, coriander, and chili flakes, whisk, and return to a boil. Remove from the heat, strain into a bowl, and nestle the bowl in an ice-water bath to chill.

Remove the fennel from the brine and rinse. Place the fennel and the pickle in a sous vide bag. Place the bag in the chamber vacuum sealer and vacuum seal. Refrigerate the bag overnight to pickle the fennel. The fennel and pickling liquid can be transferred to an airtight container and refrigerated for up to 3 months.

THE REMARKABLE VEG BLANC

The discovery of veg blanc—one of our most useful ways to prepare vegetables—came in response to a surprise, but the method's evolution has been spurred by our desire to continually improve, explore, become more efficient.

One day a few years back, per se received an unexpected delivery of fifty pounds of cardoons. We love the cardoon, a thistle in the artichoke family prized for its celery-like stalks and artichoke-like flavor, but we couldn't possibly use that much before it would spoil. Someone recalled a recipe for *cardons stérilisés*, or preserved cardoons, and eventually located it in a French cookbook called *Flaveurs* by Swiss chef Philippe Rochat. It was a simple recipe, with trimmed cardoons, water, salt, sugar, and ascorbic acid all placed in a canning jar and boiled for about half an hour to make the vegetables shelf stable for the season.

It worked well. And with some experimentation and adjustments (increasing the concentration of the salt, sugar, and ascorbic acid), it worked even better. We knew this would be a great medium for vegetables cooked sous vide.

Because the cardoons are in the thistle family like artichokes, we tried putting turned artichokes in the mixture. Artichokes oxidize, or discolor, very quickly. Common practice is to put them into water acidulated with lemon juice. When we put them in this new mixture, not only did they stay white, but hearts that had oxidized would be completely refreshed after a few minutes. We named this new liquid veg blanc and began using it with nearly *all* our nongreen vegetables—onions, potatoes, carrots, salsify, sunchokes, you name it. All yielded great results. To reiterate, virtually all nongreen vegetables are sealed and cured or cooked in veg blanc.

Cèpes are a mushroom we love for their meaty texture and flavor, but their season is very short, especially in spring. Compressed in veg blanc, however, they'll keep beautifully for weeks. So now we buy them in abundance when they're in season and the veg blanc extends their season by a month or more.

Even vegetables served raw, like radish or fennel, are compressed in veg blanc for a brief "cure," for anywhere from a few minutes to a few hours, depending on the porousness of the vegetable and how it has been prepared. When treated this way, they come out of the bag seasoned throughout and beautifully crisp.

Of course, one thing leads to something just a little better. Why don't we *flavor* that water first? Infuse the water with fennel fronds, make a veg blanc using this fennel-frond water to cook fennel bulb.

Or must it be water? What if we juiced carrots and added the dry ingredients for the veg blanc, for a "Carrot Veg Blanc," and cooked the carrots in this? It turned out to be brilliant.

We've been working with Bruno Goussault of Cuisine Solutions since we began exploring sous vide cooking. Since then, we've learned so much from him, such as his technique of cryoconcentrating vegetable essences (he freezes vegetable juices, separating the flavorful solids from the water to make intense concentrates). And from this we've learned that rather than juicing a vegetable, we can make a concentrated infusion by vacuum sealing the typically discarded elements of a vegetable with veg blanc and cooking them for a few hours; the intensely flavored juice is wrung from the solids. For example, in the Tout Artichaut recipe (page 148), we take all the artichoke leaves left over from turning artichokes—there are piles of them—and cook them. We then strain the infused cooking liquid, or *cuisson*, and use it as the flavor base for a sauce, mounting it with butter and thickening it with a liaison (see page 108). It's hard to give Bruno enough credit for all he taught us.

We use the same principle with Belgian endive, leeks, or mushrooms, cooking them in veg blanc, then using the *cuisson* to make a vinaigrette or glaze by utilizing one of our liaisons. One simple technique yields exceptional results. And an unexpected fifty pounds of cardoons can transform a kitchen for years.

Veg Blanc, Powdered and Prepared

Makes 600 grams powder base (enough for 10,000 grams prepared veg blanc)

POWDER BASE
300 grams kosher salt
250 grams sugar

50 grams ascorbic acid

Filtered water

PREPARED VEG BLANC

FOR THE POWDER BASE

Mix all the ingredients together and store in an airtight container at room temperature.

FOR THE PREPARED VEG BLANC

For every 100 grams prepared veg blanc needed, whisk together 100 grams filtered water and 6 grams of the powder base.

Fermented Parsnips

150 grams parsnips or
    parsnip peel
2.25 grams kosher salt

This is a very gentle cure. Most pickles use at least 3% salt, but this fermented parsnip requires only 1.5% salt.

If using whole parsnips, using a vegetable peeler, peel along the length of the parsnips to create thin shavings, 3½ to 4 inches (9 to 10 centimeters) long. Season with the salt. Place in an 8 by 12-inch (20 by 30-centimeter) sous vide bag. Place the bag in a chamber vacuum sealer and vacuum seal, then place in a dehydrator and dehydrate at 160°F (71°C) for 2 weeks. The bag will expand as the parsnip ferments and may look as if it might burst. After 2 weeks, pierce the bag to release the pressure. The parsnips will smell pungent. The fermented parsnips can be used right away or refrigerated in a covered container for up to 3 months.

Ají Dulce Chili Paste

Makes 800 grams

500 grams ají dulce
    peppers
120 grams distilled white
    vinegar
120 grams water
40 grams sugar
25 grams kosher salt

5 grams garlic
2.5 grams citric acid
10 grams Pre-Hy
    (page 109)

While we don't think of pastes as pickles, these peppers are, in fact, combined with vinegar, citric acid, salt, sugar, and an aromatic—thus a pickle no matter the texture, and one that will keep, like a pickle, in the fridge for several months. This particularly delicious condiment is made from maybe our favorite pepper, which is becoming increasingly popular around the country.

Use the paste as you would any pepper pastes you have in your pantry, like sambal or sriracha. It's a go-to flavor booster for anything, and does so without heat. Ají dulci is not spicy but rather sweet, with a beautiful floral aroma. Use it in any tomato-based sauce or to season spicy lobster broth. We make this in the fall and usually have 40 quarts to last us through the winter.

Stem the peppers and wash them thoroughly. Place the peppers, vinegar, water, sugar, salt, garlic, citric acid, and Pre-Hy in a blender and puree until blended but not completely smooth. Transfer the mixture to a 2-quart (2-liter) saucepot and bring to a boil over high heat. Reduce the heat to medium and cook for 5 minutes. Immediately transfer the paste to a bowl and nestle the bowl in an ice-water bath to chill. Store in an airtight container in the refrigerator for up to several months and use as needed.

Pickled Mustard Seeds

Makes 250 grams

125 grams yellow
  mustard seeds
	250 grams champagne
	  vinegar
		125 grams water

125 grams brown mustard seeds	125 grams sugar	10 grams kosher salt

We mainly use these as a textural and visual element in our Smoked Montana Rainbow Trout Chaud-Froid (page 126), but they can be added to most any vinaigrette or sauce where appropriate. They're fabulous in a gribiche sauce.

Place the yellow and brown mustard seeds in a 1-quart (1-liter) saucepot and cover with cold water. Bring the water to a rolling boil, then drain immediately. Repeat this process twice more.

In a small clean pot, combine the vinegar, sugar, water, and salt and bring to a boil, whisking to ensure the sugar and salt have dissolved. Add the blanched mustard seeds and return to a rolling boil. Boil vigorously for 5 minutes.

Transfer to a storage container and let cool, uncovered, to room temperature. Cover the container with a lid and refrigerate for up to 1 month. Drain the mustard seeds before using.

ON BRINING AND CURING FISH

We used to have any number of ways to handle fish, but during the past ten years or so, we've refined and streamlined our methods, thanks to the influence of both our chefs de cuisine. We now submerge almost all fish in a 10% brine for between 10 and 30 minutes, depending on the thickness of the fillet.

David Breeden, chef de cuisine at The French Laundry, is obsessive about this. Coming from Tennessee country, where fishing in the rivers was part of life, he'll tell you, "I'm very particular with fish." He's so concerned about bacteria and spoilage and cleanliness that his fish go straight into a brine when he's done cutting them, and they wait there while he washes his station down. This is standard practice among all our fish butchers, even with lobster. It makes sense—ocean fish is returned to ocean water.

The primary reason for the 10% brine, for both freshwater and saltwater fish, is cleanliness, eliminating any surface bacteria that could affect the delicate flesh. But there are other benefits, too. The brine improves the texture of the fish as it draws out moisture, and the salt in the brine seasons the fish, improving its flavor. It also helps to set the albumen, the protein in the fish's flesh that congeals when exposed to heat, which gives cooked fish a better appearance. We then refrigerate it for 12 hours to allow moisture to evaporate.

And finally, the dehydration caused by brining makes the fish easier and better to cook. If you take a piece of fish off the bone and try to sauté it, no matter how hot the pan, the fish is going to steam due to the moisture in its flesh. Brining first will remove this excess moisture.

This from David, a man after my own heart: "If you take a nice pavé of halibut, and brine it first? Then refrigerate it overnight? You coat that fish in some mayonnaise and crushed Ritz crackers and broil it? You're going to have a piece of fish like you've *never* had before."

Corey loves to serve crudo, such as the hiramasa on page 110. He packs this fish in what we call our citrus cure—3 parts sugar to 2 parts salt, and the zest from a lemon, a lime, and an orange. Fish he wants to serve raw will almost always get 30 minutes or so in this cure. The salt takes care of any residual bacteria and, much as it does in a brine, improves texture and flavor through concentration and seasoning.

Brining is so important that all three of us—David, Corey, and myself—recommend brining all fish, even it will be packed in a dry cure. (The single exception is tuna; its lean red flesh doesn't like a brine.)

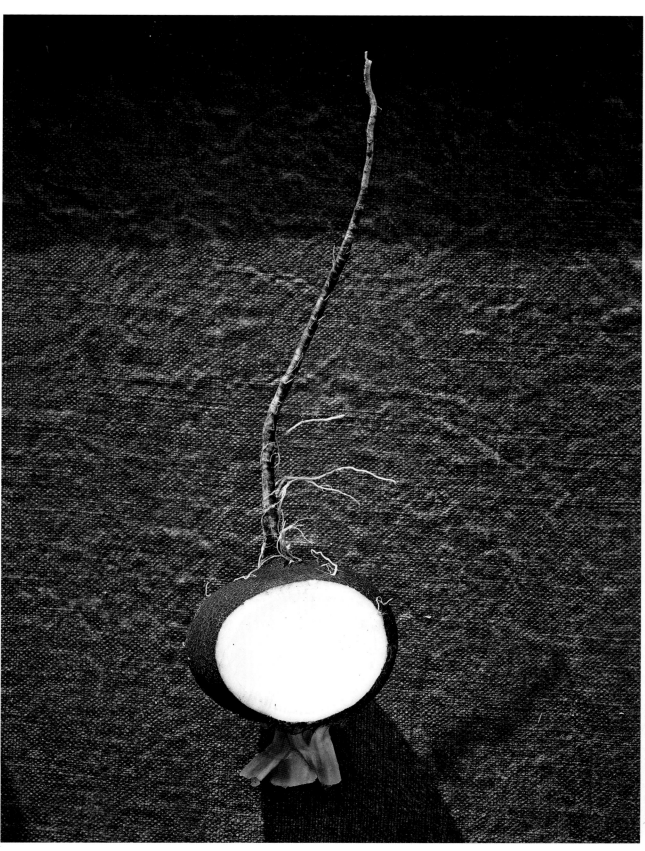

MOLOKAI SWEET POTATO MILLE-FEUILLE

Compressed Asian Pear, Chrysanthemum Shoots, and Caramelized Onion Jus

Makes 6 servings

MILLE-FEUILLE

175 grams clarified butter (page 53)

400 grams peeled Molokai sweet potato, about 2½ inches (6.5 centimeters) in diameter

200 grams peeled russet potato, about 2½ inches (6.5 centimeters) in diameter

8 grams kosher salt

COMPRESSED ASIAN PEAR

90 grams water

90 grams sugar

30 grams yuzu juice

Sea salt

1 Asian pear

CARAMELIZED ONION JUS

100 grams sherry vinegar, plus more to taste

875 grams water

600 grams sweet onion essence (page 288)

600 grams mushroom essence (page 289)

15 grams dehydrated caramelized onions (recipe follows)

7 grams thyme sprigs

3 garlic cloves, skin on, smashed

1 bay leaf

12 grams Pre-Hy (page 109)

Kosher salt

CREAMED ARROWLEAF SPINACH

75 grams whole butter

100 grams diced leek (white and light green portions only), rinsed to remove any dirt

200 grams heavy cream

500 grams stemmed arrowleaf spinach leaves

8 grams Pre-Hy (page 109)

Kosher salt

TO COMPLETE

40 grams potato flakes

1 recipe cornstarch–egg white paste (page 235)

30 grams clarified butter (page 53), or more as needed

Chrysanthemum shoots

SPECIAL EQUIPMENT

Chamber vacuum sealer (optional)

Japanese mandoline

Immersion circulator (optional)

Flower-shaped cutter, just over ½ inch (13 millimeters) in diameter

Combi oven (optional)

This dish originated because of the shape of the vegetables we were using. We've always done some form of mille-feuille potato, a shingled or scalloped dish. When we found ourselves with a colorful variety of small marble potatoes, we scalloped them in a sheet pan, making a virtue of their varying sizes and colors. When we discovered the richly flavored purple Molokai sweet potato, we used this same technique. We love its deep coloring, its sweetness, and the savory depth of the spinach, pear, and onion jus that makes this vegetarian dish as satisfying as a meat course.

FOR THE MILLE-FEUILLE

If you have a chamber vacuum sealer, put an eighth sheet pan in a 12 by 15-inch (30 by 40-centimeter) sous vide bag, place in the sealer chamber, and vacuum seal. If you do not have a chamber vacuum sealer, spray an eighth sheet pan with nonstick spray. Line the pan with two layers of plastic wrap, extending it over the sides.

Put the clarified butter in a wide 3-quart (3-liter) saucepot, heat just enough to melt the butter, and keep warm.

Set a Japanese mandoline over a bowl. Slice the potatoes lengthwise into 1-millimeter-thick (paper-thin) slices. Adjust the blade as necessary to be certain that the slices are solid and of even thickness. Season with the salt. Gently toss the potato slices in the pan with the clarified butter to coat.

Overlap (shingle) the potato slices, alternating between the sweet potatoes and the russet potatoes (use 2 slices of sweet potato, then 1 slice of russet), in even rows to cover the bottom of the prepared sheet pan in a solid layer. Cover the potatoes with a piece of parchment paper, set a second eighth sheet pan on top, and press down to secure the potato slices in place. Remove the top pan and the parchment and arrange a second layer of potato slices over the first. Continue to layer the potatoes, pressing with the parchment and sheet pan after each layer is complete. The final layer of potatoes should be level with the rim of the pan.

(continued)

If you have a chamber vacuum sealer, set an immersion circulator in a water bath and heat the water to 88°C (190.4°F). Wrap the entire sheet pan twice in plastic wrap, place it in a 12 by 15-inch (30 by 40-centimeter) sous vide bag, and vacuum seal. Cook in the water bath for 1½ hours. Remove from the water bath and let rest for 15 minutes, then submerge in an ice-water bath until cold. Refrigerate for up to 2 days.

If you do not have a chamber vacuum sealer, preheat the oven to 300°F (150°C). Place a piece of parchment on top of the mille-feuille and seal the pan with a piece of aluminum foil. Bake for about 1 hour, until a cake tester inserted into the potatoes meets no resistance. Remove the foil but leave the parchment over the top. Set a second eighth sheet pan on the parchment and add weight to the pan to compress the potatoes; let stand for about 30 minutes. Transfer the potatoes with the weights to the refrigerator and refrigerate for at least 6 hours or up to 2 days.

FOR THE COMPRESSED ASIAN PEAR

Combine the water, sugar, and yuzu juice in a 2-quart (2-liter) saucepot and warm over medium-high heat, stirring often, just enough to dissolve the sugar. Pour the syrup into a bowl and season to taste with sea salt. Nestle the bowl in an ice-water bath and let cool completely.

Peel the pear and slice it just under ¼ inch (6 millimeters) thick on a Japanese mandoline. If you have a chamber vacuum sealer, put the slices of pear and the syrup in a sous vide bag. Place in the sealer chamber and vacuum seal. The pears can be used immediately or refrigerated for up to 3 days. Punch it with a flower-shaped cutter just over ½ inch (13 millimeters) in diameter just before using.

If you do not have a chamber vacuum sealer, punch the pear with a flower-shaped cutter just over ½ inch (13 millimeters) in diameter and place the pieces directly in the syrup. Refrigerate in a covered container for at least 24 hours or up to 3 days.

FOR THE CARAMELIZED ONION JUS

Reduce the vinegar in a 4-quart (4-liter) saucepot over high heat until the pan is almost dry.

Add the water, onion essence, mushroom essence, dehydrated caramelized onions, thyme, garlic, and bay leaf to the saucepot. Bring to a boil, then reduce the heat and simmer for about 15 minutes.

Place a dampened tea towel in a strainer set over a medium bowl. Strain the liquid into a 2-quart (2-liter) saucepot. Bring to a simmer and reduce to 300 grams.

Strain the liquid into a blender. With the blender running on medium speed, add the Pre-Hy and blend to combine. Season with additional vinegar and salt to taste. Strain through a chinois into a container and cover.

Refrigerate for up to 3 days.

FOR THE CREAMED ARROWLEAF SPINACH

Heat the butter in a 1-quart (1-liter) saucepot over medium-high heat until it begins to brown. Add the leek to the saucepot and sweat over low heat until tender, about 30 minutes.

Add the cream to the saucepot and bring it to a boil. Cook, stirring often, until the cream mixture is very thick. It will have the consistency of a glaze and look as though it is about to split.

Bring a pot of water to a boil. Blanch the spinach in the boiling water until tender, about 3 minutes. Drain the spinach and transfer to a clean kitchen towel. Wring out any excess moisture. Place 135 grams of the spinach in the blender. Add the glazed leek and Pre-Hy; blend until smooth, using the tamper to help the mixture combine. Taste the creamed spinach and season with salt. Keep in a warm spot for up to 4 hours before serving or transfer to an airtight container and refrigerate for up to 2 days.

TO COMPLETE

Warm the caramelized onion jus and the creamed spinach in separate saucepots, if needed. Fill a disposable piping bag with the creamed spinach and pipe it into a small squeeze bottle.

Remove the mille-feuille from the refrigerator and work with the potatoes while they are cold. Remove the weights or plastic. Lift the potatoes from the pan and place on a cutting board. Trim just enough of the mille-feuille to smooth the edges. Cut crosswise in half, then cut each half crosswise into 3 equal portions.

Lightly crush the potato flakes in your hands and place in a shallow bowl. Put the cornstarch paste in a separate shallow bowl. Dip the bottom of each mille-feuille in the cornstarch paste, then dip in the potato flakes to coat.

Heat the clarified butter in a large sauté pan over medium heat. Working in batches, add the mille-feuille to the pan, crust-side down, and sauté for 2 to 3 minutes, until the bottom is golden brown. Transfer the mille-feuille to a cutting board, crust-side down, and cut each piece into 3 equal pieces. Drain briefly on paper towels. Repeat with the remaining mille-feuille. If the mille-feuille have cooled before you're ready to serve them, transfer them to a rack set over a sheet pan and rewarm in a preheated 375°F (190°C) oven for about 6 minutes, until warmed throughout.

Arrange the mille-feuille on the serving plates. Garnish with pieces of the Asian pear, dots of the creamed spinach, and chrysanthemum shoots. Spoon a few pools of the caramelized onion jus onto each plate.

Dehydrated Caramelized Onions

Makes 60 grams

700 grams yellow onions
10 grams canola oil
500 grams water

SPECIAL EQUIPMENT
Japanese mandoline
Dehydrator

Cut ¼ inch (6 millimeters) from the root end and ½ inch (1.25 centimeters) from the stem end of the onions. Halve them through the root and peel them. Using a Japanese mandoline, slice the onions lengthwise into pieces as long and thin as possible.

Spread the onions in a shallow layer in a wide saucepot. Add the oil and cook over medium-low heat, stirring often, for 8 to 10 minutes, until the natural sugars in the onions caramelize to a rich golden brown without burning.

Once a layer of caramelization or fond has formed on the bottom of the pan, add one-third of the water and use a silicone spatula to deglaze the pan. Cook until the pan is dry. If the pan begins to scorch, transfer the onions to a clean pan. Cook until the onions are a very dark brown, about 1 hour 20 minutes total, deglazing twice more when the fond builds up on the bottom of the pan.

Line a sheet pan with a nonstick silicone baking mat and spread the onions in a 9 by 12-inch (23 by 30-centimeter) layer over the mat. Dry in a dehydrator set to 150°F (65.5°C) for 14 to 18 hours, until the onions are very dry. The onions must be crisp when cool.

Use the dehydrated caramelized onions as is, or grind into a powder in a spice grinder to use as a seasoning. Store in an airtight container at room temperature for up to 3 months.

YUKON GOLD POTATO RÔTI À LA BROCHE

Broccoli Spigarello, Cashew Milk, and Black Winter Truffle

Makes 6 servings

TAMARI-MARINATED YUKON GOLD POTATOES

6 Yukon Gold potatoes, 3½ to 4 inches (9 to 10 centimeters) long and about 2½ inches (6.5 centimeters) wide

If vacuum-sealing

55 grams sugar

225 grams tamari

135 grams mirin

95 grams sake

Without vacuum-sealing

110 grams sugar

450 grams tamari

270 grams mirin

190 grams sake

CASHEW MILK

200 grams cashews

375 grams water

2 grams Pre-Hy (page 109)

1.5 grams kosher salt

10 grams minced black winter truffle (optional)

TO COMPLETE

Clarified butter (page 53)

30 leaves broccoli spigarello

Kosher salt

18 brassica flowers

SPECIAL EQUIPMENT

Chamber vacuum sealer (optional)

iSi siphon

2 cream chargers

In this dish, potatoes are marinated in tamari, modeled after *nikujaga*, braised meat and potatoes in mirin, soy, and sake—one of Corey's favorite Japanese dishes. The tamari brings a meaty umami to the potatoes. After marinating for 12 hours, they're cooked in a rotisserie. They're fantastic, especially with the sautéed broccoli spigarello. We finish the dish with toasted cashews, spoonfuls of delicious cashew milk (water, roasted cashews, and truffle), and flowers. Corey can make this vegan by substituting extra-virgin olive oil for the clarified butter.

FOR THE TAMARI-MARINATED YUKON GOLD POTATOES

Peel the potatoes and trim them to about 130 grams each, keeping them as long as possible. Scrub the potatoes with a new scouring pad to smooth away any sharp edges.

Place the sugar in a 2-quart (2-liter) saucepot and add enough tamari to cover; reserve the remaining tamari. Heat over medium heat, stirring, until the sugar has dissolved, then transfer to a medium bowl and stir in the mirin, sake, and remaining tamari.

If you have a chamber vacuum sealer, place the potatoes and the marinade in a sous vide bag. Place in the sealer chamber and vacuum seal.

If you do not have a chamber vacuum sealer, arrange the potatoes in a container and pour the marinade over. Press a piece of plastic wrap against the potatoes and weight with a small plate to keep the potatoes submerged in the marinade.

Marinate the potatoes in the refrigerator for at least 12 hours or up to 3 days.

FOR THE CASHEW MILK

Preheat the oven to 350°F (180°C). Line a quarter sheet pan with a piece of parchment paper or a nonstick silicone baking mat.

Spread the cashews over the prepared pan. Toast the nuts in the oven until they are golden brown, about 12 minutes. Remove 50 grams of the cashews and reserve for garnishing the dish and toast the remaining cashews until they are dark brown, 3 to 6 minutes more.

(continued)

Put the water in a food processor and add the dark toasted nuts while still warm. Pulse the cashews just until the nuts are coarsely chopped and broken up; do not puree. Pour the cashew milk into a clean dry siphon and seal the lid tightly. Charge the siphon with two cream chargers, shaking the siphon vigorously between charges and after charging, to ensure it is fully aerated for use. Allow the cashew milk to sit in the siphon, undisturbed, for about 1 hour, giving the cashew milk time to settle.

Line a strainer with a double layer of dampened cheesecloth and set it over a bowl. Release the gas from the siphon. Carefully open the lid and pour the cashew milk through the cheesecloth. Squeeze the cheesecloth well to extract as much liquid as possible. Discard the cashews.

Pour 200 grams of the cashew milk into a blender. With the blender on medium speed, add the Pre-Hy and blend until incorporated. Pour into a bowl and stir in the salt and truffle (if using).

The cashew milk can be refrigerated in an airtight container for up to 3 days. Rewarm in a small saucepot before serving.

TO COMPLETE

To spit-roast the potatoes: At the restaurant, we spit-roast the potatoes on the middle spit in the middle setting of our rotisserie on a high flame; the soy marinade will burn if the potatoes are too close to the fire. Brush the potatoes with clarified butter, roast for 25 minutes, then brush with butter and roast, brushing with additional butter every 10 minutes, for 20 to 25 minutes more, until the potatoes have a rich golden brown exterior with a tender, creamy interior.

To oven-roast the potatoes: Preheat the oven to 400°F (205°C). Put a cooling rack over a sheet pan and place a piece of aluminum foil on top of the rack.

Place the potatoes on the foil and brush them generously on all sides with clarified butter. Bake for 20 minutes, brush with clarified butter, and turn and rotate the potatoes. Bake for 10 minutes more, then brush, turn, and rotate again. Roast until the potatoes have a rich golden brown exterior and a tender, creamy interior, about 10 minutes more.

Just before serving, remove the tougher stem from the bottom of each leaf of broccoli spigarello and rinse the leaves. If the leaves are very large, split them in half lengthwise and dry thoroughly with a clean kitchen towel.

Heat a large sauté pan over high heat. Add enough clarified butter to lightly coat the bottom of the pan. When the butter is shimmering, add the broccoli spigarello leaves. Do not overcrowd the pan, or the broccoli will steam rather than sauté. Sprinkle with salt. Cook for 10 to 20 seconds, until the leaves are lightly wilted. Remove from the pan.

Slice the potatoes in half lengthwise. Place one half on each plate and angle the other on top. Drape the broccoli spigarello over the potatoes and garnish with 3 or 4 of the reserved toasted cashews. Finish with a spoonful of the cashew milk and the brassica flowers.

CELERY ROOT PASTRAMI

Pumpernickel Melba, Petite Lettuces, Persian Cucumbers, and Burgundy Mustard

Makes 6 servings

PASTRAMI SPICE

40 grams black peppercorns

40 grams coriander seeds

20 grams juniper berries

10 grams yellow mustard seeds

10 grams brown mustard seeds

CELERY ROOT PASTRAMI

500 grams water

5 grams kosher salt

13 grams liquid smoke

2 (250-gram) peeled celery roots

Cornstarch–egg white paste (page 235)

PUMPERNICKEL MELBA

Clarified butter (page 53)

Kosher salt

Pumpernickel or rye loaf, frozen

BURGUNDY MUSTARD CONDIMENT

190 grams clover honey

190 grams water

3.75 grams agar-agar

190 grams Burgundy mustard

75 grams whole-grain mustard

38 grams preserved horseradish

15 grams champagne vinegar

7.5 grams fleur de sel

7.5 grams lemon juice

4.5 grams Pre-Hy (page 109)

TO COMPLETE

24 small romaine or Little Gem lettuce leaves

Clarified butter (page 53)

72 slices pickled Persian cucumbers (see page 183)

Extra-virgin olive oil

Red wine vinegar

SPECIAL EQUIPMENT

Chamber vacuum sealer

Electric slicer

3-inch (75-millimeter) fluted round cutter

Press pan (optional)

As vegetables move increasingly toward the center of the plate, Corey looks for inspiration in classic American meat staples to develop new vegetable dishes that have the impact of a meat course. Here he treats the versatile celery root like a beef brisket, corning it and roasting it with pastrami spices. It's a pastrami on rye, per se–style, by way of Katz's Deli.

The celery root is fragrant, delicious, and satisfying, and it can be used in so many ways. A classic celeriac salad is one of my favorites; it can also be sliced and deep-fried or boiled and mashed. Here it's brined, cooked, then dehydrated to intensify its flavor and give it a denser texture, a technique both kitchens use with many vegetables.

The great technique here is one used with so many of our root vegetables and squashes: they're cooked, then dehydrated. After the celery root is brined, it is painted with our standard cornstarch-and-egg-white slurry, then roasted. It's then partially dehydrated, which intensifies its flavor and gives it a satisfying bite.

FOR THE PASTRAMI SPICE

Place all the ingredients for the pastrami spice in a spice grinder and grind to a fine powder. Store at room temperature in an airtight container.

FOR THE CELERY ROOT PASTRAMI

Bring the water with the salt to a boil in a 1½-quart (2-liter) saucepot over medium-high heat. Turn off the heat and add 17 grams of the pastrami spice and the liquid smoke, stirring well to disperse them evenly in the brine. Submerge in an ice-water bath until cold.

Place the celery roots and pastrami brine in a 12 by 15-inch (30 by 40-centimeter) sous vide bag. Place in a chamber vacuum sealer and vacuum seal. Brine for 8 hours in the refrigerator, then drain the celery roots and dry on paper towels. It is important to remove the celery root from the brine after 8 hours or it will become too salty.

Preheat the oven to 325°F (163°C). Line a sheet pan with aluminum foil and top with a cooling rack.

Put the remaining pastrami spice in a bowl. Holding one celery root over a bowl of the cornstarch paste, completely cover the outside of the celery root with the paste, allowing the excess to drip back into the

bowl. Place the celery root in the pastrami spice and pack the spice generously onto the celery root to coat completely. Set the coated celery root on the rack on the prepared pan and repeat to coat the second celery root.

Roast the celery roots on the rack until just tender when tested with a cake tester, 4½ to 5 hours.

Most of the coating will have fallen off the celery roots, but remove any that is still attached. Dry the celery roots in a dehydrator set to 160°F (71°C) for about 5 hours, until partially dried, shriveled on the outside but still "meaty" in texture. Let cool to room temperature. Cut off the top and bottom of each celery root to make them flat.

Using an electric slicer, slice 1.5-millimeter-thick rounds from the celery roots, beginning at the root end (the wider end). You will need a total of 54 rounds.

FOR THE PUMPERNICKEL MELBA

Preheat the oven to 300°F (150°C). Lay two nonstick silicone baking mats on the work surface. Brush a thin layer of clarified butter over both baking mats and season lightly with salt.

Using an electric slicer, cut the frozen bread into six 1.5-millimeter-thick slices. The outer pieces work best for this application, as there are no air bubbles. Using a 3-inch (75-millimeter) fluted round cutter, punch a disc from each slice of bread.

Place one of the buttered baking mats, buttered-side up, on an inverted half sheet pan and arrange the bread on the mat. Cover with the second baking mat, buttered-side down, and set a stainless-steel press pan or a second half sheet pan on top to keep the melbas flat. Be certain that both sheet pans have completely flat bottoms.

Bake for 7 to 8 minutes, checking the color every 2 to 3 minutes, until the bread is dark brown and crisp. Remove from the oven and let cool.

The melbas can be stored in an airtight container, layered with paper towels, at room temperature for up to 2 days.

FOR THE BURGUNDY MUSTARD CONDIMENT

Combine the honey and the water in a 2-quart (2-liter) saucepot and bring to a boil over medium-high heat. Whisk in the agar-agar. While whisking continuously, boil vigorously for 1 minute to activate the agar-agar. Transfer to a bowl and nestle the bowl in an ice-water bath. Chill, undisturbed, until the honey is completely firm and set.

Cut the set honey into roughly 1-inch (2.5-centimeter) cubes and transfer to a blender. Add the Burgundy mustard, whole-grain mustard, horseradish, vinegar, fleur de sel, lemon juice, and Pre-Hy and blend until smooth. Pass the puree through a chinois into a container. Place the container, uncovered, in the chamber vacuum sealer. Run a complete cycle on full pressure to remove any air bubbles incorporated during blending. This will give the puree clarity and shine.

Transfer the mustard condiment to a piping bag, pipe into a small squeeze bottle, and refrigerate until serving, up to 3 days.

TO COMPLETE

Wash the lettuce leaves, place them in a small container of ice water, and place the container, uncovered, in the chamber vacuum sealer. Run a complete cycle on full pressure to compress the lettuce. Dry the lettuce on paper towels.

Melt enough clarified butter to coat the bottom of a large sauté pan over medium-low heat. Add a single layer of celery root and cook just to warm through, turning to heat both sides. Remove from the pan and drain on paper towels. Repeat with the remaining celery root, adding butter as needed to warm all the slices.

Place 12 slices of pickled cucumber in a ring on each serving plate, overlapping them slightly. Top the pickled cucumber ring with a pumpernickel melba. Fold each slice of celery root in half, then into quarters, and place 6 of these celery root "rosettes" around the perimeter of each melba. Place 3 celery root rosettes in the center.

Dress the lettuce leaves with olive oil and vinegar and tuck them into the celery root rosettes. Garnish with dots of the Burgundy mustard condiment in a ring around the pastrami.

CHARCOAL-GRILLED HONEYNUT SQUASH

Anson Mills Farro Verde, Lacinato Kale, and Preserved Yuzu Emulsion

Makes 6 servings

PRESERVED YUZU

52 grams kosher salt

68 grams sugar

2 yuzu, about 70 grams each

CIDER VINEGAR GASTRIQUE

450 grams apple cider vinegar

300 grams glucose syrup

180 grams sugar

CHARCOAL-GRILLED HONEYNUT SQUASH

6 (275- to 300-gram) honeynut squash, about 8 inches long, with the stem ends attached

780 grams prepared veg blanc (see page 185)

FARRO VERDE

100 grams farro

150 grams sweet onion essence (page 288)

Minced shallots

Olive oil

Red wine vinegar

Kosher salt

BRAISED LACINATO KALE

35 grams extra-virgin olive oil

100 grams stemmed lacinato kale leaves

Kosher salt

20 grams thinly sliced shallot (sliced on a Japanese mandoline)

10 grams thinly sliced garlic (sliced on a Japanese mandoline)

0.1 grams minced chili flakes

50 grams Sauvignon Blanc

200 grams sweet onion essence (page 288)

PRESERVED YUZU EMULSION

100 grams water

100 grams yuzu juice, preferably Muen yuzu juice

38 grams sliced shallots

2 small bay leaves

32 grams heavy cream

170 grams whole butter, cut into small cubes and chilled

Kosher salt

TO COMPLETE

24 young kale leaves

Extra-virgin olive oil

Red wine vinegar

Kosher salt

SPECIAL EQUIPMENT

Chamber vacuum sealer

Immersion circulator

Dehydrator

This dish is just an unconventional way of looking at a vegetable, as well as trying to get the most flavor out of a squash. The squash is vacuum sealed in veg blanc and cooked, then dehydrated somewhat to intensify its flavor. It's then resealed with a cider vinegar gastrique, which the partially dried squash will absorb to make it very flavorful. For even more flavor, we grill it, basting it with more of the gastrique. It's then stuffed with kale and farro, from the bottom, so it can be sliced and served with a tart yuzu emulsion. We're proud to be serving this squash, which was bred by Row 7, the seed company created by Dan Barber, Michael Mazourek, and Matthew Goldfarb to grow food for flavor. It's one of our favorite vegetables. (Note that the preserved yuzu must be frozen for 3 months before using, so plan ahead!)

FOR THE PRESERVED YUZU

Combine the salt and sugar in a small bowl. Slice an X through the stem end of each yuzu, cutting about three-quarters of the way down and ending about ½ inch (1.25 centimeters) from the bottom. Pull the quarters of one yuzu outward and generously pack the center with about half the sugar and salt mixture. Repeat the process with the other yuzu. Place both yuzu in an 8 by 10-inch (20 by 25-centimeter) sous vide bag and pack any remaining salt and sugar mixture around them. Place in the sealer chamber and vacuum seal. Place the bag in the freezer and freeze for 3 months.

Defrost the yuzu and discard the syrup in the bag, reserving the yuzu peel, pith, and pulp.

FOR THE CIDER VINEGAR GASTRIQUE

Place the vinegar, glucose syrup, and sugar in a small saucepot and bring to a boil over high heat. Reduce the heat to medium-low and slowly simmer for about 15 minutes, until thick and syrupy. Transfer to a bowl and nestle the bowl in an ice-water bath to chill. Set aside while you prepare the squash.

FOR THE CHARCOAL-GRILLED HONEYNUT SQUASH

Set an immersion circulator in a water bath and heat the water to 88°C (190°F).

Leaving the stalks attached, peel the squash with a vegetable peeler, making sure no white skin remains on the orange flesh. Using a small 1-inch (2.5-centimeter) round cutter, punch a hole in the bottom of each squash. Scoop out the seeds using the handle of a spoon or a melon baller. Put the squash in a 12 by 18-inch (roughly 30 by 46-centimeter) sous vide bag with the veg blanc. Place in the chamber vacuum sealer and vacuum seal. Cook in the water bath for 30 minutes, or until tender. Place the bag of squash in an ice-water bath to chill. Remove the squash from the bag and pat dry on paper towels; discard the veg blanc.

Skewer the squash (just beneath the stalk) and tie butcher's twine around the skewer to secure the squash. Hang in a dehydrator set to 65.5°C (150°F) and dry for 3½ to 4½ hours.

Return the water bath to 88°C (190°F).

Remove the squash from the dehydrator and place the squash and 780 grams of the cider vinegar gastrique in a 12 by 18-inch (roughly 30 by 46-centimeter) sous vide bag. Place in the sealer chamber and vacuum seal. Cook with the immersion circulator in an 88°C (190°F) water bath for 12 minutes, until it is tender when touched. Transfer the squash and gastrique to a container.

The squash can be used right away or refrigerated in the gastrique for up to 3 days.

FOR THE FARRO VERDE

Place the farro and the sweet onion essence in a small saucepot. Bring to a boil over high heat. Cover the saucepot tightly with aluminum foil and reduce the heat to its lowest setting. Cook the farro for 30 minutes, or until tender. Dress the farro with minced shallots, olive oil, vinegar, and salt to taste. Let cool in the saucepot. Set aside at room temperature for up to 4 hours.

FOR THE BRAISED LACINATO KALE

Preheat the oven to 350°F (180°C).

Heat a large saucepot over medium-high heat. Add about 15 grams of the olive oil and half the kale. Sprinkle with salt and toast for about 1 minute, until slightly wilted. Transfer the kale to a strainer. Repeat with the remaining kale and 15 grams of the olive oil, then add the kale to the strainer.

Sweat the shallot and the garlic in the remaining 5 grams olive oil over medium heat for about 30 seconds and season with salt. Add the chili flakes and toast lightly for about 30 seconds. Return all the kale to the saucepot and cook over medium heat until wilted, about 2 minutes.

Add the white wine, increase the heat to medium-high, and reduce until the pan is almost dry, about 1 minute. Add the sweet onion essence and bring to a boil. Cook for about 1 minute. Remove from the heat and cover with a cartouche. Braise in the oven, stirring every 5 minutes, for about 20 minutes, until the kale is tender with a "saucy" consistency. Remove from the oven and let cool, then coarsely chop the kale.

Mix the chopped kale into the farro. The kale-farro mixture can be used immediately to stuff the squash or refrigerated in an airtight container for up to 3 days.

FOR THE PRESERVED YUZU EMULSION

Cut the preserved yuzu into ½-inch (1.25-centimeter) dice. Combine 135 grams of the diced preserved yuzu, the water, yuzu juice, shallots, and bay leaves in a medium saucepot and bring to a boil over high heat. Reduce the heat to medium-low and reduce the mixture by a third to about 240 grams, about 10 minutes.

Add the cream. Reduce the mixture by about half to 135 grams. Remove the pan from the heat and whisk in the cold butter until fully emulsified. Strain the emulsion through a chinois into a container and season with salt. Cover and keep in a warm spot for up to 4 hours before serving.

TO COMPLETE

Prepare a fire (see page 270).

Remove the squash from the gastrique, reserving the gastrique for glazing. Transfer the kale-farro mixture to a piping bag and pipe it into the cavities of the squash, filling them. (Alternatively, the mixture can be spooned into the squash.) Grill the squash on the charcoal grill, glazing it with the gastrique, until it is charred and caramelized on the surface.

Toss the young kale leaves with olive oil, vinegar, and salt to taste.

For each serving, slice the squash crosswise into 8 pieces and carefully transfer it to a serving plate. Arrange the slices so they overlap slightly from bottom to top, keeping the shape of the whole squash. Garnish with the young kale leaves and spoon the preserved yuzu emulsion to the side.

FISH

ATLANTIC SKATE WING DORÉ

Musquee de Provence Pumpkin Farce and Pumpkin Seed–Brown Butter Sauce

Makes 6 servings

MUSQUEE DE PROVENCE PUMPKIN FARCE

125 grams strained Musquee de Provence pumpkin juice

38 grams semolina flour

6 grams kosher salt

160 grams mousse base (page 253), made with pike

SKATE

Two 250-gram (large side) skate fillets

Kosher salt

CURED PUMPKIN PUNCHES

1 (200-gram) square piece peeled Musquee de Provence pumpkin, at least ½ inch thick

300 grams prepared veg blanc (see page 185)

TOASTED PUMPKIN SEED GASTRIQUE

30 grams hulled raw pumpkin seeds

75 grams Banyuls vinegar

37 grams sugar

75 grams veal stock (page 287)

25 grams whole butter

20 grams toasted pumpkin seed oil

Lemon juice

Kosher salt

TO COMPLETE

Wondra flour

Canola oil

Kosher salt

30 grams whole butter

_____

SPECIAL EQUIPMENT

Electric slicer (preferred) or Japanese mandoline

1¼-inch (30-millimeter) plain round cutter

Skate is typically cooked flat, so we wanted a more unusual way to serve it. David decided to roll it around a stuffing of cooked pumpkin and pike mousse that's very delicate. The sauce is a traditional browned butter, flavored with Banyuls vinegar balanced with sugar to make a light gastrique, which we finish with veal stock and mount with butter and pumpkin seed oil.

FOR THE MUSQUEE DE PROVENCE PUMPKIN FARCE

Bring the pumpkin juice to a simmer in a 1-quart (1-liter) saucepot and whisk in the semolina flour and salt. Cook for 2 to 3 minutes, stirring continuously to prevent scorching, until the juice has thickened and the semolina is fully hydrated. The mixture will be very thick.

Spread the farce in a container and nestle the container in an ice-water bath to chill. Once fully chilled, transfer the farce to the bowl of a stand mixer fitted with the paddle and add the mousse base. Mix until homogenous. Transfer to a disposable piping bag and refrigerate for up to 1 day.

FOR THE SKATE

Clean the skate fillets by removing the skin and bloodline. Lightly pound each fillet between two pieces of plastic wrap to an even ¼-inch (6-millimeter) thickness. Square off each fillet.

Lay a long piece of plastic wrap vertically on a work surface. Season the skate with salt and place it skin-side up on the plastic wrap. Pipe a ¾-inch-wide (2-centimeter) strip of the pumpkin farce across the skate, about ½ inch (1.25 centimeters) from the top of the fillet.

Using the plastic wrap for support, tightly wrap the skate around the farce to reach one complete turn. The fillet should overlap itself by ¼ to ½ inch (6 millimeters to 1.25 centimeters). Continue to tightly roll the fillet in the plastic. Twist the ends of the plastic to compress the fish and tie the ends tightly with butcher's twine, as close to the roll as possible. Repeat with the second fillet. Refrigerate for at least 4 hours or up to overnight.

(continued)

FOR THE CURED PUMPKIN PUNCHES

Using an electric slicer or a Japanese mandoline, cut the pumpkin into 2-millimeter-thick slices. Using a 1¼-inch (30-millimeter) plain round cutter, punch 12 circles from the slices. Punch 6 of the circles with the cutter offset from the center to form a moon shape.

Place the punches in a container, cover with the veg blanc, and refrigerate for at least 1 hour or up to 1 day to macerate.

FOR THE TOASTED PUMPKIN SEED GASTRIQUE

Preheat the oven to 320°F (160°C).

Spread the pumpkin seeds over a sheet pan and toast in the oven for 15 minutes, or until golden brown and fragrant. Let cool, then coarsely chop the seeds. Shake the chopped seeds in a strainer to remove any dust.

Combine the vinegar and sugar in a small saucepot and reduce to a gastrique (a thick syrup) over medium-high heat. Add the veal stock and remove from the heat. Whisk in the butter to emulsify. Stir in the chopped pumpkin seeds. Transfer to a bowl and pour in the pumpkin seed oil to "break the sauce." Season with lemon juice and salt to taste. Keep the sauce warm.

TO COMPLETE

Remove the fish from the refrigerator 30 minutes before cooking. Dry the pumpkin punches on paper towels.

Set a small cooling rack on a quarter sheet pan. Spread Wondra flour on a small tray. Roll the skate in the flour to lightly coat.

Heat a medium sauté pan over medium-high heat and add canola oil to generously cover the bottom of the pan. Remove the plastic from the fish, season with salt, and place in the pan. Using a small offset spatula, gently roll the fish to achieve even caramelization. Add the butter and baste the fish with the fat several times. This should be done quickly to avoid overcooking. To test for doneness, slide a cake tester into the center of the farce, then remove it and touch the tester to your lip; it should be hot. Tilt the pan over the rack, allowing the fish to slide out onto the rack. Rest in a warm place for 5 minutes. Slice each skate roll into 3 pieces.

Spoon the gastrique into the center of each serving plate and top with a piece of skate. Garnish with the cured pumpkin punches.

HEARTH-ROASTED ALASKAN KING CRAB

Sweet-and-Sour Kumquat Glaze, Broccoli Pudding, and Broccoli Buds

Makes 6 servings

**SWEET-AND-SOUR
KUMQUAT MARMALADE
AND GLAZE**

250 grams kumquats

285 grams sugar

125 grams orange juice

12 grams fleur de sel

6 grams apple pectin

2 grams citric acid

30 grams yuzu juice

80 grams ají dulce chili
paste (page 186)

CRAB LEGS

1 (8-pound/3,600-gram)
king crab, or 6 king crab
merus (see Note)

**GARDEN BROCCOLI
PUDDING**

3 quarts (3 liters) water

30 grams kosher salt,
plus more to taste

10 grams thyme sprigs

10 grams garlic cloves,
skin on, smashed

2 grams chili flakes

225 grams broccoli floret
tips and tender stems,
chopped

25 grams stemmed
arrowleaf spinach
leaves

5 grams agar-agar

TO COMPLETE

2 or 3 stalks Broccolini

Canola oil

Kosher salt

SPECIAL EQUIPMENT

Meat grinder with a small
die

Chamber vacuum sealer
(optional)

At The French Laundry, we cook this crab in a chestnut pan so that it picks up flavors from the hearth, then glaze it with a marmalade made from kumquats that grow just down the street. We put them through a grinder, seeds and all, add sugar, orange juice, and salt, then let it sit overnight. The next day, we bring it to a boil with a little pectin to make sure it's thick enough to glaze the crab.

What makes the marmalade so good are the ají dulce peppers used to finish it. David was originally introduced to these sweet, intensely flavored peppers by Ken Vedrinski of the Woodlands Inn in Summerville, South Carolina, but hadn't seen them since working there. Years later, on a shopping trip for per se at the Union Square Greenmarket, he smelled something familiar. It was those peppers. He walked all the way across the square and found the farmer selling them, bought all he could, then sent some to our gardeners so they could start growing their own. We now grow two hundred ají dulce plants a year, with most of the peppers going to the bottled sauce made and sold by Ad Hoc. One restaurant feeds another.

The broccoli, cooked with some chili flakes, is vibrantly green because we use just the florets and also add some spinach to the puree, which is thickened with agar to a very light pudding consistency.

FOR THE SWEET-AND-SOUR KUMQUAT MARMALADE AND GLAZE

Grind the kumquats through the small die of a meat grinder into a bowl. Mix with 250 grams of the sugar, the orange juice, and the fleur de sel and macerate at room temperature for 2 hours. Transfer the mixture to a 2-quart (2-liter) saucepot and slowly bring to a boil over medium-low heat.

Thoroughly mix the remaining 35 grams sugar, the apple pectin, and the citric acid. Dust the pectin mixture over the surface of the marmalade in an even layer and whisk until evenly incorporated. Bring to a boil, stirring frequently, then reduce the heat and simmer for 5 minutes.

To make the glaze, stir in the yuzu juice and ají dulce paste to combine. Use immediately or refrigerate in a covered container for several months.

FOR THE CRAB LEGS

Wear thick rubber gloves or use a clean kitchen towel to protect your hands. Cut the crab legs from the body, leaving the shoulders attached to the body. Bend the tip of the leg backward and remove the shell. Bend the second joint and pull off the shell. Break the third joint and pull it away, bringing the long pieces of cartilage with it. Break off the portions of exposed crabmeat. They will not be used in this recipe but can be frozen for up to 1 month for other uses.

The largest section of the leg will remain. Hold the shell perpendicular to the table, with the side that was connected to the body facing downward. Shake the merus a couple of times to free the last piece of meat; it should come out of the shell fairly easily. If it does not come right out, use your fingers or some tweezers to help remove it from the shell.

Arrange the merus on a paper towel–lined tray, cover with plastic wrap, and refrigerate for up to 1 day.

FOR THE GARDEN BROCCOLI PUDDING

Place the water, salt, thyme, garlic, and chili flakes in a pot and bring to a boil. Strain through a chinois into another saucepot and return to a rolling boil. Add the broccoli and spinach and boil until the broccoli is completely tender, 2 to 3 minutes. Drain the broccoli and spinach in a chinois set over a bowl, pressing on the broccoli and spinach to extract all the liquid. Transfer 250 grams of the cooking liquid to a blender and add the broccoli and spinach.

Beginning on low speed and gradually increasing to high, blend until completely smooth, about 1 minute. With the blender running, shear in the agar-agar through the hole in the lid and blend on high speed for 2 minutes, until the agar-agar is activated. Pour the mixture into a bowl and nestle the bowl in an ice-water bath. Chill until the broccoli pudding base is completely firm and set.

Cut the broccoli pudding base into smaller pieces and transfer to the blender. Beginning on low speed and gradually increasing to high, blend until completely smooth, using the tamper to keep the puree moving. Adjust the seasoning with additional salt.

If you have a chamber vacuum sealer, pass the pudding through a chinois into a container and place the container, uncovered, in the sealer chamber. Run a complete cycle on full pressure to remove any air bubbles incorporated during blending. This will give the puree clarity and shine. If you don't have a chamber vacuum sealer, transfer the pudding to an airtight container and lay a piece of plastic directly against the surface of the pudding to prevent a skin from forming.

Keep at room temperature for up to 4 hours before serving, or refrigerate up to 1 day.

TO COMPLETE

Prepare a fire (see page 270).

Using a small pair of kitchen scissors, cut the buds off the Broccolini until you have about 2 tablespoons. Refrigerate until plating the dish.

In a small pot, gently reheat the broccoli pudding over medium-low heat. Transfer to a small container, cover, and keep in a warm spot until ready to plate.

If necessary, reheat the glaze.

Lightly coat the crab with canola oil and season with salt. Place the crab on a hot grate over the coals, red-side down. The crab will begin to plump and become firm. After 1 to 2 minutes, when the crab has caramelized and is almost cooked through (the back side will still be somewhat translucent and raw), flip and cook for 30 seconds to 1 minute, until cooked through. Remove from the hearth or grill and place on a cutting board to rest for 2 to 3 minutes.

Hold a spoonful of the broccoli pudding at a slight angle (almost perpendicular) above the point you want the pudding on the plate and allow the pudding to slide onto the plate. Sweep the spoon through the pudding twice, from the center outward.

Spoon a generous coating of the glaze over the top of each crab leg. Trim the ends of the legs. Garnish each leg with the Broccolini buds and place one leg alongside the pudding on each plate.

> **NOTE**
>
> The merus is the largest section of a king crab leg. To buy the merus only, cleaned and separated from the other portions of the crab, see Sources, page 366.

CHARCOAL-GRILLED JAPANESE SEA SNAILS À LA FRANÇAISE

Escargot Butter Sauce, Warm Puff Pastry, and Garlic Confit

Makes 6 servings

SEA SNAILS

6 Japanese sea snails in
   the shell, about
   375 grams each

2 quarts (2 liters) water

20 grams fleur de sel

80 grams kombu

PUFF PASTRY

1 (10- to 12-inch/25- to
   30-centimeter) sheet
   puff pastry, homemade
   or store-bought

GARLIC CONFIT

9 large garlic cloves

Clarified butter (page 53),
   melted

**ESCARGOT BUTTER
SAUCE**

200 grams warm water

100 grams heavy cream

20 grams Burgundy
   mustard

24 grams lemon juice

350 grams whole butter,
   cut into cubes

16 grams Pre-Hy (page
   109)

30 grams coarsely
   chopped shallots

30 grams coarsely
   chopped flat-leaf
   parsley

20 grams coarsely
   chopped garlic

10 grams fleur de sel

TO COMPLETE

Canola oil

75 grams whole butter

30 grams Sauvignon
   Blanc

Flat-leaf parsley leaves

SPECIAL EQUIPMENT

Pressure cooker

Chamber vacuum sealer
   (optional)

2½-inch (60-millimeter)
   fluted barquette cutter

4 ring molds, ½ inch
   (13 millimeters) tall

Weighted press pan
   (optional)

The Japanese sea snail, *ezo-bora*, has a fabulous texture and sea flavor, and it is very versatile. We cook them in a pressure cooker with something akin to seawater: a mixture of salt, water, and seaweed. Then they're cooled and trimmed, and after that, you can do anything with them—grill, fry, braise, glaze. We like to serve these à la française, as one would escargot, with garlic butter and parsley. Here we reheat the snails by sautéing them in butter, then deglazing the pan with wine, and serve them with the butter sauce, some warm puff pastry, garlic confit, and a few leaves of fresh parsley.

FOR THE SEA SNAILS

Rinse the snails in cool water. Combine the water, fleur de sel, and kombu in a medium pot and bring to a boil. Place the snails in a pressure cooker and pour the hot liquid over them. The water may not cover the snails completely. Cook on high pressure according to the manufacturer's instructions for 30 minutes, then carefully release the pressure. Remove a snail to check for doneness. The small plate at the base of the snail will come off easily if they are properly cooked. If they need further cooking, return them to the pressure cooker and cook at high pressure for 5 minutes more. Transfer the snails to a container, pour the cooking liquid over them, and let cool, uncovered.

Remove a snail from the cooking liquid, reserving the liquid. Hold the cone of the shell vertically (the snail will be at the bottom) and gently shake up and down to loosen the snail from the shell. It may be necessary to use your fingers to gently separate the snail. When the snail begins to emerge, turn the opening of the shell downward and continue to shake the shell, using your fingers to coax the snail from the shell. Repeat to remove all the snails from their shells.

To clean the snails, use small, sharp kitchen scissors to snip the "skirt" surrounding the main mass of meat. Removing the skirt will also detach most of the organs. Position the snails on a cutting board, with the arch facing up. Halve the snails lengthwise. This will expose the remaining organs. Use a knife to cut away the section of organs.

(continued)

If you have a chamber vacuum sealer, place the snails and their cooking liquid in a sous vide bag. Place the bag in the sealer chamber and vacuum seal. If you do not have a chamber vacuum sealer, return the snails to the container with the cooking liquid and cover.

Refrigerate for several hours to chill completely or for up to 3 days.

FOR THE PUFF PASTRY

Preheat the oven to 450°F (232°C). Lightly spray a sheet pan with non-stick spray, line the pan with parchment paper, and lightly spray the parchment.

Roll the puff pastry to ⅛-inch (3-millimeter) thickness. Using a 2½-inch (60-millimeter) fluted barquette cutter, punch out 6 pieces of the puff pastry and place them on the prepared sheet pan.

Put one ½-inch-high (13-millimeter) ring mold in each corner of the pan. Lightly spray the underside of another sheet pan with nonstick spray and adhere a piece of parchment paper to the sprayed surface. Rest the sheet tray, parchment-side down, on the ring molds. The ring molds will hold the pan above the pastry. Place a weight, such as a press pan or a heavy pan, on top to hold the pan firmly in place.

Bake the puff pastry for 12 minutes, then check to see if it is golden brown; if not, return it to the oven for 2 to 3 minutes more, until golden brown. Remove from the oven and transfer the puff pastry to a cooling rack. Let cool. These can be baked in the morning, stored on paper towels in an airtight container at room temperature, and gently reheated before serving.

FOR THE GARLIC CONFIT

Halve the garlic cloves lengthwise. Peel them and trim the root from each half. Using a tourné knife, carefully remove and discard the germ. Place the garlic in a small pot and cover with cold water. Bring to a boil over medium-high heat. Drain immediately and return the garlic to the pot. Repeat the process twice. The garlic should be just tender.

Return the garlic to the pot and cover with clarified butter. Slowly bring the butter to a simmer over medium-low heat and cook until the garlic is completely tender but still holds its shape, about 5 minutes. Remove from the heat. If using within a few hours, keep in a warm spot.

The garlic can be refrigerated in the butter for up to 3 days. Rewarm the garlic confit enough to melt the butter before using.

FOR THE ESCARGOT BUTTER SAUCE

Combine the water, cream, mustard, and lemon juice in a 1-quart (1-liter) saucepot and bring to a simmer. Whisk in the butter a little at a time to emulsify. Whisk in the Pre-Hy. Transfer to a blender and blend on low speed until emulsified. Add the shallots, parsley, garlic, and fleur de sel and pulse to combine. Keep in a warm spot for up to 6 hours before serving.

TO COMPLETE

If the puff pastries have cooled, reheat them in a 250°F (121°C) oven for 4 to 5 minutes. If necessary, rewarm the garlic confit enough to melt the clarified butter. Remove the garlic cloves from the butter.

Drain the snails and dry on paper towels. Cut them into small bite-size pieces. Coat the bottom of a small sauté pan with canola oil and heat over medium heat. Add the snails and lightly caramelize, turning them to color all surfaces. Add the whole butter to the pan and swirl to melt and foam. Add the wine and the garlic confit and cook to evaporate the wine. Transfer the snails and garlic confit to a tray.

Spoon the butter sauce into the bottom of each serving bowl. Divide the snails and garlic confit among the bowls. Place a warm puff pastry to the side and garnish with parsley.

CATALINA ISLAND SPINY LOBSTER

Green Rhubarb and Garden Celery

Makes 6 servings

CATALINA SPINY LOBSTER

6 (2-pound/900-gram)
spiny lobsters, or
6 small spiny lobster
tails, about 250 grams
each

GREEN RHUBARB

300 grams white verjus

240 grams water

100 grams orange juice

60 grams sugar

4 grams fleur de sel

4 green rhubarb stalks, at
least 7 inches
(18 centimeters) long
and about ½ inch
(1.25 centimeters) wide

HORSERADISH GASTRIQUE

10 grams drained
preserved horseradish

12 grams Ultra-Tex 8

25 grams Pre-Hy (page
109)

10 grams coarsely
chopped yellow celery
leaves

BUTTER POACH

1,000 grams beurre
monté (page 220)

75 grams lemon juice

75 grams kosher salt

TO COMPLETE

Pickled yellow celery (see
page 183)

Yellow celery leaves from
1 head of celery

Burgundy amaranth

Maldon salt

SPECIAL EQUIPMENT

Butcher's scissors

Chamber vacuum sealer
(optional)

Immersion circulator
(optional)

Infrared thermometer gun
or instant-read
thermometer

This dish is all about the lobster itself. The texture of the muscle, the structure of it, and the way it breaks down as you eat it are just beautiful. I love the freshness—you can smell the ocean as you eat it. The tail is poached in the classic beurre monté at a low temperature until those proteins just set throughout and the natural sweetness of the flesh is realized. It's a very specific point in the cooking. Here we serve it with green rhubarb, which is a variety of rhubarb, not unripe rhubarb. It's very sour and, unlike regular rhubarb, keeps its shape when cooked. We add verjus, salt, and sugar to it. We also include fresh celery, which mimics the rhubarb in shape, and fresh horseradish. It's almost like cocktail sauce.

FOR THE CATALINA SPINY LOBSTER

If using whole lobsters, break back the middle piece of the tail fin of the lobster. Pull it away, which will bring the entrails with it. Using butcher's scissors, cut the spikes from each side of the shell. Cut through the shell along one side of the tail, being careful not to cut into the lobster flesh. Repeat on the other side of the tail. Pull the shell from the underside of the lobster, beginning at the head end and pulling back toward the tail. Remove the tail from the shell.

The tails can be refrigerated in an airtight container for up to 1 day. The lobster bodies will not be used in this recipe but can be reserved for stock.

FOR THE GREEN RHUBARB

Combine the verjus, water, orange juice, sugar, and fleur de sel in a 1-quart (1-liter) saucepot and bring to a simmer over medium heat, stirring to dissolve the salt and sugar. Transfer the cuisson to a bowl and nestle the bowl in an ice-water bath to chill.

While the cuisson is chilling, cut the rhubarb on the bias into 2-inch (5-centimeter) pieces. You will need at least 12 pieces.

If you have a chamber vacuum sealer, set an immersion circulator in a water bath and heat the water to 88°C (190.4°F). Place the rhubarb pieces and chilled cuisson in a sous vide bag. Place the bag in the sealer chamber and vacuum seal. Cook in the water bath for about 5 minutes, or until tender. Immediately submerge the bag in an ice-water bath to chill.

If you do not have a chamber vacuum sealer, arrange the rhubarb in a single layer in a saucepot or rondeau. Add the cuisson. Cover with a cartouche and bring to a simmer over low heat. Cook the rhubarb for 2 to 3 minutes, turning as needed to ensure even cooking.

Reserve 250 grams of the rhubarb cuisson for the gastrique. The rhubarb and remaining cuisson can be refrigerated for up to 1 day. Bring to room temperature before serving.

FOR THE HORSERADISH GASTRIQUE

Put the reserved 250 grams rhubarb cuisson in a blender and add the horseradish. With the blender running on medium-low speed, shear in the Ultra-Tex. Blend for 1 minute to hydrate the Ultra-Tex. Add the Pre-Hy and blend briefly on low speed just to incorporate. Pass the gastrique through a chinois into a container.

If you have a chamber vacuum sealer, place the container, uncovered, in the sealer chamber. Run a complete cycle on full pressure to remove any air bubbles incorporated during blending. This will give the gastrique clarity and shine.

Stir in the celery leaves. The gastrique can be refrigerated in an airtight container for up to 2 days.

FOR THE BUTTER POACH

Remove the lobster tails from the refrigerator to temper, about 20 minutes.

Whisk the beurre monté, lemon juice, and salt together in a pot wide enough to comfortably hold all six lobster tails in a single layer. Warm the beurre monté to about 140°F (60°C), checking the temperature with an infrared or instant-read thermometer, then gently lower the lobster tails into the butter. Continue to monitor the temperature of the beurre monté, adjusting the heat as needed to maintain the temperature. If it becomes too hot, remove the pot from the burner to bring the temperature down. After 12 minutes, check the tails for doneness. The flesh should feel firm to the touch. Insert a cake tester into the thickest part of the tail, then touch the tester to your upper lip; if the tails are done, it should feel warm. If necessary, continue poaching the tails, checking them every 2 minutes, until cooked.

Using a spider, remove the lobster tails from the beurre monté and place them on a cooling rack set over a sheet pan to drain; discard the beurre monté.

TO COMPLETE

Drain the rhubarb pieces and dry on paper towels. Place in a medium bowl and dress with enough of the horseradish gastrique to completely coat.

Arrange 2 pieces of the rhubarb on each serving plate. Garnish with pickled celery, celery leaves, and burgundy amaranth.

Season the lobster tails with Maldon salt and arrange alongside the rhubarb and celery. Spoon additional gastrique over the lobster at the table.

BUTTER-POACHED LOBSTER AND BEURRE MONTÉ

I'd always hated the way we cooked lobster in the restaurants I'd worked in—going all the way back to my summers at Clarke Cook House and the Dunes Club in Narragansett, Rhode Island, in the mid-1970s. We'd boil them ahead of time, 7 minutes a pound, chill them, then reheat the cut-up cooked lobster in our Newburg sauce. The result was rubbery and had a reheated flavor that I didn't like.

I spent a year and a half cooking in France in the early 1980s, when I was in my late twenties. At Taillevent in Paris, I'd learned about beurre monté, what we call the workhorse sauce in *The French Laundry Cookbook* (and which some refer to as *beurre fondue*), since it had become such an important part of my kitchen. It's simply butter melted in such a way that it doesn't break; the name comes from the term *monté au beurre*, or whisking whole butter into a sauce to finish it. At Taillevent we used this creamy, homogenous butter to enrich sauces *à la minute*, and for any number of preparations. I thought it was brilliant.

My favorite way to eat boiled lobster was simply with "drawn butter" (clarified butter), so it seemed natural, when I was refiguring how to make lobster better than the boil-and-reheat version ubiquitous in America, to think, *Why don't I cook this in butter?*

I first figured out how to get the meat out of the shell without cooking it—putting the lobsters in boiling-hot water with vinegar added for a couple of minutes is enough to cook the exterior so that it pulls cleanly away from the shell but remains mainly raw. Now I could poach the lobster in beurre monté, and it worked *beautifully*.

But even this technique has evolved. Our first method was to poach the lobster in a pot of beurre monté. The gentle heat kept the meat from becoming tough. When we discovered the magic of sous vide cooking, we put the lobster meat in a bag with some of the beurre monté and held it at 60°C (140°F) until we needed to serve it. But we go through so many lobsters every night, we put the immersion circulators into the beurre monté itself so that we had butter at the perfect temperature all night long.

Now the combi oven can keep a hotel pan filled with beurre monté at the perfect temperature throughout service, and that's how we cook lobsters today. But for small batches, it's just as easy to cook them the old-fashioned way.

And don't forget how all-purpose that beurre monté is—we hold our 6-minute eggs in it, baste meats with it, and finish sauces with it. Take a look in both kitchens before service, and you'll see somebody whisking pounds and pounds of beurre monté and distributing it among the stations.

Beurre Monté

Yield varies

Whole butter, cut into
⅜-inch (1-centimeter)
cubes and chilled

No matter what quantity of beurre monté you will be making, you need a thin layer of water at the bottom of a pot to start the emulsification process.

Put the water in a saucepot or rondeau and bring it to a simmer. Reduce the heat to low and begin whisking in the butter, piece by piece, to emulsify. Once you have established the emulsion, continue whisking in pieces of the butter until you have the quantity of beurre monté you need. It is important to keep the heat gentle and consistent in order to maintain the emulsification. Make the beurre monté close to the time it will be used, and hold it in a warm spot. Leftover beurre monté can be clarified (see page 53).

Oven Method for Classical Sauce Vin Blanc

Our job as chefs is not necessarily to make something that's different, but rather to make the best possible dish we can make, whether it's the elaborate suckling-pig preparation (see page 262) or the most beautiful hollandaise sauce you've ever had.

In our search for the new, we stand to lose a lot of these flavors and textures that are so emotionally satisfying. Something that's new isn't always satisfying. So we try to be progressive and at the same time have our feet deeply embedded in the classics.

Every time I go to Restaurant Paul Bocuse and have the sauce vin blanc with the rouget, I think, *My God, why don't we make this sauce anymore?* So we do.

Moreover, it connects me with my past because we make it just as my chef at the Polo Lounge, Patrice Boely, taught me to do it: in the oven.

Patrice was a mischief maker and might throw cayenne peppers on your flattop so that you could hardly breathe while you cooked. He was also a fabulous chef and teacher. Because I needed every burner available and couldn't tie them up by making my lobster stock and sauce, he showed me an ingenious way to make it in the oven instead: gently sauté the chopped lobster bones with aromatics until they turn red, then add vermouth and cream and pop it in the oven. In an hour I could strain my perfect sauce vin blanc. It was brilliant. We still use the method at The French Laundry today.

Preheat the oven to 300°F (150°C).

Sauté chopped lobster bones in butter with carrot, onion, and mushroom, just until the lobster bones turn red (choose a pot that will contain all the ingredients efficiently). Cover with equal parts cream and Noilly Prat dry vermouth. Bring just to a simmer, then put it in the oven uncovered for an hour. Strain and reduce the sauce vin blanc to the desired flavor. Thicken as necessary.

THE LESSONS OF A DISHWASHER

The Six Disciplines for Success

WHEN I WAS FIFTEEN and still in high school, my mom gave me a night job as a dishwasher at a restaurant she managed, the Redwood Inn, in Palm Beach, Florida. We—my two brothers, my sister, my mom, and I—lived on the island of Palm Beach in a small bungalow near enough to the restaurant that I could walk.

After I graduated from high school, I had a short stint as a carpenter's apprentice, then went back to work for my mom, washing dishes at the Palm Beach Yacht Club in West Palm Beach. I'd cross the bridge over the Intracoastal Waterway, then head north on Flagler Drive to the club. The dining room was small, about forty seats, with two cooks, four servers, and a bartender. Lunch service only. A small, square building and a dock managed by Captain John. Every day was pretty much the same, and I found that I liked this. I liked routine.

The first thing I'd do was clean the bathrooms. My mom was very particular; those bathrooms had to be spotless. Then I'd sweep the kitchen, help prep the food, take out the trash—each task always pretty much at the same time of day, every day.

Lunch service would begin and I'd work my station—the dishwasher's station—pretty much as I would work at all the stations throughout my career, with everything in its place. If I wasn't organized, I'd get behind, and then the cooks wouldn't have their cookware and the servers wouldn't have plates and silverware and the bartender wouldn't have the glasses he needed. So I'd have a kind of template. I'd put my entrée plate here, the salad plate here, my silverware soaking bins here, places for both clean dishes and dishes to wash. This way the servers always knew where to stack the dirty dishes. If I wasn't organized, how could they be organized?

I'd scrape the plates, give them a rinse, then stack them in the dishwasher in exactly the same way. Each time I'd run it—restaurant dishwashers run in cycles of a minute or less—I'd know if I'd done a good enough job scraping and rinsing; if I hadn't, I'd have to rewash them, costing us all time.

I wanted to do a good job to please my mother, but she was, without my knowing it, giving me all the skills I'd need to survive and thrive in the world. She was telling me in her way that every day, I had to ask myself, *What do I have to do to become better at what I do?*

I washed dishes for about eight months. Then one day, my mother pulled me aside, nodded to the guy who was her head chef, and said quietly to me, "Watch him. Watch what he does."

Her instincts were right—the chef quit soon after and took the other cook with him. Mom tapped me to take his place. My good friend Prezempko (pronounced "Shempko") was looking for a job. I told him he was hired. We went out that night and partied. *We were going to become chefs!*

And we did, though we had zero qualifications and didn't know what we were doing. I'd call my older brother, Joseph, who was a cook at La Petite Marmite, a well-known fine-dining restaurant in Palm Beach on Worth Avenue, and say, "Joseph, how do you roast a prime rib?!" I can't tell you what I owe Joseph. There aren't words for it. You know how big brothers are to little brothers? But Joseph was so patient with me. He's the one who taught me how to make a hollandaise sauce. He worked at night, so he could come to the yacht club and teach me how to cook a prime rib, make roux, or whip up a hollandaise. That was 1974.

Twenty years later, I opened The French Laundry. I might never have gotten there without my mother's awareness and my brother's kindness and patience with his little brother.

And exactly *thirty* years later, as I was about to open per se, I'd learned enough to know to do at least one important thing for my new staff there. I needed to close The French Laundry, one of the most sought-after restaurants in the country, so I could fly the key staff—the captains, the expediters, the sous chefs, one or two of each position (it was kind of like Noah's ark)—to inoculate and train the staff of the new restaurant in the philosophy, culture, techniques, and standards developed at The French Laundry. To my knowledge, this had never happened before, closing down a restaurant like The French Laundry to open a new restaurant, but it was critical to me to connect the two, and training the new staff in the philosophy of The French Laundry was one of the fundamental pieces of a successful opening.

But on the first night of the friends and family meal, our first trial run, it was clear I'd made a huge error: in the migration of so many people to New York City—finding lodging for them, setting them up in a new space—I'd forgotten one person, maybe the most important person of all: the dishwasher. At our restaurants, the dishwashers are known as porters. At per se, we had dozens and dozens of different plates and dishes and specialized servicewear, so many that the dishwashers, who were used to five or ten pieces, couldn't wash them efficiently so that they would be available for the servers when they needed them. I'd forgotten what had been so fundamental to my own development as a chef. I'd forgotten my dishwasher, the lead porter, Juan Venegas.

The next day, I flew him out to train the staff to wash and care for the immense volume of plates, glassware, silverware, serving pieces, and cookware. When he arrived the next day, I brought him into the new restaurant, called everyone around, and said, "This man is the most important person in the French Laundry kitchen."

And over the next ten years, as per se and our other endeavors grew—and as I continued to be asked how I've gotten where I am—I returned over and over to my eight months as a dishwasher, lessons that served me well as a cook, and lessons that continue to serve me well as a restaurateur, businessman, and entrepreneur. The lessons I learned as a dishwasher, I realized, epitomize my entire philosophy, the six disciplines I believe are the keys to being successful not just at the dishwasher's station or as chef de cuisine at the pass of a three-star restaurant, but anywhere.

The six disciplines that have always directed me:

Organization. That's number one. I learned it at the dishwasher station at the yacht club. But the servers also had to be organized; they had to drop their stuff in the right place or *I* couldn't be organized, so my being organized encouraged them to be organized.

Next, **efficiency.** This is never clearer, or more important, than in a kitchen. There is so much work to be done in a kitchen—and done rapidly—that if you aren't organized, you can't possibly be efficient, and if you aren't efficient, you will very quickly be buried. And when *you're* buried, everyone else gets buried. And it's chaos.

Efficiency was critical to me as a dishwasher. There had to be efficiency in the way I racked my dishes. How many do I put in a rack, what size are they, when do you rack side to side, when do you rack back to back? How do you manage the different shapes of the plates and dishes and bowls so that you can get as much into the dishwasher as efficiently as possible, but without *over*filling it, which could result in some dishes needing to be rewashed?

Critical feedback. That's a gentle way of saying "criticism." Somewhere along the way, the notion of criticism has become bad, but for me, that critical feedback, *criticism*, is *good*. More than that—it's essential for success. Without our failures, we don't have the opportunity to learn. The bigger the mistake, the faster you modify your behavior. Everyone wants to be praised; no one *likes* to be criticized. But criticism is, for me, the best form of teaching, of learning.

As a dishwasher, I got my criticism from the dishes themselves. If I didn't scrape them correctly, if I didn't rinse them correctly, or spot the lipstick on the glass that needed extra attention, they'd come out of the dishwasher dirty. So after a minute, or however long the dishwasher ran, I got my critical feedback. If I'd done something wrong, it was obvious—the dishes couldn't be used. I had to wash them again, and do a better job of it next time, or the afternoon would devolve into chaos.

Routine. Doing your daily tasks in the same order, every day, increases your efficiency and your proficiency. It's how surgeons organize complex cases. It's how a good cook organizes his or her time. When I was in the kitchen at The French Laundry, you could set a clock by when you saw me filleting the salmon. Creating and maintaining a daily routine allows you to take a deeper pleasure in what seem to be rote or monotonous tasks, such as peeling a liter of raw fava beans. Routine tasks could become rituals, doing the same tasks at the same time of day. This allows everyone to work efficiently together. The back waiter in charge of polishing the wineglasses could always polish the glasses at four thirty because he or she knew that I always washed those glasses at four.

Repetition, and the appreciation of the repetition, is essential for me, and must be for anyone aspiring to be a professional cook and chef. As a doctor practices medicine and a lawyer practices law, we practice the craft of cooking. Doing the same job over and over and over and over again. For hours, for days. For weeks and years, for the rest of your life. I embraced repetition. It didn't matter if I was cleaning the bathroom, racking dishes, or peeling asparagus for the chef—I loved the repetition. That's what dominates the life of a chef.

When we're young cooks, we have it in our minds that there's going to be something different every day, but in reality, that's not the case. You chop your carrots every day; you chop your onions every day; you chop your parsley every day; you cut your fish every day; you fill your oil bottles every day. All those things, every day, no shortcuts, and that's how you get good. And more—that's how you get *better*. Not just getting through those cases of asparagus, those cases of artichokes, but rather pushing yourself and trying to make your cuts closer and closer to perfect each time. A little better, every day.

And finally, **teamwork.** Almost no one works in solitude. We work together. I had to recognize and acknowledge that I, as a dishwasher, was as important as anybody on the team. If the dishwasher doesn't do his or her job, everyone else *will* fail. You, the dishwasher, were the linchpin of the kitchen. *Just like everybody else.* You had to be successful at your job or nobody else could be successful at theirs. As the proverb goes: If you want to go fast, travel alone. If you want to go far, you need a team.

I couldn't have told you any of this back then. I didn't know most of my success would come from those six disciplines—organization, efficiency, critical feedback, routine, repetition, teamwork—and my mom didn't teach me those disciplines when she told me to get behind that dish station. But somehow, in so many ways, she helped me to discover them on my own, and they have directed my life. I miss her every day. Thank you, Mom.

JAPANESE SAYORI

Spicy Mango Puree, Coconut Pudding, Toasted Quinoa, and Thai Basil

Makes 6 servings

SPICY MANGO PUREE

400 grams ¼-inch-dice
(6-millimeter) peeled
mango

200 grams orange juice

50 grams mirin

40 grams rice wine
vinegar

25 grams lime juice, plus
more to taste

15 grams kanzuri

8 grams fleur de sel, plus
more to taste

7 grams agar-agar

COCONUT PUREE

300 grams full-fat
coconut milk

200 grams coconut water

20 grams lime juice, plus
more to taste

10 grams sugar

8 grams kosher salt

7 grams agar-agar

Fleur de sel

SAYORI

6 Japanese sayori, brined
(see page 187)

TOASTED QUINOA

120 grams uncooked
quinoa

220 grams water

5 grams kosher salt

TO COMPLETE

Dry sake

Canola oil

Kosher salt

3 or 4 Thai basil sprigs
with buds

SPECIAL EQUIPMENT

Chamber vacuum sealer
(optional)

Metal skewers

This fish is also called Japanese halfbeak, because the upper beak is half as long as the lower. It's got an almost crunchy texture. We put it on a skewer and grill it for a simple fish course, and serve it with coconut and mango purees and crunchy quinoa.

FOR THE SPICY MANGO PUREE
Combine the mango, orange juice, mirin, vinegar, lime juice, kanzuri, and fleur de sel in a 1-quart (1-liter) saucepot and bring to a simmer over medium-low heat. Cook for about 5 minutes, until the mango is tender. Increase the heat to medium-high and whisk in the agar-agar. While whisking continuously, boil vigorously for 1 minute to activate the agar-agar. Immediately pour the liquid into a bowl and nestle the bowl in an ice-water bath. Chill, undisturbed, until the mango puree base is completely firm and set.

Cut the mango puree base into smaller pieces and transfer to a blender. Beginning on low speed and gradually increasing to high, blend until completely smooth, using the tamper to keep the puree moving. Season to taste with additional fleur de sel and lime juice. Pass the puree through a chinois into a medium bowl.

If you have a chamber vacuum sealer, place the bowl, uncovered, in the sealer chamber. Run a complete cycle on full pressure to remove any air bubbles incorporated during blending. This will give the puree clarity and shine.

Fill a disposable piping bag with the puree and pipe the puree into a small squeeze bottle.

Refrigerate for up to 3 days.

FOR THE COCONUT PUREE
Combine the coconut milk, coconut water, lime juice, sugar, salt, and agar-agar in a 1-quart (1-liter) saucepot and bring to a boil over medium-high heat. While whisking continuously, boil vigorously for 1 minute to activate the agar-agar. Immediately pour the liquid into a bowl and nestle the bowl in an ice-water bath. Chill, undisturbed, until the coconut puree base is completely firm and set.

Cut the coconut puree base into smaller pieces and transfer to the blender. Beginning on low speed and gradually increasing to high, blend until completely smooth, using the tamper to keep the puree moving. Season to taste with fleur de sel and additional lime juice. Pass through a chinois into a medium bowl.

If you have a chamber vacuum sealer, place the bowl, uncovered, in the sealer chamber. Run a complete cycle on full pressure to remove any air bubbles incorporated during blending. This will give the puree clarity and shine.

Fill a disposable piping bag with the puree and pipe the puree into a small squeeze bottle. Refrigerate for up to 3 days.

FOR THE SAYORI

Set up a cutting board with a damp towel wrapped around it (this will help prevent any slipping). Work with one fish at a time, keeping the others refrigerated.

Under cold running water, use a scaler or the back of a knife to gently scrape the skin of the fish from the tail toward the head, to remove any scales. Once the scales have been removed, pat the fish dry and place it on the cutting board. Remove the tail and head, cutting just under the gills. Make a cut along the belly of the fish and gently remove the entrails. Rinse the fish under cool running water and pat dry. Make a small cut, 2 to 3 millimeters deep, down the backbone of the fish. Starting at the head of the fish, slice toward the tail in one fluid movement, following the line of the cut down the backbone and keeping the knife lightly pressed against the backbone as you make your cut to remove as much flesh as possible. Set the fillet to the side and repeat to remove the remaining fillet. Trim the fillets of any fat or cartilage and put them on a tray. Refrigerate the fillets while you fillet the remaining fish.

Working with one fillet at a time and keeping the others refrigerated, slice the belly bones off the fillet. To remove the pin bones, use fish tweezers or needlenose pliers to firmly pull each bone out, pulling toward the head of the fillet and touching the flesh as little as possible. Working from the head, grip the skin and peel it toward the tail to remove it in one piece. Set the fillet in a shallow container and repeat with the remaining fillets.

Refrigerate, covered, for up to 4 hours.

FOR THE QUINOA

Heat a 1-quart (1-liter) saucepot over medium-high heat. Toast the quinoa in the dry pan, swirling the pan regularly to prevent burning, until it becomes fragrant, with a nutty aroma, 2 to 3 minutes. Add the water and salt to the pot and bring to a boil. Cover and reduce the heat to medium-low. Simmer for 10 to 15 minutes, until all the water has been absorbed and the quinoa is tender. Fluff with a fork or spatula and keep covered until plating.

TO COMPLETE

Prepare a fire (see page 270), with the grate positioned 2 to 3 inches (5 to 7.5 centimeters) above the flame.

Remove the container of sayori from the refrigerator and pour in sake to cover. Marinate for 15 minutes. Weave a metal skewer in and out of each fillet at 1-inch (2.5-centimeter) intervals. Brush the skin side of the fillets with canola oil and lightly season with salt. When the coals are hot, place the fish over the fire, skin-side down, resting the skewers on the edge of the hibachi or grill, and cook for 2 to 3 minutes, until the skin has started to blister. Turn the fish and "kiss" (briefly cook) the fillets on the other side. Remove the skewers from the grill and gently remove the fish from the skewers.

Place 2 fillets on each of six small serving plates and garnish with the coconut and mango purees. Pull the buds and small leaves from the sprigs of basil and sprinkle them over the plate, along with the quinoa.

PAUPIETTE OF DOVER SOLE

Satsuma Mandarins, Rumi Saffron, and Citrus Butter

Makes 6 servings

LOBSTER-STUFFED DOVER SOLE

150 grams cooked lobster knuckle or claw meat, coarsely chopped

200 grams mousse base (page 253), made with pike

Zest of 1 lemon

2 grams coarsely chopped flat-leaf parsley leaves

2 grams coarsely chopped chervil leaves

2 grams coarsely chopped tarragon leaves

4 grams kosher salt

6 Dover sole fillets, about 200 grams each, skinned and brined (see page 187)

BROWN BUTTER–SALSIFY PUREE

300 grams whole butter

250 grams chopped peeled salsify

300 grams heavy cream

150 grams water

8 grams kosher salt

Lemon juice

SATSUMA SUPRÊMES

2 medium satsumas

200 grams orange juice

SAFFRON-ORANGE BUTTER

265 grams orange juice

8 grams lemon juice, plus more to taste

1 gram saffron

1 gram Espelette pepper

160 grams whole butter

35 grams heavy cream

3 grams fleur de sel, plus more to taste

25 grams Pre-Hy (page 109)

TO COMPLETE

Whole butter, at soft room temperature

Calendula leaves

Saffron threads

SPECIAL EQUIPMENT
Milk frother

The paupiette of sole is a nod to the classical kitchen of Escoffier. Those dishes always feel right. This one has a lobster stuffing that was inspired by one from Michel Roux Sr.'s book *Sauces*. David purchased his copy in 1997 and got lost in the pages for a few years. Here the fish is folded around a lobster mousse with fines herbes and served with a salsify puree (sunchoke and cauliflower can be used instead), a saffron butter, and satsuma suprêmes with calendula leaves.

What makes this dish special to us is the extraordinary saffron we get from Rumi Spice, a company started by Kimberly Jung. Kimberly is an amazing woman who, after serving in the military as a route clearance platoon leader, sweeping for roadside bombs in Afghanistan, went to Harvard Business School and put what she calls her "wild and precious life" (words from the Mary Oliver poem "The Summer Day") in the service of the Afghan farmers. These farmers were empowered to grow crocuses for saffron instead of poppies for opium, which helps to give them a life independent of the Taliban. With over two thousand employees, Rumi Spice is the largest private employer of Afghan women. This connection makes this an especially important dish to us.

FOR THE LOBSTER-STUFFED DOVER SOLE

Stir together the lobster meat, mousse base, lemon zest, parsley, chervil, tarragon, and salt in a medium bowl to combine. Transfer to a disposable piping bag.

Lay a long piece of plastic wrap vertically on a work surface. Lay the sole fillets on the plastic wrap, skin-side up. Lay another piece of plastic wrap over the fish and lightly pound the fillets with a mallet to an even thickness, just under ⅛ inch (3 millimeters). Remove the top piece of plastic. Divide the lobster mousse among the fillets, piping a small mound in the center of each fillet. Using the plastic wrap to help, gently fold the head end of each fillet over the mousse and press the ends of the fillet together to meet.

Refrigerate in a covered container for up to 8 hours.

FOR THE BROWN BUTTER-SALSIFY PUREE

Melt the butter in a medium pot over medium heat. Cook until the butter begins to brown, whisking occasionally and scraping the bottom of

the pot to be certain the milk solids do not stick. Add the salsify to the pot, reduce the heat to low, and cook until the salsify is tender, without letting it take on too much color, 5 to 7 minutes. Add the cream, water, and salt and bring to a simmer. Simmer gently until the cream has thickened and glazes the salsify. Transfer the contents of the pot to a blender and blend on high speed until very smooth, about 1 minute. Add lemon juice to taste. Keep in a warm spot for up to 4 hours before serving.

The puree can be refrigerated in an airtight container for up to 3 days. Rewarm before serving.

FOR THE SATSUMA SUPRÊMES

Peel the satsumas and separate the wedges. Soak them in warm water for 2 to 3 minutes to soften any pith left on them. Remove from the water and use a small paring knife to gently scrape away and discard any pith. Place the segments in a container and pour the orange juice over the top.

The suprêmes in the orange juice can be refrigerated for up to 1 day.

FOR THE SAFFRON-ORANGE BUTTER

Put the orange juice and lemon juice in a 1-quart (1-liter) saucepot and stir in the saffron and Espelette pepper. Reduce rapidly over medium-high heat to 150 grams. Transfer the reduction to the blender without straining it.

Add the butter, cream, fleur de sel, and Pre-Hy to the blender and blend on high speed for 30 seconds. Adjust the seasoning with additional lemon juice and fleur de sel. Strain into a high-sided container, cover, and keep in a warm place for up to 4 hours before serving.

The butter can be refrigerated for up to 3 days. Rewarm and blend before serving.

TO COMPLETE

Preheat the oven to 300°F (150°C). Generously butter a gratin dish.

Generously butter the sole fillets and place one in the prepared gratin dish, then stand the remaining in the dish. Bake until the fish is opaque and the filling is cooked through, 13 to 15 minutes. To check, insert a cake tester into the center of a filled fillet and touch it to your lip; it should be warm. If any of the filling is poking out or the fillets won't sit flat, trim the sides of the fillets.

Bring the satsuma suprêmes to room temperature, if necessary.

Spoon a dollop of the salsify puree just off-center into each bowl. Position a piece of the fish on the puree. Lay 3 satsuma suprêmes to the side.

Holding a milk frother between the edge of the container and a spoon, foam the soubise until it is very bubbly. Spoon the soubise into the bottom of each bowl. Garnish with calendula leaves and saffron threads.

ROUGET EN ÉCAILLES DE POMME DE TERRE

Roasted Caper Cream, Crispy Capers, and Meyer Lemon

Makes 6 servings

MEYER LEMON

1 Meyer lemon

80 grams sugar

40 grams water

40 grams Meyer lemon juice

POTATO SCALES

2 large Yukon Gold potatoes

1,000 grams (1 quart/ 1 liter) prepared veg blanc (see page 185)

Cornstarch–egg white paste (recipe follows)

ROUGET

6 rouget fillets, brined (see page 187)

ROASTED CAPER CREAM

225 grams whole butter

75 grams drained Spanish capers

3 grams coarsely chopped shallot

75 grams heavy cream

30 grams roasted garlic puree (page 133)

25 grams Pre-Hy (page 109)

5 grams fleur de sel

8 grams coarsely chopped flat-leaf parsley leaves

Zest of 1 lemon

25 grams lemon juice

3 grams colatura (anchovy essence)

TO COMPLETE

Canola oil, for deep-frying and sautéing

50 grams drained Spanish capers

Kosher salt

30 grams whole butter

3 thyme sprigs

1 garlic clove, skin on, crushed

Flat-leaf parsley leaves

SPECIAL EQUIPMENT

Chamber vacuum sealer (optional)

Japanese mandoline or electric slicer

¾-inch (20-millimeter) plain round cutter

This is a tribute to Paul Bocuse and one of his best dishes, sautéed rouget covered in potato "scales" (the *écailles* in the recipe's title). Or you could also say it's yet another version of fish and chips. Monsieur Paul would have served it with a classic sauce vin blanc, but we like to serve it with a roasted caper emulsion scented with anchovy. The fish is so delicate that David prefers to cook it "scales"-side down and only bastes the top to finish it.

FOR THE MEYER LEMON

Partially freeze the Meyer lemon, until it is firm but still soft enough to cut. (Freezing the lemon will allow you to cut beautiful wedges, but also tenderizes the lemon.)

Combine the sugar, water, and lemon juice in a 1-quart (1-liter) saucepot and heat over medium-low heat, stirring, just to dissolve the sugar. Strain the simple syrup into a small bowl or container and nestle the bowl in an ice-water bath to chill.

Cut the frozen lemon into 6 wedges and carefully remove any seeds or pith from around the core of the lemon. Cut away the ends of 4 of the wedges and cut the center sections crosswise into 5 or 6 slices each, about ⅛ inch (3 millimeters) thick. Cut away and discard the flesh and pith from the remaining 2 wedges. Dice the zest into ⅛-inch (3-millimeter) brunoise. Place the lemon slices and zest in a deli container or other container and pour in the chilled simple syrup.

If you have a chamber vacuum sealer, place the container, uncovered, in the sealer chamber and run a complete cycle on full pressure. If you do not have a chamber vacuum sealer, cover and refrigerate the lemons in the simple syrup overnight. The lemons will absorb the simple syrup, enhancing the sweet-tart flavor of the Meyer lemon.

The lemon slices can be refrigerated for up to 1 day.

FOR THE POTATO SCALES

Using a Japanese mandoline or electric slicer, cut the potatoes lengthwise into 2-millimeter-thick slices. The potato slices need to be as uniform in thickness as possible to allow for even cooking and coloration.

(continued)

Arrange the slices in stacks of 5 and punch them with a ¾-inch (20-millimeter) plain round cutter. You will need 90 to 120 rounds. Stack the rounds in a container deep enough to accommodate the potatoes and the veg blanc.

Bring the veg blanc to a boil and pour it over the stack of potatoes. Let cool to room temperature or until the potato is slightly cooked with no raw potato flavor but still has a bite to it. If the potatoes do not sit long enough, they will oxidize as they cool.

Line a sheet pan with a clean kitchen towel. Drain the potatoes in a basket strainer and place them in a single layer on the towel. Pat dry and immediately refrigerate, uncovered, for 10 minutes.

Lightly brush half of a cutting board with half the cornstarch paste. Arrange the potato discs in straight lines over the paste. Brush each of the potato discs with the cornstarch paste.

FOR THE ROUGET

Line a sheet pan with parchment paper.

Remove one rouget fillet from the refrigerator and place it, skin-side up, on the uncovered side of the cutting board. Place a single disc of potato at the narrow end of the fillet. From there, begin shingling the discs over the skin, overlapping them by about one-quarter and gradually increasing the number of discs as the fillet gets wider. The discs should hang just slightly over the edge of the fillet. Depending on the size of the fillet, you may need 15 or more discs to cover the top. Transfer the fillet to the prepared pan and repeat with the remaining fillets and potato discs.

Refrigerate the fillets, uncovered, overnight.

FOR THE ROASTED CAPER CREAM

Melt 75 grams of the butter in a 1-quart (1-liter) saucepot over medium heat. Cook until the butter is golden brown. Add the capers and shallot and cook in the brown butter, swirling the pan, until fragrant and roasted. Reduce the heat to low.

Add the cream to the pan. When the cream is warm, whisk in the remaining 150 grams butter, the roasted garlic puree, Pre-Hy, and fleur de sel. Transfer the sauce to a blender and blend on high speed just until emulsified, less than 1 minute. Add the parsley, lemon zest, lemon juice, and colatura and blend on medium speed until emulsified, less than 1 minute. Keep in a warm spot for up to 4 hours before serving.

The caper cream can be refrigerated in an airtight container for up to 3 days. Rewarm and blend before serving.

TO COMPLETE

Fill a high-sided small pot with 2 to 3 inches (5 to 7.5 centimeters) of canola oil. Heat the oil to 375°F (190°C).

Dry the capers well on a paper towel. Add them to the hot oil and fry until they puff and become crispy and the bubbles in the oil subside, 1 to 2 minutes. Drain the capers on paper towels.

Season the rouget fillets with salt. Heat a large sauté pan over medium heat. Pour in about ⅛ inch (3 millimeters) of canola oil, just enough to reach up the sides of the potato discs but not the fish. When the oil is shimmering, but not smoking, add the rouget to the pan, potato-side down. The pan should be hot enough and the potato "scales" dry enough that they do not stick to the pan when added. Cook the fish until the potatoes are golden brown and crispy, about 5 minutes.

Drain the excess oil from the pan and add the butter, thyme, and garlic. Cook until the butter foams. Baste the fish with the melted butter three or four times, until the fillets are warm in the center and just firm to the touch. Remove the fillets from the pan and drain on paper towels.

Remove the Meyer lemon slices from their syrup and drain on paper towels.

Place a rouget fillet, potato-side up, on each serving plate. Garnish the top of the fillets and the plates with the Meyer lemon slices, diced zest, crispy capers, and parsley leaves. Finish each plate with a spoonful of the caper cream.

Cornstarch–Egg White Paste

Makes 170 grams

100 grams egg whites	70 grams cornstarch

Whisk the egg whites and cornstarch together in a small bowl until thoroughly combined. If not using immediately, whisk the paste again just before using.

HERB-CRUSTED ATLANTIC COD

Brandade Tortellini, Mussels a la Plancha, and Bouillabaisse Sauce

Makes 8 servings

HERB CRUST

75 grams panko breadcrumbs

4 grams Chowry salt (recipe follows)

1.5 grams finely minced rosemary

6 grams finely minced basil leaves

2 grams finely minced savory leaves

2 grams finely minced thyme leaves

4 grams finely minced flat-leaf parsley leaves

7 grams finely minced garlic chives

BRANDADE TORTELLINI

90 grams ½-inch-dice (1.25-centimeter) peeled Yukon Gold potato

250 grams skinless deboned Atlantic cod, smoked (see page 239)

1 large egg yolk

1.5 grams finely minced shallot

0.5 grams Chowry salt (recipe follows)

5 grams Burgundy mustard

5 grams roasted garlic puree (page 133)

Kosher salt

3 sheets basic pasta dough (page 169)

BOUILLABAISSE SAUCE

80 grams whole butter, diced

250 grams lobster bodies, cleaned and cut into 1-inch (2.5-centimeter) pieces

100 grams sliced shallots

15 grams thinly sliced garlic (cut on a Japanese mandoline)

10 grams sliced peeled fresh ginger

0.2 grams chili flakes

1 gram saffron

2 grams coriander seeds, toasted

2 grams fennel seed, toasted

120 grams ¼-inch-dice (6-millimeter) onions

100 grams ¼-inch-dice (6-millimeter) fennel

60 grams ¼-inch-dice (6-millimeter) leeks

60 grams ¼-inch-dice (6-millimeter) sweet carrots

80 grams ¼-inch-dice (6-millimeter) red bell peppers

200 grams ¼-inch-dice (6-millimeter) tomatoes

1 small bay leaf

7 grams kosher salt, or to taste

30 grams tomato paste

16 mussels, in their shells

200 grams Sauvignon Blanc

500 grams lobster stock (page 287)

10 grams tarragon sprigs

5 grams thyme sprigs

1 strip lemon zest (removed with a vegetable peeler)

12 grams Pre-Hy (page 109)

60 grams extra-virgin olive oil

3 grams lemon juice

PARSLEY-GARLIC OIL

100 grams extra-virgin olive oil

15 grams grated garlic (grated on a rasp grater)

3 grams kosher salt

30 grams finely minced flat-leaf parsley

0.2 grams finely minced chili flakes

0.2 grams finely minced dried oregano

COD

8 (35- to 50-gram) pieces trimmed skinless Atlantic cod (see Note)

Cornstarch–egg white paste (page 235)

50 grams clarified butter (page 53)

3 garlic cloves, skin on, crushed

85 grams whole butter, diced

3 thyme sprigs

TO COMPLETE

250 grams beurre monté (page 220)

Extra-virgin olive oil

Lemon juice

SPECIAL EQUIPMENT

Immersion circulator

Chamber vacuum sealer

#806 (½-inch/ 13-millimeter) plain piping tip

2-inch (50-millimeter) flower-shaped cutter

Jonathan Benno, the original chef de cuisine at per se, loved cod and bouillabaisse, and he made it almost every Sunday for the team's dinner. Corey developed this dish because of that fond memory. The cod in this dish is prepared two ways: beautiful medallions are cut from the center of the loin, and, at the restaurant, the trimmings are smoked and mixed with potatoes to make a brandade filling for tortellini. They are both served in a bouillabaisse sauce made with a fortified lobster stock and marinated mussels.

This dish uses "Chowry salt," Corey's take on the Lawry's seasoned salt his mother used when he was growing up, which he loved on the old-school prime rib at Lawry's restaurant. But on the East Coast he couldn't find the salt. So he made his own, which includes turmeric, various powdered peppers, oregano, garlic powder, and onion powder. We season all kinds of meat and fish with it. It's great on lamb and makes a great blackening seasoning for fish, because it's about 20 percent sugar.

FOR THE HERB CRUST

Rub the panko between your hands until all the crumbs are uniform in size and no bigger than coriander seeds. Put the panko in a small bowl and whisk in the Chowry salt. Lightly dry the herbs on paper towels and whisk them into the panko mixture.

Store in an airtight container at room temperature for up to 3 days.

FOR THE BRANDADE TORTELLINI

For this recipe, you will need only 16 finished tortellini; you will have extra dough and brandade. Extra tortellini can be frozen for a future use.

Set an immersion circulator in a water bath and heat the water to 100°C (212°F). Place the potato in a sous vide bag. Place the bag in a chamber vacuum sealer and vacuum seal. Cook in the water bath for about 45 minutes, until tender; the potato should be soft enough to easily flatten with your thumb. While still hot, pass the potato through a fine-mesh tamis into a small bowl.

Finely shred the smoked cod with your fingertips and add it to the bowl with the potato. Add the egg yolk, shallot, Chowry salt, mustard, and roasted garlic puree and mix together with a silicone spatula. Season with kosher salt to taste.

(continued)

Transfer the brandade to a piping bag fitted with a #806 (½-inch/ 13-millimeter) plain piping tip. Pipe the brandade into 5-gram mounds onto a plastic Lexan lid or a parchment–lined sheet pan sprayed with nonstick spray. Cover and refrigerate until cold, or for up to 1 day. (It's important that the brandade is cold, or it will not hold its shape when the tortellini are formed.)

To shape the tortellini, work with one sheet of pasta at a time and keep the others covered with a damp kitchen towel to prevent them from drying out. Punch the pasta into discs with a 2-inch (50-millimeter) flower-shaped cutter. As they are cut, place the pasta discs under a damp kitchen towel to prevent them from drying out. Each disc will have a dull side and a shiny side.

Place a disc of pasta on the work surface, dull-side up, and set a mound of the brandade in the center. Dip your finger in a small bowl of water and run it along the edge of the top half of the pasta disc. Pull the bottom edge of the pasta up and over the filling to meet the dampened side, lining up the fluted edges. Lift the pasta and seal the tortellini by carefully molding the pasta over the filling, pressing out any pockets of air and pushing the brandade toward the center to plump the pasta. Press the edges lightly to seal the dough. Using your thumb, on the straight edge of the pasta, press the center of the pasta upward until it forms a V. Bring the tips of the pasta together and seal to form a circular shape. Place the shaped tortellini on a nonstick sheet pan. Repeat with the remaining pasta discs and brandade. Don't let the tortellini touch each other, or they may stick together.

Freeze the tortellini on the sheet pan. Once frozen, they can be cooked directly or removed from the sheet pan and stored in a resealable plastic bag in the freezer for up to 2 days. Cook them from frozen.

FOR THE BOUILLABAISSE SAUCE

Heat a small rondeau over medium heat. Add 40 grams of the butter and cook until just after it foams, 2 to 4 minutes; the butter should smell nutty. Add the lobster bodies, shallots, garlic, and ginger, reduce the heat to low, and sweat the vegetables, stirring often and keeping them in an even layer on the bottom of the pot to prevent them from sticking to the side and burning, for about 10 minutes, until tender and translucent. Add the chili flakes and saffron and lightly toast for 2 to 3 minutes, until fragrant. Add the coriander and fennel seed.

Add the onions, fennel, leeks, carrots, bell peppers, tomatoes, bay leaf, and salt. Increase the heat to medium-low and cook until all the moisture at the bottom of the rondeau is gone and a light fond has formed, about 30 minutes.

Stir in the tomato paste. Add the mussels and white wine. Increase the heat to medium-high, cover, and steam until the mussels have opened, about 2 minutes. Remove the mussels and set aside to cool to room temperature; reserve to add to the parsley-garlic oil.

Add the lobster stock to the rondeau and bring to a simmer. Cook for 30 minutes, skimming the surface as needed. Pour the contents of the pot through a china cap, pressing on the solids with a wooden spoon to extract all the liquid.

Strain the liquid through a chinois into a small saucepot and return it to the stovetop. Slowly simmer the liquid, skimming the surface often, until it has reduced to 300 grams. Remove from the heat. Add the tarragon, thyme, and lemon zest, cover with a lid, and steep for 5 minutes. Taste the sauce; at this point, it should taste slightly overseasoned. Strain the sauce through a chinois into a blender. With the blender running on low speed, add the Pre-Hy and the remaining 40 grams butter, one cube at a time. Drizzle in the olive oil. Add the lemon juice and adjust the seasoning with additional salt to taste.

The sauce can be refrigerated in an airtight container for up to 3 days.

FOR THE PARSLEY-GARLIC OIL

Combine the olive oil, garlic, and salt in a small saucepot. Cook over medium heat, stirring continuously with a silicone spatula, until the oil is warm and the garlic is toasted to a golden brown, about 3 minutes.

Remove the pan from the heat and immediately add the parsley. Once the parsley has stopped bubbling, add the chili flakes and oregano. Pour into an airtight container and let cool to room temperature. Remove the reserved mussels from their shells and trim off any beard. Add the mussels to the oil and cover the container.

Refrigerate for up to 1 day.

FOR THE COD

Spread the herb crust over a plate. Brush the top of each piece of cod with cornstarch paste and dip the coated surface into the herb crust.

Heat a medium sauté pan over medium-high heat and add the clarified butter. Once hot, with a whisper of smoke, place the cod in the pan, crust-side down, add the garlic, and sauté until the crust is golden brown. Add the whole butter and the thyme and flip the pieces of cod. Baste the fish with the butter for about 1 minute, until the cod just begins to flake and is translucent in the center.

TO COMPLETE

Bring a large pot of salted water to a boil. Add 16 of the frozen tortellini, return the water to a boil, then adjust the heat to maintain a simmer and cook until the pasta is tender, 2 to 3 minutes. Transfer the cooked tortellini to a small pot of warm beurre monté to coat.

Reheat the bouillabaisse sauce.

Lightly oil a plancha and heat over a gas flame on high. Remove the mussels from the parsley-garlic oil, place them on the hot plancha, and cook to caramelize both sides. Remove and finish with a squeeze of lemon juice.

Pour 35 to 40 grams of the bouillabaisse sauce into each serving bowl. Place a piece of the cod in the center of the bowl, crust-side up, and arrange 2 tortellini around the cod. Garnish with the caramelized mussels.

NOTE

To make round fillets of cod, roll a loin of cod in plastic wrap, twisting and tying the ends to make a cylinder. Put the cod in the freezer until partially frozen to set the shape, then unwrap it and cut it crosswise into 50-gram rounds.

Chowry Salt

Makes about 170 grams

75 grams kosher salt	10 grams onion powder	2 grams pimentón (Spanish smoked paprika)
28 grams paprika	7 grams ground turmeric	
25 grams sugar	5 grams Espelette pepper	
10 grams garlic powder		1 gram ground oregano

Chowry salt can be used to season grilled meats, fish, or vegetables.

Whisk all the ingredients together in a bowl. Store in an airtight container at room temperature.

Smoking Fish

Fish fillets should be brined and/or cured, rinsed, and dried in the refrigerator near the fan, uncovered, for 6 to 12 hours. A thin skin (pellicle) should form on the fish; this will allow the smoke to adhere to the fillet. If you have a smoker, follow the same directions below.

Preheat the oven to 140°F (60°C) to smoke trout or cod, or to 167°F (75°C) if cooking sturgeon; set the fan to low. Adjust your oven racks so that the rack that will hold the fish is positioned about 6 inches (15 centimeters) over the rack that will hold the wood chips.

Place a cooling rack on a half sheet pan, line the rack with a tea towel, and arrange the fillets, skin-side down, on the towel.

Spread a shallow layer of wood chips in a small metal pan (the size of a pie tin). Using a grill lighter or culinary torch, set the chips on fire. Allow them to fully catch fire, then cover the pan with a tray to put out the fire.

Carefully uncover the chips and allow the discolored smoke to dissipate. Place the pan of chips to the left side of the lower rack in the oven and place the pan of fish on the right side of the top rack in the oven.

Smoke the fish for about 20 minutes, until the flesh is cooked and has a deep, smoky scent. Remove the fish from the oven, let cool to room temperature, then refrigerate in an airtight container until fully chilled. The fish can be vacuum-packed and refrigerated for up to 1 month or stored in an airtight container in the refrigerator for up to 3 days.

THE FRENCH LAUNDRY KITCHEN

The Evolution of Equipment and Space

IN MANY WAYS the French Laundry kitchens define the eras of the restaurant. There was the opening kitchen, in 1994, which was really Sally Schmitt's, where the salon is now. That was a 300-square-foot kitchen. The refrigeration was all on wheels. The hood was blue. We did stocks overnight on the ten-burner stove, and on a hot summer day, forget about it. The pilot lights didn't work, so I kept some butane clickers on the shelf above the stove to light the burners, and one night, one of them exploded from the heat—shrapnel right into my back, left a huge bruise. I liked that kitchen.

Almost as soon as we were open, I began building the second kitchen, which really allowed us to come into our own by giving us the space we needed. We had a prep room where big kettles of Veal #1 and Veal #2 simmered, burners that worked, big screened windows that let air and light in. I put in skylights. It was a beautiful kitchen, which I knew it had to be, if I were going to attract the kind of staff who were willing to work 12 to 14 hours a day at the level I needed.

In 2004, we undertook the first major rehabilitation of the kitchen, putting in an energy system called a geothermal loop, which would be our first commitment to sustainable heating, cooling, and refrigeration. The new system involved fourteen bores extending 450 feet into the earth below The French Laundry, eliminating all the exterior fans required for heating, cooling, and refrigeration—giving the grounds a serenity they hadn't known before. We added buildings for offices, a wine cellar, bathrooms for employees and guests. And we put in a new breezeway.

In 2014, I decided we needed a major makeover in order to keep pushing ourselves and continue the refinements. This took a lot of courage. Why undertake a multimillion-dollar reconstruction, disrupt a property that means so much to me, disrupt lives, tie up available cash while reducing cash flow? When we started this renovation, I was in my late fifties, and the restaurant was critically and financially successful. Why *do* it?

Because if I hadn't, we'd just be what we were before. Staying the same doesn't open up opportunities, doesn't require new thinking, or create new challenges. Being alive means changing, always evolving. In order to undertake this two-year job, we had to build what I consider the fourth kitchen, four shipping containers outfitted with all that we needed to keep The French Laundry open.

The current kitchen, our fifth, opened in 2017. Every detail of the new kitchen is important to me, down to the terrazzo floor with steel dividers eliminating the grout normally used in tiling (which is hard to clean and can trap bacteria), up to the skylight and chandelier and the ceiling whose white waves mimic the abundant white linen at The French Laundry. We put in solar panels that became the roof of the office building, which produce 16 kilowatts of energy every day—that's a lot of electricity, cutting out a chunk of our fossil fuel use, another part of our commitment to sustainability. We more than doubled the size of our geothermal loop, which takes care of all our refrigeration, air-conditioning, and heating—including the radiant-heated floors and the climate control in the wine cellar—and also heats about 60 percent of our water. The wood that now covers the outside of the building was preserved using the Japanese technique of wood preservation called *shou sugi ban*, so the exterior is beautiful and will last 150 years with no painting or maintenance.

And the most dramatic innovation in the kitchen was the elimination of ventilation hoods—our ceiling is ventilated. This opens lines of sight we've never had in any kitchen. And being able to see all the moving people and parts of the kitchen helps you work more efficiently. It gives you more room physically and in your mind.

The kitchen begins and ends in the dishwashers' station, one of its most important parts. As there was in the last kitchen, we have an immediate pass-through into the kitchen so that the chefs working first course and fish can put their used cookware in the window, eliminating the need for dishwashers to walk down the line collecting pots and pans, and clean cookware can be moved from the dishwashers back to the kitchen.

But there's more to the pass-through. It requires all pans to be passed back and forth, so that meat and garde manger stations pass to fish and first course, which then moves the pans to the pass-through dish station, all the chefs working together, all having to be aware of where each chef is in his or her service.

We have pass-through ovens as well. If the chef on the meat station opens his oven at the same time as the chef on fish, they can see each other. Though across from each other at the range, they share ovens.

I put a wood-burning hearth into this kitchen, something I'd never dreamed I'd do back when I built the second kitchen. But I love being able to serve fire-roasted meats and to give my chefs a new dimension to their cooking. Managing a continuously changing fire, and managing the varying cuts throughout service, requires intensely engaged cooking.

I've also put in a plancha, or griddle, which gets very hot, for searing scallops or griddling ramps, and it can be used at a lower heat to simmer stocks during the day. We also have a combi oven, which has been the most transformative cooking device in my lifetime, taking us beyond sous vide.

We have two big Bonnet ranges, one gas and one induction. Induction uses magnetism to heat the pan, so the only thing that gets hot is the pan itself, making this range and the area around it much cooler than the main course range. This is key because the pastry station is on the other side, and these chefs need a cool kitchen.

We've reduced the depth of the refrigerated drawers so that each station can fit more of them. We've elevated the drawers to leave foot room below the benches themselves; we've raised the benches so the chefs don't have to spend their time bent way down over their work surface. And we've installed lighting at foot level, which adds a dramatic visual element to the kitchen.

Everything was done for a reason, not least of all for simplicity, as I've realized that cooking will continue to evolve and we don't always know in what ways. In the per se kitchen, we built two holding tanks into the back of the main cooking area to fit the immersion circulators used for sous vide cooking. But combi ovens have replaced most of our sous vide cooking, something we couldn't have envisioned in 2004, so we find other uses for these permanent vessels. The French Laundry kitchen was built to evolve.

THE PER SE KITCHEN

Efficiency and Collaboration

THE PER SE KITCHEN is one of the best kitchens I've ever designed. It's fifteen years old, but it's still modern, in the quality and use of materials.

I eliminated walk-ins in this kitchen, thanks to the fabulous Traulsen refrigeration units, which allow each member of the team to be in charge of all the raw products they need. The fish butcher has a Traulsen, an ice machine, everything in the place where it's needed. The chef is self-contained. Their efficiency is enhanced because they're not going back and forth to the walk-in or the ice machine, where everyone else is going. This also gives each chef a sense of responsibility—that is that person's refrigerator, and if anything's out of place, dirty, or not labeled correctly, that chef is the only one responsible.

We have enclosed rooms for the butchery of both meats and fish. We have a central kitchen to serve the private dining rooms and use it as an additional prep and cooking area, and it's where we set up family meal every day at three forty-five.

And there is a smaller kitchen behind that where stocks are made and the big combi ovens do much of the initial cooking.

Through a corridor, past the business offices, is the bakery, including small cooled rooms for chocolate and sugar work. Putting the bakery in back, giving it its own production facility, allows us to produce the extraordinary amount of food for Bouchon Bakery that we didn't even know we'd need at the time we installed the facility, but can now accomplish.

And as is well known, there's a big-screen monitor looking out over the pass at both restaurants. I'm often asked whether I put them in to keep an eye on the staff. If I had to worry about that, we'd never have been successful in the first place! I put them there to connect the two kitchens, to connect their work, a visual reinforcement that we are not two separate restaurants but rather extensions of one entity. It works so well that I put monitors in the Bouchon restaurants, as well as at TAK Room and The Surf Club Restaurant in Florida. It's all about sharing.

BREAD AND BUTTER

For most of its history, The French Laundry had a traditional bread service, meaning bread was offered near the beginning of the meal, and then throughout the meal as needed. But the custom began to concern me.

Most people arrive at The French Laundry or per se having planned for a substantial meal and so are very hungry. After being served the cornet and the Oysters and Pearls, they were offered bread, which, of course, they ate. It's so good! But they were filling up on it. And once the courses began, they would *stop* eating the bread, so we ended up discarding it or donating it to city meal programs. I didn't like either outcome.

I wanted our guests to appreciate bread and butter as much as butter-poached lobster and Keith Martin's lamb. Our bread is made by our head executive baker, François Hiegel, and I'm so proud of what he and his team do. And our butter! Diane St. Clair's butter, handmade in Orwell, Vermont, on her Animal Farm, is the best butter in the world, in my opinion.

What if we give bread and butter the same weight as the other dishes on the menu, I thought, even print it on the menu, as a course of its own? This would allow us not only to feature the extraordinary craftsmanship of two members of our team, but also to tell their stories to each diner, François's journey from Alsace to Yountville, his work overseeing all of the restaurants' bread, and Diane's Animal Farm butter, some of it from a cow that is, I'm honored to say, named Keller.

In our redefined bread service, François makes an individual roll of great delicacy and aesthetic beauty, usually a lamination of two different-colored doughs, with a delicate exterior and a soft crumb. Each guest receives one roll, along with Diane's butter. (This also gave us an opportunity to design a new plate for this course.)

In addition to the day's featured roll, François makes a few different breads each day, which we can serve with specific courses if we wish, or if someone requests traditional bread service, we can accommodate them. But our focus is on that singular artisan roll.

People don't give a lot of thought to the baker, to the butter maker, but they ought to.

MEAT

"THE WHOLE BIRD"

Poached Breast with Leg Rillettes, Crispy Skin, and Sauce Suprême

Makes 4 servings

POULARDE

1 (3½- to
4-pound/1,500- to
1,800-gram) poularde

POULARDE LEG CONFIT

150 grams kosher salt

45 grams sugar

1.5 grams thyme leaves

1.5 grams lemon zest
(grated on a rasp
grater)

1 gram freshly ground
black pepper

2 garlic cloves

5 grams thyme sprigs

2 bay leaves

Duck fat (optional)

POULARDE STOCK

1,200 grams chicken
stock (page 285)

LEG RILLETTES

100 grams mousse base
(recipe follows), made
with 200 grams reserved
poularde leg meat

5 grams Burgundy
mustard

2.5 grams roasted garlic
puree (page 133)

1.5 grams kosher salt

1 gram minced shallot

Two grinds black pepper

SAUCE SUPRÊME

200 grams heavy cream

100 grams whole butter,
cut into cubes and
chilled

Lemon juice

Kosher salt

Armagnac

TO COMPLETE

Activa GS
(transglutaminase), for
dusting

Burgundy mustard

SPECIAL EQUIPMENT

Meat grinder with a
medium die, chilled in
the refrigerator

Chamber vacuum sealer
(optional)

Immersion circulator
(optional)

Poularde—a chicken slaughtered before reaching sexual maturity at around three months—from Four Story Hill Farm is exquisite, and Corey has developed an ingenious dish that puts the whole bird to work and a whole bird on the plate. Legs are both confited and used to make a mousse; the confit and mousse are then combined into a kind of rillette. These are spread on top of the breast, which is then poached gently. The skin is ground and rendered into cracklings, then used to coat the layer of rillettes. It's both an ode to the poularde as well as a show of respect to Sylvia and Stephen Pryzant, who in raising this bird achieved a kind of benchmark for the breed. I couldn't name a single chef in the country who had poularde on their menu before the Pryzants came along.

Of course, the beauty of this dish is that here two elements, the chicken and the sauce, are in fact extraordinary creations. The piece of chicken comprises every part of the chicken.

And the sauce. A *sauce suprême*, chicken stock thickened with a roux and finished with cream, is an elegant French sauce. Here Corey combines this classical idea with an Asian technique used for tonkatsu ramen broth. In classic French cuisine, stocks are simmered gently and skimmed continually to remove fat and impurities, while tonkatsu ramen broth is boiled heavily so the fat is emulsified into the broth. Corey takes that idea and applies it here, boiling his stock ramen-style (see page 285), but then goes further: he blends more chicken fat into the stock with a hand blender as he's chilling it. To finish the sauce, he combines this rich stock with reduced cream, mounts it with butter, and flavors it with lemon zest and Armagnac, creating this wonderfully rich and delicate version of *sauce suprême*.

I should note that Corey calls this "*sauce suprême*" knowing that it's nothing like the classic—but for good reason. He once served it at a dinner attended by Daniel Boulud and Jean-Georges Vongerichten, two of New York's best French-born chefs, and they kept delighting in the sauce and calling it an incredible *sauce suprême*. Corey tried to explain that they were mistaken, but they insisted it was the best *sauce suprême*. He was so honored, he continues to call it by this name.

FOR THE POULARDE

Cut the legs from the poularde. Remove and reserve the skin from the legs. One leg will be used for the confit and the other to make the mousse base. Remove and reserve the skin from the rest of the poularde. Cut off each side of the breast, keeping the small tender attached to each breast.

(continued)

Remove the bones from one leg and weigh the meat. You will need 200 grams to make the mousse base; if you do not have 200 grams, trim off some of the meat that remains on the carcass. Rinse the bones and feet (if they were on your poularde) under cold running water to remove all visible blood. Remove and discard any organs still attached to the bones. Cut the bones into 1-inch (2.5-centimeter) pieces and reserve them for the poularde stock.

Keep all parts of the poularde refrigerated in an airtight container until you are ready to use them, up to 2 days.

Grind the skin through the chilled medium die of a meat grinder and place it in a 2-quart (2-liter) saucepot. Cook over low heat for about 30 minutes to render. The fat will separate and the skin will become crisp and golden brown. Strain the fat through a chinois or fine-mesh strainer into a bowl and let cool to room temperature; reserve the fat for the stock. Drain the fried skin on paper towels and let cool until crisp, then chop it very finely and reserve it for finishing the dish.

FOR THE POULARDE LEG CONFIT

Mix the salt, sugar, thyme, lemon zest, and pepper in a bowl. On a piece of plastic wrap, make a bed of just less than half of this cure. Lay the bone-in poularde leg on the bed of cure and pat the remaining cure over and around the sides of the leg. Cover with the plastic wrap and refrigerate for about 2½ hours.

Rinse and dry the cured poularde leg.

If you have a chamber vacuum sealer, set an immersion circulator in a water bath and heat the water to 80°C (176°F). Place the cured poularde leg, garlic, thyme, and bay leaves in a sous vide bag. Place the bag in the sealer chamber and vacuum seal. Cook in the water bath for 5 hours.

If you do not have a chamber vacuum sealer, preheat the oven to 200°F (93°C). Place the cured poularde leg, garlic cloves, thyme sprigs, and bay leaves in a small heavy-bottomed pan and add duck fat to cover. Cover with a cartouche and cook in the oven for about 2 hours, until completely tender.

Remove the bag from the water bath or the pan from the oven and let the leg cool in the fat. Remove the leg from the fat and dry it on a clean kitchen towel. Carefully pick the meat from the bones, removing any veins. Shred the meat as finely as possible and chop. Reserve the meat for the rillettes.

FOR THE POULARDE STOCK

Combine the reserved poularde bones and feet (if using) and the chicken stock in a 2-quart (2-liter) saucepot and bring to a rapid boil over high heat. Boil for about 30 minutes, until the stock has reduced by half. Do not skim or reduce the heat at any point.

Strain the stock through a chinois or fine-mesh strainer into a clean pot, bring to a boil, and reduce the stock by about two-thirds to about 200 grams. Strain the reduced stock into a narrow vessel and nestle the container in an ice-water bath to cool.

When the stock has cooled, using a hand blender, blend in 55 grams of the reserved rendered poularde fat on high speed.

Refrigerate the stock in an airtight container until ready to use, up to 3 days. Once the emulsion is set, it can be reheated or cooled without any risk of breaking.

FOR THE LEG RILLETTES

Combine 75 to 100 grams of the chopped poularde leg confit with the mousse base, mustard, roasted garlic puree, salt, shallot, and pepper and mix until completely homogenous. Transfer to a disposable piping bag and refrigerate until ready to use, up to 1 day.

FOR THE SAUCE SUPRÊME

Bring the cream to a gentle boil in a 2-quart (2-liter) saucepot over medium-high heat, adjusting the heat as necessary, and reduce the cream by a little more than half to about 75 grams. Add 200 grams of the poularde stock to the pan and reduce the sauce by half. Rapidly stir the butter into the sauce (this will improve the richness, body, and shine of the sauce). Season with lemon juice, salt, and Armagnac to taste. Keep in a warm spot until serving.

TO COMPLETE

Lay the two poularde breasts on the work surface with the tenders facing up. Using a paring knife, very carefully remove the white tendon on each tender. Peel the tenders back but leave them attached to the breasts. Lightly spray the exposed side of the breasts with water and sprinkle the surface lightly with Activa (shake it through a small fine-mesh strainer or from a shaker). Fold the tenders back into place. Turn the breasts over.

Wipe the work surface with a slightly dampened kitchen towel. Lay out two pieces of plastic wrap, each about 9 inches (23 centimeters) long. Smooth the plastic so that there are no creases. Spray the plastic lightly with nonstick spray. Lay a breast on each piece of plastic, about one-third of the way up from the bottom edge. The length of the breast should run the direction of the length of the plastic. Pipe a line of the rillettes down the center of each breast. Use a small offset spatula to spread the rillettes evenly into a ¼-inch (6-millimeter) layer across each breast, spreading it to the edges of the breasts. Fold the top of the plastic up and over each breast to meet the other side.

Continue to "flip" the breasts in the plastic, keeping the bottom of the breast flat and the rillettes in a natural dome. Keep the plastic wrap tight. Pull the ends of the plastic tightly, then trim them and tuck under the breast to hold its shape.

If you have a chamber vacuum sealer, set an immersion circulator in a water bath and heat the water to 60°C (140°F). Place the breasts in a sous vide bag. Place the bag in the sealer chamber and vacuum seal. Cook in the water bath for 45 minutes. Remove the bag and let rest until cool enough to handle. Remove the breasts from the bag and remove the plastic wrap.

If you do not have a chamber vacuum sealer, preheat the oven to 180°F (80°C). Put the poularde in a wide 2-quart (2-liter) saucepot (just large enough to hold the pieces of poularde without their touching each other) and add enough water to cover by 1 inch (2.5 centimeters). Remove the poularde and set aside in a bowl. Bring the stock to 180°F (80°C). Return the poularde to the pot, cover with a lid, and place in the oven. Poach for 30 to 40 minutes, until an instant-read thermometer inserted into a breast reads 160°F (71°C). Remove the poularde breast from the stock and let rest until cool enough to handle. Remove the breasts from the plastic wrap.

Slice each breast in half on a slight bias. Using a small pastry brush, lightly brush the top of the breast with mustard. Carefully cover the top of the breast with the reserved crispy skin. Spoon the sauce suprême on each serving plate and place a piece of the poularde alongside.

Mousse Base

Makes 370 grams

200 grams lean protein	4 grams kosher salt	***SPECIAL EQUIPMENT***
30 grams egg whites	90 grams heavy cream	Meat grinder with a medium die
5 grams potato starch	40 grams crème fraîche, preferably Kendall Farms	

This recipe works well with all types of lean protein, including chicken, pike, scallops, raw lobster, beef, or veal.

Refrigerate a medium die for a meat grinder, food processor bowl, and food processor blade until cold. Cut the protein into ½-inch (1.25-centimeter) dice. Grind the protein twice through the chilled medium die into a bowl.

Transfer the protein to the chilled food processor bowl and process until smooth. Add the egg whites and process briefly to emulsify. Using a silicone spatula, scrape the bowl and the lid of the food processor. Add the potato starch and salt and process briefly to combine. It is important not to overwork the mousse, as the friction of the blade will overheat the mousse and cause it to break.

With the machine running, slowly add the cream to maintain the emulsification. Scrape the sides and the lid of the food processor again. Add the crème fraîche and process until the mousse becomes smooth and develops a nice shine.

Transfer the mousse to a bowl and nestle the bowl in an ice-water bath to chill. Press a piece of plastic wrap directly against the surface of the mousse, smoothing out any air bubbles, and refrigerate until cold. For longer storage, transfer the mousse to an airtight container, press a piece of plastic wrap directly against the surface, cover, and refrigerate for up to 3 days.

STEPHEN AND SYLVIA PRYZANT

*Four Story Hill Farm,
Damascus, Pennsylvania*

Stephen and Sylvia met in Israel in the 1970s, when Stephen spent two years working on a kibbutz and Sylvia was a student in Tel Aviv. For Stephen, working on a farm was transformative. He learned that he loved working with animals. He brought Sylvia, who was born in North Africa and spent her youth there and in France, back to his hometown of New York City. While he worked as a director of food services for a nursing home in Brooklyn, they hunted for land to buy on which to raise animals. They found a piece of land with an old barn on it and put a double-wide trailer on the property. Sylvia and Stephen began building the farm, while Stephen also maintained his job in Brooklyn.

Just as they were raising their first animals, their barn was crushed by a snowstorm. And that winter, Stephen lost his job. They now had no other choice but to commit to their ultimate desire of a life spent raising animals.

Tom Colicchio was one of the first chefs Stephen and Sylvia contacted. He told me about them, and I began ordering their veal in the mid-1990s, shortly after I opened The French Laundry. That's how long our relationship goes back.

Currently they raise 18 head of beef cattle, 120 pigs, and a lot of poultry. So much poultry that they often have to ask their neighbor down the street to help them process the birds. They don't only raise the poulardes we use at per se; they also process the birds themselves and drive hours to New York City to deliver them personally, so they know their cared-for cargo is perfectly handled all the way to its final destination. And they love knowing how carefully Corey will prepare and serve their birds.

The Pryzants' devotion to raising the best birds lured Sylvia back to France, where she studied how the famous Bresse chickens were cared for, and Four Story Hill Farm began raising their first milk-fed poussins. The poulardes she raises for us have lots of room to run around, are fed a natural diet, and are slaughtered before they reach sexual maturity (which happens at around twenty-three weeks).

This is not a job for them—it's more like a calling. This is not a nine-to-five, or even the one-p.m.-to-one-a.m. job of a young chef. Those animals need caring for constantly. And Stephen and Sylvia custom butcher fifty-two weeks a year. They are always working.

"Our relationship with our chefs transcends friendship," Sylvia says. "We enjoy a wonderful warm and friendly relationship, but our goal in our craft is to maintain a high level of excellence in their honor. No matter what, we're only as good as our last delivery."

WOLFE RANCH WHITE QUAIL

Blueberry and Barley Farce, Garden Turnips and Greens, and Foie Gras "Mignonette"

BARLEY

60 grams sweet yellow onion

20 grams clarified butter (page 53)

8 grams kosher salt

140 grams pearl barley

140 grams chicken stock (page 285)

140 grams water

BLUEBERRY AND BARLEY FARCE

Marinated Meat

150 grams ½-inch-dice (1.25-centimeter) boneless, skinless chicken thighs

50 grams ½-inch-dice (1.25-centimeter) fatty slab bacon

30 grams ½-inch-dice (1.25-centimeter) slab fatback

3 grams kosher salt

1 gram freshly ground black pepper

Blueberries and Onions

5 grams whole butter

20 grams coarsely chopped sweet yellow onion

5 grams kosher salt

20 grams dried blueberries

60 grams heavy cream

20 grams diced brioche, crust removed

QUAIL

3 Wolfe Ranch white quail, about 300 grams each

FOIE GRAS "MIGNONETTE" SAUCE

25 grams whole butter

135 grams foie gras

35 grams ¼-inch-dice (6-millimeter) shallots

2.5 grams black peppercorns

2 thyme sprigs

100 grams cognac, plus more to taste

12 grams all-purpose flour

500 grams veal stock (page 287), warmed

60 grams crème fraîche

Sherry vinegar

Kosher salt

Coarsely ground black pepper

CREAMED BARLEY

175 grams sweet onion béchamel (page 111)

Kosher salt

Champagne vinegar

TURNIPS

6 petite Hakurei or Tokyo turnips, with their greens

Canola oil, for sautéing

50 grams chicken stock (page 285)

5 grams whole butter

Kosher salt

TO COMPLETE

Canola oil, for sautéing

75 grams whole butter

4 thyme sprigs

3 garlic cloves, skin on, lightly smashed

SPECIAL EQUIPMENT

Meat grinder with a medium die, chilled in the refrigerator

We love Brent Wolfe's quail—Brent has been a partner for twenty-two years—and serve it a number of ways. Because the quail is fed barley, we like to feature barley in the garnish for this dish, making a creamed barley using a turnip béchamel and also including the grain in the farce we layer between the quail breast and skin. The farce contains blueberries as well as brioche, which makes for a wonderful and enriching panade. The sauce is rich with foie gras and brandy and aromatics, and named for the classic sauce that features black pepper.

FOR THE BARLEY

Mince the onion to the consistency of a paste. Melt the butter in a 2-quart (2-liter) saucepot over medium-low heat. Add the onion and salt. Sweat the onion in the butter, stirring occasionally, for about 2 minutes, until translucent.

Stir in the barley and toast, stirring occasionally, for 2 to 3 minutes, until you smell a nutty aroma. Add the chicken stock and water and bring to a boil. Reduce the heat, cover with a lid, and simmer gently for 25 to 30 minutes, until the barley is tender and all the liquid has been absorbed. Spread the barley on a tray and refrigerate until cold.

Reserve 30 grams of the barley for the farce and refrigerate the remaining barley in an airtight container for the creamed barley.

FOR THE BLUEBERRY AND BARLEY FARCE

Prepare the marinated meat: Combine the chicken thighs, slab bacon, fatback, salt, and pepper in a bowl, cover, and refrigerate.

Prepare the blueberries and onions: Melt the butter in a medium sauté pan over medium-low heat. Add the onion and salt and sweat for about 5 minutes, until translucent and fragrant.

Add the blueberries and cream and bring to a boil. Add the diced brioche and the reserved 30 grams cooked barley and stir until the mixture is combined and the bread soaks up the cream. Remove from the heat, spread on a tray, and refrigerate until cold.

(continued)

Grind the marinated meats twice through the chilled medium die of a meat grinder into a bowl. Add the blueberries and onions to the ground meat and grind once more. Transfer the farce to a disposable piping bag and refrigerate.

FOR THE QUAIL

Using butcher's shears or a small knife, cut off the first two joints of the wings and reserve in the refrigerator for the sauce. Place the bird on the work surface with the legs toward you. Cut through the skin between the leg and breast on one side, leaving as much skin attached to the breast as possible. Feel for the joint between the thigh and the body and use your fingers to separate the bones at the joint. Repeat on the other side (this makes it easier to cut off the legs). Using the shears or knife, remove the legs and reserve in the refrigerator for the sauce. Cut off the bottom half of the backbone extending over the cavity and discard it. You are now left with the "crown." Repeat with the remaining quail.

Starting at the narrow point of the breast, closest to the cavity opening, gently peel the skin back from the breast and over the top of the crown, leaving the opposite end of the skin attached to the body. Pipe 70 grams of the farce over the breast meat. Using a small offset spatula, spread the farce to cover the entire breast in an even layer about ⅛ inch (3 millimeters) thick. Repeat with the remaining quail. Place the quail on a tray and refrigerate them for about 30 minutes, until the farce is slightly firm, then pull the skin back over the farce to encase it.

Refrigerate the quail overnight, uncovered, positioning them close to the refrigerator's fan to help dry the skin.

FOR THE FOIE GRAS "MIGNONETTE" SAUCE

Melt the butter over medium heat in a rondeau large enough to hold the quail wings and legs in one layer. Add 200 grams of the reserved quail wings and legs to the pan in a single layer. Lightly caramelize the wings and legs, turning them frequently, for about 15 minutes, until rich golden brown on all sides.

Add 25 grams of the foie gras and the shallots, peppercorns, and thyme and stir over low heat for about 2 minutes, until the shallots are tender and the aromatics become fragrant.

Carefully add the cognac to the pan and ignite. Cook to burn off the alcohol and reduce the liquid until the pan is almost dry. Add the flour and stir with a flat wooden or silicone spatula, scraping the bottom to prevent sticking, and allow the flour to soak up the rendered foie gras fat and remaining butter.

Strain the veal stock through a chinois into the rondeau; whisk to fully incorporate. Rinse the chinois. Bring the sauce to a simmer and cook gently, skimming off any excess fat and impurities that rise to the surface, for 20 minutes.

Strain the sauce through the chinois into a blender, lightly pressing on the solids to extract as much essence as possible. Blend, beginning on low speed and gradually increasing to high. Add the remaining 110 grams foie gras and the crème fraîche through the opening in the blender cap and puree until fully incorporated and smooth. Rinse the chinois.

Season the sauce to taste with cognac, vinegar, and salt. Strain through the chinois into a container and finish with ground black pepper to taste.

The sauce can be refrigerated in an airtight container for up to 3 days. This makes more sauce than you will need, but extra sauce can be frozen, then defrosted in the refrigerator and warmed gently.

FOR THE CREAMED BARLEY

Warm the sweet onion béchamel in a 2-quart (2-liter) saucepot over low heat. Fold the remaining cooked barley into the béchamel. The béchamel should just bind the barley, but not be too loose. The mixture should be stiff enough to shape into a quenelle. Gently warm the barley over medium heat, stirring regularly, until hot, 2 to 4 minutes. Adjust the seasoning with salt and vinegar to taste. Cover the pot and keep warm.

FOR THE TURNIPS

Cut the greens from the turnips, leaving about ½ inch (1.25 centimeters) attached. Discard the stems and reserve the greens. Wash the turnips and greens in cold water. Quarter the turnips.

Heat a medium sauté pan over medium heat. Add enough canola oil to lightly coat the bottom of the pan. Add the turnip quarters and sauté until golden brown on all sides, about 5 minutes. Move the turnips to one side of the pan and add the turnip greens to the other side.

Add the chicken stock and butter to the greens and cook, turning them occasionally, for about 2 minutes to wilt. Season with salt to taste.

Transfer the turnips and greens to paper towels to drain excess liquid. Keep in a warm spot until serving.

TO COMPLETE

Remove the quail from the refrigerator to temper for about 30 minutes, to a cool room temperature. Preheat the oven to 450°F (232°C) with the fan set to low.

Heat a large sauté pan over medium-high heat. Pour ¼ inch (6 millimeters) of canola oil into the pan. When the oil is nearly smoking, add the quail to the pan, placing them so one side of each breast is fully in contact with the side of the pan, which will prop up the birds and hold them in place. Cook until the skin is dark golden brown, then rotate the birds to brown the opposite sides of the breasts. Continue to rotate the birds as needed for even browning of the breasts.

Turn the birds to sit flat in the pan, breast-side up, and place the pan in the oven. Roast for 3 minutes. Carefully remove the pan from the oven and baste the birds with the fat in the pan; return to the oven and roast for 3 minutes more. At this point, the birds should be nearly cooked. To test, insert a cake tester into the thickest part of the breast, closest to the breastbone, then touch it to your lip; it should be warm.

Remove the quail from the oven, transfer them to a tray, and drain the fat from the pan. Return the pan to medium heat, add the butter, thyme, and garlic to the pan, and allow the butter to foam. Return the birds to the pan, breast-side up, and baste with the butter three or four times.

Return the birds to the tray, standing them on their neck ends (cavity side up) and propping them up against each other. Pour the butter and aromatics from the pan into the cavities and rest in a warm spot for 8 to 10 minutes.

Remove each side of the breasts by slicing down from the breastbone along the body until the breast comes free from the crown. Trim the edges and any small pieces of bone or cartilage still attached to the meat.

Place a quenelle of the creamed barley on each serving plate. Place a piece of the quail breast on top farce-side down, pressing it lightly to flatten the barley slightly. Arrange the greens on the plates, trailing them behind the quail, and arrange the pieces of turnip around the greens. Finish with a spoonful of the sauce.

BRENT WOLFE

Wolfe Quail,
Vacaville, California

When he was a boy, Brent Wolfe loved animals and had pets of all kinds—cats, dogs, snakes, possums, tortoises he'd find trying to cross the road near his family's home in San Rafael, California, north of San Francisco. Around 1971, when he was ten, his pal bought some chickens to raise. Brent asked his parents if he could, too. His parents, children of a local feed store owner and a veterinarian, said sure. Brent loved raising his birds so much that when a chicken industry event came to the Cow Palace, an indoor arena south of San Francisco, his mother dropped him off there at eight in the morning and said, "I'll see you tonight at five."

Alone and bored after the first hour of a trade show filled with adults, he got to talking to Albert Marsh, a quail farmer who made his money manufacturing incubators and hatchers for eggs. Marsh demoed his devices all day at the trade show, hatching eggs for interested customers. At the end of the day, Brent asked what Marsh was going to do with the quail chicks he'd hatched. "Garbage," the man said. "I can't fly them back to Anaheim." Brent asked if he could have them. His mom arrived at five to pick him up, and drove home with Brent—and his twenty-seven new charges. And that's how he got into the quail business.

"I've lived with these birds my whole life," he says.

By the time Brent got out of college, he'd decided to forgo his plans of becoming a veterinarian and try to make a go of quail farming. He still had his small original colony of quail in the backyard, which his youngest brother had taken care of while Brent was in college.

When Brent was twenty-one, his father helped him to buy a 2.5-acre "ranchette" so that Brent could expand his business beyond the family's backyard. He sold his quail eggs to sushi restaurants in San Francisco. His biggest client was a man named Sun Myung Moon and his Unification Church; Brent had no idea.

Early in his breeding career, Brent was told by a French chef in Sausalito that his quail were too small, so he began breeding for size, but he still didn't know what to do with them. Except for a few forward-thinking restaurants, no one was putting quail on their menus in the mid-1980s. Brent's mom had a suggestion, reminding Brent that his childhood friend John Bertolli had a brother who was a chef.

Paul Bertolli was a young chef at a Berkeley restaurant called Chez Panisse. Brent thought he'd give it a shot, and went to speak to Paul. Paul was interested. The creator of Chez Panisse, Alice Waters, sent a partner up to see how Brent raised his birds, approved, and Brent had his first big client at the seminal restaurant.

Chef-patrons such as Mark Miller and Bradley Ogden ate at Chez Panisse, and soon *they* were buying Brent's quail. Ogden began making a name for himself at the Campton Place hotel. When Wolfgang Puck came to town, he ate at Ogden's restaurant and tasted the quail. He called Brent the next morning at seven—Brent thought it was a crank call—and said, "I must have your quail for Spago!" Brent recalls. "And that's when the business really took off," he says.

Brent continued to raise birds, eventually buying four different ranches; he has plans to buy another soon. We cherish his quail—it's big and meaty, with a very pure poultry flavor. He breeds for size and consistency, and his genetics have evolved more docile birds, quiet by nature, that process better (they generate less adrenaline at slaughter, which can lower the pH of the meat), and therefore taste better. And they also happen to be easier and more fun to work with. He continues to sell only about 1,500 to 1,700 birds a week in all.

I still remember the first time he came to dine at The French Laundry (Brent doesn't remember this part of the story, but I definitely do). I'd been trying to work with pheasant, even hanging them to age—a common practice for a bird that doesn't have a lot of flavor—without success, and asked for his help. He hadn't farmed pheasant since he was a teenager, but when he arrived with his girlfriend for dinner, he entered through the kitchen—with two wild pheasants he'd shot himself to bring me as a gift! One was dressed, and one he'd left in full plume. He and his girlfriend arrived in the kitchen and gave me the birds, and I personally escorted them to the dining room, dead wild birds in my hand. The dining room went silent!

He told me not to serve them to customers—they had shot in them. I told him I had Swiss royalty dining soon, and that they were used to eating wild game and would appreciate these fine birds.

THE PORCELET AND OTHER WHOLE ANIMAL PREPARATIONS

"Porcelet," suckling pig, is a milk-fed piglet raised on a Canadian farm for D'Artagnan, a company started by Ariane Daguin. (Ariane, it should be noted, is among those who helped transform the food world with this company, which began by selling foie gras. I remember when she was selling it out of the back of her car.)

This particular dish, and this very special cut of pork—the entire, bone-in middle section of the baby pig—is a great example of the way our kitchen can combine various parts of the animal in a single portion. I've been doing this since we began bringing whole baby lambs into The French Laundry in the spring, and composing a dish using all its parts, sautéed chop, braised breast and shoulder, rillettes from the trim, a small slice of sautéed kidney (I love kidney), and sauce made from the bones and braising liquid.

Now we like to combine various parts into a single sliceable portion. But the cooking of the various muscles requires different times and temperatures, so Corey and his team came up with this great method of total utilization—and an enormously elegant three-star service.

First the tenderloin spine and the last ten ribs are removed and saved for stock. The loin is then removed whole, leaving only the fat skin and belly. This is all cooked sous vide low and slow till everything is very tender.

The belly meat is separated from the skin and coarsely chopped to be garnish for a pork mousseline (the tenderloin is too small to feature on its own and so becomes a part of the belly mixture). The skin is scraped of excess fat so that it will crisp up nicely.

We put it all back together in a quarter sheet pan: skin-side down; a layer of the belly mousseline; the raw loin, which has been butterflied

and pounded to a uniform thickness and the width and length of the sheet pan. Finally, we top this with a layer of shingled bacon.

We vacuum seal this sheet pan and cook it again just until the loin is done, then weight it down as it chills. Once it's chilled, it can be portioned to size and sautéed at service. The piece in this photograph has five layers: crispy skin; a very thin layer of fat; the thickest layer of mousseline forcemeat made from the trim and belly; a layer of loin; and on the very bottom, a layer of bacon.

We can serve this in various ways. Here it's shown with fava tendrils that have been wilted with shallot, chopped, then creamed with sou-béch (see page 111) and shaped into a quenelle; a crispy romano bean, breaded and fried; and a classic sauce périgourdine (veal stock, red wine, and truffles, reduced to sauce consistency, mounted with butter, and seasoned with sherry vinegar).

This, like the baby spring lamb and Corey's poularde preparation (see page 251), comes under the mantle of serving as much of the animal as possible in a single dish, which is ultimately a way to show our respect to the animal itself and the people who raise it.

SALT-AND-RYE-BAKED LAMB NECK

Riz Rouge, Tender Garden Roots, and Navarin Bouillon

Makes 4 to 6 servings

RYE BREAD

270 grams all-purpose flour

270 grams rye flour

270 grams spelt flour

24 grams kosher salt

17 grams caraway seeds

2 grams SAF Gold instant yeast

600 grams sourdough starter or rye levain (follow the recipe for liquid levain on page 272 of *Bouchon Bakery*, using rye flour instead of all-purpose flour)

540 grams water

LAMB NECK

1 (2-pound) piece lamb neck, lightly trimmed of excess fat

Sel gris

3 grams caraway seeds

NAVARIN BOUILLON

40 grams clarified butter (page 53)

450 grams ½-inch-dice (1.25-centimeter) peeled purple-top turnips

300 grams ½-inch-dice (1.25-centimeter) peeled bunch carrots

60 grams thinly sliced garlic

20 grams whole butter

10 grams sugar

3 thyme sprigs

8 grams black peppercorns

2 bay leaves

8 flat-leaf parsley sprigs

200 grams Cabernet Sauvignon

60 grams red wine vinegar

1,000 grams (1 quart/ 1 liter) mushroom essence (page 289)

50 grams red beet juice

45 grams sherry vinegar, plus more to taste

20 grams tamari

115 grams egg whites

25 grams cornstarch

15 grams fleur de sel

RIZ ROUGE

450 grams water

150 grams riz rouge

4 grams kosher salt

TENDER GARDEN ROOTS

18 baby turnips, stems trimmed to ¼ inch (6 millimeters)

18 baby radishes, stems trimmed to ¼ inch (6 millimeters)

18 small Nantes carrots, about 2 inches (5 centimeters) long, stems trimmed to ¼ inch (6 millimeters)

Canola oil

30 grams whole butter

3 garlic cloves, crushed

4 or 5 thyme sprigs

I think this simple piece of lamb neck baked in rye bread is a stunner. We prepared this dish for the first time in the early days at per se for a special guest who was very fond of extravagant presentations. It is simply a piece of meat wrapped in a generous portion of dough and slowly baked for a very long time. It is served off the bone with a stew of tender root vegetables and rice, and the bread itself is served as an accompaniment to soak up the jus.

FOR THE RYE BREAD

Mix all the ingredients together in the bowl of a stand mixer fitted with the paddle. Mix on low speed for 4 minutes, then increase the speed to medium-low and mix for 5 minutes more, scraping the sides and bottom of the bowl as needed.

Cover the bowl with a clean kitchen towel and place it in a warm place to proof for 1 hour, or until it has doubled in size. Fold the edges of the dough toward the center and punch down the dough. Flip the dough over, cover, and proof for 1 hour more, or until doubled in size. Fold in the edges of the dough and punch down again. Turn the dough over in the bowl, cover the bowl with plastic wrap, and refrigerate for at least 6 hours or up to 1 day.

FOR THE LAMB NECK

Preheat the oven to 350°F (180°C). Spray a 2-quart (2-liter) ovenproof metal bowl with nonstick spray or use a lined banneton basket.

Remove the rye bread dough from the refrigerator. On a lightly floured work surface, press the dough out into a sheet about ¾ inch (2 centimeters) thick and large enough to wrap around the lamb neck completely. Season the lamb liberally with sel gris and place it in the center of the dough. Wrap the dough around the neck completely and place it seam-side down in the prepared bowl. Set in a warm spot to proof for 30 minutes.

Sprinkle the caraway seeds over the top and place the bowl in the oven. Bake for 40 minutes, until the crust is set and light golden brown in color, then reduce the oven temperature to 300°F (150°C) and bake for 4 hours more. Remove from the oven and let rest for 30 minutes.

FOR THE NAVARIN BOUILLON

Heat a 4-quart (4-liter) saucepot over medium-high heat and add the clarified butter. Add the turnips, carrots, and garlic and caramelize in the butter, stirring regularly to prevent sticking, until deep golden brown, 4 to 7 minutes. Add the whole butter, sugar, thyme, peppercorns, bay leaves, and parsley sprigs and cook until the aromatics become fragrant, 1 to 2 minutes.

Add the red wine and the red wine vinegar and reduce until the pan is dry. Add the mushroom essence, beet juice, sherry vinegar, and tamari and bring to a simmer. Remove the pot from the heat, cover with a lid, and steep for 30 minutes.

Strain the liquid through a chinois into a clean 2-quart (2-liter) saucepot, pressing lightly on the solids to extract the liquid. Reserve one-quarter of the strained broth in a separate container.

Place the egg whites in a medium bowl and whisk lightly just to break them up. Whisk the reserved broth into the egg whites to temper them. Quickly whisk the tempered egg whites into the pot of broth.

Place the pot over medium-high heat and cook, dragging a flat-sided silicone spatula over the bottom of the pot frequently to prevent the egg whites from scorching, until the egg whites rise to the top of the broth and form a raft. Simmer gently, without stirring, for 15 minutes or until clear, monitoring the broth carefully and adjusting the heat as necessary to keep the raft in one piece. If the broth bubbles too aggressively, it will break the raft. The resulting consommé will become perfectly clear; check the consommé by spooning a small bit from the side of the pot.

Line a colander or perforated pan with a dampened tea towel and set it over a clean saucepot. (Dampening the towel will prevent it from absorbing the consommé.) Carefully pour the contents of the pot through the towel; the raft should come out in one piece. Discard the raft.

Measure 100 grams of the consommé into a small bowl and let cool to room temperature. Whisk in the cornstarch until smooth, then whisk the mixture into the consommé in the pot. Bring to a simmer over medium heat and cook gently for 4 to 5 minutes, until the sauce has thickened. Strain through a chinois into a saucepot and add the fleur de sel and additional sherry vinegar to taste. Cover with a lid to keep warm for up to 1 hour before serving.

The bouillon can be refrigerated in an airtight container for up to 3 days or frozen for longer storage.

FOR THE RIZ ROUGE

Preheat the oven to 350°F (180°C).

Bring the water to a boil in a 2-quart (2-liter) saucepot. Stir in the rice and salt. Cover the saucepot and transfer to the oven. Bake for 35 to 45 minutes, until all the water has been absorbed and the rice is tender and fluffy. Remove from the oven and let rest, covered, for 10 minutes.

FOR THE TENDER GARDEN ROOTS

Wash the vegetables in cold water and rub them with a clean kitchen towel to remove any hairs or dirt.

Heat a large sauté pan over medium-high heat. Add enough canola oil to coat the bottom of the pan. Add the vegetables and roll them in the pan to caramelize on all sides. Reduce the heat to medium-low and cook until the vegetables are tender, about 7 minutes. Test them with a cake tester; it should slide in easily.

Add the butter. When it foams, add the garlic and thyme to the pan. Roll the vegetables in the butter for about 1 minute, then drain on paper towels.

TO COMPLETE

If necessary, rewarm the bouillon in a saucepot.

Cut off the top of the bread and reserve. Remove the neck from the bread and set aside. Strain the cooking juices in the bread into the bouillon. Pick the meat from the neck and shred or coarsely chop it into smaller pieces.

Arrange the rice, meat, and root vegetables in each serving bowl. Ladle in the bouillon. Slice the bread into smaller pieces and serve it on the side.

LOW AND SLOW

Whether using an immersion circulator for traditional sous vide cooking or achieving the same precise-temperature cooking with a combi oven, we stick to six base temperatures as guidelines.

Exact times depend on the thickness or overall mass and bone density of the item being cooked, but with precise-temperature cooking, you have a broad window in terms of hitting the temperature and texture you're after because the carryover cooking isn't as extreme as it would be with conventional higher-temperature methods.

"The Veg Temp": 88°C (190°F), 15 to 60 minutes. Good for pretty much all nongreen vegetables—root vegetables, artichokes, hearts of palm, white asparagus, cèpe confit, Belgian endive. About the only vegetable we cook at a higher temperature is the potato, 100°C (212°F) for 45 minutes. The starches in potatoes prefer the higher temperature.

"The Custard Temp": 83°C (181.4°F), 15 to 40 minutes. The perfect temperature for custards and preparations in which eggs are mixed with other ingredients, such as the Sunchoke Custard (page 159) or our classic truffle custard.

"The Confit Temp": 80°C (176°F), 5 to 8 hours. Used for whole muscles cooked in the style of confit, meaning cooked low and slow in their own fat, which keeps the meat moist and tender. Specific cuts include pork necks, duck and rabbit legs, and lamb shoulders. The time can vary slightly depending on the size, the muscle density, and whether or not the meat is on the bone.

"The Workhorse Temp": 64°C (147.2°F), 60 to 90 minutes for cuts served rosé; typically 48 hours for braises. Our standard braising temperature for all long-braised fatty meats such as brisket, short ribs, and tongue. This sous vide method produces a much more succulent result than traditional braising, because the low temperature doesn't force the meat fibers to contract as they do when cooked at higher temperatures, which squeezes the fat out of the meat. Do look at the classic Escoffier braising method, however, which I think is superior to all.

In addition to braises, meats that are traditionally served rosé, or medium—such as lamb saddles, lamb racks, veal chops, and the fatty calotte of beef—are cooked at this temperature, and then finished gently over fire or in a sauté pan with butter.

"The Service Temp": 60°C (140°F), 10 to 90 minutes. For somewhat leaner and more compact and tight-fibered cuts of meat such as sirloins, eye of the rib (both from the same heavy-load muscle, the longissimus dorsi), and the tenderloin. The cuts are then rested, and finished over fire or in a sauté pan with butter.

Fillets of fish such as sole, turbot, sturgeon, and John Dory, and some shellfish such as lobster tail and king crab, are also cooked at this temperature, but for shorter times, usually 10 to 15 minutes. We generally enrobe the fish in a mousse or confit it au naturel.

"The Slow-Poached Temp": 35°C (95°F), 15 to 45 minutes. Discovered by chef Eli Kaimeh, a former chef de cuisine at per se, this temperature is perfect for activating and just setting the proteins in an ingredient such as the bone marrow for the crispy bone marrow on our calotte (see page 279) or an à la minute lardo made from cured pork fatback. It is also a great way to just set the protein in a fatty fillet of wild salmon or sea trout that will then be poached and served chilled or at room temperature, such as in a chaud-froid (see page 126). This results in a perfectly cooked and buttery fish that flakes ever so delicately. A favorite of both of my chefs.

FIRE AND SMOKE

The French Laundry and per se have different kitchens, so their ability to use fire and smoke varies. The French Laundry has the luxury of a hearth. Per se does not. So when per se staff want to cook over fire, they generally use a hibachi charcoal grill.

Both kitchens are fans of binchotan, the compressed Japanese charcoal that burns especially hot and clean. The high heat of it, however, is best suited to searing food over glowing coals. Cooking over binchotan is not the right choice for larger cuts of meat or fish, unless they have been poached or confited first and then seared over the charcoal as the *arroser* step, the third step in the three-step cooking process. Almost all our meats go through the initial cooking step, then a resting step, followed by finishing the dish for service, often by basting—thus the term *arroser*, French for "to baste"—but the finishing step could be searing or cooking over smoke instead.

For the satisfying, primal flavor of foods that are actually cooked over smoky embers, you must use wood, and cook either directly over the embers or indirectly on a rack or shelf perched high above the fire where the heat is affecting the food but the main impact comes from the subtle waves of smoke caressing the meat. We love this kind of influence. Just smelling the smoke in the air makes the mouth water. Hearing the crackle of the fire and seeing the meat sizzle whets the appetite. Cooking in this ancient way involves all the senses. In our hearth at The French Laundry, that's easy to achieve. At per se, the kitchen uses smaller pieces of wood in tandem with the charcoal in the Japanese grill.

When recipes in the book call for starting a fire, we recommend using a charcoal chimney. These chimneys are great because you can load them with the charcoal and place them over an open burner. When the coals are glowing orange, you can dump them into your grilling vessel.

The vessel could be a Japanese hibachi, an American-style kettle grill, or a solid piece of earth with a couple of bricks in it to elevate the rack—it's really that simple. Once the bed of charcoal is glowing, you can add your flavor influencer—the wood. We prefer fruitwood such as apple or fig, but also like the clean flavor of almond wood, and we will even use grape knots left over from the trimming of the vines after our annual harvest in the valley (see the roasted venison on page 272). Once the flavor influencer has burned completely and turned to embers, you're ready to cook. Just top them with the rack or grate, let it heat for a few minutes, then grill.

Most important, though, is to pay attention to the dance between fire and food. The heat is different every time and always changing, requiring the cook to be very engaged in the cooking, very aware. That's what's so great about cooking over fire.

VENISON RACK ROASTED OVER GRAPEVINES

Glazed Endive, Date Marbles, and Paradigm Grape "Beurre Rouge"

Makes 8 servings

PLUMPED SULTANAS

35 sultanas (golden raisins)

50 grams white verjus

50 grams water

25 grams sugar

PISTACHIO-DATE FARCE

70 grams Sicilian pistachios

160 grams Medjool dates

5 grams cilantro leaves, coarsely chopped

5 grams fleur de sel

Canola oil (optional)

BRAISED ENDIVES

500 grams orange juice

125 grams water

50 grams sugar

10 grams tarragon leaves

7.5 grams kosher salt

5 grams fennel seed

3 grams coriander seeds

1 gram star anise

2 grams citric acid

8 heads white Belgium endive

PARADIGM GRAPE "BEURRE ROUGE"

500 grams red beet juice

250 grams dark raisins, dried on the vine, preferably from Paradigm Winery

125 grams sliced shallots

200 grams Cabernet Sauvignon

200 grams port

200 grams balsamic vinegar

100 grams red verjus

15 black peppercorns

125 grams wildflower honey

250 grams whole butter, cut into ½-inch (1.25-centimeter) dice and chilled

50 grams Burgundy mustard

Kosher salt

Lemon juice

VENISON

1 rack Broken Arrow Ranch venison or frenched rack of venison, chine and featherbones removed

1.5 kilograms dried grapevine knots or hardwood

Binchotan charcoal

500 grams almond wood "kindling"

Sel gris

Freshly ground black pepper

300 grams fresh grapevines and leaves

TO COMPLETE

2 heads white Belgian endive

Concord grapes

8 chives

SPECIAL EQUIPMENT

Immersion circulator

Chamber vacuum sealer

Our venison comes from Broken Arrow Ranch, an extraordinary company founded by Mike Hughes that hunts venison and other wild animals in the Texas Hill Country and has a mobile unit that dresses the animals immediately. The quality of animals procured this way is unequaled.

We tie the venison crosswise for the most compact shape and even cooking and serve it with a sauce made from Paradigm Winery grapes that have been dried on the vine and intensely flavored. Paradigm, our neighbor just a couple of miles up the road from The French Laundry, is run by a Napa family whose roots here go back more than a century. We love that we're able to smoke the meat over grape knots, gnarled pieces of grapevine pruned by the winery. They're great to smoke with, as are grape leaves. Of course, charcoal is fine, too, if that's what you have.

FOR THE PLUMPED SULTANAS

Combine the sultanas, verjus, water, and sugar in a small pot. Bring to a simmer over medium heat. Remove from the heat, cover with a lid, and steep for 10 to 12 minutes, until the sultanas have been rehydrated by the liquid. Set aside at room temperature for up to a few hours before serving, or transfer to an airtight container and refrigerate for up to 1 month.

FOR THE PISTACHIO-DATE FARCE

Preheat the oven to 320°F (160°C). Line a sheet pan with parchment paper.

Spread the pistachios over the lined sheet pan. Toast the nuts in the oven for 10 to 14 minutes. Allow the nuts to cool, then coarsely chop them into pieces just larger than sunflower seeds. Shake the chopped pistachios in a strainer to remove any dust.

Soak the dates in warm water to cover for about 5 minutes, to soften the outer skin. Using a small tourné knife, peel the skin and discard. Pit the dates and coarsely chop them. Place the dates, pistachios, cilantro, and fleur de sel in a bowl. With a spoon or a gloved hand, gently mix the ingredients just until they hold together.

(continued)

Form the farce into 8 rounds the size of the eye of the venison, either by simply patting them into shape or by rolling the farce between two pieces of lightly oiled plastic wrap, then using an appropriate-size cutter, lightly rubbed with oil, to punch out rounds to match the size of the eye of the venison. Place the rounds of farce on a sheet pan and cover with plastic wrap.

The rounds can be refrigerated for up to 3 days.

FOR THE BRAISED ENDIVES

Combine the orange juice, water, sugar, tarragon, salt, fennel, coriander, star anise, and citric acid in a 1-quart (1-liter) saucepot and bring to a boil over medium heat. Immediately remove from the heat, cover with a lid, and steep for 10 minutes. Strain the liquid into a bowl and nestle the bowl in an ice-water bath to chill.

Set an immersion circulator in a water bath and heat the water to 31°C (88°F). Place the endives and chilled liquid in a sous vide bag. Place in a chamber vacuum sealer and vacuum seal. Cook in the water bath for 20 minutes, until the endives are very tender. Transfer the endives to a container and keep warm until serving, or submerge the bag in an ice-water bath to chill, then refrigerate for up to 3 days. Rewarm before serving.

FOR THE PARADIGM GRAPE "BEURRE ROUGE"

Combine the beet juice, raisins, shallots, Cabernet Sauvignon, port, vinegar, verjus, and peppercorns in a 2-quart (2-liter) saucepot and bring to a boil over medium-high heat. Rapidly reduce the liquid until it becomes a thick syrup, 30 to 35 minutes. Whisk in the honey to fully incorporate.

Reduce the heat to medium and start whisking in the butter, 1 or 2 cubes at a time, ensuring each cube is emulsified before adding the next. After you have added about one-quarter of the butter, you can increase the number of cubes added at a time. Once all the butter has been incorporated, whisk in the mustard. Strain the sauce through a chinois into a small pot, using a ladle to help pass it through. Adjust the seasoning with salt and lemon juice to taste. Keep in a warm spot if serving within a few hours or transfer to an airtight container and refrigerate for up to 1 day.

FOR THE VENISON

If your venison has not been frenched, remove the venison rack from the bag and dry it thoroughly with a lint-free kitchen towel. Place the venison bone-side up on a cutting board, with the tips of the bones facing to the left (alternate if you are left-handed). Trim the thick band of connective tissue from the bottom of the eye of the rack. This will loosen the cap. Turn the rack so the bones are facing away from you.

Turn the rack over. Beginning at the shoulder end, make incisions under the shoulder blade to loosen the cap, working toward the end of the cap. Grip the cap and make delicate cuts to free it from the ribeye, making sure to keep the knife against the bones to remove as much of the cap as possible.

Once the cap is removed, turn the rack bone-side up and run the tip of the knife down and across the ribs just below the eye, making incisions between each set of bones. Score a line down the back center of each bone. Using a tourné knife, scrape the bones, working to the left and right of the scored line.

Turn the rack meat-side up. Run the knife across the bones, making an incision between the bones parallel to the incision on the silver skin side of the rack.

Using a clean kitchen towel, pull the meat back from the bones, working from the silver skin side to the cap side and trimming as necessary to remove.

Scrape the bones with a small tourné knife, making sure each bone is free of meat and pearly white. Remove the thicker silver skin from the eye, being careful not to remove too much meat.

Place the venison meat-side down, with the bones facing away from you. Using butcher's twine, make individual ties between each bone to set the shape of the ribeye, ensuring that the twine goes over the base of each bone. Make another tie on the opposite side of each bone, centering the meat and bone that will later be carved into a chop. Refrigerate the venison until 1 hour before serving, then remove the venison from the refrigerator to temper.

Arrange the grapevine knots and a few sticks of binchotan in the hearth. Using small dried kindling, light the fire to catch the vines and charcoal. Allow them to burn for about 30 minutes, until they are fiery red and smoking and have started producing coals. Add more vines as needed to produce enough coals for cooking.

Season all sides of the venison with sel gris and pepper and place on a grate or rack 6 to 10 inches (15 to 25 centimeters) above the smoking grape knots, depending on the level of the heat. Add the fresh grapevines and leaves to the fire to smolder.

Roast the meat, rotating and turning it every 5 minutes to ensure even roasting on each side, until cooked to 130°F (54°C) for medium-rare, 15 to 20 minutes, depending on the size of the rack and the strength of the heat. Remove the venison from the grate and rest in a warm place for at least 15 minutes before carving.

TO COMPLETE
While the venison is resting, separate the leaves of the raw endives. Using small kitchen shears, cut 14 leaves into small spear shapes.

Using small tweezers, gently remove the seeds from the grapes from the point where the grape was attached to the vine. There will be three or four seeds in each grape.

Rewarm the braised endives, if necessary. Remove them from the cooking liquid and peel back the outermost layer of leaves. Firmly wrap a chive twice around the base of each endive, tying it gently and snipping any excess chive from the knot.

Rewarm the "beurre rouge" and bring the plumped sultanas to room temperature, if necessary.

When the venison is rested, cut the strings and remove them from the rack. Place the rack on a cutting board with the meat toward you; hold the bones to steady the roast. With a sharp slicing knife, cut the rack into individual chops. Lay the chops on their sides on a paper towel and top the eye of each chop with a round of the date farce.

Place a chop and one braised endive on each serving plate. Garnish the plates with the endive spears, plumped sultanas, and Concord grapes. Finish with a spoonful of the "beurre rouge."

SCHNITZEL

Corned Veal Heart "Schnitzel," Caramelized Oxheart Cabbage, and Red Cabbage Essence

THE SCHNITZEL

David first cooks the corned heart sous vide, then cuts it very thin so that it's tender. He makes a mousseline farce of veal pureed with egg white, salt, and crème fraîche, then folds in minced veal heart trimmings and fermented cabbage for its acidity. He sandwiches this mousseline between the two thin slices of heart, then batters and fries it like schnitzel.

GREEN CABBAGE LAYER

Oxheart cabbage is cooked simply over high heat, almost like a stir-fry, until beautifully browned and caramelized, then mixed with cauliflower puree for creaminess.

THE GARNISH AND SAUCE

Red cabbage leaves are cut into rounds and quick-pickled in an apple cider vinegar, mustard, shallot, and dill brine, giving them a pleasing crisp texture. Red cabbage juice becomes the base for the sauce, along with Riesling (a nod to eastern France, where these flavors are so predominant), vinegar, and rich veal stock. The aromatics are onion, garlic, apple, juniper, and importantly, bacon.

For this four-star version of a simple country dish—corned beef and cabbage—David corns a veal heart, a lean, flavorful muscle, in a brine (coriander, allspice, black pepper, ginger, pink curing salt), and then treats it like schnitzel. But making cabbage the star is the remarkable part of this dish. It's used in four ways: sautéed (a variety called oxheart, named for its shape); fermented; mixed into the farce; and as the basis for the sauce.

SNAKE RIVER FARMS CALOTTE DE BOEUF

Wilted Bok Choy, Scallion Mousseline, Szechuan Peppercorn Jus, and Crispy Bone Marrow

Makes 6 servings

CRISPY BONE MARROW

750 grams beef marrow bone, cut crosswise into 2-inch-wide (5-centimeter) pieces

200 grams milk brine (recipe follows)

SCALLION OIL

82 grams thinly sliced scallion greens

15 grams baby spinach

270 grams canola oil

4 grams kosher salt

SCALLION REDUCTION

160 grams Sauvignon Blanc

80 grams champagne vinegar

40 grams thinly sliced scallions

2 grams black peppercorns

2 thyme sprigs

SCALLION MOUSSELINE

200 grams egg yolks

40 grams clarified butter (page 53), melted

25 grams heavy cream

30 grams chicken stock (page 285)

15 grams lemon juice

15 grams kosher salt

SZECHUAN PEPPERCORN JUS

90 grams rice wine vinegar, plus more to taste

60 grams glucose syrup

30 grams tamari

50 grams thinly sliced shallots

15 grams scallion greens, cut into 2-inch (5-centimeter) pieces

10 grams garlic cloves, skin on, crushed

5 grams ½-inch-dice (1.25-centimeter) peeled fresh ginger

25 grams sugar

1 gram black peppercorns

250 grams veal stock (page 287)

25 grams oyster sauce

20 grams sweet soy sauce

Kosher salt

CALOTTE DE BOEUF

2 garlic cloves, skin on, crushed

1 bay leaf

5 thyme sprigs

10 Szechuan peppercorns

1 (450- to 480-gram) piece Snake River Farms calotte de boeuf

Kosher salt

100 grams rendered beef fat

BOK CHOY

45 grams whole butter

18 small bok choy leaves

Kosher salt

Red wine vinegar

TO COMPLETE

Canola oil, for deep-frying

Cornstarch–egg white paste (page 235)

50 grams finely ground dried potato flakes

Kosher salt

4 grams black peppercorns, coarsely crushed

4 grams Szechuan peppercorns, coarsely crushed

45 grams minced shallots

Sel gris

SPECIAL EQUIPMENT

Immersion circulator

Chamber vacuum sealer

iSi siphon

2 cream chargers

This is probably my favorite cut of beef, essentially the beautifully marbled cap over the ribeye. This is cooked vacuum sealed, then finished over a charcoal fire. Corey loves pepper—whether the black pepper crab of Singapore or a steak and peppercorns—so he created a super-peppery sauce for the beef that includes Szechuan peppercorns. He serves it with fried bone marrow, dredged in potato flakes to ensure crispness, sautéed bok choy, scallion mousseline, and scallion oil. The scallion oil makes use of the green scallion tops that we have in abundance, and the technique is a great way to make an oil using any green (kale aïoli made from kale oil is fantastic, for instance; see page 156).

I'm really proud of this cut, the calotte (the French term for what we call the deckle in the United States). My brothers used to fight over this part of the rib steak or rib roast because it was the fattiest, most wonderful part of the steak. I begged Snake River Farms for years to sell me just this cut, but they didn't think they could offer it because it was part of a traditional rib steak. Now they do sell it to me, and it also allows them to sell a true eye of the rib, giving the two cuts and giving us this amazing calotte, which we can cook to a gorgeous medium-rare.

FOR THE BONE MARROW

Whether your bones are fresh or frozen, soak them in cold water for 2 to 4 hours to clean them. Once soaked, use your thumb to push the bone marrow out of the individual pieces of bone. Place the bone marrow in a bowl of ice water in the sink and place a clean kitchen towel on top of the bone marrow to ensure it stays submerged. Let cold water flow in a steady stream from the faucet over the bone marrow for at least 8 hours or up to overnight.

Set an immersion circulator in a water bath and heat the water to 30°C (86°F; the temperature is very low to purify and clean the bone marrow). Place the bone marrow and milk brine in a sous vide bag. Place in a chamber vacuum sealer and vacuum seal. Cook in the water bath for 2 hours. Immediately submerge the bag in an ice-water bath to chill.

Drain the bone marrow and rinse under cold water for a few minutes to wash away any residual milk brine.

The cooked bone marrow can be refrigerated in a bowl of ice water, covered with a clean kitchen towel, for up to 3 days.

(continued)

FOR THE SCALLION OIL

Put all the ingredients for the scallion oil in a blender. Blend on high speed for at least 5 minutes, or until the greens warm and "cook," to remove their raw, spicy flavor.

Pour the mixture into a bowl and nestle the bowl in an ice-water bath. Chill, stirring from time to time, until cool. Refrigerate for 8 hours or overnight. Place a large dampened coffee filter in a strainer set over a container. Pour in the scallion oil and refrigerate for at least 8 hours or up to overnight to extract the oil.

Refrigerate the oil in an airtight container for up to 3 weeks or freeze for up to 3 months. Bring to room temperature before using.

FOR THE SCALLION REDUCTION

Combine all the ingredients for the scallion reduction in a 2-quart (2-liter) saucepot and cook over medium heat for 6 to 8 minutes, until the liquid has reduced by just less than half.

Transfer to a bowl and nestle the bowl in an ice-water bath to cool. The reduction can be strained and used immediately or refrigerated with the solids in an airtight container for up to 5 days and strained before using.

FOR THE SCALLION MOUSSELINE

Combine 100 grams of the strained scallion reduction and the egg yolks in a sabayon pot or double boiler and whisk over medium heat for about 3 minutes, until the sabayon becomes light and frothy. Make sure to rotate the pot continuously to prevent hot spots and scrambling. As the sabayon thickens, remove the pot from the direct heat and continue to whisk until smooth, light, and fluffy (ribbon stage), about 2 minutes. Gradually whisk in the melted clarified butter and 160 grams of the scallion oil. The sabayon will become very thick, with a consistency similar to that of mayonnaise. Whisk in the cream, chicken stock, lemon juice, and salt. The mousseline should be able to hold its shape when piped.

Strain the mousseline through a chinois and transfer it to a disposable piping bag, then pipe it into a siphon. Charge the siphon with two whipped cream chargers, shaking vigorously between charges and after charging to ensure it is fully aerated for use. Reserve in a warm place for up to 4 hours.

FOR THE SZECHUAN PEPPERCORN JUS

Combine the vinegar, glucose syrup, tamari, shallots, scallion greens, garlic, ginger, sugar, and black peppercorns in a 1-quart (1-liter) saucepot. Bring to a boil over medium-high heat and reduce, adjusting the heat as necessary, for about 5 minutes.

Add the veal stock, oyster sauce, and sweet soy sauce and reduce over medium-low heat for about 20 minutes, skimming off any impurities that rise to the surface with a small ladle, until the liquid has reduced to 250 grams. Season with additional vinegar and salt to taste; the reduction should have an intense but balanced flavor. Strain the reduction and keep in a warm spot for up to 4 hours before serving, or transfer to an airtight container and refrigerate for up to 5 days. (Szechuan peppercorns and shallots will be added before serving.)

FOR THE CALOTTE DE BOEUF

Set the immersion circulator in a water bath and heat the water to 64°C (147.2°F). Make a sachet by placing the garlic, bay leaf, thyme, and Szechuan peppercorns in a disposable tea bag. Season the calotte liberally with salt and place it in the sous vide bag with the beef fat and sachet. Place in a chamber vacuum sealer and vacuum seal. Cook in the water bath for 1 hour.

Remove the bag from the water bath and let the meat rest in the bag on a cooling rack set over a sheet pan for about 30 minutes.

FOR THE BOK CHOY

Melt the butter in a medium sauté pan over medium heat. When it foams, add the bok choy and sauté for about 90 seconds, turning the leaves to prevent them from taking on any color. The stem of the bok choy should still have a bite to it, and the leaves should just be wilted. Sprinkle with salt and vinegar. Remove from the pan and drain on paper towels. Keep in a warm spot until serving.

TO COMPLETE

Prepare a fire (see page 270). Fill a deep fryer with canola oil and heat the oil to 375°F (190°C). Place a cooling rack on a sheet pan.

Remove the bone marrow from the ice water and dry well. Cut each piece of bone marrow into thirds. Toss them in the cornstarch paste to coat and place on the rack to allow the excess paste to drip off, then dredge in the potato flakes to coat. Fry the bone marrow in the hot oil until a crisp, golden brown crust has formed and the bone marrow has softened. Remove from the oil and drain on paper towels. Sprinkle with salt.

Remove the calotte from the bag and pat off any excess fat with paper towels. Sprinkle with salt and grill to color the exterior of the meat. Remove the meat and let it rest for 5 to 10 minutes before serving.

Reheat the Szechuan peppercorn jus, if needed, and stir in half the crushed black peppercorns, half the crushed Szechuan peppercorns, and the shallots. Let the jus sit for 5 minutes, then taste and add more of the peppercorns as desired.

Cut the calotte against the grain into 6 pieces. Season with sel gris.

Arrange the calotte, bok choy, and bone marrow on each serving plate. Spoon the Szechuan peppercorn jus on the plate and siphon a mound of the scallion mousseline to the side.

Milk Brine

Makes about 960 grams

525 grams water	3 grams pink salt (optional)	1 small bay leaf
135 grams heavy cream		1 gram black peppercorns
33 grams kosher salt	3 grams lemon zest	
20 grams sugar	2 grams thyme sprigs	300 grams ice cubes

Combine the water, cream, kosher salt, sugar, pink salt (if using), lemon zest, thyme, bay leaf, and peppercorns in a 2-quart (2-liter) saucepot and bring to a boil, stirring from time to time. Strain the liquid into a bowl and add the ice. As the ice melts, stir the brine occasionally to combine. Use immediately or refrigerate in an airtight container for up to 1 day.

STEAK AND POTATOES

100-Day Dry-Aged Côte de Boeuf, Braised Brisket "Tater Tots," and Gem Lettuce Salad with Tony's Green Goddess Dressing

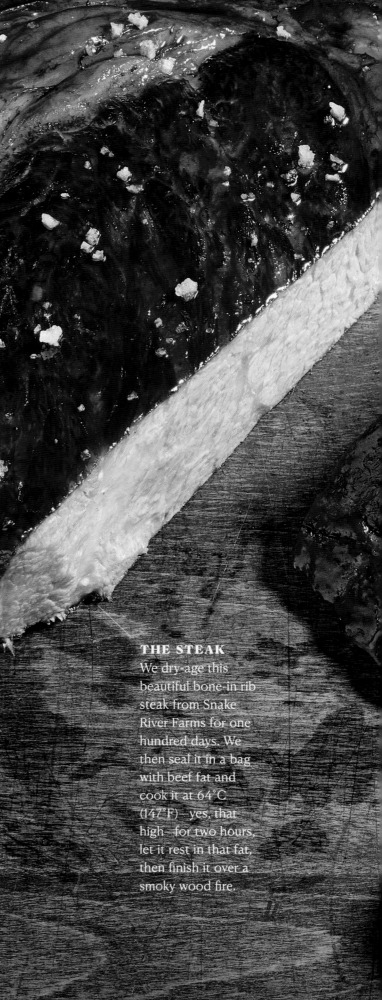

THE STEAK
We dry-age this beautiful bone-in rib steak from Snake River Farms for one hundred days. We then seal it in a bag with beef fat and cook it at 64°C (147°F)—yes, that high—for two hours, let it rest in that fat, then finish it over a smoky wood fire.

GREEN GODDESS DRESSING

Equal weights diced sweet onion and Heinz tarragon vinegar, along with sliced garlic, capers, and anchovies, plus a hit of salt and sugar are combined, macerated, and blended until chunky, then mixed with avocado, mayonnaise, and crème fraîche. Fresh chopped watercress, parsley, tarragon, and dill finish the sauce, which then coats a half head of Gem lettuce.

TATER TOTS

Russet potatoes are cooked whole, then peeled, grated, and mixed with about 20 percent braised beef brisket. They're shaped, then coated in dried potato flakes, using a standard breading procedure, and deep-fried for service.

We always like to serve a main meat course. Here David returns to the story of his father's favorite restaurant, Augustino's Ristorante, in Greeneville, Tennessee, where his father would dip his steak in their Green Goddess dressing. (David would eventually wash dishes there when he was sixteen.) He swears by their take on the famous salad dressing from the 1970s, and in keeping with the '70s motif, he serves it with tater tots.

SAUCE ON THE SIDE!

Extra Green Goddess dressing, of course

STOCKS AND ESSENCES

PERHAPS THE BIGGEST CHANGE in our stocks came in 2019, when we started TKMM Stock Co. in Portland, Oregon, to make our veal stock. It now arrives in 2-liter cryovaced pouches, and former employees who return are astonished when we open one for them and it smells exactly like The French Laundry of 1996, with the scent of Veal #1 and Veal #2 reducing in the screened-in porch. We started the company out of practical concerns. We simply had to make so much stock each week that it prevented our cooks from accomplishing what they needed to, in terms of both space and time. And those giant, unwieldy stockpots could result in dangerous spills. All this was solved with a stock of the same—or even better—quality.

Perhaps our most important discovery was figuring out the amount of cooking time required to make stock from 500 pounds of bones. In the early days of The French Laundry, we'd cook the aromatic vegetables for nearly as long as the bones. But vegetables release pretty much all their flavor in 45 to 60 minutes. So today we only add the vegetables at the end of the stock making.

Our master method creates a very neutral, highly gelatinous base, which is flavored with vegetables (and 10% roasted bones if we want a roasted stock). We use the following percentages for our master stock recipe: 100% bones, washed well in hot water; 40% beef tendons (or calves' feet) for gelatin; and 240% water. Cover the ingredients with water in a stockpot and bring to a boil, skimming any protein that rises to the surface. When the pot is simmering, mix 10% tomato paste with enough water so that it will distribute evenly in the stock and add it to the pot. We use 25 kilograms of bones and 60 liters of water and cook this at a solid simmer for 14 hours.

We then strain it and add a kilogram each of carrots, onions, and leeks, all cut into small pieces, about 1-inch dice. We also add crushed garlic, peppercorns, thyme, parsley stems, and bay leaves, simmer it for an hour, then strain through a chinois two or three times until the sediment is filtered out.

Essences have changed as well. When we make an essence, we tend to use only the main ingredients (mushrooms, corncobs, onions) and water. We've simplified and refined.

The following stocks and essences are what we use when making small batches of specific stocks.

Golden Chicken Stock

Makes about 5,500 grams (5½ quarts/5.5 liters)

2,500 grams chicken
  wings

450 grams chicken feet

3,750 grams (3¾ quarts/
  3.75 liters) cold water

2,000 grams ice cubes

225 grams carrots,
  cut into 1-inch
  (2.5-centimeter) dice

225 grams leeks (white
  and light green portions
  only), cut into 1-inch
  (2.5-centimeter) dice
  and rinsed to remove
  any dirt

225 grams onions,
  cut into 1-inch
  (2.5-centimeter) dice

20 grams garlic cloves,
  roots removed, crushed

20 grams fresh thyme

20 black peppercorns

1 bay leaf

We call this golden because of the color that the abundant carrots give to the stock (as always, we add the vegetables at the end). It's also very concentrated (we often water it down if its flavor could become too pronounced if used in, say, making risotto) and, from the additional chicken feet, very gelatinous. For chefs at The French Laundry (per se also has a fortified chicken stock—see Ramen-Style Stock—that is based on the golden chicken stock), it's an all-purpose tool each night on the line, used for braising and glazing and finishing. Because it's so rich and flavorful, we can use more stock and less butter to obtain a beautiful glaze, and a very nutritious one that the vegetables can absorb.

Rinse the chicken wings and feet thoroughly under hot running water to remove visible blood and place in a 15-quart (15-liter) stockpot. Cover with the cold water. Set the stockpot slightly off center over the burner. (This will cause any impurities that rise to gather at one side of the pot, making them easier to skim off.) Bring slowly to a simmer, skimming continually. Once the liquid is at a simmer, add the ice; this will cause the fat to congeal. Remove the fat and skim off as much of the impurities from the surface as possible. Bring the stock back to a simmer and cook gently for 90 minutes. Remove any excess fat as necessary.

Add the carrots, leeks, onions, garlic, thyme, and bay leaf and slowly bring the liquid back to a simmer, skimming frequently. Simmer for 35 to 45 minutes, skimming often. Turn off the heat and let the stock rest for about 20 minutes; this allows any particles left in the stock to settle at the bottom of the pot.

Set a chinois over a large container. Carefully ladle the stock off the top, disturbing the bones as little as possible so that the impurities that have settled to the bottom are not mixed into the stock. Once you reach the bones, tilt the pot to reach the stock; once again, be extremely careful not to move the bones. Do not press on the solids in the strainer or force through any liquid that does not pass through on its own. Discard any stock at the bottom of the pot that is cloudy with impurities. Nestle the container in an ice-water bath to chill.

Cover the container with a lid and store the stock in the refrigerator for up to 3 days or freeze for longer storage.

RAMEN-STYLE STOCK, AKA SUPER STOCK

We still make classical veal stock–based sauces, like a bordelaise or périgourdine, but we don't make a veal stock at The French Laundry anymore, because we founded a stock company to produce restaurant-quality stocks, which saves a lot of time, doesn't tie up burner space for hours and hours, and eliminates the accidents that could occasionally happen when you're working with giant kettles of boiling liquid. The veal stock is absolutely perfect. But even meat-based sauces and the quick stocks of the early days are evolving.

Corey Chow, chef de cuisine at per se, has developed an extraordinarily rich chicken stock that he uses like a mother sauce at per se. It's antithetical to the classical stock technique, which seeks a very clean, clear stock through cooking the meat and bones at a very low temperature to avoid agitation of the water, and frequent skimming of the fat and protein that rise to the surface.

Corey's stock does exactly the opposite. Taking his cue from Japanese ramen stock, he cooks his stock at a vigorous boil, emulsifying the fat into the stock for a very rich, smooth result. And Corey not only boils his stock—he adds extra fat to it.

We can't write about this stock without mentioning the scholarship program created by TKRG (the name of our restaurant group) that sends our employees around the world to study what they're interested in. They can write a proposal to work with a restaurant or farmer or forager abroad and, if it's approved, have their trip paid for by the scholarship. Elaine Smyth, one of the team members on this book, earned a scholarship to work with cacao farmers in Peru and Chef Olivier Roellinger in Brittany. Sarah Hsieh, who crafts the foie gras dishes included in this book (see page 144), went to London on a scholarship to work with Calum Franklin at the Holborn Dining Room, a master of the *pâté en croûte*.

Perhaps one of the most impactful uses of our scholarship, an extreme example of its power to transform a young chef, was sending Grant Achatz to work with Ferran Adrià, the godfather of modernist cuisine, at El Bulli, his groundbreaking restaurant in Roses, Spain. Grant would never have been able to afford that trip on his own, and it was a defining experience for him. So much so that when he returned, he no longer fit into The French Laundry—it was time for him to leave. He moved to Chicago, where he ultimately opened the Michelin three-star modernist restaurant Alinea.

In Corey's case, he won a scholarship to Copenhagen, where Matt Orlando, chef and owner of Amass, opened up for him the world of whole-ingredient utilization (see his carrot oil, made from the peelings of carrots, on page 119, and his pea granité on page 25). The week before Corey began at the restaurant, Amass had hosted a pop-up ramen restaurant, where Orlando had watched this stock being made. Corey took that idea and refined it for per se by emulsifying even more fat into the stock. He calls it "Super Stock." This chicken stock is so flavorful we usually prefer it to a fumet.

Corey starts with per se's classic chicken stock: 60 blanched chicken carcasses, 18 quarts mirepoix, and aromatic herbs, covered with water, brought to a boil, simmered for 45 minutes, then strained.

For his ramen-style stock, he combines 4 kilos of meaty chicken bones, 8 liters golden chicken stock, and 500 grams duck fat, brings it all to a boil, and maintains the boil until the stock has reduced by half. The stock then goes into an ice bath and, using an immersion blender, is blended continuously until chilled.

With the resulting stock, Corey can achieve all kinds of effects. He can add it to a béarnaise reduction in place of butter, finishing the béarnaise "jus" with fresh tarragon. He can put it in an iSi siphon and make a thick, foamy sauce. He might use it to bind pasta and finish it with black truffle. He can use it as is, like a broth, perhaps seasoned with fresh herbs or with pastrami spices. He can pour it over roasted lobster bones for an intense, meaty lobster stock. It would even work with halibut bones. There's almost nothing you can't do with this stock.

Clam Stock

Makes 400 grams

1,000 grams clams, preferably littleneck clams	8 grams 1-inch (2.5-centimeter) flat-leaf parsley stems	**SPECIAL EQUIPMENT** Combi oven
100 grams thinly sliced shallots	3 grams black peppercorns, coarsely crushed	
25 grams garlic cloves, skin on, crushed	150 grams Sauvignon Blanc	
2 grams 1-inch (2.5-centimeter) pieces thyme sprig		

This method can be used for any bivalve, and it's very standard—shallots, herbs, white wine—and also very quick. If we're making a striped bass dish with a nage, we'll use the bones for a classic fumet, but generally, whether for a sauce or soup, clam or other stock made from a bivalve is preferred.

Place the clams in a bowl in the sink and rinse them under cold running water until the water runs clear with no dirt or silt, at least 30 minutes. Place the shallots, garlic, thyme, parsley, peppercorns, and white wine in a hotel pan and top with a perforated hotel pan. Place the clams in the perforated hotel pan and cover with a plastic lid. Steam in a combi oven set at 100°C (212°F) for 5 minutes. If the clams have all opened, they are cooked. If not, cook for a further 2 minutes, then check again; cook longer as necessary until all the shells open. (The cooking time on the clams can vary greatly from 5 to 15 minutes, sometimes even longer.) Remove the pan from the oven and remove the lid. Set the clams aside. The clams will not be used in this recipe, but can be removed from their shells once cool and reserved for another use. They will keep in an airtight container in the refrigerator overnight.

Remove the perforated pan and nestle the hotel pan with the clam stock in an ice-water bath to cool (or transfer the stock to a bowl and set that in an ice-water bath). Line a strainer with a dampened tea towel and set it over an airtight container. Strain the cooled stock through the tea towel. Cover and refrigerate for up to 3 days or freeze for up to 3 months.

Classic Lobster Stock

Makes about 1,000 grams

Clarified butter (page 53)

1,250 grams lobster bodies, leg sections only, free of gills and viscera, rinsed and dried

125 grams whole butter

750 grams ripe beefsteak tomatoes, diced, or canned crushed San Marzano tomatoes with their juices

300 grams sweet carrots, diced

20 grams tarragon tops (hard bottom stems removed)

5 quarts (5 liters) water

This is straight out of *The French Laundry Cookbook*—and it still works as the creamy lobster broth in the "Macaroni and Cheese." To this day, I taste it whenever I'm in the kitchen. I once made David throw out a whole batch because he'd over-reduced it, and he had to tell Chef Benno that he wouldn't have the lobster dish on his menu that night. I am very particular about it. Because we go through so many lobsters, we have the luxury of using the legs and lower carapace, trimmed of all lung, because that's where the flavor is concentrated. Aside from not over-reducing the stock, the most important thing to avoid is cooking the legs in a too-hot pan. They can scorch and give the stock a harsh flavor. Adding whole butter after the legs have turned red helps to keep the heat down.

Heat a 6-quart (6-liter) rondeau over medium-high heat. When the pan is hot, add a thin layer of clarified butter to coat. Add the lobster bodies and gently sauté for 3 minutes, until the bodies are bright red but not browned. Reduce the heat to medium, add the whole butter, and cook until the butter is foamy and the shells are aromatic, about 3 minutes.

Add the tomatoes, carrots, and tarragon and cook, stirring frequently, until the tomatoes break down. Add the water and bring to a boil. Reduce the heat and simmer for about 30 minutes.

Remove from the heat and pour the stock through a china cap or colander, using a sturdy wooden spoon to crush the solids in the strainer to extract as much of the lobster essence as possible. Discard the solids. Strain the lobster stock through a chinois, swirling the strainer continuously but not forcing the stock or any solids through. Strain again through a chinois into a 4-quart (4-liter) saucepot. Bring to a boil, reduce the heat slightly, and cook until the stock has reduced by half, skimming the surface frequently to remove the impurities.

Strain the stock through the chinois into a 2-quart (2 liter) saucepot and cook until reduced by half again, skimming as needed. Strain the stock into a bowl and nestle the bowl in an ice-water bath to cool. Refrigerate in an airtight container for up to 3 days or freeze for up to 3 months.

Veal Stock

Makes about 1,750 grams

4.5 kilograms veal bones, necks, and backs

1 calf's foot, spilt

450 grams tomato paste

340 grams carrots, cut into 1-inch (2.5-centimeter) dice

340 grams leeks (white and light green sections only), cut into 1-inch (2.5-centimeter) dice and rinsed to remove any dirt

225 grams onions, cut into 1-inch (2.5-centimeter) dice

1 head garlic, root end and excess skin removed, halved horizontally and broken into pieces

42 grams flat-leaf parsley sprigs

14 grams thyme sprigs

2 bay leaves

255 grams tomatoes, cut into 1-inch (2.5-centimeter) chunks

While we created a company to make this stock, we occasionally make small batches of it ourselves. We've included it here because it's such a fundamental sauce to us—and remains very much the *fond de cuisine* it has always been.

Rinse the bones under cold running water and put them in a stockpot with at least a 19-quart (19-liter) capacity. Add the calf's foot and fill the pot with cold water, adding twice as much water as you have bones. Slowly bring the water to a simmer, moving the bones around from time to time, but do not stir, as this would disperse the impurities. Skim the scum that rises to the surface. As soon as the liquid comes to a simmer, remove the pot from the heat.

Drain the bones in a china cap and immediately rinse to remove any scum. Clean the stockpot.

FOR VEAL #1

Return the bones to the stockpot and add 11½ quarts (11.5 liters) cold water. Set the stockpot slightly off center over the burner. (This will cause any impurities that rise to gather at one side of the pot, making them easier to skim off.) Bring the liquid to a simmer. Skim the surface, then stir in the tomato paste. Add the carrots, leeks, onions, garlic, parsley, thyme, bay leaves, and tomatoes, bring back to a simmer, and simmer for 6 hours, skimming often.

Strain the liquid through a china cap into a container, then strain it through a chinois into a second container. Do not press on the solids in the strainer or force through any liquid that does not pass on its own;

reserve the bones and aromatics. You should have 7½ to 9½ quarts (7.5 to 9.5 liters) of liquid.

Place the liquid in a saucepot and reduce over low heat as you cook Veal #2. It is not critical how much the stock reduces at this point.

FOR VEAL #2 (THE REMOUILLAGE)

Clean the stockpot and return the bones and aromatics to the pot. Add 11½ quarts (11.5 liters) cold water and slowly bring the water to a simmer, skimming often. Simmer for 6 hours, skimming frequently.

Strain the liquid through a china cap, then a chinois as you did for Veal #1. You should have 7½ to 9½ quarts (7.5 to 9.5 liters) of liquid.

FOR THE "MARRIAGE" OF VEAL #1 AND VEAL #2

Clean the stockpot. Combine Veal #1 and Veal #2 in the pot. Slowly bring to a simmer and cook until the stock reduces to about 1¾ quarts (1.75 liters). It should have a rich brown color and saucelike consistency. Transfer the sauce to a container and nestle the container in an ice-water bath to chill. Cover and refrigerate for up to 3 days or freeze for longer storage.

Corn Essence

Makes 3,000 grams

1,800 grams stripped corncobs	**SPECIAL EQUIPMENT**
3 quarts (3 liters) cold water	Pressure cooker

"Essence," because that's what it is. We just want the corn, so all you need are cobs and water.

Place the corncobs in a pressure cooker and cover with the water. Cook on high pressure according to the manufacturer's instructions for 30 minutes, then carefully release the pressure.

Sandwich a tea towel between two basket strainers and place it over a 6-quart (6-liter) container. Strain the stock through the towel. Nestle the container in an ice-water bath to chill. Cover and refrigerate the stock for up to 3 days or freeze for up to 3 months.

Sweet Onion Essence

Makes about 600 grams

2,000 grams peeled yellow onions	5 grams thyme sprigs	**SPECIAL EQUIPMENT**
250 grams water	3 small bay leaves	Meat grinder with a medium die
40 grams peeled garlic cloves		Pressure cooker

In the restaurants, we make large quantities of onion essence, so we strain the stock through a tea towel–lined perforated hotel pan. We top the onions with another hotel pan and weight it, then let it stand for 30 minutes to extract as much essence as possible. The best way to get flavor is through single ingredients, but here we're adding a few aromatics. Reduced down, this essence is almost like a demi-glace—it's so full and sweet. You can add kombu for more body and a meaty umami flavor. This, too, is used in braising and glazing and sauce making. As with all essences, this can be thickened with a liaison to make its own sauce.

Cut the onions in half through the root end. Trim off the root end and stem end and discard. Cut the onions into pieces that will fit into the meat grinder. Grind through the medium die into a bowl.

Place the water, garlic, thyme, bay leaves, and onions in a pressure cooker. Cook on high pressure on the 10-minute setting according to the manufacturer's instructions, then carefully release the pressure.

Line a fine-mesh strainer with a tea towel and set it over a medium bowl. Strain the stock through the tea towel and let cool, then wring the tea towel to extract all the stock from the onions. Discard the solids in the towel.

Store the stock in an airtight container in the refrigerator for up to 3 days or freeze for 3 months.

Mushroom Essence

Makes 600 grams

750 grams button
mushrooms

150 grams water

SPECIAL EQUIPMENT

Meat grinder with a fine
die

This is the veal stock of the vegetable world. Like most essences, it's been streamlined. Have a look at the mushroom stock in *The French Laundry Cookbook*—there are many ingredients and hours of cooking and reduction on the stove. Here, we use nothing but mushrooms, ground, and just a small amount of water to get them weeping. We squeeze them aggressively to get all the liquid we can out of them. And the solids are still pretty tasty and make a great vegetarian meat loaf or stroganoff for a satisfying vegetarian staff meal.

Wash and dry the mushrooms. Grind them through the fine die of a meat grinder. Place the mushrooms and water in a 4-quart (4-liter) saucepot and bring to a boil over medium heat. Reduce the heat to maintain a simmer and cook, stirring from time to time, for about 5 minutes, until the mushrooms are cooked. Cover the saucepot with a lid and steep for about 30 minutes.

Line a fine-mesh strainer with a tea towel and set over a medium bowl. Pour the mushroom mixture into the strainer and allow the mushrooms to sit for about 1 hour to drain thoroughly.

Lift, twist, and squeeze the tea towel to drain any remaining essence from the mushrooms; discard the mushrooms. Store the essence in an airtight container in the refrigerator for up to 3 days.

Tomato Water

Yield varies

Tomatoes or tomato
trimmings

Kosher salt

At the restaurant, we make tomato water with our tomato trimmings, including the flesh, seeds, and skin, but you can also use whole ripe tomatoes cut into smaller pieces. Tomato is mostly water, so you just need to separate it from the cellulose. Tomato water is used in tandem with liaisons and to marinate tomatoes and is delicious in a broken basil vinaigrette. Set it as is with gelatin (3 sheets for 500 grams) for a beautiful jelly for caviar. Or make a tomato velouté for agnolotti (mix it with 25% cream and 15% beurre manié and cook it out, then finish it in a blender with extra-virgin olive oil).

Weigh the tomatoes and add 1 percent salt by weight. Toss to combine. Transfer the salted tomatoes to a blender and blend. Refrigerate the mixture overnight.

The following day, line a strainer with a tea towel and set it over a container. Pour the tomato mixture into the towel and let stand for a few hours to extract all the tomato water. Refrigerate the tomato water in an airtight container for up to 1 week or freeze for up to 3 months.

DESSERTS

ELWYN BOYLES

THINK LIKE A PASTRY CHEF

WHEN I AM NOT IN THE KITCHEN and I have ideas, I make drawings. In the kitchen, I can put my ideas into action right away, but if I'm traveling or at home and I have an idea I don't want to forget, I make a drawing, such as the Strawberry Tea illustration.

My idea for that dessert began with a flavor combination: strawberry and tea, a common English pairing in everyday life. Starting with that first concept, I then considered what structures I could fit those flavors into. For this dessert, I immediately thought of a big pyramid as the dominant focal point, and I carried on from there, ending up with the complex and beautiful dish on page 334. Illustrating helps me create.

But I also use drawings for teaching and for sharing ideas between the two restaurants, as one more way to keep us connected. For example, I sent Anna Bolz, the per se pastry chef, my illustration for the Victoria Sponge, with its reimagining of how to serve a slice of cake. Anna may like an idea for one dish and then realize she can apply it to a different dessert, such as using the Victoria Sponge construction in her red velvet cake.

I'm passable at hand-drawn illustrations (I grew up with a professional designer for a father), but I prefer to use the iPad app called Paper, which is how these illustrations were created. This system of think-draw-share is a great one for collaborating on our creations.

ALL DESSERTS

To begin: Start with a focal point, a pure, simple idea, such as a flavor pairing or "cake."

Next: Interpret that idea. Desserts are structured architecturally, so we begin with shapes, both geometric and abstract. We then build them vertically, and we build them laterally. We continue the composition by giving those shapes colors, flavors, and textures.

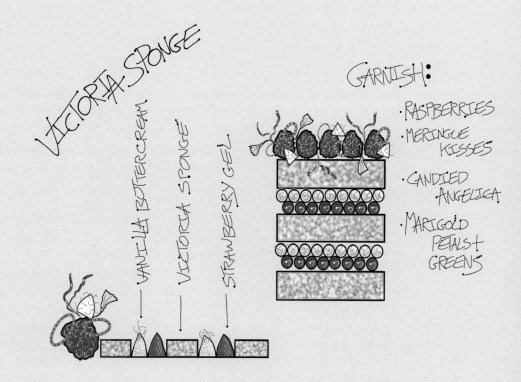

See photograph on page 336

VICTORIA SPONGE ILLUSTRATION: Here, the focal point was "cake." How do we serve this old-fashioned cake, which is typically layered with jam and cream?

We started our architectural structure with bars of cake, and between them we piped slim cylinders of buttercream and jam.

We then added myriad garnishes, which exist in both lateral and vertical dimensions. Notice the two views—the overhead view shows how the dessert should look arrayed on the plate. The cross-section view shows how high the raspberries and rows of buttercream and jam should be relative to the bars of cake. The illustration conveys all the proportions for the dessert ingredients.

Flavor combination: Strawberries, cream
Texture: Tender cake, silky buttercream, moist jam with fresh raspberry, chewy candied angelica, crisp meringue kisses

GÂTEAU OPÉRA: Again, the focal point is "cake," but this time, a classic French cake with many layers.

Here, the architectural structure is built on very precise layers cut into a very precise rectangle. We elaborate by using crackers as a primary garnish, which have a neutral flavor and great crunch. In the drawing, we can see that their varying shapes offset the squareness of the cake. The additional garnishes add to the visual appeal of the dish by providing more contrast in shape and texture.

Flavor combination: Coffee, whiskey, chocolate, almonds, thyme
Texture: Moist cake, dense ganache, creamy buttercream, crunchy crackers, soft green almonds

STRAWBERRY TEA: The starting point here was a notion I'd had for a while, which was to pair the flavors strawberry and tea—specifically soba and matcha—and to use panna cotta as the vehicle.

The key shape would be an oval pyramid, created by layering the flavored panna cottas using gelatin, and then carving out the shape with a spoon, as we do the trifle (see page 314). We would expand the concept with a delicate soba tea pavlova, for gentle crunch, and then surround these structures with all kinds of strawberry confections.

Flavor combination: Strawberry, tea
Texture: Light, airy panna cotta, crunchy pavlova, chewy strawberry net (like fruit leather), dense, fruity strawberry

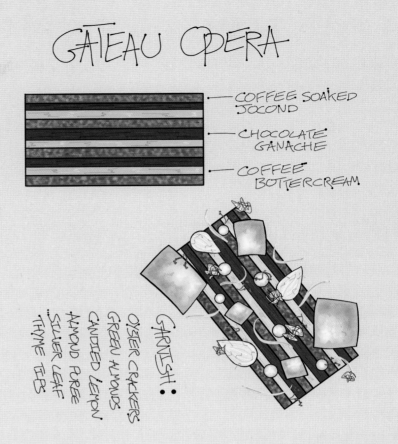

GÂTEAU OPÉRA

COFFEE SOAKED JOCOND

CHOCOLATE GANACHE

COFFEE BOTTERCREAM

GARNISH:
OYSTER CRACKERS
GREEN ALMONDS
CANDIED LEMON
ALMOND PUREE
SILVER LEAF
THYME TIPS

See photograph on page 341

STRAWBERRY TEA

TWO TEA PANNA

STRAWBERRY LACE

SOBA PAVLOVA

STRAWBERRY BLOSSOM

CANDIED HIBISCUS

ALPINES

HERB SCENTED STRAWBERRIES

See photograph on page 334

PEAR SOUP

Sweet Steamed Rice, Compressed Pears, and Lime Laces

Makes 8 servings

PLUM-PICKLED GINGER

250 grams young ginger

5 medium very ripe Santa
   Rosa plums

500 grams apple cider
   vinegar

200 grams water

200 grams sugar

15 grams kosher salt

YUZU PEEL CONFIT

5 yuzu

250 grams sugar

50 grams glucose syrup

250 grams water

**CAPE GOOSEBERRY
RAISINS**

250 grams water

250 grams sugar

15 grams ground ginger

24 Cape gooseberries

COMPRESSED PEARS

100 grams water

100 grams sugar

5 grams ascorbic acid

3 slightly underripe
   Bartlett pears

PEAR SOUP

4 ripe Bartlett pears

500 grams water

6 grams ascorbic acid

1 (3-inch) cinnamon stick

30 black peppercorns

2 star anise pods

½ vanilla bean, split
   lengthwise

20 grams mirin

18 grams rice wine
   vinegar

2 grams kosher salt

50 grams sugar

8 strips lime zest

LIME LACES

5 large egg yolks

600 grams lime juice

1,200 grams sugar

SWEET STEAMED RICE

125 grams sushi rice,
   preferably Nishiki

153 grams water

21 grams rice wine
   vinegar

4.5 grams kosher salt

25 grams sugar

TO COMPLETE

1 yuzu

Black salt

40 Cape gooseberries,
   husks removed

Extra-virgin olive oil

SPECIAL EQUIPMENT

Japanese mandoline

#022 melon baller

Chamber vacuum sealer
   (optional)

The first rendition of this dish was developed many years ago, for the dessert tasting menu, which included five dessert courses. It was intended to balance the sweeter dishes and verges on savory. So this is a sour-salty pear soup, powerfully flavored with star anise, cinnamon, black pepper, and mirin. Also in the bowl are steamed sticky rice balls with black salt and yuzu, and compressed Bartlett pears, very crunchy and bright. We also add fresh Cape gooseberries (also called ground cherries), chewy Cape gooseberry raisins coated in a spicy ginger syrup, lots of citrus zest, and, for richness, olive oil.

The egg yolk laces came about simply because I'd asked Elwyn if he'd ever confited egg yolks; we cured them, but I was curious about treating them like a preserve. My thoughts had gone back to cooking at La Réserve in the mid-1980s, and a Vietnamese chef there who made noodles from egg yolks—I couldn't have told you how he made them. Six weeks later, Elwyn came back with these bright yellow laces, made from egg yolk that had been poached in a very dense sugar syrup. Brilliant. So this was a technique that originated before the dessert that would feature it, from my memories of a cook thirty years ago.

FOR THE PLUM-PICKLED GINGER

Wash the ginger and, using a spoon, scrape away the peel. Using a Japanese mandoline, slice the ginger into very thin sheets, working in the direction of the fibers, which is normally lengthwise (this yields a more tender piece of pickled ginger). Place the ginger in a bowl.

Halve and pit the plums, then thinly slice them. Place the plums in a 2-quart (2-liter) saucepot. Add the vinegar and water. Bring to a boil, then reduce the heat to maintain a very low simmer and cook for about 10 minutes.

Strain the plum base into a clean pot and discard the pulp. Add the sugar and salt to the pot and bring to a boil. Pour the boiling liquid over the sliced ginger and let cool to room temperature. Refrigerate in a covered container for at least 3 days and up to 1 month before using.

FOR THE YUZU PEEL CONFIT

Cut off a small slice from the top and bottom of a yuzu, so that both ends are flat. Take a sharp paring knife and position the knife along the

top edge of the yuzu, wedging it between the white pith and the flesh of the fruit. Cut downward around the flesh to remove the peel and pith without taking the flesh. Continue to work around the fruit. Repeat with the remaining yuzu. (The yuzu flesh can be juiced and used as you would lemon or lime juice; it makes a unique twist on traditional lemonade.)

If some flesh remains on the pith, trim it away with the knife. Trim any uneven edges and cut the peel and pith into a brunoise just under ¼ inch (6 millimeters). Place the yuzu peel and 500 grams water in a small pot and bring to a boil, then drain and return the yuzu peel to the pot. Repeat this process twice more.

Meanwhile, in another 1-quart (1-liter) saucepot, combine the sugar, glucose syrup, and the 250 grams water and bring to a gentle simmer. Add the blanched yuzu peel and simmer gently for 15 to 20 minutes, until the peel is tender. Remove from the heat and let cool.

Refrigerate the candied yuzu in its syrup in a covered container for up to 6 months. Extra confit can be used in any recipe where candied fruit is used.

FOR THE CAPE GOOSEBERRY RAISINS
Combine the water, sugar, and ground ginger in a 1-quart (1-liter) saucepot. Bring to a simmer, stirring occasionally to dissolve the sugar. Pour the syrup into a bowl and nestle the bowl in an ice-water bath to cool completely. Put the gooseberries in a bowl and pour the ginger syrup over them. Cover and refrigerate for 24 hours.

Preheat the oven to 212°F (100°C). Line a half sheet pan with a nonstick silicone baking mat.

Drain the gooseberries and transfer them to the sheet pan. Bake for 2 to 3 hours, until the gooseberries have dried to the texture of a commercial raisin, agitating the pan and rolling the gooseberries every 20 minutes to crystallize the sugar. Remove from the oven and let cool. Refrigerate in a covered container for up to 1 week.

FOR THE COMPRESSED PEARS
Combine the water, sugar, and ascorbic acid in a small pot and bring to a simmer, stirring occasionally to dissolve the sugar. Pour the syrup into a bowl and nestle the bowl in an ice-water bath to cool completely.

Peel the pears. Using a #022 melon baller, scoop at least 48 round balls of pear, dropping them directly into the chilled syrup as you work.

If you have a chamber vacuum sealer, place the pears and syrup into a sous vide bag. Place in the sealer chamber and vacuum seal. Refrigerate until cold or for up to 3 days.

If you don't have a chamber vacuum sealer, cover the bowl and refrigerate the pears in the syrup for at least 24 hours and up to 3 days before using.

FOR THE PEAR SOUP
Peel the pears and quarter them lengthwise. Core and thinly slice them. You will need 600 grams for this recipe; reserve any excess pear for another use. Place the sliced pears in a 2-quart (2-liter) saucepot with the water, ascorbic acid, cinnamon, peppercorns, and star anise. Scrape the vanilla seeds into the pot and add the pod. Bring to a simmer, then simmer gently, skimming the surface as needed, for about 25 minutes, until the pears have broken down. Remove from the heat, strain the liquid into another pot, and discard the pulp. Add the mirin, vinegar, salt, sugar, and lime zest to the pot and bring to a gentle boil, stirring to dissolve the salt and sugar. Remove from the heat and strain the soup through a chinois or fine-mesh strainer. Weigh the soup; if you have less than 500 grams, add cold water to reach 500 grams. Pour the soup into an airtight container and nestle the bowl in an ice-water bath to cool. Refrigerate until cold or for up to 3 days.

FOR THE LIME LACES
Put the egg yolks in a bowl and break them up with a spoon. Do not use a whisk, as this will create small air bubbles throughout the yolks, which will lead to imperfect laces. Pass the yolks through a sieve into a disposable piping bag.

Combine the lime juice and sugar in a wide, shallow 10- to 12-inch (25- to 30-centimeter) saucepot or rondeau. The mixture should reach a depth of about 1 inch (2.5 centimeters). Bring to a gentle boil over low heat, stirring frequently and skimming the surface to keep the liquid clear. Take care not to overheat the syrup; bubbles forming in the syrup will make it difficult to form long, smooth laces. Stir frequently to avoid caramelizing the sugar, which would darken the syrup and discolor the laces.

Turn off the heat. Once the syrup has stopped boiling, return it to very low heat to keep it just below the boiling point. You may see a few small bubbles rising, but no bubbles should break the surface.

Cut a tiny hole in the tip of the piping bag. Hold the bag upright over the center of the saucepot, close to the syrup. In a smooth, continuous motion, pipe a long, thin spiral of egg yolk, working from the center out toward the edges of the saucepot. Poach the egg yolk in the lime syrup for 1 minute, then, using a fork and beginning in the center of the pan, twirl the cooked lace around the fork as you would if you were eating pasta. Transfer the lace to a plastic container and repeat this process until you have 8 laces. Cover the container and refrigerate for up to 1 day.

FOR THE SWEET STEAMED RICE

Preheat the oven to 400°F (205°C).

Place the rice in a sieve and rinse under cold running water for about 20 seconds. Place the rice in a medium saucepot with a tight-fitting lid. Stir in the water, 13 grams of the vinegar, and 1.5 grams of the salt. With the saucepot uncovered, bring the water to a boil, stirring occasionally to prevent the rice from sticking to the bottom of the saucepot. When the water reaches a boil, quickly cover the saucepot with the lid and place it in the oven. Bake for 15 minutes. Remove from the oven and let rest, covered, for 3 minutes. Remove the lid and gently spoon the cooked rice onto a large plate.

Using two silicone spatulas, season the rice with the sugar and the remaining 3 grams salt and 8 grams vinegar. Gently fluff and fold the seasonings into the rice, being careful not to break the grains. Let the rice cool to room temperature.

Have a bowl of water at your side. Brush your hands with the water to prevent the rice from sticking, then gently form sixteen 13-gram balls of rice without exerting too much pressure on the rice, which would cause them to become dense rather than airy in texture. Place in an airtight container and hold at room temperature for up to 4 hours before serving.

TO COMPLETE

Remove the laces from the refrigerator 30 minutes before serving and, using a rasp grater, grate zest from the yuzu over the laces. Let the laces come to room temperature. Slice enough pieces of pickled ginger lengthwise to make 24 thin ribbons. Sprinkle the rice balls with black salt.

Add the larger components to each serving bowl first and end with the smallest garnishes to prevent the details from being covered. Arrange 2 rice balls on opposite sides of each bowl. Scatter the pear balls and fresh Cape gooseberries between and around them, creating a flat layer of garnish over the bottom of the bowl. Spoon in the pear soup. Arrange the ginger ribbons over the garnishes and scatter the gooseberry raisins and yuzu confit over the top. Grate some yuzu zest over the dish. Finish the soup with a few drops of olive oil. Wrap a lime lace around the end of a pair of chopsticks and position them on top of the bowl.

> ### NOTE
> The lime laces will be piped and cooked in a lime-sugar syrup. It is important to use a wide, shallow, 10- to 12-inch (25- to 30-centimeter) rondeau so you're able to hold the piping bag close enough to the syrup to pipe a long lace.

PEACHES 'N' CREAM

Whipped Ricotta and Pecan Sandies

Makes 10 servings

CANNED PEACHES

1,000 grams water

200 grams granulated sugar

20 grams ascorbic acid

5 freestone yellow peaches

PECAN SANDIES

240 grams whole butter, at room temperature

63 grams confectioners' sugar, plus extra for dusting

5 grams kosher salt

284 grams all-purpose flour

100 grams raw pecans, chopped

WHIPPED RICOTTA

15 grams granulated sugar

15 grams water

300 grams whole-milk ricotta

Seeds from 1 vanilla bean

Zest of 1 lemon

200 grams mascarpone cheese

100 grams crème fraîche

PEACH-SCENTED JELLY

3 sheets silver leaf gelatin

50 grams lemon juice

TO COMPLETE

Fresh basil buds

Maldon salt

SPECIAL EQUIPMENT

Combi oven (optional)

The Napa Valley has some of the most amazing peaches you will ever taste, and at The French Laundry we are lucky enough to get the best of the bunch, all picked at perfect ripeness. But when they're in the full flow of the summer season, they drop off the trees in such abundance that we can't possibly serve them all. So we do what farms and households have been doing for hundreds of years: we put them up—preserve them. The process actually intensifies the flavor of the peaches and gives us the syrup they're preserved in as a fabulous by-product to include with their preparation. We usually can about 15 quarts of peaches in the summer; then we serve them around Christmastime, a special summer treat near the winter holidays. (Use perfectly ripe peaches with no bruises for canning. Firmer varieties work best; if they're too soft, they can lose their shape.)

The syrup is seasoned with lemon and sugar, thickened with gelatin, and brought just to the setting point to create a thick, shiny glaze over the cold peaches. We finish the peach with basil buds from the garden (Genovese basil produces a white flower, Thai basil and lime basil produce a beautiful pink flower, and opal basil has a purple flower). We serve it with something creamy, here our housemade ricotta with mascarpone and crème fraîche, seasoned with vanilla and citrus. And for crunch, pecan sandies seem to be everyone's favorite.

FOR THE CANNED PEACHES

Stir together the water and sugar in a 2-quart (2-liter) saucepot (this is a 20% sugar solution). Heat just enough to dissolve the sugar without reducing the liquid and keep warm while you blanch the peaches.

Prepare an ice-water bath and have it close to the cooktop. Bring a large pot of water to a rolling boil. Dissolve the ascorbic acid in 4,000 grams (4 quarts/4 liters) water in a 6-quart (6-liter) container and set aside.

Score the skin (not the flesh) of the bottom of each peach with a small 1-inch (2.5-centimeter) X. Drop 2 of the peaches into the boiling water and blanch for 30 to 40 seconds (see Note). Using a long-handled slotted spoon, immediately transfer the peaches to the ice-water bath to prevent further cooking. Using a paring knife, gently peel the peaches and set them on a tray. Repeat to blanch and peel the remaining peaches.

Cut the peaches vertically in half; separate the halves and remove the pits. Check the inside of the peaches to ensure they are good quality, with no mold or bugs. Drop the peaches into the ascorbic acid solution to prevent oxidation while you sterilize the jar.

If you have a combi oven, sterilize a clean 1-quart (1-liter) mason jar at 100°C (212°F) for 10 minutes. Otherwise, place a wire rack at the bottom of a large pot, fill the pot with enough water to submerge the jar, and bring the water to a boil. Place the jar on the rack in the pot, making sure it is submerged, and boil for 10 minutes. During the last minute, add a slotted spoon to sterilize it as well.

Meanwhile, bring the sugar solution to a gentle simmer. Remove the peaches from the ascorbic acid solution and place them in the sugar solution. Gently simmer for 3 minutes, then remove the pan from the heat. Using clean tongs, transfer the jar to a clean kitchen towel.

Keeping the jar free from any foreign contamination at this point is crucial; you want to keep a clean, sterile environment within the jar. Tilt the jar and, using the sanitized slotted spoon, gently scoop one peach half at a time from the sugar solution and lower it into the jar, rounded-side down, until all the peach halves are in the jar. Return the sugar solution to a boil, then pour it into the jar, covering the peaches and leaving 1 inch (2.5 centimeters) of headspace at the top of the jar. Gently tap the jar on the counter to remove any air bubbles trapped by the peaches.

Place the lid on the jar and tighten it to fingertip-tight (just until you feel resistance) to allow air to escape during the canning process. If you have a combi oven, process the jar at 100°C (212°F) for 20 minutes. Otherwise, check the pot you used to sterilize the jar; if there is not enough water to keep the jar submerged, add additional water. Bring the water to a boil. Stand the canning jar on the rack in the pot, making sure it is submerged, and boil for 20 minutes.

Remove the jar, tighten the lid all the way, and stand the jar upside down on the counter. Let cool to room temperature. Turn the jar right-side up, clean the outside of the jar, check the lid for a proper seal, and label it with the date. Press the center of the lid; if it pops, the jar is not properly sealed. Remove the cap, reseal it, then steam or process in boiling water as before.

Properly sealed, the peaches will keep without refrigeration in an area not exposed to light for up to 6 months. The ideal temperature for long-term storage is 40° to 70°F (4.5° to 21°C). After the jar has been opened, the peaches will keep in the refrigerator for up to 1 week. Always use a clean utensil, never your fingers, to remove peaches from the jar.

FOR THE PECAN SANDIES

Preheat the oven to 325°F (163°C). Line a sheet pan with a nonstick silicone baking mat.

In the bowl of a stand mixer fitted with the paddle, combine the butter, confectioners' sugar, and salt. Beginning on low speed and gradually increasing to medium, cream the mixture until light and fluffy, about 3 minutes. Add the flour and pecans and mix on low speed until just combined, being careful not to crush the pecans. Transfer the dough to a work surface and press it with the heel of your hand as necessary to bring it together.

Place the pecan dough between two sheets of parchment paper and roll it out to ¼ inch (6 millimeters) thick, doing your best to keep a rectangular shape. From time to time, lift the top sheet of parchment and, using a dough cutter, push the edges to straighten them. (Keeping the dough a uniform rectangle will give a higher yield when cutting the cookies.) Slide the parchment onto a sheet pan and refrigerate for at least 1 hour and up to 24 hours, or wrap in plastic wrap and freeze for up to 3 months. (If frozen, defrost before baking.)

Cut the cookie dough into 2 by ½-inch (5 by 1.25-centimeter) batons. Using a small offset spatula, transfer them to the lined sheet pan, leaving 1 inch (2.5 centimeters) between them. Bake for 10 to 13 minutes, until golden.

Meanwhile, put some confectioners' sugar in a small fine-mesh sieve. Remove the cookies from the oven and, while they are still hot, immediately dust the tops with confectioners' sugar. Let cool.

The cookies can be stored in an airtight container for up to 3 days.

FOR THE WHIPPED RICOTTA

Heat the sugar and water in a small saucepot just enough to dissolve the sugar. Remove from the heat and let the simple syrup cool completely.

In the bowl of the stand mixer fitted with the whisk, whisk together the ricotta, vanilla seeds, and lemon zest until well combined. Add the mas-

carpone and whisk until smooth. Add the crème fraîche and whisk until smooth. Finally, whisk in the simple syrup. Refrigerate in an airtight container for up to 5 days.

FOR THE PEACH-SCENTED JELLY

Submerge the gelatin in a bowl of ice water to bloom (soften) for about 5 minutes.

Set a cooling rack over a half sheet pan. Open the jar of peaches and pour 250 grams of the syrup into a small saucepot. Arrange the peach halves cut-side up on the rack and refrigerate while you make the jelly.

Add the lemon juice to the syrup in the saucepot and bring to a simmer. Remove from the heat. Remove the softened gelatin from the ice water and squeeze out any excess water. Add the gelatin to the hot syrup and whisk to dissolve. Strain the syrup through a chinois or fine-mesh strainer into a bowl and nestle the bowl in an ice-water bath to cool, stirring from time to time. Watch closely; as the syrup cools, it will begin to set, and you need to catch it right at the setting point, when it has thickened and begun to gel but still has fluidity. When the syrup reaches this point, remove the peaches from the fridge and spoon the syrup over them in a thick layer. Refrigerate to set the jelly completely, at least 4 hours and up to 24 hours.

TO COMPLETE

Remove the peaches from the refrigerator. Crush the basil buds lightly between your fingers to release their scent and flavor and sprinkle them over the peaches. Finish each peach with a little Maldon salt.

Place a large spoonful of the whipped ricotta in each serving bowl or on serving plates. Gently rest a peach half on top, cut-side up. Serve with a stack of pecan sandies on a plate alongside.

> ### NOTE
> Blanching peaches loosens their skins, making them easier to peel. The heat helps to separate the skin from the peach so the peels slip off.

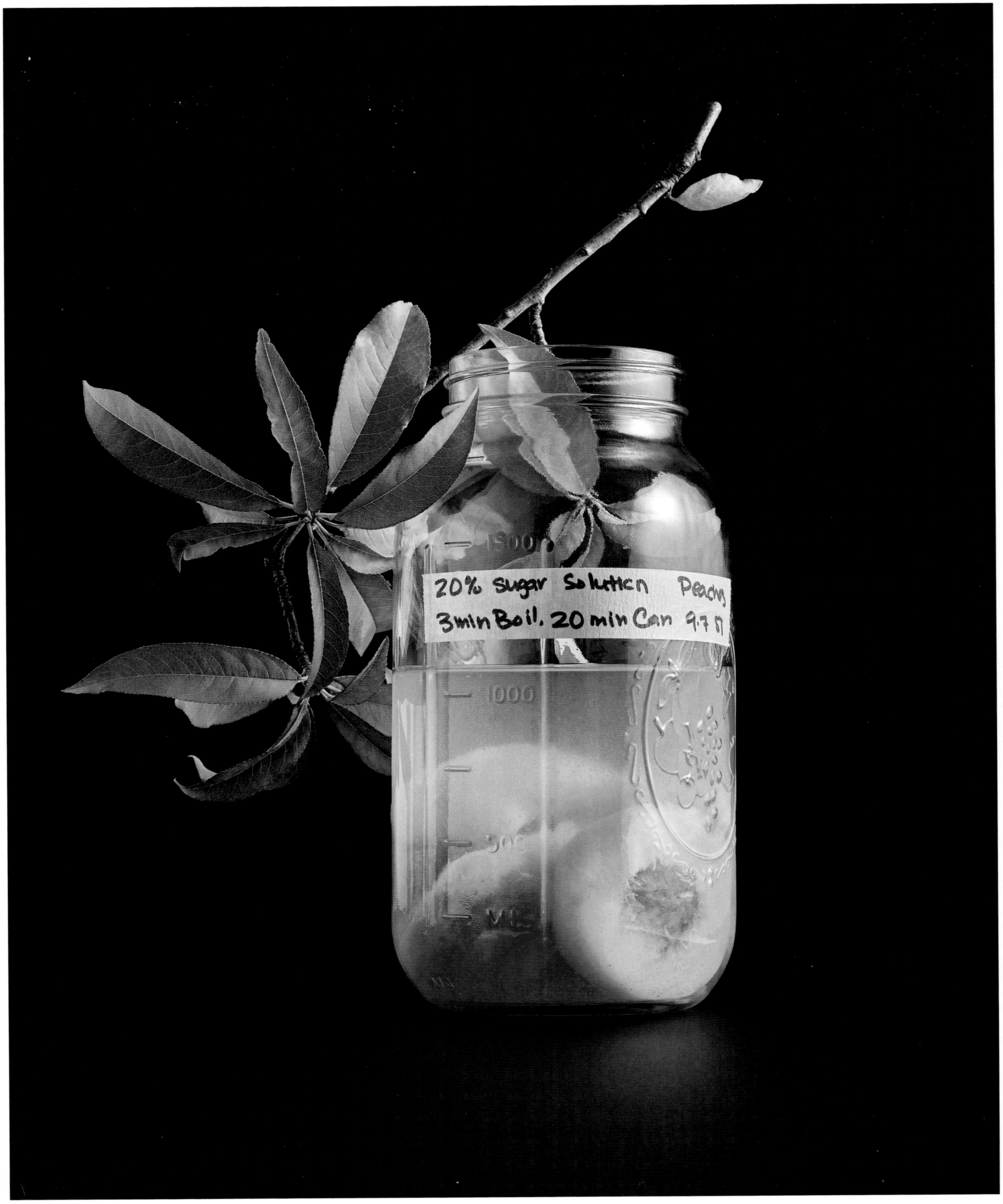
20% Sugar Solution
3min Boil. 20 min Can
1000

RHUBARB AND CUSTARD

Rose Water Whip, Green Tea Sponge, Turkish Delight, and Rhubarb Fritters

TRIFLE SPONGE

132 grams eggs

80 grams sugar

80 grams all-purpose flour

ROSE WATER BASE

600 grams water

200 grams pink rose water, store-bought or homemade (recipe follows)

200 grams ¼-inch-thick (6-millimeter) slices fresh rhubarb

100 grams grenadine

3 strips lemon zest

100 grams lemon juice

½ vanilla bean, split lengthwise

100 grams sugar

ROSE WATER SOAK

5 sheets silver leaf gelatin

VANILLA BAVAROIS

5½ sheets silver leaf gelatin

250 grams heavy cream

2 vanilla beans, split lengthwise

250 grams whole milk

3 egg yolks

85 grams sugar

25 grams egg whites

ROSE WATER JELLY

2 sheets silver leaf gelatin

GREEN TEA SPONGE

150 grams water

68 grams matcha green tea powder

170 grams eggs

250 grams sugar

93 grams canola oil

120 grams Greek yogurt

55 grams lime juice

193 grams all-purpose flour

70 grams bread flour

4 grams baking soda

1.25 grams baking powder

2.5 grams kosher salt

TURKISH DELIGHT

15 sheets silver leaf gelatin

72 grams cornstarch, plus extra for dusting

50 grams lemon juice

100 grams pink rose water, store-bought or homemade (recipe follows)

80 grams water

600 grams sugar

RHUBARB AND ROSE WATER WHIP

125 grams fresh rhubarb, chopped

150 grams pink rose water, store-bought or homemade (recipe follows)

100 grams water

Zest of ½ lemon, removed with a vegetable peeler

25 grams lemon juice

¼ vanilla bean, split lengthwise

50 grams sugar

2½ grams kosher salt

2.3 grams Versawhip

0.75 grams xanthan gum

RHUBARB FRITTER BATTER

84 grams eggs

25 grams sugar

7 grams vanilla paste

245 grams whole milk

210 grams all-purpose flour

5 grams baking soda

1 gram kosher salt

TO COMPLETE

Cornstarch, for dusting

Peeled fresh rhubarb

Lime juice

Canola oil, for deep-frying

Yellow and green celery leaves

Verbena blossoms

10 (2½ by ½-inch/6.5 by 1.25-centimeter) fresh rhubarb batons

All-purpose flour

Sugar

Ground ginger

SPECIAL EQUIPMENT

Chamber vacuum sealer (optional)

This dessert takes inspiration from a trifle and uses the same trifle sponge, well soaked in jelly and then topped with a bavarois to emulate the custard in a trifle.

We then wanted to have some fun and expand it, adding a multitude of textures and techniques all springing up from the rhubarb and rose theme: a green tea sponge cake; Turkish delight; rhubarb and rose water whipped juice; a rhubarb fritter; and a garnish of diced fresh rhubarb, yellow and green celery leaves, and verbena blossoms. A lot going on here. It doesn't look like a trifle but it eats like one, even with all the complex flavors.

Celery is great with dessert. It's a little bit bitter, so when you eat it, it cuts through the sweetness of the other ingredients to bring it all together. The Turkish delight and the sourness of the raw rhubarb dressed with a little lime add to the complexity. And why the rhubarb fritter? Because Elwyn would traditionally eat warm stewed rhubarb with warm custard. We often return to childhood for inspiration, just as Elwyn has here.

FOR THE TRIFLE SPONGE

Preheat the oven to 325°F (163°C). Line a quarter sheet pan with a non-stick silicone baking mat and spray with nonstick spray.

Bring water to a simmer in the bottom of a double boiler. Crack the eggs into the top of the double boiler. Whisk in the sugar and place over the simmering water. Cook, whisking briskly to warm the eggs, for about 5 minutes, until the mixture is hot to the touch and the eggs have started to become light with some aeration; you should be able to hold your finger in the egg mixture for 7 seconds before feeling discomfort.

Transfer the egg mixture to the bowl of a stand mixer fitted with the whisk and whip on high speed until pale and voluminous, 8 to 10 minutes. Gently, so as not to deflate the mixture, use a silicone spatula to transfer it to a medium bowl. While folding with a silicone spatula, gradually sift the flour over the egg mixture and fold until the flour is fully incorporated and the mixture is smooth. Scrape the sides and bottom of the bowl to incorporate any pockets of flour and ensure that no flour is left at the bottom of the bowl.

Gently transfer the batter to the prepared quarter sheet pan, spreading it to the edges of the pan and smoothing the top with a small offset spatula into an even layer. Be gentle when working with the batter so you do not lose volume; you want the lightest sponge possible.

Bake until the cake springs back when gently touched, 10 to 12 minutes; it will not take on much color but will have a light golden shine. Remove from the oven and let cool in the pan on a cooling rack. While the cake is still warm, run a small knife around the edges of the cake to loosen it. Place a piece of parchment paper on top of the cake and invert the cake onto the back of another quarter sheet pan. Remove the pan covering the cake and place the cake in the freezer for 30 minutes, or until it is cold and firm. Once cold, remove the cake from the freezer and peel off the baking mat. Invert the cake onto another piece of parchment and peel the parchment off the top, removing some of the "skin" from the surface of the cake with it. If there is any skin left on the cake, remove it by scraping the surface of the cake with a knife. (It is important to remove the skin, as it breaks down to a sludgy texture when soaked.)

If you have a chamber vacuum sealer, place a quarter sheet pan inside a large sous vide bag and vacuum seal to line the pan.

If you do not have a chamber vacuum sealer, cut a piece of plastic wrap that is at least 2 inches (5 centimeters) longer and wider than a quarter sheet pan. Lay it on the work surface, smoothing out any wrinkles. Top with a second layer of plastic wrap. Spray the quarter sheet pan with a light coating of nonstick spray. Lay the double layer of plastic wrap in the pan, pressing it into the corners. Trim the plastic wrap to give you a 1-inch (2.5-centimeter) overhang on all sides and fold the plastic back against the outside of the pan.

Place the cake, peeled-side up, into the lined pan and set aside at room temperature while you make the jelly.

The trifle sponge can be well wrapped in plastic wrap to preserve flavor and freshness (see Note) and refrigerated for up to 24 hours or frozen for up to 2 weeks. Defrost the trifle sponge in the refrigerator, still in the plastic wrap (this way, any condensation will form on the outside and not on the sponge).

NOTE

The plastic wrap is critical for keeping moisture off the sponge. The freezer is a humid environment; water in the form of frost or ice crystals can attach itself to the sponge and lead to a compromised product.

FOR THE ROSE WATER BASE

Combine the water, rose water, rhubarb, grenadine, lemon zest, and lemon juice in a medium pot. Scrape the vanilla seeds into the pot and add the pod. Bring the mixture to a gentle boil, then reduce the heat to maintain a simmer and cook for 3 minutes. Remove from the heat, cover with a lid, and steep for 10 minutes. Stir in the sugar and return the mixture to a boil, stirring to dissolve the sugar. Remove from the heat and set aside to cool to room temperature. Strain the rose water base through a chinois into a bowl.

FOR THE ROSE WATER SOAK

Submerge the gelatin in a bowl of ice water to bloom (soften) for about 5 minutes.

Pour 500 grams of the rose water base into a 1-quart (1-liter) saucepot (reserve the remainder for the rose water jelly). Warm over medium heat until hot. Remove the softened gelatin from the ice water and squeeze out any excess water. Add the gelatin to the rose water base and stir to dissolve. Pass the rose water soak through a sieve into a bowl.

While the soak is still warm, pour it over the cake in the quarter sheet pan, pouring systematically around the pan from left to right and then top to bottom and making sure every inch of the cake is completely soaked. If the soak starts to pool on the cake, gently massage it into the cake with your fingers. The cake should be saturated.

If the surface of the cake is not completely smooth after soaking, take a small offset spatula and smooth the surface. Refrigerate the cake to set the soak, about 2 hours.

FOR THE VANILLA BAVAROIS

Submerge the gelatin in a bowl of ice water to bloom (soften) for about 5 minutes.

In the bowl of a stand mixer fitted with the whisk, whip the cream to soft peaks. Refrigerate.

Scrape the seeds from the vanilla beans into a 1-quart (1-liter) saucepot and add the pods and the milk. Bring the milk to a boil over medium heat. Place the egg yolks in a bowl with 35 grams of the sugar and whisk until lightened in color. While whisking continuously, gradually add the hot milk to the egg yolks to temper them.

Return the mixture to the pot and cook over medium heat, whisking continuously, until the mixture has thickened and coats the back of a spoon. Remove the softened gelatin from the ice water and squeeze out any excess water. Add the gelatin and stir it into the anglaise. Strain the anglaise through a sieve into a bowl. Nestle the bowl in an ice-water bath and let cool to about 80°F (26.7°C); any hotter, and it could melt the meringue once it is added.

Pour the egg whites into the clean bowl of the stand mixer fitted with the whisk and begin whipping on medium speed. When the whites begin to appear frothy, pour in one-third of the remaining sugar and whip until the whites become foamy. Add half of the remaining sugar and whip until the whites reaches soft peaks. Add the remaining sugar and whip for 4 minutes more.

Using a whisk, fold one-third of the meringue into the cooled anglaise, then fold in the remaining meringue, followed by the whipped cream.

The bavarois will set quickly, so work fast. Using an offset spatula, quickly spread it over the surface of the cake in an even layer, stopping ¼ inch (6 millimeters) from the top of the pan to leave enough space to accommodate the jelly layer. Refrigerate until set, about 1 hour.

FOR THE ROSE WATER JELLY

Submerge the gelatin in a bowl of ice water to bloom (soften) for about 5 minutes.

Place 250 grams of the rose water base in a 1-quart (1-liter) saucepot and heat over medium heat until warm. Remove the softened gelatin from the ice water and squeeze out any excess water. Add the gelatin to the rose water base and stir gently to avoid incorporating air bubbles. Pass through a sieve into a bowl and nestle the bowl in an ice-water bath. Let cool to 70°F (21°C), stirring occasionally (stir gently to avoid incorporating air bubbles into the jelly). The jelly should become more viscous as it cools and feel cold to the touch when it has cooled sufficiently.

Pour an even layer of the jelly over the vanilla bavarois layer. Refrigerate until the jelly is set, about 1 hour. Keep the pan flat and do not move it to ensure that the jelly sets in an even layer. Once the rhubarb and custard is set, put the pan in an airtight container, cover, and refrigerate overnight to fully firm up.

FOR THE GREEN TEA SPONGE

Preheat the oven to 350°F (180°C). Line a quarter sheet pan with a nonstick silicone baking mat and spray with nonstick spray.

Place the water in a 1-quart (1-liter) saucepot and bring the water to 160° to 165°F (71° to 74°C) over medium heat. (Warming the water will help the green tea powder dissolve more easily.) Add the green tea powder and whisk until no lumps remain. Using a silicone spatula, pass the resulting paste through an extra-fine sieve into a bowl to remove any last lumps.

In the bowl of the stand mixer fitted with the whisk, whip the eggs and sugar on medium-high speed until the mixture holds a soft peak. With the mixer running, slowly drizzle in the canola oil and whip until it is emulsified.

Add 150 grams of the egg mixture to the bowl with the green tea paste and whisk to loosen the paste. (This will enable the paste to fully incorporate with the remaining ingredients.) Whisk in the yogurt, followed by the lime juice, and whisk to combine. Scrape the edges and the bottom of the bowl thoroughly to be sure that all the ingredients are well incorporated. Add the green tea mixture to the mixer bowl with the remaining egg mixture and whip to combine.

Combine the all-purpose flour, bread flour, baking soda, baking powder, and salt in a medium bowl. Sift the flour mixture into the bowl of the stand mixer. Begin mixing on low speed and gradually increase the speed, mixing just enough to incorporate the dry ingredients.

Spread the batter over the prepared pan and bake until the surface of the cake springs back when gently touched and a cake tester inserted into the center comes out clean, 15 to 20 minutes. Remove from the oven and let cool in the pan.

The cake can be well wrapped in plastic wrap to preserve flavor and freshness (see Note) and refrigerated for up to 24 hours or frozen for up to 2 weeks. Defrost the cake in the refrigerator, still in the plastic wrap (this way, any condensation will form on the outside and not on the cake).

FOR THE TURKISH DELIGHT

If you have a chamber vacuum sealer, place a quarter sheet pan inside a large sous vide bag and vacuum seal to line the pan. Spray the lined pan with nonstick spray.

(continued)

If you do not have chamber vacuum sealer, cut a piece of plastic wrap that is at least 2 inches (5 centimeters) longer and wider than a quarter sheet pan. Lay it on the work surface, smoothing out any wrinkles. Top with two additional layers of plastic wrap. Spray the quarter sheet pan with a light coating of nonstick spray. Lay the triple layer of plastic wrap in the pan, pressing it into the corners. Trim the plastic wrap to give you a 1-inch (2.5-centimeter) overhang on all sides and fold the plastic back against the outside of the pan.

Submerge the gelatin in a bowl of ice water to bloom (soften) for about 5 minutes.

Stir together the cornstarch, lemon juice, and 50 grams of the rose water in a bowl to make a slurry. Combine the water, sugar, and the remaining 50 grams of rose water in a small pot and bring to a boil. Stay by the pot, because the mixture will bubble up and could boil over. Once the mixture is at a boil, stir in the slurry and boil for 3 minutes. Remove the syrup from the heat. Remove the softened gelatin from the ice water and squeeze out any excess water. Add the gelatin to the syrup and stir just until dissolved. Pour the syrup into the prepared pan and set aside at room temperature overnight to set and dry.

Dredge the top of the Turkish delight in cornstarch. Cut the bag (if used) from around the pan and invert the Turkish delight onto the work surface; remove the bag or plastic wrap. Dredge the bottom and sides in cornstarch as well. Refrigerate in an airtight container for up to 5 days.

FOR THE RHUBARB AND ROSE WATER WHIP

Place the rhubarb, rose water, water, lemon zest, and lemon juice in a 1-quart (1-liter) saucepot. Scrape the vanilla seeds into the pot and add the pod. Bring the mixture to a boil. Reduce the heat to maintain a slow simmer and cook for 15 minutes, or until the chopped rhubarb breaks down, releasing its flavor. Remove from the heat, cover with a lid, and let cool to room temperature.

Strain the rhubarb infusion into a clean 1-quart (1-liter) saucepot and mix in the sugar and salt. Heat the infusion, stirring, just to dissolve the sugar. Strain the infusion and refrigerate until completely cold.

Place 300 grams of the chilled infusion in a blender. With the blender running on low speed, shear in the Versawhip and xanthan gum, then blend on medium speed for 2 minutes. Transfer the mixture to the bowl

of the stand mixer fitted with the whisk. Whip on high speed until the base reaches its full volume and stops rising up the sides of the bowl. Transfer to a container, cover, and refrigerate for up to 4 hours before serving. Rewhip if needed before using.

FOR THE RHUBARB FRITTER BATTER

Whisk the eggs and sugar in a medium bowl and set aside. Combine the vanilla and milk in a small bowl. Combine the flour, baking soda, and salt in a separate bowl. In three additions, whisk the milk mixture and the flour mixture into the egg mixture, alternating between them. Refrigerate, covered, for up to 12 hours before frying.

TO COMPLETE

Remove the rhubarb and custard from the sheet pan by lifting it out with the plastic wrap (or cutting the bag away from the pan) and place on a cutting board. Peel back the plastic from the sides. Using a large chef's knife dipped in hot water and dried on a kitchen towel, trim the sides so you have a 7 by 10-inch (18 by 25-centimeter) rectangle. Slice this crosswise into ten 1-inch-wide (2.5-centimeter) pieces, cleaning and drying your knife between cuts for even cuts with visible layers. The cake can be cut up to 24 hours ahead, placed on a sheet pan, wrapped well in plastic wrap, and refrigerated until serving.

Cut fifty ⅜-inch (1-centimeter) cubes of Turkish delight and coat them evenly in cornstarch. Set aside at room temperature until serving.

Cut the peeled rhubarb into ⅛-inch (3-millimeter) dice and dress in a little lime juice. You will need about 40 grams (¼ cup) for garnishing. Refrigerate until serving.

Remove the green tea sponge from the pan and remove the parchment paper. Using a long serrated knife, cut off the top skin and ½ inch (1.25 centimeters) from each side. Cut ten 5 by ⅜-inch (12.5 by 1-centimeter) strips of sponge. If cut ahead of serving, lay them on their sides in a container, cover with a lid, and hold at room temperature.

Fill a medium fry pot with 2½ inches (6.5 centimeters) canola oil. Heat the oil to 350°F (180°C).

Place a slice of the rhubarb and custard in the center of each serving plate on a diagonal. Offset a slice of the green tea sponge alongside the custard. Carefully sprinkle the fresh rhubarb dice on top of the green tea sponge and garnish with pieces of Turkish delight and celery leaves.

Spoon a dollop of the rhubarb and rose water whip on each plate and garnish the whip with verbena blossoms.

Lightly dust the rhubarb batons in flour and dip them into the rhubarb fritter batter. Gently drop them into the hot oil and fry until golden, about 3 minutes. Remove the fritters with a slotted spoon or spider and drain on paper towels. After 1 minute, roll the fritters in sugar seasoned with a little ginger and place one on each plate. Serve immediately.

Pink Rose Water Distillation

Yield varies

Strong-fragranced
 unsprayed rose petals,
 for scent

Bright red unsprayed
 rose petals, for color

The variety of rose is important. We use two varieties for pink rose water: one should be selected for its scent, as floral and strong as possible; the other for its color, as bright red as possible.

The roses should be picked as soon as they open in the morning, to capture the maximum flavor from the scent, then distilled as soon as possible with this very basic method.

Lay the rose petals for scent in a 2-inch-deep (5-centimeter) layer in the bottom of a large pot and cover with cold water.

Place a metal ring in the center of the petals and set a small metal bowl on top. Place the pot on a burner and bring the water just to a simmer. Immediately place a large, round-bottomed metal bowl full of ice over the top of the pot. The flavor of the rose petals is evaporated in the steam, which then condenses on the bottom of the cold bowl and drips into the small metal bowl.

The rose water that collects in the small bowl will be clear. To color it pink, transfer the rose water to a small pot and heat until it steams; do not bring it to a boil, as this would draw unwanted bitter flavors from the petals. Add the red rose petals, remove from the heat, and cover the pot with plastic wrap. Let sit for 30 minutes to tint the rose water. Strain through a chinois.

Store in an airtight container in the refrigerator for up to 3 days.

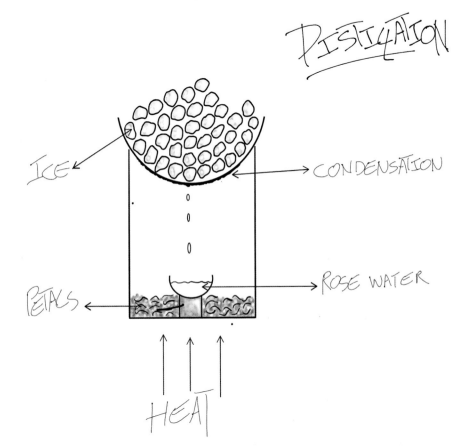

BLACKCURRANT AND CHAMPAGNE TRIFLE

Makes 4 to 6 servings

TRIFLE SPONGE

188 grams eggs

113 grams sugar

113 grams all-purpose flour

BLACKCURRANT JAM

63 grams sugar

5 grams apple pectin

250 grams blackcurrant puree, preferably Boiron

SHERRY SOAK

½ sheet silver leaf gelatin

53 grams water

45 grams sugar

1 strip lime zest

¼ vanilla bean, split lengthwise

38 grams sweet sherry

ROSÉ JELLY

3 sheets silver leaf gelatin

40 grams sugar

Zest of 1 lime, removed with a vegetable peeler

25 grams lime juice

½ vanilla bean, split lengthwise

330 grams rosé champagne

VANILLA CUSTARD

1 sheet silver leaf gelatin

50 grams sugar

50 grams eggs

24 grams egg yolks

20 grams Bird's custard powder

250 grams whole milk

½ vanilla bean, split lengthwise

75 grams crème fraîche

WHIPPED CREAM

120 grams heavy cream (preferably 40% fat), or more as needed

25 grams sugar

1.2 grams whipped cream stabilizer (optional)

SPECIAL EQUIPMENT

Two 10-millimeter-thick confectionary rulers (optional)

1-quart (1-liter) glass bowl, about 5 inches (12.5 centimeters) high and 4 inches (10 centimeters) wide

#804 (⅜-inch/ 10-millimeter) plain piping tip

#803 (5/16-inch/ 8-millimeter) plain piping tip

This classic British trifle follows very closely the one made by pastry chef Wally Ladd at the Connaught Hotel in London, where Elwyn worked for two years. It was one of the great classical French restaurants that helped to get England's food and restaurant scene back on track after the devastation of the Second World War and rationing. The dessert here is scarcely refined in any way from what was developed at the Connaught during the twentieth century.

It's a traditional trifle sponge—saturated with a sherry soak (sherry, vanilla, and sugar, along with gelatin to maintain the trifle's body)—rosé champagne jelly, pastry cream, and Chantilly. Elwyn adds crème fraîche to the custard to lighten it, and incorporates a jelly in this version because that's what his mom did. Growing up in Wales and Cambridge, this was Elwyn's favorite dessert, and the custard is made with the addition of some Bird's custard powder to give people a little taste of things he loved from childhood.

We prepare this in a glass bowl and serve it tableside by spooning out elegant quenelles of trifle—the trick here is to capture all the layers in one giant spoonful.

FOR THE TRIFLE SPONGE

Preheat the oven to 325°F (163°C). Line an eighth sheet pan with parchment paper and spray with nonstick spray.

Bring water to a simmer in the bottom of a double boiler. Crack the eggs into the top of the double boiler. Whisk in the sugar and place over the simmering water. Cook, whisking briskly to avoid scrambling the eggs, for about 2 minutes, until the mixture is hot to the touch and the sugar has dissolved.

Immediately transfer the hot egg mixture to the bowl of a stand mixer fitted with the whisk and whip on high speed for 8 to 10 minutes, until it reaches its full volume and stops rising up the sides of the bowl. Gently, so as not to deflate the mixture, use a silicone spatula to transfer it to a medium bowl. While folding with a silicone spatula, gradually sift the flour over the egg mixture and fold until the flour is fully incorporated and the mixture is smooth. Scrape the sides and bottom of the bowl to incorporate any pockets of flour and ensure that no flour is left at the bottom of the bowl.

(continued)

Gently transfer the batter to the prepared pan, spreading it to the edges of the pan and smoothing the top with a small offset spatula into an even layer. Be gentle when working with the batter so you do not lose volume; you want the lightest sponge possible. Bake for 15 to 17 minutes, until the cake is golden brown and springs back when gently touched and a cake tester inserted into the center comes out clean. Remove from the oven and let cool slightly in the pan on a cooling rack. While the cake is still warm, run a small knife around the edges of the cake to loosen it. Place a piece of parchment paper on top of the cake; it is important that the paper is not sprayed or greased so that it will stick to the top of the cake. Position a small cutting board over the parchment and invert the cake onto the cutting board. Remove the pan and place the cake in the freezer for 30 minutes, or until it is cold and firm. Once cold, remove the cake from the freezer and invert the cake. Peel back the parchment, removing some of the "skin" from the surface of the cake with it. If there is any skin left on the cake, remove it by scraping the surface with a knife. (It is important to remove the skin, as it breaks down to a sludgy texture when soaked.)

The trifle sponge can be well wrapped in plastic wrap to preserve flavor and freshness (see Note on page 308) and refrigerated for up to 24 hours or frozen for up to 2 weeks. Defrost the trifle sponge in the refrigerator, still in the plastic wrap (this way, any condensation will form on the outside and not on the sponge).

FOR THE BLACKCURRANT JAM

Combine half the sugar and the apple pectin in a small bowl and mix well to disperse the pectin throughout the sugar. (This will help to avoid lumps in your jam.)

Combine the blackcurrant puree with the remaining sugar in a nonreactive pot (see Note), such as stainless steel or enamel-lined cast iron, preferably with a copper core. While whisking, bring the puree to a rolling boil over medium-high heat. Remove from the heat and whisk in the pectin mixture. Return to the heat and continue to whisk as it comes to a boil; boil for 30 seconds to thicken.

> ### NOTE
> Pots made from metals such an aluminum or untreated cast iron can react with the acid in the fruit and leach a metallic flavor into your jam.

Pour the jam into a bowl and immediately press plastic wrap against the surface to prevent a skin from forming. Let cool to room temperature.

Once cool, the jam is ready to spread on the sponge. It can be refrigerated in an airtight container for up to 1 week. Let stand at room temperature for 2 hours before using.

FOR THE SHERRY SOAK

Submerge the gelatin in a bowl of ice water to bloom (soften) for about 5 minutes.

Put the water, sugar, and lime zest in a 1-quart (1-liter) saucepot. Scrape the vanilla seeds into the pot and add the pod. Bring the mixture to a full boil, then remove the saucepot from the heat. Remove the softened gelatin from the ice water and squeeze out any excess water. Add the gelatin to the saucepot and whisk to dissolve. Strain into a small bowl and let cool to room temperature. Stir in the sherry. If not using immediately, the soak can be refrigerated in an airtight container for up to 1 week. Bring it back to room temperature before using.

Using a long, sharp serrated knife, slice the sponge horizontally through the center, creating two even layers. (We use 10-millimeter-thick confectionary rulers as a guide to divide it cleanly in half.)

Remove the top layer of the sponge. Using an offset spatula, spread 125 grams of blackcurrant jam evenly over the bottom layer of the sponge. Place the top layer of sponge on top, peeled-side up, and press down, working outward from the center to the edges to flatten and secure the sponge. Trim the sides of the sponge and cut it into nine 1-inch (2.5-centimeter) cubes. (Any remaining sponge can be wrapped and frozen for up to 2 weeks.)

Arrange the cubes randomly in a 1-quart (1-liter) trifle bowl, about 5 inches (12.5 centimeters) high and 4 inches (10 centimeters) wide. Pour the sherry soak over the cake. Allow the cake to soak up the liquid for a few minutes, then gently press the cake cubes down to absorb the last of the soak and to create a flat surface for the rosé jelly. (The gelatin in the soak helps keep the rosé jelly in a distinct layer and prevents it from combining with the soak and sponge layer.) Place the trifle bowl in the refrigerator to allow the soak to set while making the rosé jelly.

FOR THE ROSÉ JELLY

Submerge the gelatin in a bowl of ice water to bloom (soften) for about 5 minutes.

Put the sugar, lime zest, and lime juice in a 1-quart (1-liter) saucepot. Scrape the vanilla seeds into the pot and add the pod and 75 grams of the rosé. Warm over low heat, stirring to dissolve the sugar, then increase the heat and bring the mixture to a boil. Remove the saucepot from the heat. Remove the softened gelatin from the ice water and squeeze out any excess water. Add the gelatin to the saucepot and stir to dissolve. Strain into a bowl. Stir in the remaining 255 grams rosé. Nestle the bowl in an ice-water bath. Let cool, stirring often so that the jelly does not begin to set on the sides of the bowl. After 12 to 14 minutes, the jelly will start to thicken. Watch carefully; if the jelly sets up too much, you won't be able to pour it into an even layer. Look for the vanilla seeds to be suspended throughout the jelly rather than sinking to the bottom.

Remove the trifle dish from the refrigerator and carefully pour the jelly over the soaked cake in an even layer. Refrigerate for 1 hour to set the jelly.

FOR THE VANILLA CUSTARD

Submerge the gelatin in a bowl of ice water to bloom (soften) for about 5 minutes.

Place the sugar, eggs, and egg yolks in a small bowl and whisk until lightened in color. Whisk in the custard powder until smooth; set aside. Pour the milk into a 1-quart (1-liter) saucepot. Scrape the vanilla seeds into the milk and add the pod. Bring the milk to a simmer over medium heat. While whisking continuously, gradually pour the hot milk into the egg mixture to temper the eggs.

Return the mixture to the pan and cook over medium heat, whisking vigorously, for about 1 minute, until the custard is thick. Taste the custard to be certain that the starch has been cooked completely and no starchy taste remains. Remove the softened gelatin from the ice water (reserve the ice water) and squeeze out any excess water. Add the gelatin to the custard and whisk to dissolve. Pour the hot custard into a bowl and nestle the bowl in an ice-water bath. Let cool to room temperature, removing the bowl from the water every few minutes and whisking to avoid the formation of lumps. At this point, the cooled custard can be refrigerated in an airtight container with a piece of plastic wrap pressed directly against the surface for up to 4 days. Gently stir the custard until it has a creamy consistency before adding the crème fraîche.

Whip the crème fraîche until it holds soft peaks to incorporate air (this will result in a lighter custard). Using a large whisk, gently fold the crème fraîche into the custard to incorporate it while maintaining its volume. Transfer the custard to a disposable piping bag fitted with a #804 (⅜-inch/10-millimeter) plain piping tip.

Remove the trifle dish from the refrigerator. Beginning in the center and working outward, pipe the custard in a spiral over the rosé jelly layer. Gently smooth the custard using a small offset spatula to create a flat surface without penetrating the layer of jelly. Refrigerate for 1 hour to chill completely.

FOR THE WHIPPED CREAM

Place the cream in the bowl of a stand mixer fitted with the whisk. Mix the sugar and stabilizer (if using) together in a small bowl. Using a whisk, mix the stabilizer and sugar into the cream to combine. Whip on medium speed until the cream holds stiff peaks. Transfer the whipped cream to a disposable piping bag fitted with a #803 (⁵⁄₁₆-inch/ 8-millimeter) plain piping tip.

TO COMPLETE

Remove the trifle dish from the refrigerator. Beginning in the center and working outward, pipe the whipped cream in a spiral over the pastry cream. Sweep a long offset spatula over the whipped cream from one side of the bowl to the other to create a flat surface. Run the offset spatula under hot tap water to warm it, then dry it with a paper towel. Sweep the warmed spatula over the whipped cream again to give the trifle a perfectly smooth finish. (If the whipped cream does not reach the top of the serving vessel, whip additional cream and add it to the top to create a smooth finish that aligns with the top of the vessel.)

Before serving, refrigerate the trifle for 2 hours if you prepared the whipped cream without stabilizer or for up to 6 hours for whipped cream with stabilizer.

THE EVOLUTION OF DESSERT

When I opened The French Laundry, I wanted every part of the meal to surprise, astonish, and delight each person who came to the restaurant. But I also followed what I knew to be true: the law of diminishing returns.

The more you experience something, the more palate fatigue sets in. This means that the longer you eat one thing, the less you pay attention to it, but I wanted my guests to pay attention to every bite. This meant I had to serve small, focused courses—brilliant-orange carrot soup served in an espresso cup (remember *those*?), a tiny spool of linguine in a clam shell—and, therefore, many of them.

I felt every part of the meal deserved this kind of attention. That's why I developed a cheese course that was actually a composed dish, a beautiful cheddar melting between toasted brioche, beside a small cup of peeled cherry tomatoes in tomato consommé, a reimagined Caesar salad to feature a great Parmesan.

And I called on Stephen Durfee, The French Laundry's original pastry chef, to move off the hot line to take over the final section of the meal. I wanted dessert service to mirror the rest of the meal, and he refined our desserts, like the pineapple chop, and reinventions of classics like *île flottante*.

But as we've evolved, and as the diner has evolved, our thinking about dessert has changed. We now serve several kinds of desserts all at once. It's an extravaganza, like the Fourth of July fireworks finale. Our executive pastry chef, Elwyn Boyles, introduced it. So now, rather than sending out four separate dessert courses, we serve four different sweets as one course: a chocolate dessert, a seasonal fruit, an ice cream, and a cake or cookie. Followed by mignardises and bonbons, of course!

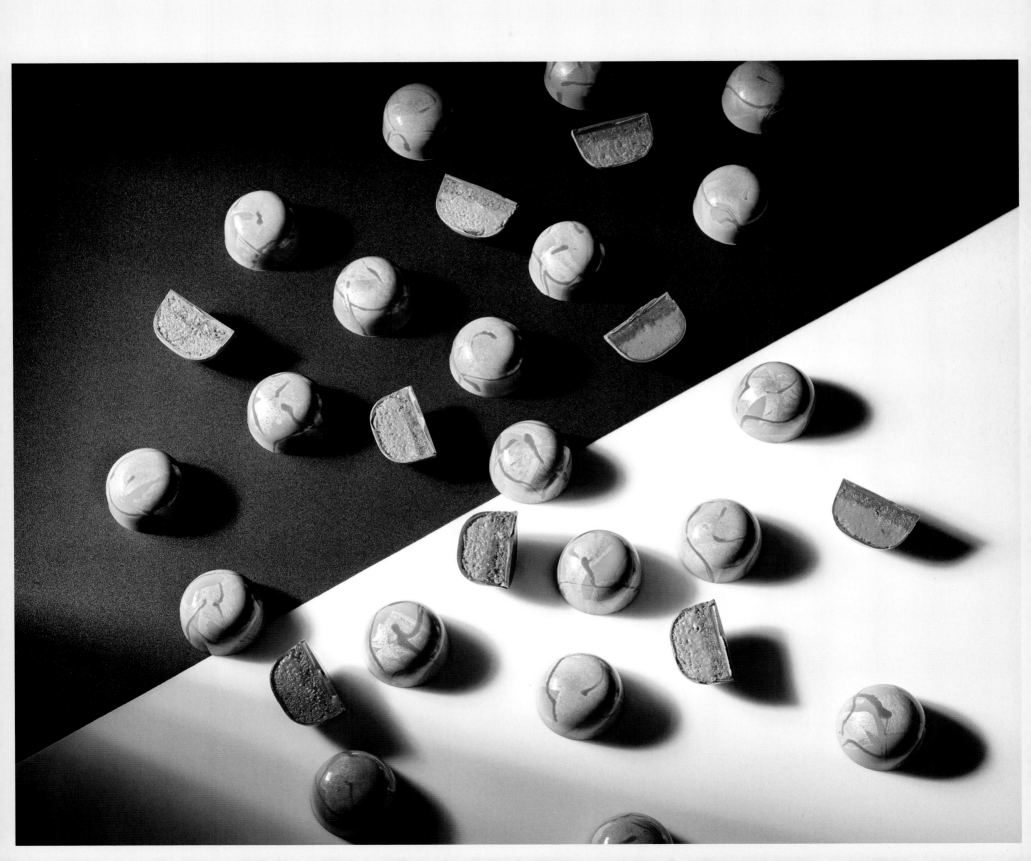

VANILLA ICE CREAM

Cookie Crumb and Cured Egg Yolk

Makes 22 sandwiches

**SUGAR-CURED
EGG YOLKS**

500 grams granulated
sugar

166 grams kosher salt

3 large eggs

COOKIE CRUMB

60 grams whole butter, at
room temperature

60 grams Demerara
sugar

60 grams all-purpose
flour

VANILLA ICE CREAM

1 Madagascar vanilla
bean, split

½ Tahitian vanilla bean,
split

625 grams whole milk

450 grams heavy cream

40 grams dextrose

10 grams Trimoline invert
sugar

270 grams granulated
sugar

10 large egg yolks

Zest of ½ lime

4 grams kosher salt

PUFF PASTRY

1 (16½ by 7-inch/42 by
18-centimeter) sheet
puff pastry, ¼ inch
(6 millimeters) thick,
homemade or
store-bought

TO COMPLETE

Cracked black pepper

SPECIAL EQUIPMENT

Acetate sheets

Ice cream machine

Eight ½-inch-tall
(13-millimeter) metal
blocks or rings

I've wanted to serve ice cream ever since I opened per se, and I began to wonder how this amazing confection got cut out of fine-dining desserts. I just love ice cream: the texture of it, the way milk and cream can carry flavor, and also the way it returns you to childhood pleasures. Elwyn and his team perfected vanilla ice cream over the course of about three years, starting with a standard crème anglaise—2,000 grams whole milk and heavy cream, 20 egg yolks, 250 grams sugar, vanilla bean—making minute changes and asking the staff to taste and rate each new ice cream. Does it feel heavy? Does it cling to the mouth? Is the sugar content right? What's the best vanilla bean to use? What are the best sugars in what proportions?

Here's the result.

Elwyn confided that he actually uses a little lime zest to season it. "It's the greatest secret," he says. He adds lime zest after the custard has cooked, just to lightly infuse it, 30 minutes or so. You shouldn't even know that it's there.

We serve the ice cream between layers of crisp puff pastry, baked under a weight to keep it from rising too much and creating a uniform thickness. And we top it with bright yellow gratings of cured egg yolk.

The ice cream itself is powerfully flavored. It's both light and rich at the same time, with spice from the vanilla bean, freshness from the lime, richness from the yolk. Sweet but not too sweet. Enough sugar to allow it to be soft and creamy, the perfect texture, without being sickly sweet. We think it's close to perfectly balanced.

FOR THE SUGAR-CURED EGG YOLKS

Whisk the sugar and salt in a medium bowl.

Spread half the mixture over the bottom of a pan that is about 8 by 8 inches (20 by 20 centimeters) and at least 2 inches (5 centimeters) deep. Using the bottom of an eggshell, press three divots in the mixture, leaving ample room between them and stopping ½ inch (1.25 centimeters) from the bottom of the pan, forming a bed to softly cradle the raw yolks. The yolks will be stored at room temperature. Place the pan in the location where you will keep it; it is best not to move the pan once the egg yolks are added.

Crack the eggs into a small bowl, separate the yolks, remove the chalazae (the white membranes attached to the yolks), and gently place a raw yolk into each divot. Carefully sprinkle the remaining salt-sugar mixture over the raw yolks to completely enclose the yolks. Do not agitate the container, as this could break the yolks.

Cure the yolks, untouched and uncovered, at room temperature for 7 days. The salt will pull the moisture from the yolks and keep them shelf stable. Remove the yolks from the salt-sugar mixture and brush off any of the mixture clinging to the yolks. Rinse the yolks quickly in cold water just to remove any remaining salt and sugar (you do not want to rehydrate the yolks). Dry on a paper towel to remove the moisture; water left on the yolks could soak in and cause mold.

Preheat the oven to 212°F (100°C). Line a pan with parchment paper or a nonstick silicone baking mat.

Place the yolks on the pan and dry them in the oven for 10 minutes. Let the yolks cool to room temperature. Refrigerate in a sealed container for up to 1 week.

FOR THE COOKIE CRUMB

Cut two 16½ by 7-inch (42 by 18-centimeter) pieces of acetate. Fill a saucepot with 1 inch (2.5 centimeters) of water and bring to a simmer.

Place the butter in a bowl and place the bowl over the simmering water, making sure the bottom of the bowl does not touch the water. Stir with a silicone spatula for 3 to 4 seconds to further soften the butter. Continue as necessary until the butter is soft and loose but still emulsified.

Using the spatula, stir in the Demerara sugar and mix thoroughly. Add 15 grams of the flour and mix well. Repeat until all the flour is incorporated.

Place the large piece of acetate with the longer side running horizontally on the work surface. Center the dough on the acetate. Center the smaller piece of acetate with the longer side running horizontally over the dough.

Using a rolling pin, roll the dough to a ¹⁄₁₆-inch-thick (1.5-millimeter) layer that is the same size as the top piece of acetate. Any dough that extends past it can be wiped away with a finger. Move the acetate and dough to a half sheet pan, wrap securely in plastic wrap, and freeze for up to 1 month.

FOR THE VANILLA ICE CREAM

Set a medium bowl in an ice-water bath and place it near the cooktop.

Scrape the vanilla seeds into a medium pot and add the pods. Add the milk, cream, dextrose, and Trimoline and bring to a full boil. Meanwhile, in a second medium bowl, whisk together the granulated sugar and egg yolks for about 20 seconds.

When the milk mixture comes to a boil, remove it from the heat. While whisking continuously, ladle one-quarter of the milk mixture into the egg yolk mixture to temper the eggs. Repeat, whisking in one-quarter of the liquid at a time.

Return the yolk mixture to the pot and cook over medium-low heat, whisking continuously, until the anglaise has thickened enough to coat the back of a spoon. (Whisking continuously will keep the temperature of the anglaise even throughout and avoid overcooking the yolks.) The temperature of the mixture should reach 185°F (85°C).

Immediately pour the anglaise into the chilled bowl over the ice-water bath. Whisk for 30 seconds to release the heat and stop the cooking. Whisk in the lime zest and salt. Chill the anglaise completely, then strain it into an airtight container and refrigerate overnight to allow the flavors to mature.

Put a plastic storage container to hold the ice cream in the freezer for at least 2 hours. Line a quarter sheet pan with a piece of plastic wrap at least 13 by 16 inches (33 by 41 centimeters) that extends past the edges of the pan and use your palms to smooth the plastic, working outward from the center. Cut an 8 by 12-inch (20 by 30-centimeter) piece of acetate and place it over the plastic wrap. The acetate is stronger than the plastic wrap and will not wrinkle, giving you a clean, smooth sheet of ice cream. Freeze the pan for at least 2 hours.

Freeze the anglaise in an ice cream machine. Transfer the ice cream to the chilled container and freeze for 1 hour to set slightly.

Work quickly to prevent the ice cream from softening and melting, which would degrade its texture once it refreezes. Spoon the ice cream onto the frozen sheet pan. Use a silicone spatula to spread the ice cream into a solid, even layer. Tap the pan against the counter to be certain there are not any gaps between the ice cream and the pan. Using a large offset spatula, smooth the top of the ice cream into a flat, even layer. A small offset spatula can be used after for a final smoothing.

smoothing. Wrap the pan in plastic wrap and freeze the ice cream until frozen solid, at least 3 hours.

Meanwhile, line two quarter sheet pans with 8 by 12-inch (20 by 30-centimeter) pieces of acetate and freeze them for 2 to 3 hours; put a cutting board in the freezer as well.

Once your ice cream, pans, and cutting board are fully frozen, you are ready to portion your ice cream. It is important to work in a room that is not too hot and to work quickly. Remove the cutting board from the freezer and place a piece of parchment paper over it. Remove the ice cream from the freezer and invert it onto the frozen cutting board. Lift off the pan, peel off the plastic wrap, then gently peel off the acetate.

Using a large chef's knife, trim the ice cream to a 6 by 11-inch (15 by 28-centimeter) sheet. Cut it lengthwise into two 3-inch-wide (7.5-centimeter) strips. Then cut each strip crosswise into 3 by 1-inch (7.5 by 2.5-centimeter) rectangles, wiping the blade with a damp towel between cuts (you should have 22 rectangles). As you cut, use an offset spatula to immediately transfer the rectangles to the sheet pans in the freezer. Keep the ice cream rectangles frozen while you bake the puff pastry.

FOR THE PUFF PASTRY

Place the sheet of puff pastry on a cutting board. Lay the frozen sheet of cookie crumb over the pastry and place the cutting board in the freezer for 1 hour.

Preheat the oven to 350°F (180°C). Cut four 17 by 12-inch (43 by 30-centimeter) pieces of parchment paper. Spray two half sheet pans with nonstick spray and line them with the parchment. Place a metal block or tart ring that is ½ inch (13 millimeters) high in each corner of both pans.

Transfer the frozen pastry and cutting board to the refrigerator for about 5 minutes to defrost slightly. The pastry should remain partially frozen so you can make clean cuts, which will lead to better, cleaner rising as the pastry bakes.

Remove the cutting board from the refrigerator and cut the sheet lengthwise into two 3½-inch-wide (9-centimeter) strips. Cut each strip into 11 rectangles that are 1½ inches (4 centimeters) wide. Evenly space

11 of the puff pastry rectangles on each of the two prepared pans. The uncooked pastry can be securely wrapped on the sheet pan and frozen for up to 1 month.

Spray the undersides of two separate sheet pans with nonstick spray and adhere a piece of parchment paper to the sprayed surface. Rest one pan, parchment-side down, over each of the sheets with the pastry. The spacers will hold the pans above the pastry.

Bake the pastry for 34 minutes. The pastry will rise and touch the top pan, which will give it a flat, even surface. The cookie crumb should be golden brown from the heat generated by the top pan. If the cookie crumb is soft or pliable, return the pan to the oven and cook for 2 minutes, then check again and repeat as needed to finish the cooking.

Remove the sheet pans from the oven and very slowly remove the top sheet pan. If the pastry sticks to the bottom of the top sheet pan, use an offset spatula to nudge it off and into the bottom sheet pan. Reduce the oven temperature to 310°F (155°C).

Return the pan of puff pastry to the oven and bake for 7 minutes, or until the cookie crumb has dried and set. Remove from the oven and let cool on the sheet pan to room temperature.

TO COMPLETE

Using a serrated knife, cut the puff pastry horizontally through the center, to create a top and bottom for your sandwich, and place the pieces side by side. Remove the ice cream rectangles from the freezer. Using a small offset spatula, place a piece of ice cream on the bottom half of each sandwich. Top with the top pieces, cookie crumb–side up. Rest at room temperature for 3 minutes, then gently press the top of each sandwich in the center to seal, without breaking or damaging the pastry. Wrap the sandwiches on the sheet pan in plastic wrap or transfer to an airtight container and return to the freezer until serving or for up to 3 days.

Remove the ice cream sandwiches from the freezer and stand them on their sides, placing them next to each other so they are touching. Using a rasp grater, shave the cured egg yolks evenly over the exposed ice cream and sprinkle with cracked black pepper. Carefully transfer the ice cream sandwiches to individual plates and serve.

CRÈME BRÛLÉE ICE CREAM

Sugar Tuile

Makes 12 servings

SUGAR TUILE

200 grams pouring
 fondant

100 grams glucose syrup

100 grams isomalt

**CRÈME BRÛLÉE
ICE CREAM**

390 grams whole milk

390 grams heavy cream

1 Madagascar vanilla
 bean, split lengthwise

2 grams kosher salt

155 grams Demerara
 sugar

15 grams Bird's custard
 powder

40 grams glucose powder

155 grams egg yolks

40 grams Trimoline invert
 sugar

SPECIAL EQUIPMENT

Acetate sheets

Twelve 2-inch
 (50-millimeter) metal
 rings, 1½ inches
 (40 millimeters) tall

Ice cream machine

This dessert simply takes a classical dessert and reimagines it as an ice cream course, which I love to serve (and to eat). Elwyn makes a custard that has a little more yolk in it than a traditional ice cream base, and we cook it at a slightly higher temperature to bring the egg flavor out. It's also flavored with a light caramel using Demerara sugar (what we use to top a traditional crème brûlée crust to mimic that caramel), and Elwyn likes to add a little Bird's custard powder to the mix as well.

FOR THE SUGAR TUILE

Line a sheet pan with a nonstick silicone baking mat. Place the fondant and glucose syrup in a 1-quart (1-liter) saucepot. Stir over low heat to melt and combine the ingredients. Stir in the isomalt. Cook the syrup over medium heat until it reaches 315°F (157°C). Be careful, as the mixture is extremely hot! Immediately pour the mixture over the baking mat and tilt the pan to allow the mixture to spread without reaching the edges of the mat. Let cool at room temperature until it hardens completely. The unbroken sheet of sugar can be stored in an airtight container, away from moisture, for up to 1 year.

Hit the sheet of sugar with a rolling pin to break it into smaller pieces. Put the pieces in a food processor and grind to a powder. Working in several batches, transfer the powder to a spice grinder and grind it into a finer dust. The tuile powder is most susceptible to moisture after being ground to a dust. Store in an airtight container with a food-safe silica gel pack at room temperature for up to 2 weeks. Should it clump together, it can be rubbed through a sieve to break up the clumps.

To make a tuile stencil, draw two concentric circles on a piece of acetate, with the outer ring measuring about 4½ inches (11.5 centimeters) in diameter and the inner ring 4 inches (10 centimeters) in diameter. Draw a tab extending from the outer ring (this will make it easy to lift the stencil later). Trim around the tab and the outer ring, then cut out the inner ring (an X-Acto knife works well for this).

Preheat the oven to 350°F (180°C). Line a sheet pan with a silicone baking mat. Lay the stencil on the baking mat.

(continued)

Sift the tuile powder inside the stencil to create a solid, even layer 1 to 2 millimeters thick. Lift away the stencil (this is where the tab comes in handy) and repeat, leaving ample space between each tuile.

If your oven has a light, turn it on. Place the sheet pan in the oven and bake just until the sugar melts. This should take under 1 minute; watch it carefully. If left in the oven for too long, the sugar will begin to bead up and bubble and you will not be able to remove the tuiles in one piece. Remove the sheet pan from the oven and let cool for 2 to 3 minutes.

Carefully slide a small offset spatula under the tuiles to loosen the edges and release them. Should the tuiles stiffen too much to release, return them to the oven for just a few seconds to soften. As you remove them, arrange them in single layers in an airtight container, with sheets of parchment paper between each layer and food-safe silica gel packs in the container as well. Store at room temperature away from any humidity or water. They can be held as long as they remain crisp; if the tuiles absorb any humidity, they will become sticky and soft.

FOR THE CRÈME BRÛLÉE ICE CREAM

Set a medium bowl in an ice-water bath.

Put the milk and cream in separate 1-quart (1-liter) saucepots and heat them to 165°F (74°C). Scrape the vanilla seeds into the saucepot with the milk and add the pod and the salt; keep warm.

In a small bowl, whisk together 55 grams of the Demerara sugar, the custard powder, and the glucose powder and set aside.

In a medium bowl, whisk together 55 grams of the Demerara sugar and the egg yolks and set aside.

Spread the remaining 45 grams Demerara sugar in a medium saucepot. Level the sugar to encourage even heating and coloring. Place the pan over medium-high heat. The sugar will begin to liquefy at the edges. Tilt the pan carefully to swirl the sugar toward the center to prevent any burned spots. Allow the sugar to dissolve completely and stir with a silicone spatula to melt any stubborn lumps. Cook until the caramel is a light amber.

Add about one-quarter of the cream in a very gradual stream, stirring with a silicone spatula to deglaze the pot. Continue to add the cream one-quarter at a time until it has all been added (see Note). Stir in the milk, then whisk in the Trimoline and the custard powder mixture. Return to a boil, then remove from the heat.

NOTE

The cream is added before the milk because cream is more stable than milk and will not split from the heat of caramel. If you add the cream slowly, as in this method, the sugar should not seize. If it does seize, stir and allow the sugar to melt before adding any additional cream.

While whisking continuously, slowly pour one-quarter of the hot caramel into the egg yolk mixture to temper the eggs, then return the egg yolk mixture to the pan with the remaining caramel mixture. Return the pan to the heat and cook, whisking continuously, until the custard coats the back of a metal spoon and reaches about 190°F (88°C). Immediately pour the mixture into the chilled bowl set in the ice-water bath. Whisk the custard until it begins to cool to prevent it from overcooking and scrambling, then let cool completely. Strain the custard into a covered container and refrigerate overnight for the best texture.

Place an ice cream storage container, twelve 2-inch-wide (50-millimeter) by 1½-inch-high (38-millimeter) metal rings, and a sheet pan in the freezer for at least 5 hours. The longer the rings are frozen, the longer they will hold their temperature once they are removed from the freezer.

Freeze the custard in an ice cream machine. Transfer the ice cream to the storage container and freeze with the lid off for 25 to 30 minutes, then cover and freeze for about 1 hour, until the ice cream is set but still soft enough to pipe.

Transfer the ice cream to a disposable piping bag. Remove the chilled sheet pan from the freezer and top with a piece of acetate cut to the size of the sheet pan. Set the frozen rings on the pan. Pipe the ice cream into the metal rings, filling them completely and compactly to avoid leaving any gaps on the outside of the ice cream disc. Using a small offset spatula, level the top of the ice cream. Freeze until the ice cream is very hard, at least 2 hours or up to 1 day.

TO COMPLETE

Freeze the serving plates for at least 1 hour.

Hold a ring of ice cream over the center of each chilled serving plate and allow the ice cream to slide out of the ring and onto the plate. If necessary, gently warm the outside of the ring with your palms and press the top of the ice cream gently to remove it from the ring. Top with a sugar tuile and serve immediately.

TREACLE TART

Green Apples and Rosemary-Scented Yogurt

Makes 14 slices

PIE DOUGH

270 grams whole butter

274 grams all-purpose flour

174 grams 00 flour

22 grams sugar, plus extra for sprinkling

2 grams kosher salt, plus extra for sprinkling

2 grams baking powder

50 grams cold water

18 grams white wine vinegar

2 large egg whites, for brushing

TREACLE FILLING

200 grams whole butter, cut into ½-inch (1.25-centimeter) cubes

3 large eggs

75 grams heavy cream

10 grams kosher salt

900 grams Lyle's golden syrup

Zest of 2 medium lemons

120 grams lemon juice

170 grams fine fresh breadcrumbs

ROSEMARY YOGURT

1 (4-inch/10-centimeter) rosemary sprig

250 grams Greek yogurt

TO COMPLETE

4 Granny Smith apples

Zest and juice of 1 lime

Rosemary blossoms

Apple tuiles (recipe follows; optional)

SPECIAL EQUIPMENT

Four 11 by 16-inch (28 by 41-centimeter) sheets of acetate

#805 (7⁄16-inch/ 11-millimeter) plain piping tip

This is about as old-fashioned a dessert as there is, having evolved through the centuries from a mixture of breadcrumbs, honey, and spices to the version we have today, which was made with the invention of golden syrup in England in the late nineteenth century. Golden syrup is like the corn syrup you find in American grocery stores (not to be confused with high-fructose corn syrup, a commercial product), but thicker, darker, richer, and more flavorful. The unique flavor of golden syrup and its excellent baking properties have made it a staple in every British kitchen, and treacle tart must surely be the perfect use for it.

Elwyn grew up eating Mr Kipling Treacle Tart out of a box as a rare treat. It's part of his memory and heritage, so he wanted a refined version of it. It takes many forms at the restaurants, from a simple one-bite canapé to a full-scale plated dessert. The treacle is very sweet, so it needs the balance of the acidic green apple and the crunchy, salty sablé.

This treacle is really nothing more than syrup, bread, and eggs—that's it. But we bake it in a small sheet pan, and the breadcrumbs rise to the top and get crunchy and browned. We then invert this so that we have a nice custardy layer on top.

The final flourish is the rosemary-infused yogurt. Rosemary is a great herb in desserts, as long as it's carefully used. Here it's so mild; it should be as delicate as if you were simply walking past a rosemary bush. As in the Rhubarb and Custard (page 306), precision and balance are key when using strong flavors.

FOR THE PIE DOUGH

Cut the butter into ¼-inch (6-millimeter) cubes. Spread them on a tray and place in the freezer for 30 minutes.

Place 137 grams of the all-purpose flour, 87 grams of the 00 flour, 11 grams of the sugar, 1 gram of the salt, and 1 gram of the baking powder in a food processor. Pulse a few times to combine. Add 135 grams of the butter and pulse until the butter is in pea-size pieces. Add half the water and half the vinegar and pulse until the dough begins to come together. Transfer the dough to a work surface and knead just enough to bring the dough together into a disc. Do not overmix or overwork the dough (see Note). Wrap the dough in plastic wrap and refrigerate for at least 1 hour or up to 1 day. Repeat with the remaining ingredients to make a second disc of dough.

(continued)

Remove one disc of dough from the refrigerator. Knead it slightly to soften it for rolling. Place the dough between two 11 by 16-inch (28 by 41-centimeter) sheets of acetate. With a rolling pin, press the top of the dough, working from one side of the dough to the other, to begin to flatten it; turn the dough and acetate 90 degrees and repeat. Press and shape the dough into a rectangle.

Working from the center, roll toward each corner, then roll toward each flat side, turning and flipping the dough to roll it as evenly as possible. Turning and flipping the dough often as you roll will help prevent the dough from shrinking to an uneven shape during baking. Roll to reach the full size of the acetate. The dough should be about ⅛ inch (3 millimeters) thick. There will not be a lot of extra dough. You can use a dough scraper to cut off excess dough at the edges, then lift a section of the acetate and use the scraps to fill in areas where the dough does not reach the edge.

Place the rolled dough, still in the acetate, on a half sheet pan. Wrap in plastic wrap and refrigerate for 3 hours to rest (this prevents shrinkage during baking). Repeat with the second disc of dough. After 3 hours, transfer the pans to the freezer and freeze for at least 30 minutes, until the dough freezes completely.

Preheat the oven to 325°F (163°C). If you can control the fan speed, set it to 2. Line two half sheet pans with parchment paper.

Remove one sheet of dough from the freezer. Gently peel back and remove both pieces of acetate and place the dough on a cutting board. Using a sharp knife, cut it into fourteen 7 by 1¼-inch (18 by 3-centimeter) rectangles. Place them on one of the prepared sheet pans. You must work quickly, as the dough is very thin and difficult to handle unless it is cold. Return the sheet pan to the freezer until the dough rectangles are cold. Repeat with the second sheet of dough.

Remove the pans from the freezer and, using a #805 (⁷⁄₁₆-inch/11-millimeter) plain piping tip, punch five evenly spaced holes down the center of each rectangle of dough. If the dough begins to break as it is punched, wait for a minute or two for the dough to warm slightly and become less brittle before continuing.

Lightly brush the tops of the dough rectangles with egg white, taking care not to let any get into the punched holes, and sprinkle with a little sugar and salt. Bake for 18 to 22 minutes (they will cook more slowly in a conventional oven), until cooked throughout and golden. Remove from the oven and let cool on the pan on a cooling rack. Store the cooled pastry in an airtight container, separating the layers with pieces of parchment paper, for up to 24 hours.

FOR THE TREACLE FILLING

Preheat the oven to 300°F (150°C). Spray a quarter sheet pan with non-stick spray and line it with a sheet of parchment paper that overhangs all sides by 1 inch (2.5 centimeters).

Melt the butter in a 2-quart (2-liter) saucepot over medium heat. Once the butter begins to boil, increase the heat to medium-high and cook, whisking continuously to keep the solids on the bottom of the pan from burning, for about 3 minutes, until the butter is browned. As the moisture evaporates and the butter browns, the bubbles will lessen. When the browning butter is no longer making an audible sound, lift some of the butter on a spoon and check the color. When it is caramel colored, immediately strain the butter into a bowl and set aside. The browned butter can be refrigerated in a covered container for up to 1 week. Melt the butter slowly in the microwave or over low heat before using.

Whisk together the eggs, cream, and salt in a medium bowl to combine.

Warm the golden syrup in the microwave for 40 seconds. Stir the brown butter into the warm golden syrup. Whisk the warm syrup mixture into the egg mixture to combine. Using a silicone spatula, fold in the lemon zest, lemon juice, and breadcrumbs until thoroughly combined. Pour the mixture into the prepared pan and bake for 40 to 50 minutes, until golden brown and set; the filling will jiggle as the pan is moved. The sides of the filling will be beginning to pull away from the sides of the pan. Let the treacle filling cool completely, then wrap the baking sheet in plastic wrap and refrigerate until cold or for up to 5 days.

FOR THE ROSEMARY YOGURT

Pick the rosemary leaves from the stem; finely chop the leaves and discard the stem. Mix the yogurt with the rosemary leaves in a bowl, cover, and refrigerate for 1 hour. Strain the infused yogurt into an airtight container and refrigerate for up to 3 days.

TO COMPLETE

Peel and core the apples and cut them into 3-millimeter brunoise. Place them in a small bowl and immediately dress with a little lime juice to prevent the apple from discoloring and to add an extra level of acidity. Mix in the lime zest and set aside.

Remove the treacle filling from the refrigerator. Gently pull on the exposed parchment paper to loosen all the edges. Place a cutting board over the sheet pan and invert the treacle filling onto the cutting board. Gently peel off the parchment paper, taking care not to leave any stuck to the treacle. Using a chef's knife dipped in hot water and dried on a clean kitchen towel, trim the long sides of the treacle, leaving a rectangle that is 6 inches (15 centimeters) wide. Trim the short sides just so they're even, then cut the rectangle crosswise into ¾-inch-wide (2-centimeter) bars, heating and drying the knife between cuts to keep it clean. Using an offset spatula, transfer the slices of treacle filling to serving plates.

Stand a piece of pie dough on its edge along the length of the tart filling, leaving about ½ inch (1.25 centimeters) of the filling exposed at one end. Stand a second piece of pie dough on the opposite side to sandwich the filling. Garnish the top of the tart with 3 to 5 small dollops of rosemary yogurt, evenly spaced down the length of the tart. Spoon the apple brunoise over the top of the tart and the yogurt. Garnish with fresh rosemary blossoms and, if you'd like, apple tuiles, delicately placed over the dish.

NOTE

Overmixing the dough overworks the gluten, leading to a tougher dough that will shrink more during baking. If the butter is overworked, there will be less layering of butter within the dough, making it less flaky.

Apple Tuiles

Makes about 120 using a 4-in-1 slicer or about 25 using a Swiss peeler

250 grams sugar
290 grams water
10 grams ascorbic acid
1 large, firm Granny Smith apple, without bruising

SPECIAL EQUIPMENT
Commercial 4-in-1 vegetable slicer, or 4-inch Swiss peeler
Kitchen tweezers (optional)
Combi oven (optional)
Dehydrator (optional)
6 small food-safe silica gel packs

Combine the sugar and water in a 1-quart (1-liter) saucepot and bring to a simmer over medium heat, stirring to dissolve the sugar. Add the ascorbic acid and stir to dissolve. Keep warm.

Peel the apple. If using a 4-in-1 vegetable slicer, cut the apple into long sheets or strips. Cut the sheets into 9-inch-long (23-centimeter) rectangles, and cut these rectangles lengthwise into 5-millimeter-wide strips. If using a Swiss peeler, cut the apple into strips as long as possible, then cut them into 5-millimeter-wide lengthwise strips, following the slightly curved line. Cut extra, as they break easily once they are formed.

Return the syrup to a boil, then remove it from the heat. When the bubbles in the syrup have subsided, use kitchen tweezers to submerge the apple strips in the hot syrup. Let stand for at least 10 minutes or up to 24 hours. The apples will soften and become slightly translucent.

If using a home oven or combi oven to dry the tuiles, preheat the oven to 210°F (99°C). If using a dehydrator, set the dehydrator to the maximum temperature setting. Line a half sheet pan with a nonstick silicone baking mat. Spray the mat lightly with nonstick spray and wipe off any excess, leaving only a very thin coating.

Remove the apple strips from the syrup and place them on paper towels to drain slightly. Do not pat them dry; just let the paper towels absorb some of the excess syrup. Lay the strips out flat on the prepared half sheet pan. Do not let them touch, or they will stick together during the drying process.

Dry them in the preheated oven for about 2 hours or leave them in the dehydrator overnight or for up to 18 hours, until fully dried and crisp.

Remove the apple strips from the oven, if you used it, and increase the oven temperature to 300°F (149°C). Place six small food-safe silica gel packs in an airtight container and close the lid to create a dry environment.

Reheat the apple strips in the oven just long enough to soften them, around 30 seconds. When the strips are soft and flexible, remove the pan from the oven and, working quickly, shape the tuiles, twisting and bending the strips into abstract shapes and swirls. If the strips on the pan begin to harden, return them to the oven to soften again.

Set the shaped tuiles on a clean, dry surface to cool and harden. Transfer to the airtight container and store in a dry location at room temperature for up to 1 week. Should the tuiles soften and lose their shape before serving, they can be rewarmed and reshaped as before.

STRAWBERRY TEA

Tea-Scented Yogurt, Garden Strawberries,
Candied Hibiscus, and Pavlova

**THE
STRAWBERRIES**
Mara des Bois, the
plump red ones, and
the white Alpine
strawberries are
grown in the garden
and dipped in an
herbed gel for flavor
and gloss.

**THE HIBISCUS
BLOSSOMS**
Peter Jacobsen, a
dentist-farmer in
Yountville, grows
fruit and hibiscus in
his orchards for us.
Elwyn had never
seen fresh hibiscus
before. Now they
harvest thousands
of hibiscus flowers,
which we candy and
preserve to serve
November through
Christmas.

THE PANNA COTTA

Soba and matcha teas flavor cream, which we layer using gelatin and then scoop into these conical shapes.

This elaborate plated dessert began with a simple yogurt panna cotta developed eleven years ago, a nicely balanced cream preparation that is infinitely versatile. Sometimes Elwyn adds more gelatin and pours it over a sablé Breton, then cuts it into a shape for a yogurt bar. Sometimes he pours it over rolled oats to make a granola bar. Maybe he scoops out a quenelle and dips it in jelly. Here Elwyn thought, *What if we flavor it with tea?*

For a contrast in texture, we set a small pavlova (not shown in this photograph) beside the quenelle, to add crunch and chew. We like our pavlova more delicate and creamy than a traditional one, to not overpower the flavors of the tea. We also make a net of strawberry jam, spread in a mold, and dried until crystallized—kind of like fruit leather (see illustration on page 293).

At the restaurant we serve the Victoria Sponge in a plated version, building an individual slice but keeping all the components separate. We bake the sponge in quarter sheet pans and slice it into thin rectangles. We place one rectangle of the sponge on the plate, in the lower third. Above it we pipe small kisses of the strawberry puree, then pipe kisses of the buttercream above the puree. We continue this layering until there are 3 pieces of sponge and 2 layers of filling on the plate, then garnish the top with slices of fresh strawberries, candied angelica or other candied fruit, tiny meringue dots, and marigold greens and blossoms.

VICTORIA SPONGE

Makes 8 to 12 servings

ITALIAN MERINGUE BUTTERCREAM

60 grams egg whites

33 grams water

147 grams sugar

182 grams whole butter, cut into ½-inch (1.25-centimeter) cubes, at room temperature

5 grams vanilla paste

3 grams kosher salt

STRAWBERRY PUREE

10 fresh strawberries

400 grams strawberry wine, plus extra if needed

½ vanilla bean, split lengthwise

60 grams sugar

40 grams lemon juice

10 grams apple cider vinegar

4 grams agar-agar

VICTORIA SPONGE

150 grams all-purpose flour

7 grams baking powder

4.5 grams kosher salt

165 grams whole butter, cut into 1-inch (2.5-centimeter) cubes, at soft room temperature

160 grams sugar

Zest of 1 large lemon

Zest of 1 large orange

7.5 grams vanilla paste or vanilla extract

150 grams eggs, at room temperature

5 grams orange blossom water

TO COMPLETE

Confectioners' sugar, for dusting

SPECIAL EQUIPMENT

#801 (³⁄₁₆-inch/ 5-millimeter) plain piping tip

This is a classic British dessert, named after Queen Victoria, as she was known to be partial to cake sandwiched with jam with her afternoon tea. Both restaurants have served this in the classic manner as a whole cake at special events, and as a plated dessert. In the beautifully plated dessert, we use the components to create the visual effect of a slice of cake while keeping them distinct: precisely cut pieces of Victoria sponge cake with piped buttercream and a fruit jam, fruit, and a garnish of dianthus and marigold flowers, as well as candied angelica, which we grow in the garden. The garnish is meant to complement and deepen the dessert, rather than take it away from being a simple slice of cake on a plate.

Both the sponge and the buttercream can be made in a couple of ways. The buttercream here uses an Italian meringue, in which the sugar is cooked into a syrup and that syrup is poured into the whipping egg whites. This sponge includes butter, which means the cake will be a little richer than a sponge made without the fat, and the crumb, because of the fat, will be a little tighter, which also allows us to cut the cake with more precision. The sponge still retains lightness due to the addition of baking powder to the batter.

The jam is the fruit, cooked in strawberry wine so that it releases all its juices and then strained, giving us just the rich essence of the fruit. We add agar to the essence while it's cooking so that it will set up into a brittle gel, which, when blended, becomes a beautifully textured puree (see The Liaisons, page 108).

FOR THE ITALIAN MERINGUE BUTTERCREAM

Careful timing is critical when making an Italian meringue. The syrup should reach 250°F (121°C) at the same time that the egg whites are holding a soft shape.

Place the egg whites in the bowl of a stand mixer fitted with the whisk. Combine the water and 120 grams of the sugar in a 1-quart (1-liter) saucepot and heat over medium-high heat. When the sugar syrup has reached 203°F (95°C), begin whipping the whites on medium speed. When the whites are frothy, gradually add the remaining 27 grams sugar.

When the sugar syrup reaches 250°F (121°C), remove the pan from the heat. Immediately turn the mixer to medium-low speed and slowly add the syrup, carefully pouring it between the side of the bowl and the whisk. If the syrup hits the bowl or whisk, it could harden and won't be incorporated into the egg whites. The meringue will deflate somewhat.

Increase the speed to medium and whip for 5 minutes. The meringue may feel slightly warm but should not feel hot before the butter is added. Gradually add the butter. Once incorporated, stop the mixer and scrape the sides and the bottom of the bowl well to ensure there are no pieces of butter remaining. Add the vanilla and salt and whip on medium speed for 4 to 5 minutes more, until shiny, light, and fluffy.

The buttercream can be refrigerated in an airtight container for up to 3 days.

FOR THE STRAWBERRY PUREE

Wash the strawberries and cut out the calyxes (green tops). Thinly slice the strawberries and place them in a medium pot. Add the strawberry wine. Scrape the vanilla seeds into the pot and add the pod. Place over medium-high heat and simmer gently for 5 minutes, adjusting the heat as necessary.

Remove from the heat, cover with a lid, and let stand for 5 minutes to allow the strawberries to impart more flavor to the wine. Strain the strawberry liquid through a chinois, without pressing on the berries (the strawberry pulp would cloud the gel). Discard the pulp.

Pour 300 grams of the strawberry liquid into a medium pot. If you have less than 300 grams, add more strawberry wine to reach 300 grams. Add the sugar, lemon juice, and vinegar, bring to a boil, and remove from the heat. While whisking, add the agar-agar and whisk until it is fully dissolved. Return to a boil and whisk continuously for 30 seconds to activate the agar-agar.

Remove from the heat and pour the gel into a container so it forms a layer no more than ¾ inch (2 centimeters) thick. Cover the container and refrigerate for about 2 hours, until firm and cold. Cut the gel into ½-inch (1.25-centimeter) cubes and place them in a high-powered blender. Blend until smooth and shiny, using the tamper to keep the puree moving. Strain the puree into an airtight container. Refrigerate for up to 3 days.

FOR THE VICTORIA SPONGE

Preheat the oven to 325°F (163°C). Spray two 8-inch (20-centimeter) round cake pans with nonstick spray. Line the bottom of each pan with a round of parchment paper cut to fit. Cut strips of parchment paper long enough and high enough to line the sides of the pans and spray with nonstick spray.

Sift the flour and baking powder into a bowl, stir in the salt, and set aside.

Place the butter in the bowl of a stand mixer fitted with the paddle and beat on medium speed to lighten the butter. Add the sugar, lemon zest, orange zest, and vanilla and beat for about 4 minutes, until the mixture is light and fluffy.

Put the eggs in a bowl and whisk until well combined (see Note).

With the mixer running on medium-low speed, very gradually add about half the eggs, maintaining the emulsion throughout, then stop the machine to scrape down the bowl. Return the mixer to medium-low and add the remaining eggs.

Remove the bowl from the mixer and, using a silicone spatula, fold the sifted dry ingredients into the creamed mixture (this will create a lighter sponge). When they are almost fully incorporated, fold in the orange blossom water and continue to fold until no lumps of flour or unmixed butter remain.

Divide the cake batter evenly between the two prepared pans. Using the back of a spoon, spread the cake mixture to the sides of the pans and then tap the pans on the counter to help even out the layer. Bake for about 15 minutes, until the cake is golden brown and springs back to the touch when gently pressed. Remove from the oven and let cool in the pans for 10 minutes.

Place a piece of parchment paper on a cooling rack and spray with non-stick spray. While the cakes are still warm, invert them onto the parchment paper. This will give them a smooth top. Let cool to room temperature, then invert them so they are right-side up and cover with plastic wrap. The cake layers are best on the same day you bake them.

TO COMPLETE

Remove the buttercream from the refrigerator and soften at room temperature, then whisk by hand or using the stand mixer until it is shiny, holds its shape, and has the texture of well-whipped cream before using.

For the best results, the cakes should be at cool room temperature, the buttercream should be smooth and shiny, and the strawberry puree should be cold, smooth and shiny, and firm but spreadable.

Place the flattest of the two cakes in the center of a serving plate. Spoon the strawberry puree into the center of the cake and, using a small offset spatula, spread it into an even layer, leaving a ³⁄₁₆-inch (5-millimeter) border.

Transfer the buttercream to a disposable piping bag fitted with a #801 (³⁄₁₆-inch/5-millimeter) plain piping tip. Beginning in the center of the cake, pipe concentric circles of buttercream, each touching the next, to create a solid layer of buttercream covering the layer of strawberry puree. You may have extra buttercream.

Carefully place the second layer of cake, skin-side up, on top of the buttercream and press gently to secure. As you press on the cake, the gap around the outside of the cake should fill with the puree and buttercream to reach the edge of the cake. Dust the top with confectioners' sugar.

Slice and enjoy with tea. Any leftover cake can be covered and refrigerated overnight. Return it to room temperature before serving.

NOTE

By whisking the eggs before adding them to the butter, you are able to add the eggs slowly (rather than one by one), and by having the ingredients at room temperature, there is less of a chance that the mixture will split.

GÂTEAU OPÉRA

Caramelized Oyster Crackers, Candied Lemon, and Bitter Almond Gel

Makes 18 servings

COFFEE-WHISKEY SOAK

½ sheet silver leaf gelatin

1 vanilla bean, split lengthwise

200 grams brewed coffee

20 grams granulated sugar

4 grams whiskey

ITALIAN MERINGUE COFFEE BUTTERCREAM

120 grams egg whites

66 grams water

294 grams granulated sugar

364 grams whole butter, cut into ½-inch (1.25-centimeter) cubes, at room temperature

13 grams coffee extract

2 grams kosher salt

COFFEE JOCONDE

108 grams confectioners' sugar

108 grams almond flour

164 grams eggs

28 grams whole butter, cubed

26 grams coffee extract

36 grams all-purpose flour

100 grams egg whites

38 grams granulated sugar

OPERA GANACHE

250 grams 75% dark chocolate, preferably K+M Nicaragua or Ecuador, cut into small pieces

294 grams heavy cream

10 grams granulated sugar

10 grams water

13 grams glucose syrup

31 grams Trimoline invert sugar

3 grams sorbitol (optional)

TO COMPLETE (OPTIONAL)

Caramelized Oyster Crackers (recipe follows)

Candied Lemon (recipe follows)

Bitter Almond Gel (recipe follows)

Green Almonds (recipe follows)

Thyme tips

Edible silver leaf

SPECIAL EQUIPMENT

Twelve 6-millimeter-thick confectionary rulers

This is one of the great classic cakes, perhaps even more popular than the marjolaine (see page 346). The *gâteau opéra* was developed in Paris to be "the grand opera of cakes." It has many thin layers, so that you get a little of every component in every bite. The first layer is the joconde, a French almond sponge cake saturated with a coffee-whiskey soak; the second layer is a chocolate ganache; and the third is a coffee buttercream. The joconde is very thin, bakes quickly, and has a fine crumb. The ganache is simple and clean, giving a deep dark chocolate flavor. And the buttercream begins with a Swiss meringue, in which the sugar is cooked to a syrup before being added to the egg whites. We add further interest and delight with abundant garnishes: oyster crackers for crunch, candied lemon, bitter almond gel, thyme, and green almond. You need to use a delicate hand when garnishing coffee and chocolate with lemon, almond, and thyme, but they're all very effective in the right proportions.

FOR THE COFFEE-WHISKEY SOAK

Submerge the gelatin in a bowl of ice water to bloom (soften) for about 5 minutes.

Scrape the vanilla seeds into a 1-quart (1-liter) saucepot and add the pod. Add the coffee and sugar and heat to dissolve the sugar. Remove the softened gelatin from the ice water and squeeze out any excess water. Add the gelatin to the coffee and stir to dissolve. Strain into a bowl and nestle the bowl in an ice-water bath. Stir in the whiskey. Transfer to an airtight container and refrigerate for up to 1 week.

FOR THE ITALIAN MERINGUE COFFEE BUTTERCREAM

Careful timing is critical when making an Italian meringue. The syrup should reach 250°F (121°C) at the same time that the egg whites are holding a soft shape.

Place the egg whites in the bowl of a stand mixer fitted with the whisk. Combine the water and 240 grams of the sugar in a 1-quart (1-liter) saucepot and heat over medium-high heat. When the sugar syrup has reached 203°F (95°C), begin whipping the whites on medium speed. When the whites are frothy, gradually add the remaining 54 grams sugar.

(continued)

When the sugar syrup reaches 250°F (121°C), remove the pan from the heat. Immediately turn the mixer to medium-low speed and slowly add the syrup, carefully pouring it between the side of the bowl and the whisk. If the syrup hits the bowl or whisk, it could harden and won't be incorporated into the egg whites. The meringue will deflate somewhat.

Increase the speed to medium and whip for 5 minutes. Gradually add the butter. Once incorporated, stop the mixer and scrape the sides and the bottom of the bowl well to ensure there are no pieces of butter remaining. Whip on medium speed for 2 minutes, until light and fluffy.

Weigh the buttercream. Return 500 grams to the mixer bowl and reserve any extra for another use. Add the coffee extract and salt and whisk for about 4 minutes, until well incorporated.

The buttercream can be refrigerated for up to 3 days. Remove it from the refrigerator and soften at room temperature, then whisk the buttercream by hand or in a stand mixer until shiny before using.

FOR THE COFFEE JOCONDE
Preheat the oven to 400°F (205°C).

Combine the confectioners' sugar, almond flour, eggs, butter, and coffee extract in a food processor. Process for 10 to 12 minutes, until the mixture is warm and the butter has melted. Pour the coffee base into a medium bowl. Sift the all-purpose flour into the bowl and whisk until the flour is fully incorporated without any lumps.

Put the egg whites in the clean, dry bowl of the stand mixer fitted with the whisk. Whip on medium speed until the whites become frothy, then add one-third of the granulated sugar. When the egg whites become foamy, gradually add half of the remaining sugar. When the meringue is voluminous and pillowy and has almost reached medium-stiff peaks, add the remaining sugar.

Remove the bowl from the mixer. Using a silicone spatula, fold a third of the meringue into the coffee base. Whip the remaining meringue to stiff peaks, then fold it into the coffee base.

Spray an 11⅝ by 16½-inch (30 by 42-centimeter) nonstick silicone baking mat with nonstick spray and lay it on a flat surface. Position a 6-millimeter-thick confectionary ruler on each of the long sides of the baking mat, lined up with the edges of the mat.

Ladle 250 grams of the coffee base into the center of the baking mat. Using an offset spatula, spread the mixture to reach the rulers. Rest another confectionary ruler across the two confectionary rulers and pull the top ruler back and forth to create an even 6-millimeter-thick layer of the coffee base over the baking mat.

Remove the rulers and slide the baking mat onto a half sheet pan. Bake for 4 to 5 minutes, until the cake is just cooked but before it becomes dry and crispy around the edges. Lift the baking mat from the pan and set it on the counter. Let the cake cool completely on the baking mat. Repeat to make the second layer of joconde.

FOR THE OPERA GANACHE
Bring water to a simmer in the bottom of a double boiler. Put the chocolate in the top of the double boiler and melt it gently over the simmering water.

Combine the cream, granulated sugar, water, glucose syrup, Trimoline, and sorbitol in a small pot and bring to a boil. Strain the boiling cream mixture over the melted chocolate. Remove the top of the double boiler. Using a silicone spatula, begin stirring the mixture, working from the center outward, incorporating the chocolate from around the edges of the pot. Whisk the ganache until it is glossy and smooth and has cooled to 97° to 100°F (36° to 38°C).

TO COMPLETE
Bring the coffee-whiskey soak to room temperature.

Spray a piece of parchment paper with nonstick spray and place it sprayed-side down on an inverted half sheet pan. Lift the baking mat on opposite sides and invert the cake (still on the baking mat) onto the prepared sheet pan. Carefully pull a corner of the baking mat toward you (rather than upward) to release the cake without tearing it. Spray another piece of parchment, place it over the cake, and invert the cake. Remove the top piece of parchment. Repeat with the second layer of joconde.

Transfer the joconde layers, still on parchment paper, to a cutting board and trim the edges. Cut each joconde into 3 pieces, each 4½ inches (11.5 centimeters) wide.

Spray an inverted half sheet pan with nonstick spray. Top it with a piece of parchment paper and spray the parchment. Set one piece of joconde,

lengthwise and right-side up, in the center of the parchment paper. Line the two long edges of the cake with 6-millimeter-thick confectionary rulers, one on each side.

Using an offset spatula, spread about 150 grams of the coffee buttercream over the joconde in an even layer. Rest an offset spatula on the rulers and run it back and forth to achieve a perfectly even 6-millimeter-thick layer.

Pipe a few small dots of buttercream on the top of the two confectionary rulers. Pipe several dots on the bottoms of another set of two rulers and press them over the set rulers, allowing the buttercream to act as glue and hold them together.

Pipe a small cylinder of buttercream ¼ inch (6 millimeters) high across the width of both ends of the joconde. This will close the frame and serve as a dam for the ganache. Refrigerate (leaving the bars in place) until the coffee buttercream layer is cold and set.

Remove from the refrigerator. Pour about 200 grams of the ganache over the cold coffee buttercream in an even layer to reach the top of the rulers. Rest an offset spatula on the rulers and run it back and forth to achieve a perfectly even 6-millimeter-thick layer of ganache. Immediately top the ganache with a piece of coffee joconde, top (sticky) side facing the ganache, and press lightly, working outward from the center,

to expel any air bubbles and secure the joconde to the ganache. It is crucial to work quickly. If the ganache sets before the cake layer is added, the layers will separate when the cake is cut for serving.

Using a pastry brush, soak the top of the joconde with the coffee-whiskey soak. Refrigerate for about 10 minutes, until the ganache is set. Continue to layer as before, stacking the confectionary rulers as you go, until you have three layers of buttercream and ganache and four layers of joconde. Refrigerate for about 3 hours to be certain the ganache is completely set. Remove from the refrigerator and flip the opéra over onto a cutting board. Brush what is now the top layer of joconde with the coffee-whiskey soak. Transfer the opéra to an airtight container and refrigerate for at least 3 hours or up to 3 days before serving.

Line a half sheet pan with parchment paper.

Using a chef's knife dipped in hot water and dried on a clean kitchen towel, trim the rulers off and trim the ends of the opéra, cleaning and drying the knife after each cut. Cut the opéra crosswise into ½-inch-thick (1.25-centimeter) slices, gently placing each slice on its side on the sheet pan or directly on serving plates.

If desired, garnish the slices with an arrangement of caramelized oyster crackers, candied lemon zest, dots of bitter almond gel, green almonds, fresh thyme tips, and silver leaf.

Caramelized Oyster Crackers

Yield varies

190 grams warm milk (105° to 110°F/ 40.5° to 43.3°C)

5 grams SAF instant dry yeast

250 grams all-purpose flour

75 grams bread flour

5 grams kosher salt

50 grams confectioners' sugar, for dusting

SPECIAL EQUIPMENT

Pasta machine

Mix the milk and the yeast together in a small bowl and set aside for 10 minutes to activate the yeast. The yeast should be dissolved and slightly frothy.

In the bowl of a stand mixer fitted with a dough hook, combine both flours and the salt. With the mixer running on low speed, slowly pour in the milk-yeast mixture and mix for 5 minutes (see Note), stopping to scrape the bowl as needed.

Turn the dough out onto a board and shape it into a smooth ball. Be as gentle as possible with the dough; you want to stretch it, not tear it. Transfer the dough to a medium bowl and wrap it tightly with plastic wrap. Place in a warm spot and let proof for 45 minutes to 1 hour, until the dough doubles in volume. Punch down the dough, place it in a resealable storage bag, and refrigerate for at least 2 hours or up to 2 days.

Once the dough is fully chilled, preheat the oven to 400°F (205°C). Place a sheet pan in the oven to preheat.

Using a pasta machine, roll the dough to a 2-millimeter thickness. It is important for the dough to be rolled into an even sheet; if rolled by hand, it may not puff when baked.

Using a pizza wheel, cut the dough into squares of different sizes, none exceeding ¾ inch (2 centimeters). Quickly transfer about 15 crackers of the same size to the hot sheet pan and return the pan to the oven. Bake for 1 to 2 minutes, until the crackers are fully puffed and their shape is just set. The cooking time may vary widely depending on the size of your crackers, so keep a watchful eye on them.

Reduce the oven temperature to 325°F (163°C) and bake for 2 to 5 minutes, until the crackers are firm and have not colored past a very light golden brown; they should remain nearly white. Remove the crackers from the oven and transfer to a cooling rack; return the pan to the oven to heat before baking additional crackers. Once cooled, store the crackers in an airtight container at room temperature for up to 5 days.

Just before serving, caramelize the crackers: Set the oven rack 3 to 4 inches (7.5 to 10 centimeters) below the broiler and preheat the broiler.

Lay the crackers on an unlined sheet pan and dust them liberally with confectioners' sugar. Broil until the sugar begins to caramelize. Do not leave the oven—this happens very quickly. Remove from the oven and let cool. Use the crackers the same day they are caramelized.

NOTE

Although we give an exact time for the mixing process, it is important to remember that bakers think of mixing not in terms of time but in revolutions of the dough hook. The mixing of dough is a succession of stretches and folds. The more a dough is mixed, the more uniform its structure and the smaller the gas bubbles within the dough—and, therefore, the more gas it can contain, giving it greater volume. The only way to know if you are mixing the dough right is through practice, and by keeping track of your results.

Candied Lemon

Yield varies

| 4 lemons, washed and dried | 200 grams sugar | 200 grams water |

Using a vegetable peeler, peel the lemons, keeping the pieces as long as possible; discard the flesh or reserve it for another use. Using a paring knife, remove any white pith remaining on the zest. Stack the pieces to form an orderly pile. Trim the zest to the desired length and trim the edges to straighten them. Using a very sharp knife, thinly slice the stack lengthwise into a fine julienne.

Bring a small pot of water to a boil and drop in the julienned lemon peel. Return the water to a boil, then immediately drain the lemon peel and rinse in cold water to stop the cooking process and rinse away any bitter flavor. Repeat this process twice more.

Combine the sugar and the water in a small saucepot and bring to a boil, stirring to dissolve the sugar. Add the blanched lemon peel. Reduce the heat to medium-low and simmer slowly until the peel is soft and tender, about 30 minutes.

Transfer the lemon peel and syrup to a container and let cool to room temperature. Cover and refrigerate for at least 1 hour before using. The candied lemon can be refrigerated for up to 1 month.

Green Almonds

| ½ cup shelled green almonds | Extra-virgin olive oil, to taste | Lime zest, to taste |

Blanch the almonds in boiling water. Pop them out of their peels and toss with a light coating of olive oil and lime zest to taste.

Bitter Almond Gel

Makes 500 grams

250 grams nibbed almonds or sliced blanched almonds	500 grams whole milk, plus more as needed	7 grams kosher salt
	62 grams sugar	2.5 grams almond extract
		1.75 grams agar-agar

Preheat the oven to 350°F (180°C). Line a half sheet pan with parchment paper.

Spread the almonds over the pan in an even layer. Toast them in the oven until they are very dark, about 10 minutes. When the nuts are almost toasted, bring the milk to a boil in a medium pot. Remove from the heat, add the toasted almonds, and cover the pot. Let sit until the milk has cooled to room temperature to infuse the milk with the flavor of the almonds.

Pour the nuts and milk into a bowl and nestle the bowl in an ice-water bath to cool completely. Cover and refrigerate for 24 hours. Strain the milk and weigh it; you should have 500 grams. If you do not have enough, add fresh milk to make up the difference.

Place the milk in a medium pot, add the sugar, salt, and almond extract, and bring to a boil. While whisking continuously, add the agar-agar and boil for 30 seconds to activate the agar-agar. Remove from the heat and strain into a container large enough that the mixture forms a layer no more than ¾ inch (2 centimeters) thick. Refrigerate until the bitter almond gel is completely set.

Cut the gel into ½-inch (1.25-centimeter) pieces and put them in a high-powered blender. Blend on high speed until smooth and shiny. Pass the gel through a chinois to eliminate any lumps. Transfer to a piping bag and pipe the gel into a squeeze bottle. Refrigerate until needed or for up to 2 days.

GÂTEAU MARJOLAINE

Makes 1 cake

JAPONAISE

40 grams hazelnut flour

40 grams almond flour

80 grams confectioners' sugar

100 grams egg whites

100 grams granulated sugar

CHOCOLATE GANACHE

250 grams 77% dark chocolate, preferably K+M Madagascar, chopped

230 grams heavy cream

125 grams glucose syrup

60 grams Trimoline invert sugar

5 grams sorbitol

ITALIAN MERINGUE BUTTERCREAM

120 grams egg whites

66 grams water

294 grams granulated sugar

364 grams whole butter, cut into ½-inch (1.25-centimeter) cubes, at cool room temperature

Seeds from ½ vanilla bean

2.5 grams vanilla paste

PRALINE BUTTERCREAM

75 grams praline paste

Kosher salt

TO COMPLETE

Confectioners' sugar, for dusting

SPECIAL EQUIPMENT

Combi oven (optional)

Two #802 (¼-inch/ 6-millimeter) plain piping tips

#804 (⅜-inch/ 10-millimeter) plain piping tip

I first read about the *gâteau marjolaine* in Fernand Point's *Ma Gastronomie*, given to me by my mentor, Roland Henin. In the book, Point says the marjolaine was a constant work in progress for him, always changing as he tweaked the recipe in search of the perfect cake, something he thought he never quite achieved. And that's what we've tried to continue. I wanted what he searched for, a cross between a cake and a meringue, one that's creamy, with a slight crunch, both chewy and cakelike, fully flavored with hazelnut, almond, and chocolate, balanced with salt. All those components in one bite. As I've said before, you cannot achieve perfection, because as soon as you hit the mark you were striving for, that mark moves just a little further forward. This cake hit that mark, and although the mark continues to move, it's become our signature cake, served on all birthdays celebrated at the restaurants.

We almost didn't include the recipe because Elwyn thought it might be too difficult to execute at home. Here's Elwyn on why:

"The meringue and the baking and the whipping of the egg whites are all tricky points you have to learn by sight and feel. Whipping the egg whites to just the right texture, just past firm. Kind of like Neverland—there isn't really a just-past-firm of egg whites, but that's where you need to take them. And then the folding in of the dry ingredients, just nut flour and icing sugar blended together. Simple, really. But the grade on your nuts is important—not too coarse, not ultra-fine. And then the piping—once it's ready you've only got so much time to pipe, back and forth, back and forth. You need to pipe evenly, so you get a good cross section, but if you pipe too slowly, the meringue will deflate, and the last half of the pan will collapse and won't be usable. The nuts are oily, remember, and oil also wants to break down the meringue. It seems like a very simple recipe, but the subtle differences really can set it apart. The creams inside are very easy—chocolate ganache, praline, and vanilla buttercream—you just need to be sure to season them delicately with salt."

Sounds intimidating. And Elwyn believes you have to make this every day for three or four months before you really have a solid hand. Which may be true. But when Susie tested it, she got it straightaway and didn't think it hard at all. So it's one of those great preparations that's simple to make but, happily, impossible to perfect.

We can't know what Point's best marjolaine was, but we're hoping this would come pretty close to perfect in his book.

(continued)

FOR THE JAPONAISE

Preheat a combi oven to 160°C (320°F), 40% humidity, with the fan speed set to 3, or preheat a conventional oven to 302°F (150°C). Line a half sheet pan with a sheet of parchment paper cut to fit. Use a thick black marker to draw four 3 by 9½-inch (7.5 by 24-centimeter) rectangles on the parchment, spacing each 1 inch (2.5 centimeters) apart.

Mix the hazelnut flour, almond flour, and confectioner's sugar in a medium bowl until well combined (see Note). Pass the mixture through a large-mesh sieve to lighten it and ensure that there are no clumps.

> ### NOTE
> This mixture, equal parts nut flour and confectioners' sugar, is referred to as *tant pour tant* (TPT) in French pastry kitchens.

Put the egg whites in the bowl of a stand mixer fitted with the whisk. Begin mixing on low speed. When the whites become frothy, add 13 grams of the granulated sugar. Increase the speed and continue whipping, gradually adding another 13 grams of the sugar as the whites gain volume. Once medium-stiff peaks have formed gradually, add 14 grams of the sugar. When the meringue is stiff but not dry, quickly add the remaining 60 grams sugar and whip for four more revolutions.

Transfer to a medium metal bowl and, using a silicone spatula, fold four times to soften the meringue and ensure that all the sugar is combined. Gradually fold in the nut flour mixture, retaining as much volume as possible. Transfer the mixture to a piping bag fitted with a #802 (¼-inch/6-millimeter) plain piping tip.

Place the template on a flat work surface and cover it with another sheet of parchment paper. You should be able to see the rectangles through the top sheet of parchment. Pipe the mixture across a short side of one rectangle and move the bag back and forth in a zigzag motion until the entire rectangle is covered. Repeat with the three remaining rectangles.

Slide the parchment onto a half sheet pan and bake in the combi oven for about 33 minutes or in a conventional oven for 38 minutes. Let cool on the pan to room temperature. Wrap in plastic wrap and store at room temperature for up to 1 week.

FOR THE CHOCOLATE GANACHE

Melt the chocolate in a medium metal bowl set over a saucepot of simmering water (be sure the bottom of the bowl does not touch the water) until three-quarters of the chocolate has melted. Mix the cream, glucose, Trimoline, and sorbitol together in a separate medium pot and bring to a boil.

Pour the cream mixture over the chocolate and whisk to combine. Remove the bowl from the heat and let the ganache cool to 97° to 100°F (36° to 38°C). Strain through a chinois into a blender and blend to fully emulsify.

Pour into a plastic container. Lay a piece of plastic wrap directly against the surface and place in a cool place. When it has set to the point where it holds its shape when handled but is still soft enough to pipe, it is ready to use. (The ganache is best when used at this point and should not be stored further.)

FOR THE ITALIAN MERINGUE BUTTERCREAM

Careful timing is critical when making an Italian meringue. The syrup should reach 250°F (121°C) at the same time that the egg whites are holding a soft shape.

Place the egg whites in the bowl of a stand mixer fitted with the whisk. Combine the water and 242 grams of the sugar in a 1-quart (1-liter) saucepot and heat over medium-high heat. When the sugar syrup has reached 203°F (95°C), begin whipping the whites on medium speed. When the whites are frothy, gradually add the remaining 52 grams sugar.

When the sugar syrup reaches 250°F (121°C), remove the pan from the heat. Immediately turn the mixer to medium-low speed and slowly add the syrup, carefully pouring it between the side of the bowl and the whisk. If the syrup hits the bowl or whisk, it could harden and won't be incorporated into the egg whites. The meringue will deflate somewhat.

Increase the speed to medium and whip for 5 to 6 minutes. The meringue may feel slightly warm but should not feel hot before the butter is added. Gradually add the butter. Once incorporated, stop the mixer and scrape the sides and the bottom of the bowl well to ensure there are no pieces of butter remaining. Whip on medium speed for 4 to 5 minutes more, until shiny, light, and fluffy.

Transfer 300 grams of the buttercream to a separate bowl for the praline buttercream. Add the vanilla bean seeds and vanilla paste to the mixer and whip until thoroughly combined. Transfer the buttercream to an airtight container and let cool to room temperature.

The vanilla buttercream can be refrigerated for up to 3 days. Remove it from the refrigerator and soften at room temperature, then whip using the stand mixer until shiny before using.

FOR THE PRALINE BUTTERCREAM

Return the reserved 300 grams unflavored buttercream to the mixer. Add the praline paste and salt to taste and whisk until thoroughly combined. Transfer to an airtight container and let cool to room temperature.

The praline buttercream can be refrigerated for up to 3 days. Remove it from the refrigerator and soften at room temperature, then whip using the stand mixer until shiny before using.

TO COMPLETE

Bring the praline and vanilla buttercreams to room temperature. If the buttercreams have been refrigerated, rewhip them using the stand mixer once they have reached room temperature until they are smooth, shiny, and well emulsified.

Set aside the nicest layer of japonaise, one that is flat and free from cracks and has the most even piping, to serve as the top layer.

From the bottom up, the layers will be:

> Japonaise
>
> Chocolate ganache piped with a #804 (⅜-inch/10-millimeter) plain piping tip
>
> Japonaise
>
> Vanilla buttercream piped with a #802 (¼-inch/6-millimeter) plain piping tip
>
> Japonaise
>
> Praline buttercream piped with a #802 (¼-inch/6-millimeter) plain piping tip
>
> Japonaise

Place the first layer of japonaise on a cutting board, flat-side down, and pipe on the ganache using the same technique that you used to pipe the japonaise, leaving a ⅛-inch (3-millimeter) border on all sides.

Using a small offset spatula, smooth the top of the ganache layer to create an even, flat surface. Carefully flash the top of the ganache with a blowtorch to just melt the surface; this will help the next layer adhere.

Place a second piece of japonaise over the ganache, flat-side down, and press firmly, jiggling with small movements to ensure the japonaise is well secured with no air gaps. You should press just enough that the ganache between the layers of japonaise is pushed out to the edges and the gap is filled.

Pipe a layer of the vanilla buttercream, spread it, and flash it as you did the ganache. Add a third layer of japonaise and press down.

Pipe a layer of the praline buttercream, spread it, and flash it as you did the ganache. Add the final layer of japonaise and press down gently.

Move the cutting board to the refrigerator to firm and set the marjolaine, at least 2 hours or up to 1 day. The marjolaine can be wrapped and refrigerated for up to 5 days.

Once set, remove the marjolaine from the refrigerator. Using a fine-mesh sieve, dust the top with confectioners' sugar. Using a serrated bread knife, cut it into 1-inch-thick (2.5-centimeter) slices and place one on each serving plate (see Note).

> **NOTE**
>
> For a more refined presentation, the edges of the whole cake can be trimmed and the sides coated with chocolate ganache, then garnished with chocolate shavings.

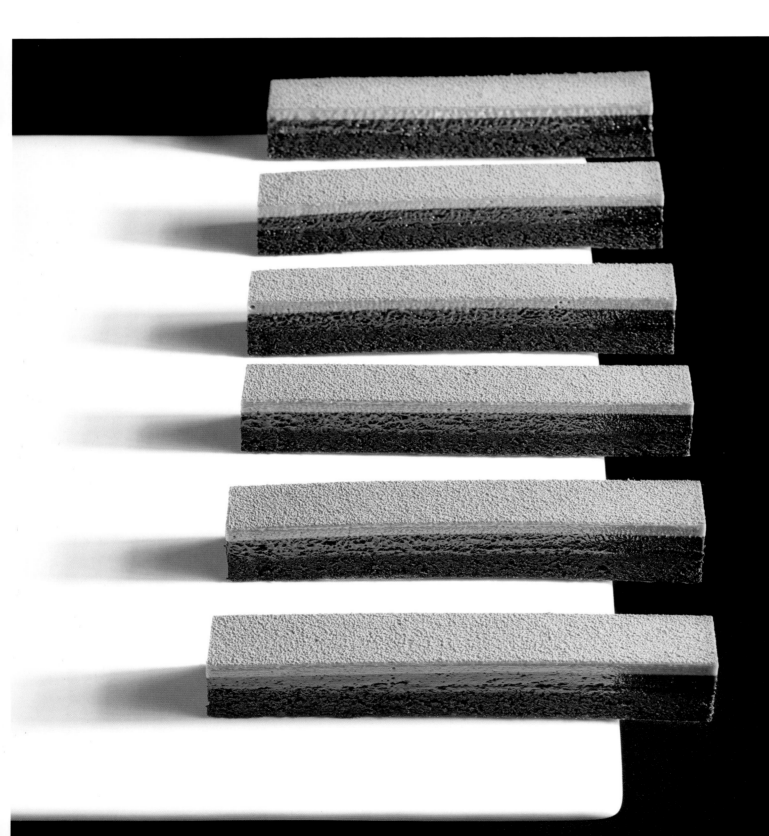

MALTED BROWNIES

Makes 20 slices

BLACKOUT SPONGE

28 grams whole butter

200 grams sugar

100 grams all-purpose flour

50 grams unsweetened alkalized cocoa powder, preferably Valrhona, sifted

5 grams baking soda

2 grams baking powder

118 grams brewed coffee, at room temperature

87 grams crème fraîche

75 grams eggs

25 grams whole milk

CHOCOLATE MARQUISE

73 grams 77% dark chocolate, preferably K+M Peru, chopped

225 grams heavy cream

135 grams whole butter

82 grams unsweetened alkalized cocoa powder, preferably Valrhona, sifted

125 grams sugar

50 grams honey

6 large egg yolks

MALT MOUSSE

80 grams white chocolate, preferably Valrhona Ivoire 35%, chopped

1.4 grams silver leaf gelatin

15 grams egg yolks

115 grams heavy cream

15 grams malted milk powder or Ovaltine

10 grams malt syrup

CHOCOLATE SPRAY

175 grams 70% dark chocolate, preferably Valrhona Guanaja 70%, chopped

75 grams cocoa butter, chopped

SPECIAL EQUIPMENT

Chamber vacuum sealer (optional)

Spray gun or paint sprayer

We call this a brownie because it has a brownie's soft cake and fudgy texture, with the marquise on top of a chocolate sponge. Malted chocolate mousse goes on top of this. The cake is a sponge recipe used in the preparation of blackout cake, a cake flavored with coffee first made in Brooklyn by Ebinger's bakery and reputed to be named after the World War II blackouts that allowed war boats to leave New York Harbor undetected. I love the precision of this dessert, with careful attention to the cuts. But it's delicious no matter how you slice it and even if you don't spray it with chocolate as the restaurant does. Temperature is key here. It should be sliced chilled, to get clean cuts, but served just below room temperature to allow the full flavor to come out.

FOR THE BLACKOUT SPONGE

Preheat the oven to 325°F (163°C). Line a quarter sheet pan with a non-stick silicone baking mat and spray with nonstick spray.

Heat the butter in a small pan over low heat just until melted. Remove from the heat.

Mix the sugar, flour, cocoa powder, baking soda, and baking powder in a medium bowl and set aside.

Mix the coffee, crème fraîche, eggs, and milk in a second bowl. Pour the wet ingredients into the dry ingredients and whisk to combine to a smooth paste, with no lumps remaining. Add the melted butter and whisk to combine. Scrape the edges and bottom of the bowl with a silicone spatula to be certain that all the dry ingredients have been incorporated. Whisk again to ensure the cake batter is smooth. Transfer the cake batter to the prepared sheet pan. Spread it evenly using an offset spatula, making sure it reaches into the corners. Tap the pan on the counter a few times to help spread the batter evenly. To check that the cake is spread evenly, stick the tip of a cake tester into each of the four corners and the center, wiping the cake tester after each test. The batter should coat the cake tester to the same height in each place.

Bake the cake for 14 to 16 minutes, until a cake tester inserted into the center comes out clean and the cake springs back when lightly touched. Set the pan on a cooling rack and let cool completely.

(continued)

Lay a piece of parchment paper on your work surface and lightly spray with nonstick spray. Run a small knife around the edges of the cake to loosen it and invert the cake onto the parchment. Carefully remove the baking mat from the cake. Lightly spray another piece of parchment with nonstick spray and place it over the cake. Gently roll a rolling pin over the parchment to slightly flatten and smooth the cake. Slide a rimless baking sheet underneath the cake and place in the freezer until frozen.

Once frozen, the cake can be wrapped in plastic wrap and stored in the freezer for up to 2 weeks.

FOR THE CHOCOLATE MARQUISE
Bring water to a gentle simmer in the bottom of a double boiler. Put the chocolate in the top of the double boiler and set it over the simmering water. Keeping the temperature below 120°F (49°C), stir the chocolate until it has almost completely melted. Remove from the heat and stir until the chocolate has completely melted. Hold the melted chocolate in a warm place.

Whip the cream to medium-soft peaks. (Note that when the amount of cream is less than 250 grams, the cream will whip more evenly if it is whipped by hand or with a handheld mixer rather than using a stand mixer.) Refrigerate.

Put the butter in a large glass bowl and warm it in the microwave until it is soft to the touch but not melted, about 30 seconds on full power if the butter is cold before microwaving. If the butter is at room temperature, warm it for a few seconds at a time, testing after each interval, to avoid melting it.

Add the cocoa powder and stir it together with the butter to make a smooth, shiny paste. If the paste is not smooth and shiny, warm it slightly over a pan of simmering water and whisk until it is.

Place the sugar, honey, and egg yolks in the bowl of a stand mixer fitted with the whisk. Whip on high speed for 7 to 8 minutes, until the mixture is thick and pale yellow, scraping down the bowl as necessary. Reduce the speed to medium-low and, with the machine running, add the melted chocolate to the bowl. Once all the chocolate has been added, stop the mixer, even if there are visible streaks of chocolate in the mixture. These will be eliminated when the mixture is folded into the cocoa powder paste.

Using a whisk, fold one-third of the chocolate mixture into the cocoa powder paste (see Note). Scrape the sides and bottom of the bowl well with a silicone spatula, then fold in the remaining chocolate mixture.

Using the whisk, fold in the whipped cream, making sure to scrape the sides and bottom of the bowl well. Whisk until no streaks remain and the marquise is smooth.

If you have a chamber vacuum sealer, place a quarter sheet pan inside a large sous vide bag and vacuum seal to line the bag.

If you do not have a chamber vacuum sealer, cut a piece of plastic wrap that is at least 2 inches (5 centimeters) longer and wider than a quarter sheet pan. Lay it on the work surface, smoothing out any wrinkles. Top with two additional layers of plastic wrap. Spray the quarter sheet pan with a light coating of nonstick spray. Lay the triple layer of plastic wrap in the pan, pressing it into the corners. Trim the plastic wrap to give you a 1-inch (2.5-centimeter) overhang on all sides and fold the plastic back against the outside of the pan.

Unwrap the blackout cake and place it in the prepared pan. The top of the cake (the sticky side) should be facing up. If it is facing downward, it will stick to the plastic and the surface of the cake will tear when you try to move it and portion it.

Pour the chocolate marquise over the blackout cake layer and, using an offset spatula, spread the marquise into an even layer. Place the sheet pan in the freezer for at least 15 minutes and up to 30 minutes to chill and firm as you make the malt mousse.

FOR THE MALT MOUSSE
Bring water to a gentle simmer in the bottom of the double boiler. Put the white chocolate in the top of the double boiler and set it over the simmering water. Keeping the temperature very low, stir the chocolate until it has almost completely melted. Remove from the heat and stir until the chocolate has completely melted. Hold the melted chocolate in a warm place.

Submerge the gelatin in a bowl of ice water to bloom (soften) for about 5 minutes.

Place the egg yolks in a small bowl and whisk. Combine 45 grams of the cream and the malted milk powder in a 1-quart (1-liter) saucepot and bring to a boil over medium heat. While whisking continuously, gradually whisk the boiling cream into the egg yolks to temper the eggs. Return the mixture to the pan and whisk continuously over medium heat for about 30 seconds until it begins to thicken. Remove the pan from the heat.

Remove the softened gelatin from the ice water and squeeze out any excess water. Whisk the gelatin into the mixture. Once the gelatin has melted, whisk in the malt syrup and strain the mixture over the melted white chocolate. Whisk until the malt base is glossy and smooth.

By hand or using a handheld mixer, whip the remaining 70 grams cream to soft peaks.

The malt base should be at about 90°F (32°C). If it is warmer than this, allow it to cool before adding the whipped cream or the cream will melt upon contact and the finished mousse will not have a light, creamy texture. Using a whisk, fold one-third of the cream into the malt base to loosen the base. Fold in the remaining cream. (Adding the cream in two parts will help retain the volume of the mousse and prevent over-whipping.)

Remove the sheet pan from the freezer and, using a silicone spatula, scrape the malt mousse onto the layer of chocolate marquise. Using an offset spatula, spread the mousse into an even layer. Return the pan to the freezer. The brownie cannot be sprayed until it is completely frozen.

For longer storage, top with a piece of parchment paper and wrap the sheet pan securely in two layers of plastic wrap. Store in the freezer for up to 2 weeks.

FOR THE CHOCOLATE SPRAY

Prepare an area for spraying. As you work, some chocolate will spray past the edges of your pan. At the restaurant, we put a trash bag on the work surface and tape one to the wall behind it to make a makeshift spraying area. If you have a deep farmhouse sink, you can put the pan in the sink and spray the brownie there (just dry the sink well beforehand).

Bring water to a gentle simmer in the bottom of the double boiler. Put the chocolate and cocoa butter in the top of the double boiler and set it over the simmering water. Warm the mixture, stirring occasionally, until the chocolate and cocoa butter are completely melted with a tem-perature of 115°F (46°C). Chocolate at this temperature is ideal for the best spray finish.

Fill your spray gun with the melted chocolate mixture and test to ensure it is coming out in an even, clean spray. Remove the sheet pan from the freezer and place it in your spraying area. Holding the spray gun about 30 inches (76 centimeters) from the brownie, spray an even coating of chocolate across the surface. As the spray hits the frozen brownie, it will form a dusty chocolate coating. Once sprayed, lift the edges of the plastic wrap (or cut the bag as needed) and carefully remove the brownie from the pan. Place the brownie on a cutting board or sheet pan, carefully remove the plastic, and place the cutting board in the refrigerator for about 2 hours to defrost the brownie.

The sprayed brownie can be refrigerated in an airtight container for up to 3 days.

TO COMPLETE

Just before serving, dip a chef's knife in hot water, dry with a clean kitchen towel, and trim the edges of the brownie. Portion the brownie into 4 by 1-inch (10 by 2.5-centimeter) rectangles, heating and drying the knife between each cut to keep the sliced edges clean. Using an offset spatula, transfer the slices of brownie to a serving platter.

> **NOTE**
>
> Folding with a whisk takes some practice. This is our preferred method because it is faster and the finished mixture will be lighter. However, you can begin folding with a whisk and finish using a silicone spatula if you find that to be an easier method.

COCONUTTY

Makes 24 cookies

COCONUT SABLÉ

170 grams whole butter, cut into ½-inch (1.25-centimeter) cubes, at room temperature

60 grams coconut oil, at room temperature

200 grams sugar

5 grams vanilla paste

1 large egg, at room temperature

300 grams all-purpose flour

90 grams unsweetened desiccated coconut

5 grams baking powder

2 grams kosher salt

TOFFEE FILLING

115 grams heavy cream, at room temperature

2.5 grams vanilla paste

125 grams sugar

165 grams Valrhona Dulcey chocolate

1.5 grams kosher salt

40 grams whole butter, at room temperature

65 grams unsweetened desiccated coconut

TO COMPLETE

750 grams tempered 70% dark chocolate (see page 357), preferably Valrhona Guanaja

100 grams unsweetened desiccated coconut, lightly toasted

SPECIAL EQUIPMENT

Acetate sheets

2-inch (50-millimeter) plain round cutter

#804 (⅜-inch/ 10-millimeter) plain piping tip

Corey created a caviar course based on the Girl Scout cookie called Samoas, and the pastry team at per se developed this cookie based on the same. Here coconut cookies sandwich chewy toffee ganache, and the assembled cookies are dipped in chocolate. The inner texture is kind of like a cross between a Mounds bar and the caramel layer in a Mars bar, so you get the best of both. This particular cookie began at per se when we first developed our biscuit box, offering a selection of cookies at the end of the meal in what was becoming an increasingly fluid dessert service. You might, for example, receive an ice cream course, a glazed peach with cream, and a cookie, a perfect series of sweets to conclude a meal.

FOR THE COCONUT SABLÉ

Place the butter in the bowl of a stand mixer fitted with the paddle. Add the coconut oil. Beat on medium speed for 3 minutes. Using a silicone spatula, scrape the sides of the bowl, then add the sugar and vanilla and cream for 4 minutes more, until the mixture is light and fluffy. Add the egg and beat for 2 minutes more, ensuring the mixture is fully combined.

Meanwhile, using a spoon or silicone spatula, mix the flour, desiccated coconut, baking powder, and salt in a medium bowl to disperse the ingredients evenly.

Stop the mixer and add the dry ingredients all at once. Mix on the lowest speed just until the dry ingredients have been fully incorporated.

Cut two large pieces of acetate in half. Turn the sablé dough out onto a work surface and divide it into two equal pieces. Place one piece on a sheet of the acetate and shape it into a flat rectangle. Top with the second sheet, then gently roll the dough to an even layer that is ⅛ inch (3 millimeters) thick. Repeat with the remaining dough. Place the sablé dough, still in the acetate, on sheet pans and freeze until firm, about 1 hour. The frozen sablé dough can be wrapped in plastic wrap and frozen for up to 2 weeks.

Preheat the oven to 350°F (180°C). Lightly coat two half sheet pans with nonstick spray and line them with parchment paper.

(continued)

Remove one sheet from the freezer and remove the acetate from one side of the dough. Flip it over onto a cutting board and remove the second piece of acetate. Punch rounds of dough using a 2-inch (50-millimeter) plain round cutter. If the dough cracks, it may be too frozen; allow it to temper for a moment before continuing. As you punch each round, transfer it to one of the prepared pans. Repeat with the second sheet of sablé, placing the rounds on the second prepared pan. The trimmed dough can be brought together, rerolled, and frozen to make more sablés.

Bake the cookies for 3 minutes. To keep the cookies flat, remove each pan from the oven and lightly tap on a heatproof surface to release any air pockets that may have started to form. Return to the oven and repeat with the second sheet. Bake for 7 to 9 minutes more, until golden brown. Let cool to room temperature before filling.

The cooled sablés can be stored in an airtight container at room temperature for up to 1 day.

FOR THE TOFFEE FILLING

Mix the cream and vanilla together in a spouted measuring cup.

Place the sugar in a medium pot over medium-high heat. Without stirring, allow the sugar to begin melting. Once it is half melted, stir and cook until it reaches a light caramel color. Mixing with a silicone spatula, gradually add the cream, about 1 tablespoon at a time to begin. (Adding the cream slowly will prevent the sugar from seizing up.)

Remove the pot from the heat and add the chocolate and salt. Mix with a spatula to fully melt and emulsify the chocolate. Transfer the mixture to a bowl and, using the spatula, stir in the butter; the heat left in the mixture will melt the butter. Using the spatula, mix in the desiccated coconut to combine. Press plastic wrap directly against the surface of the toffee filling to prevent any condensation or a skin from forming. Let the filling rest at room temperature for 45 minutes to 1 hour before assembly.

TO COMPLETE

Match the cookies in pairs and place them side by side; the bottom cookie should have the smooth side down and the top cookie should have the smooth side up. Transfer the toffee filling to a piping bag fitted with a #804 (⅜-inch/10-millimeter) plain piping tip. Pipe about 12 grams of filling onto the center of each bottom cookie. Place the top cookie over the filling and press gently to fully attach the cookie and press the toffee filling to a layer just under ¼ inch (6 millimeters) thick, with a 1-millimeter gap around the edges of the cookies. Arrange the cookies on a half sheet pan and refrigerate for 30 minutes to set.

Remove the cookies from the refrigerator about 10 minutes before coating them with chocolate. Set up a dipping station: you will need (from left to right) the cookies, the tempered chocolate in a medium bowl, a small bowl with the toasted coconut, a half sheet pan lined with parchment paper, and a dipping fork.

Hold the dipping fork in your dominant hand and a cookie in the other hand. Place the cookie, top-side up, into the center of the bowl of chocolate so it is floating on the surface. Gently press down in the center of the cookie until the bottom and sides of the cookie are completely submerged in the chocolate, taking care that none of the chocolate goes up and over onto the top of the cookie. Use the dipping fork to lift the cookie. Holding the cookie over the chocolate, tap the stem of the fork on the edge of the bowl to allow excess chocolate to drip back into the bowl. Wipe the last drip on the edge of the bowl.

Gently place the cookie in the bowl of coconut to coat the bottom and sides. The coconut will stick to the still-wet chocolate. Carefully remove the cookie and avoid leaving any chocolate in the coconut. Set the dipped cookie on the prepared pan. Repeat with the remaining cookies.

Set the pan of finished cookies in a cool place for 30 minutes to give the chocolate time to fully set. Store the cookies in an airtight container in a cool place for up to 2 days.

Tempering Dark Chocolate

Proper tempering ensures chocolate has the smooth mouthfeel, shiny appearance, and clean snap when it is broken or bitten into that we all look for in a good bar of chocolate. Dark chocolate consists of cocoa butter, cocoa solids, sugar, and often an emulsifier. It is the fat crystals in the cocoa butter that give chocolate its physical structure, and it is these crystals that we are manipulating when we temper chocolate. When you purchase chocolate, it is tempered, but melting destroys the cocoa butter crystals. If it is allowed to set straight from this state, it will cause "bloom": the surface of the chocolate will become dull, with a white coating, and upon breaking, it will crumble rather than snap. Tempering the chocolate is necessary when you are using it as a coating. It is not important if the melted chocolate is incorporated with other ingredients in baking.

A laser thermometer works well for taking accurate readings when tempering chocolate. To read the temperature, position the thermometer a few inches from the surface of the chocolate and shoot the laser eye into the middle of the surface area.

During tempering, the chocolate is taken through three stages:

Melting: 131° to 136°F (55° to 57.7°C)

Crystallization: 82° to 84°F (27.7° to 28.8°C)

Working: 88° to 90°F (31.1° to 32.2°C)

We like to use the seeding method: adding small pieces of tempered chocolate to the melted chocolate. Adding tempered pieces to the melted chocolate promotes the formation of the type of cocoa butter crystals that are needed to form a good temper. All the chocolate is chopped into small pieces. A portion (about two-thirds) of it is melted to 131° to 136°F (55° to 57.7°C) and held here for 5 minutes to allow a good amount of the cocoa butter crystals to be broken down. Then the remaining chocolate is added and mixed in, gently, to start the crystallization process. Once enough crystallization has occurred and the chocolate is at around 82° to 84°F (27.7° to 28.8°C), the chocolate is gently warmed over a water bath to 88° to 90°F (31.1° to 32.2°C). It is now "in temper" and at the working temperature.

TIMELINE

1907

John and Madeleine Lande purchase the Eagle Saloon from Pierre Guillaume, open a steam laundry, and call it "The French Laundry."

1955

Thomas Keller is born at Camp Pendleton in Oceanside, California.

1974

Don and Sally Schmitt purchase the French Laundry building and begin renovations on what will be a restaurant.

77 **Keller is twenty and works for a summer in Narragansett, Rhode Island, finding a job with Roland Henin, chef of the Dunes Club, who will become Keller's mentor.**

78 The French Laundry serves its first meals on February 9.

The French Laundry receives its first four-star rating from the *San Francisco Chronicle's* Michael Bauer, repeated every year until Bauer's retirement in 2018.

95 **Laura Cunningham is promoted to general manager of The French Laundry.**

The French Laundry opens on July 6.

Laura Cunningham joins The French Laundry.

Keller purchases The French Laundry from the Schmitts on May 1 for $1.2 million.

1994

95 **Herb Caen, an influential columnist for the *San Francisco Chronicle*, gives favorable mention to The French Laundry, awarding the restaurant its first, and defining, moment of recognition.**

96 Thomas Keller wins the James Beard Foundation Award for Best Chef: California.

97 Thomas Keller wins the James Beard Foundation Award for Outstanding Chef.

98 Bouchon Bistro opens just down the street from The French Laundry.

99 Larry Nadeau becomes the restaurant's first maître d', a critical moment in the restaurant's dining room service.

Sebastien Rouxel, the restaurant's first trained pastry chef, joins The French Laundry.

Restaurant magazine's The World's 50 Best Restaurants again names The French Laundry the world's best restaurant, the first time in its history it repeats the distinction.

04 Per se opens in New York.

Bouchon Bakery opens next door to Bouchon Bistro.

03 *Restaurant* magazine's The World's 50 Best Restaurants names The French Laundry the best restaurant in the world.

Master Sommelier Bobby Stuckey becomes the first wine director at The French Laundry to develop a world wine list, rather than a California-focused wine list.

2000

SOURCES

Throughout the book, you may find certain ingredients that are unfamiliar; in most cases, however, you will find that they are widely available online or from local farms. Always search for high-quality ingredients, whether they are pantry items or produce. In some recipes, we look for a more exacting flavor profile, and in those cases, we call for our favorite brands. Quality equipment is equally important, and this list will provide a glimpse into what we use in our kitchens.

04 The French Laundry's first kitchen remodel increases the restaurant's kitchen space to 1,100 square feet.

05 Per se is named Best New Restaurant by the James Beard Foundation.

David Breeden joins The French Laundry as a stagiaire, then commis.

06 Ad Hoc restaurant opens in Yountville.

Per se is awarded three stars from the inaugural Michelin Guide to New York City.

The French Laundry receives the Outstanding Restaurant award from the James Beard Foundation.

08 **Elwyn Boyles joins per se as a pastry chef, eventually becoming the executive pastry chef for per se and The French Laundry.**

Tucker Taylor is hired as the first official gardener for the three-acre French Laundry garden.

Chef Corey Chow joins per se as a commis.

Thomas Keller earns the Outstanding Restaurateur award from the James Beard Foundation.

The French Laundry earns three stars from the Michelin Guide in the guide's first rating of Bay Area restaurants, which it has repeated every year.

Thomas Keller is named Chevalier by the French Légion d'honneur for his work promoting French cuisine in America, the third American chef to be recognized.

12 After starting in the French Laundry kitchen, then spending eight years as captain at per se, Michael Minnillo returns to Yountville to become the general manager of The French Laundry.

David Breeden becomes the chef de cuisine of The French Laundry.

14 The French Laundry begins a major kitchen overhaul.

The French Laundry celebrates its twenty-fifth anniversary.

TAK Room restaurant opens in New York City.

19 La Calenda restaurant opens in Yountville.

18 The Surf Club Restaurant opens at the historic landmark in Surfside, Florida.

Team USA, led by the French Laundry and per se alumnus Mathew Peters, wins the Bocuse d'Or competition for the first time in the competition's thirty-year history.

The French Laundry completes a 2,000-square-foot kitchen remodel.

17 **Corey Chow becomes the chef de cuisine of per se.**

EQUIPMENT: SMALLWARES

Baking mats, silicone, for eighth, quarter, and
  half sheet pans: **Silpat**

Blender, with large and small containers and a
  tamper: **Vitamix**

Cake comb: **Ateco**

Confectionary rulers:
  TAP Plastics or Chef Rubber

Copper couplings: **NIBCO**

Cutters, round and fluted, in graduated sizes:
  Matfer Bourgeat USA or Ateco

Milk frother: **BonJour**

Offset spatula: **Triangle**

Pastry bags, disposable, 16 inch: **JB Prince**

Piping tips, assorted sizes and shapes: **Ateco**

Poultry shears: **MAC**

Rasp grater: **Microplane**

Scale, digital: **Escali**

Siphon: **iSi**

Tamis, small- and large-hole: **JB Prince**

Thermometer, instant-read:
  ThermoWorks Thermapen or Taylor

Thermometer, laser: **Etekcity Lasergrip 800**

EQUIPMENT: ELECTRIC OR LARGE EQUIPMENT

Chamber vacuum sealer: **VacMaster**

Combi oven: **Rational**

Dehydrator: **Excalibur or Cabela's**

Grinder, with small, medium, and large dies:
  Chef'sChoice Model 720 (for home use);
  Pro-Cut KG-12-FS (for restaurants)

Hibachi: **Korin**

Immersion circulator: **PolyScience**

Juicer: **Breville** (for home use); **Champion
  Classic 2000 masticating juicer or Sunkist
  J-I Commercial citrus juicer** (for restaurants)

Mandoline: **Benriner 4-blade Japanese
  mandoline**

Pressure cooker: **Duromatic**

Slicer, electric: **Chef's Choice** (for home use);
  Berkel (for restaurants)

Sprayer: **Wagner Control Stainer 150**

Stand mixer: **KitchenAid**

INGREDIENTS

Anchovy essence: **IASA**

Applewood smoke sticks: **Korin**

Bacon: **Hobbs' Applewood Smoked Meats**

Burgundy mustard: **Edmond Fallot**

Caviar: **Regiis Ova Ossetra caviar**

Chocolate: **K+M Peru Dark, Hacienda Victoria
  Milk Morceaux; Valrhona Dulcey, Ivoire,
  Opalys, Guanaja**

Coffee extract: **Trablit**

Crab merus: **Lobel's of New York**

Extra-virgin olive oil: **Manni**

Feuille de brick sheets: **JR Brick USA**

Filberts (hazelnuts): **Bazzini Nuts**

Flour
  hard wheat: **King Arthur Sir Galahad**
  soft wheat: **Gran Mugnaio "00"**
  gluten-free: **Cup4Cup**

Foie gras: **Hudson Valley Foie Gras**

Fruit purees: **Boiron**

Honey: **Marshall's Farm**

Kosher salt: **Diamond Crystal**

Koshihikari rice: **Tamaki Gold**

Lemon oil: **Agrumato**

Mirin: **Sennari Organic**

Nut oils (hazelnut, pistachio, walnut): **J. Leblanc**

Peanuts: **Virginia peanuts from Plantation
  Peanuts**

Pecans: **Pearson Farm**

Polyphosphate: **Butcher & Packer**

Quail (white quail): **Wolfe Ranch**

Red and white verjus: **Fusion Napa Valley**

Saffron: **Rumi Spice**

Silver leaf gelatin: **Gelita**

Sorbet stabilizer: **Cremodan 64**

Spruce tips: **Mikuni Wild Harvest**

Sushi rice: **Nishiki Koshihikari**

Turnips, petite: **Hakurei turnips from Johnny's
  Selected Seeds**

Vanilla beans: **Madagascar and Tahitian**

Vanilla paste: **Nielsen-Massey**

Vinegar
  aged balsamic vinegar: **Acetaia Leonardi**
  cherry balsamic vinegar: **Villa Manodori**
  red wine vinegar: **Sparrow Lane Cabernet
    Sauvignon**

White soy sauce: **Yuasa shiro shoyu**

White truffle oil: **Tartufi di Fassia**

Yeast: **SAF instant yeast**

Yogurt: **Fage whole-milk Greek yogurt,
  Straus Family Creamery whole-milk yogurt**

Yuzu juice: **Muen**